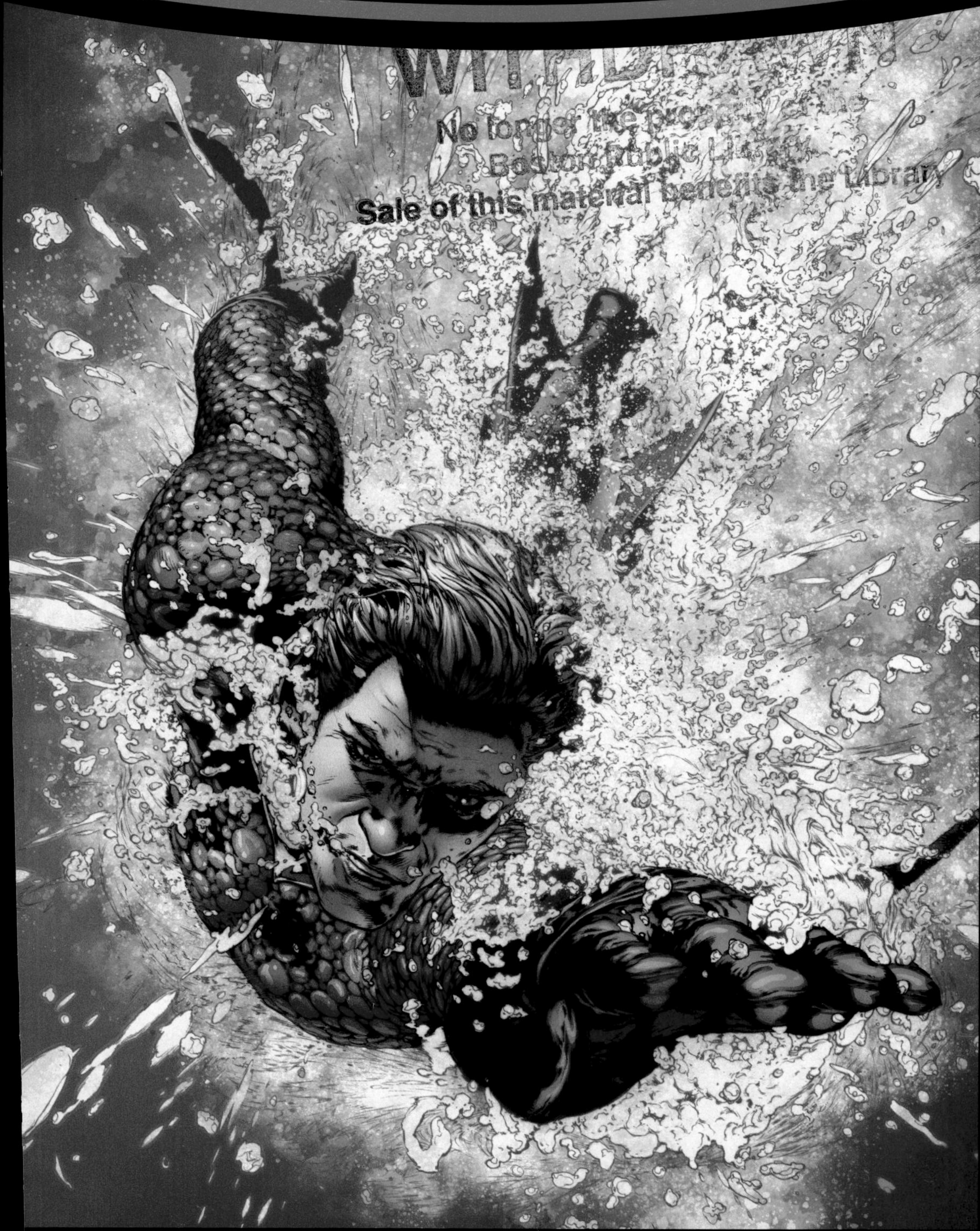

AQUAMAN

VOL.1 THE DROWNING

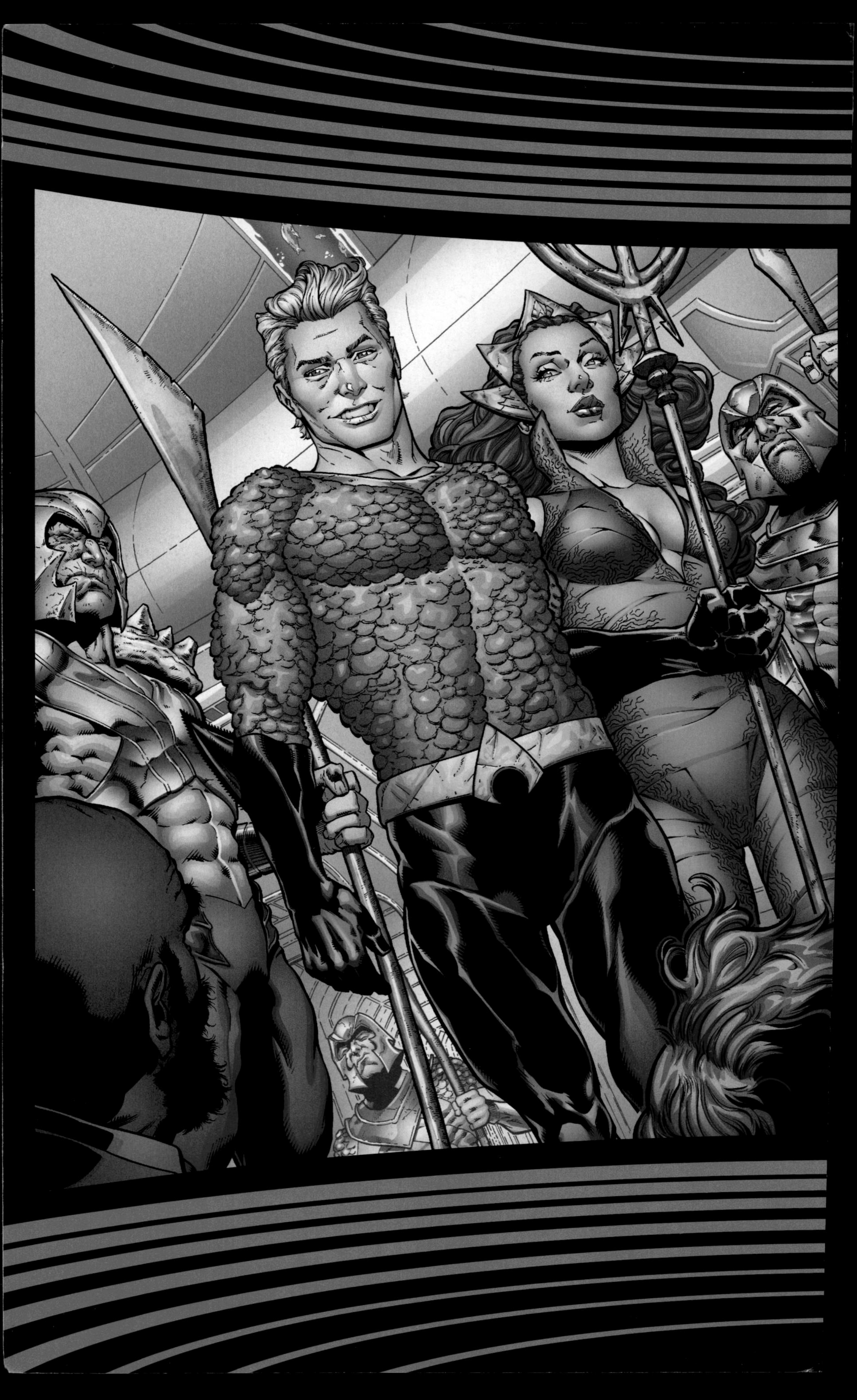

AQUAMAN
VOL.1 THE DROWNING

DAN ABNETT
writer

SCOT EATON * **OSCAR JIMÉNEZ**
MARK MORALES * **BRAD WALKER**
ANDREW HENNESSY * **WAYNE FAUCHER**
PHILIPPE BRIONES
artists

GABE ELTAEB
colorist

PAT BROSSEAU
letterer

**BRAD WALKER, ANDREW HENNESSY
& GABE ELTAEB**
series & collection cover artists

AQUAMAN created by **PAUL NORRIS**
SUPERMAN created by **JERRY SIEGEL** and **JOE SHUSTER**
By special arrangement with the Jerry Siegel family

BRIAN CUNNINGHAM Editor - Original Series • AMEDEO TURTURRO DIEGO LOPEZ Assistant Editors - Original Series
JEB WOODARD Group Editor - Collected Editions • LIZ ERICKSON Editor - Collected Edition
STEVE COOK Design Director - Books

BOB HARRAS Senior VP - Editor-in-Chief, DC Comics

DIANE NELSON President • DAN DiDIO Publisher • JIM LEE Publisher • GEOFF JOHNS President & Chief Creative Officer
AMIT DESAI Executive VP - Business & Marketing Strategy, Direct to Consumer & Global Franchise Management
SAM ADES Senior VP - Direct to Consumer • BOBBIE CHASE VP - Talent Development
MARK CHIARELLO Senior VP - Art, Design & Collected Editions • JOHN CUNNINGHAM Senior VP - Sales & Trade Marketing
ANNE DePIES Senior VP - Business Strategy, Finance & Administration • DON FALLETTI VP - Manufacturing Operations
LAWRENCE GANEM VP - Editorial Administration & Talent Relations • ALISON GILL Senior VP - Manufacturing & Operations
HANK KANALZ Senior VP - Editorial Strategy & Administration • JAY KOGAN VP - Legal Affairs
THOMAS LOFTUS VP - Business Affairs • JACK MAHAN VP - Business Affairs
NICK J. NAPOLITANO VP - Manufacturing Administration • EDDIE SCANNELL VP - Consumer Marketing
COURTNEY SIMMONS Senior VP - Publicity & Communications
JIM (SKI) SOKOLOWSKI VP - Comic Book Specialty Sales & Trade Marketing
NANCY SPEARS VP - Mass, Book, Digital Sales & Trade Marketing

AQUAMAN VOLUME 1: THE DROWNING

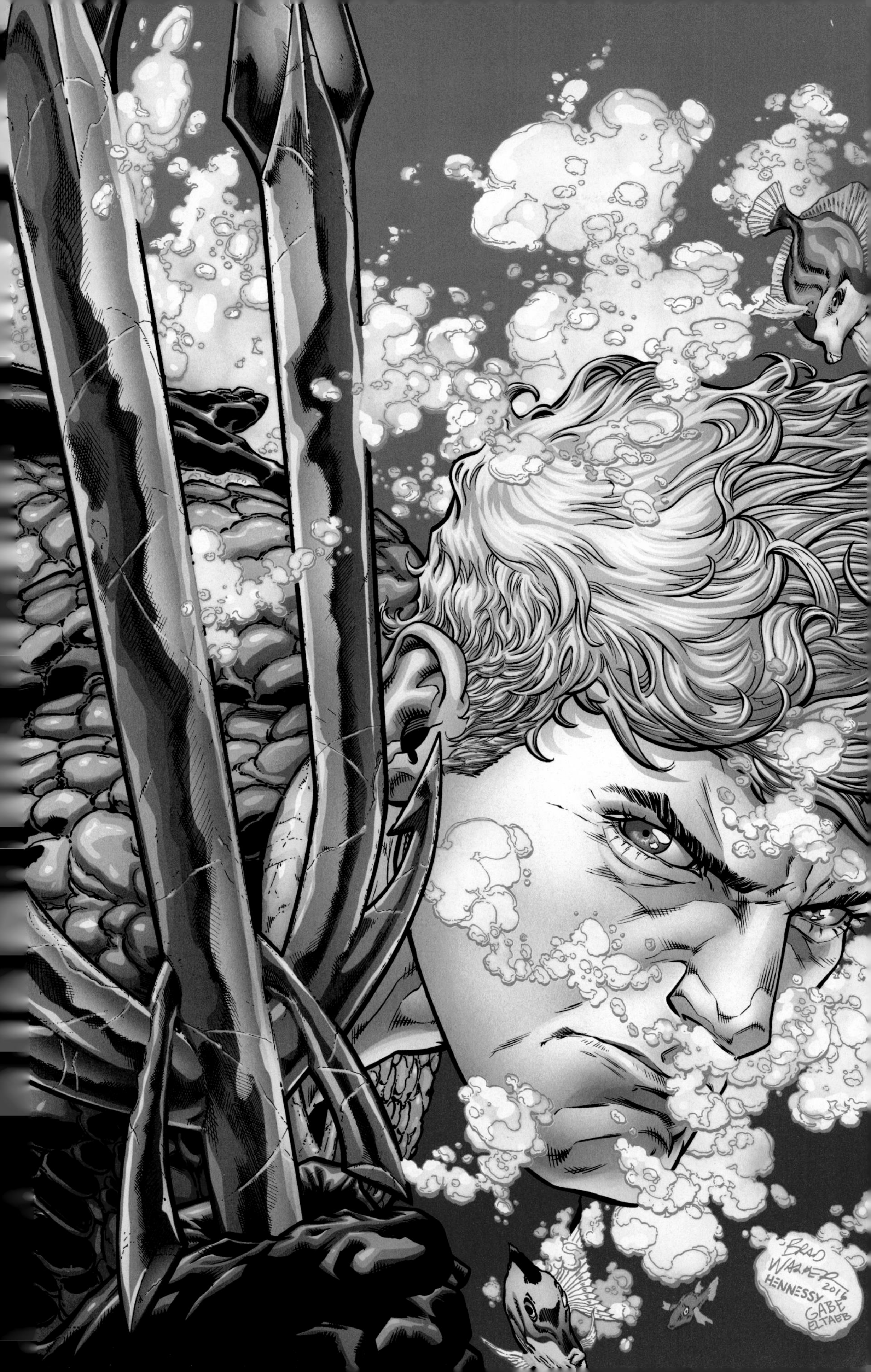
HENNESSY
2016
GABE

PROLOGUE: AFTER THE DELUGE

DAN ABNETT Writer * SCOT EATON OSCAR JIMÉNEZ Pencillers * MARK MORALES OSCAR JIMÉNEZ Inkers
GABE ELTAEB Colorist * PAT BROSSEAU Letterer

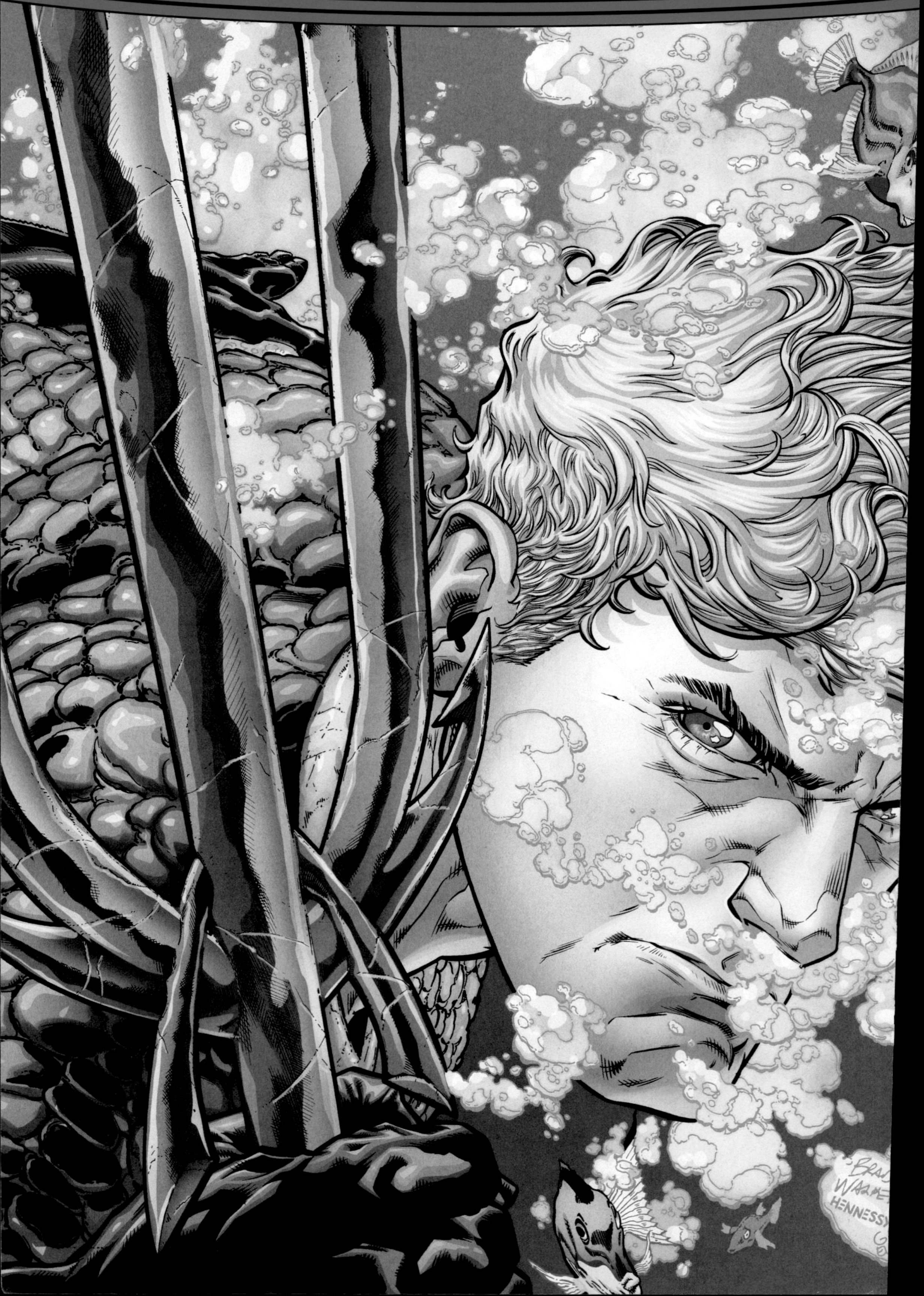

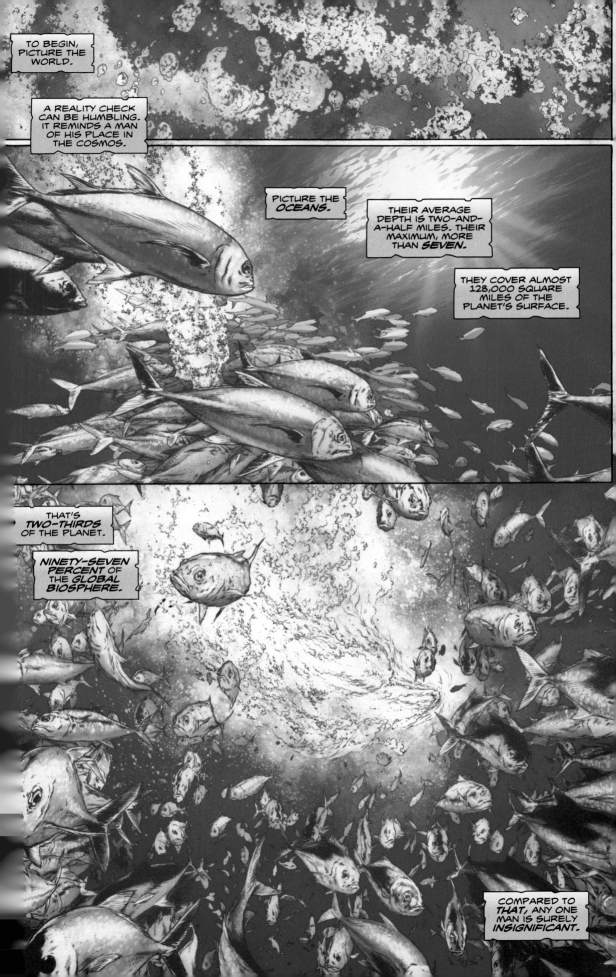

TO BEGIN, PICTURE THE WORLD.

A REALITY CHECK CAN BE HUMBLING. IT REMINDS A MAN OF HIS PLACE IN THE COSMOS.

PICTURE THE *OCEANS.*

THEIR AVERAGE DEPTH IS TWO-AND-A-HALF MILES. THEIR MAXIMUM, MORE THAN *SEVEN.*

THEY COVER ALMOST 128,000 SQUARE MILES OF THE PLANET'S SURFACE.

THAT'S *TWO-THIRDS* OF THE PLANET.

NINETY-SEVEN PERCENT OF THE *GLOBAL BIOSPHERE.*

COMPARED TO *THAT,* ANY ONE MAN IS SURELY *INSIGNIFICANT.*

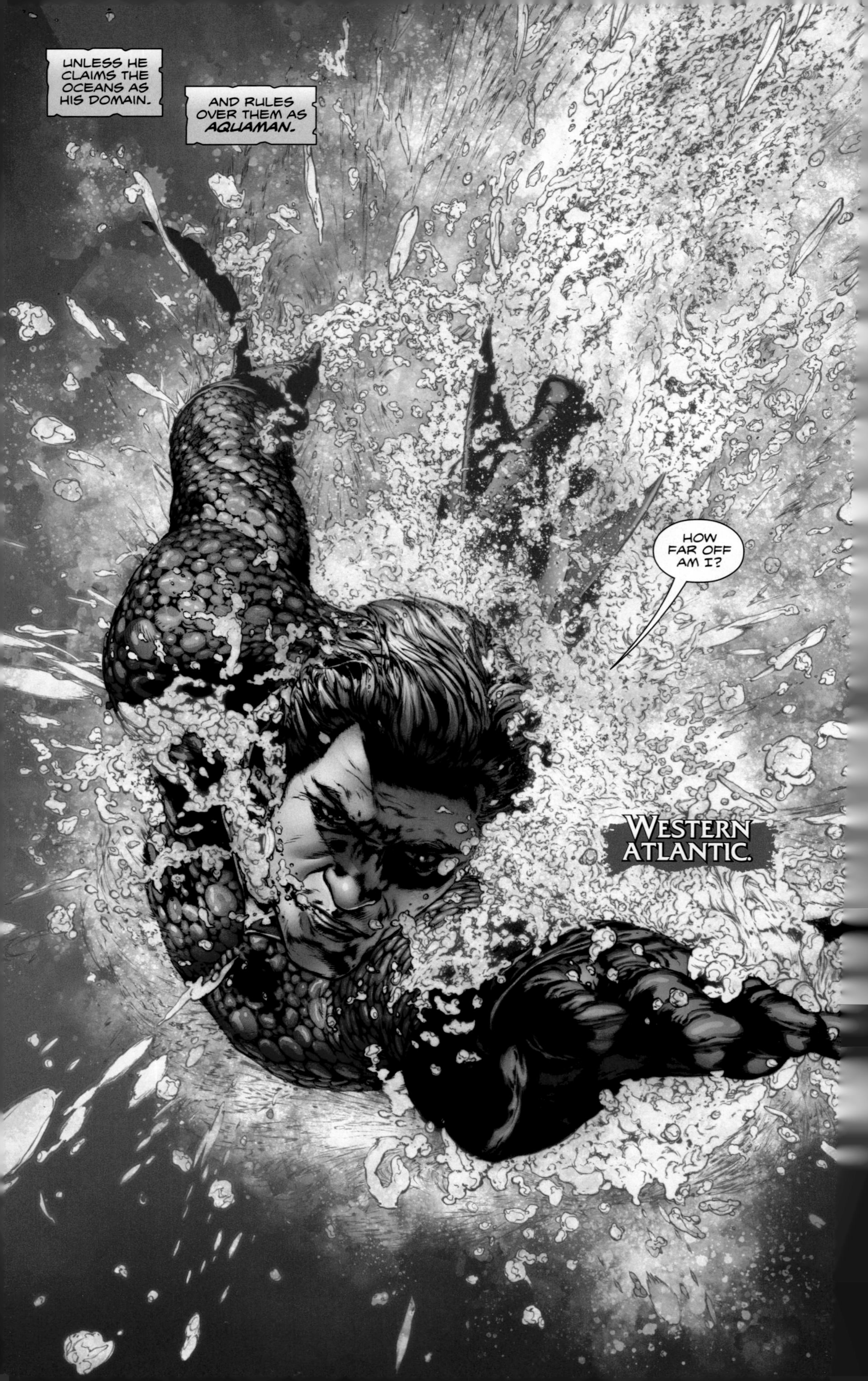
UNLESS HE CLAIMS THE OCEANS AS HIS DOMAIN.
AND RULES OVER THEM AS AQUAMAN.
HOW FAR OFF AM I?
WESTERN ATLANTIC.

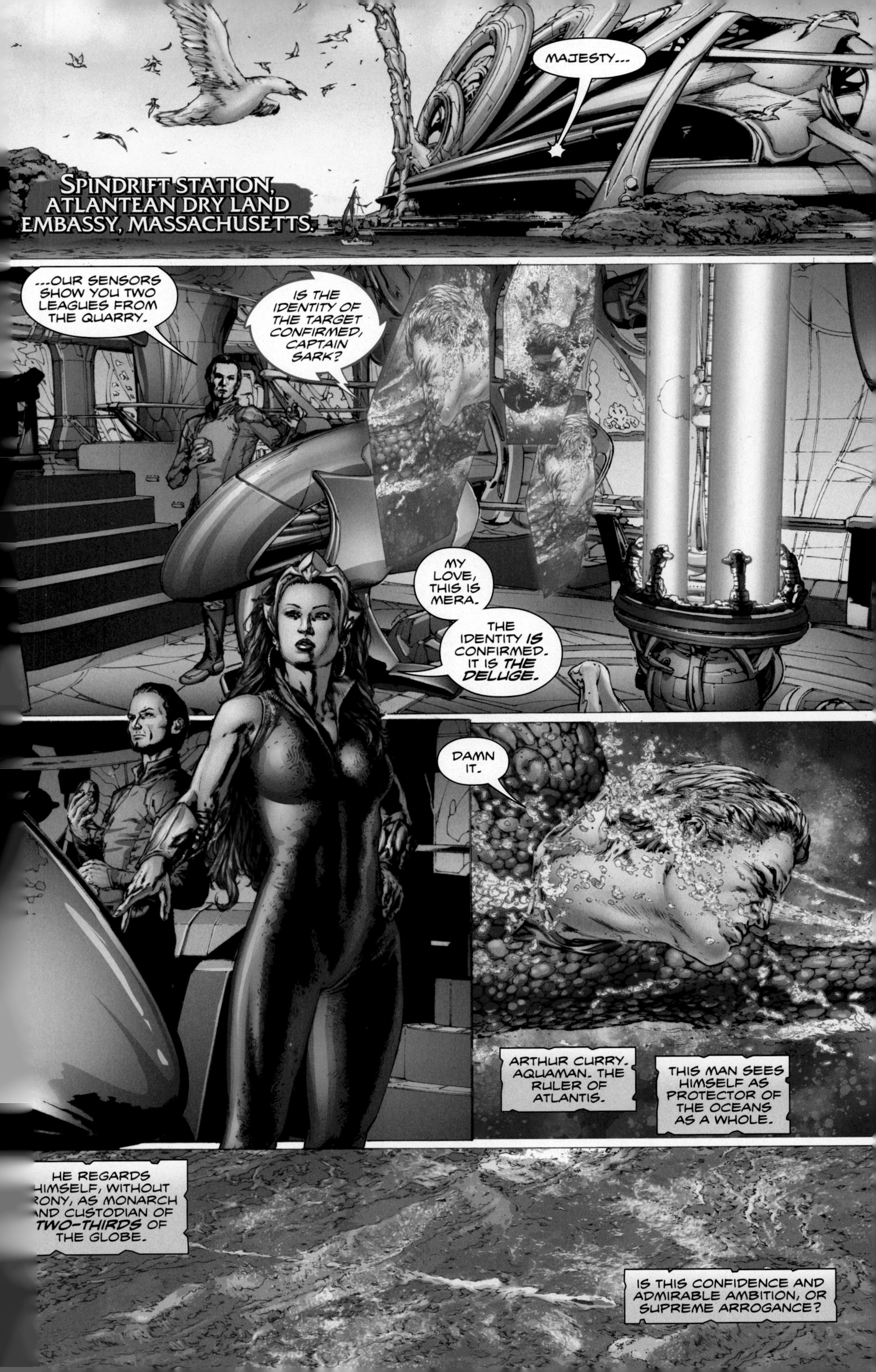
MAJESTY...
SPINDRIFT STATION, ATLANTEAN DRY LAND EMBASSY, MASSACHUSETTS.
...OUR SENSORS SHOW YOU TWO LEAGUES FROM THE QUARRY.
IS THE IDENTITY OF THE TARGET CONFIRMED, CAPTAIN SARK?
MY LOVE, THIS IS MERA.
THE IDENTITY *IS* CONFIRMED. IT IS *THE DELUGE.*
DAMN IT.
ARTHUR CURRY. AQUAMAN. THE RULER OF ATLANTIS.
THIS MAN SEES HIMSELF AS PROTECTOR OF THE OCEANS AS A WHOLE.
HE REGARDS HIMSELF, WITHOUT IRONY, AS MONARCH AND CUSTODIAN OF *TWO-THIRDS* OF THE GLOBE.
IS THIS CONFIDENCE AND ADMIRABLE AMBITION, OR SUPREME ARROGANCE?

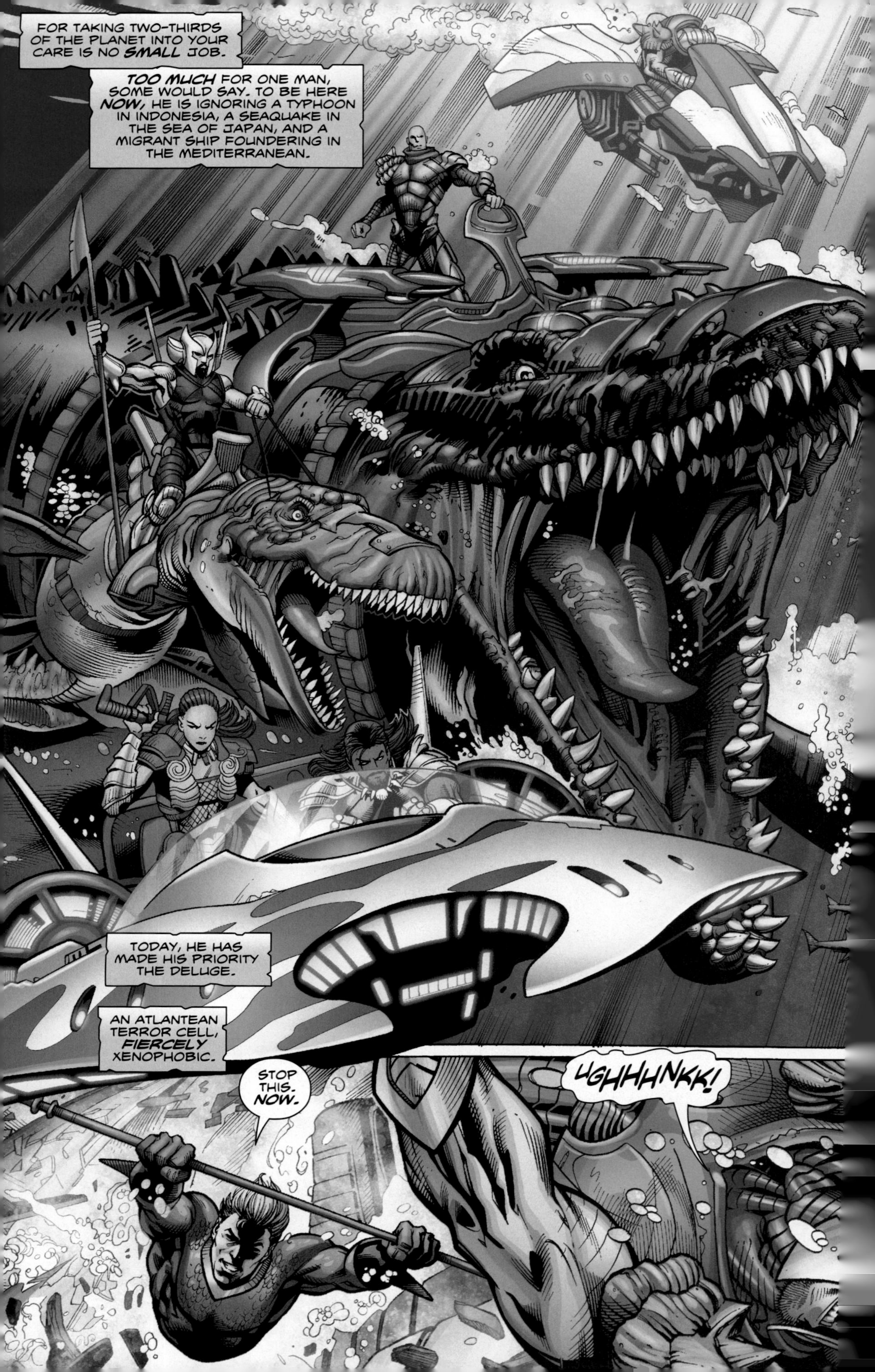
FOR TAKING TWO-THIRDS OF THE PLANET INTO YOUR CARE IS NO SMALL JOB.
TOO MUCH FOR ONE MAN, SOME WOULD SAY. TO BE HERE NOW, HE IS IGNORING A TYPHOON IN INDONESIA, A SEAQUAKE IN THE SEA OF JAPAN, AND A MIGRANT SHIP FOUNDERING IN THE MEDITERRANEAN.
TODAY, HE HAS MADE HIS PRIORITY THE DELUGE.
AN ATLANTEAN TERROR CELL, FIERCELY XENOPHOBIC.
STOP THIS. NOW.
UGHHHNKK!

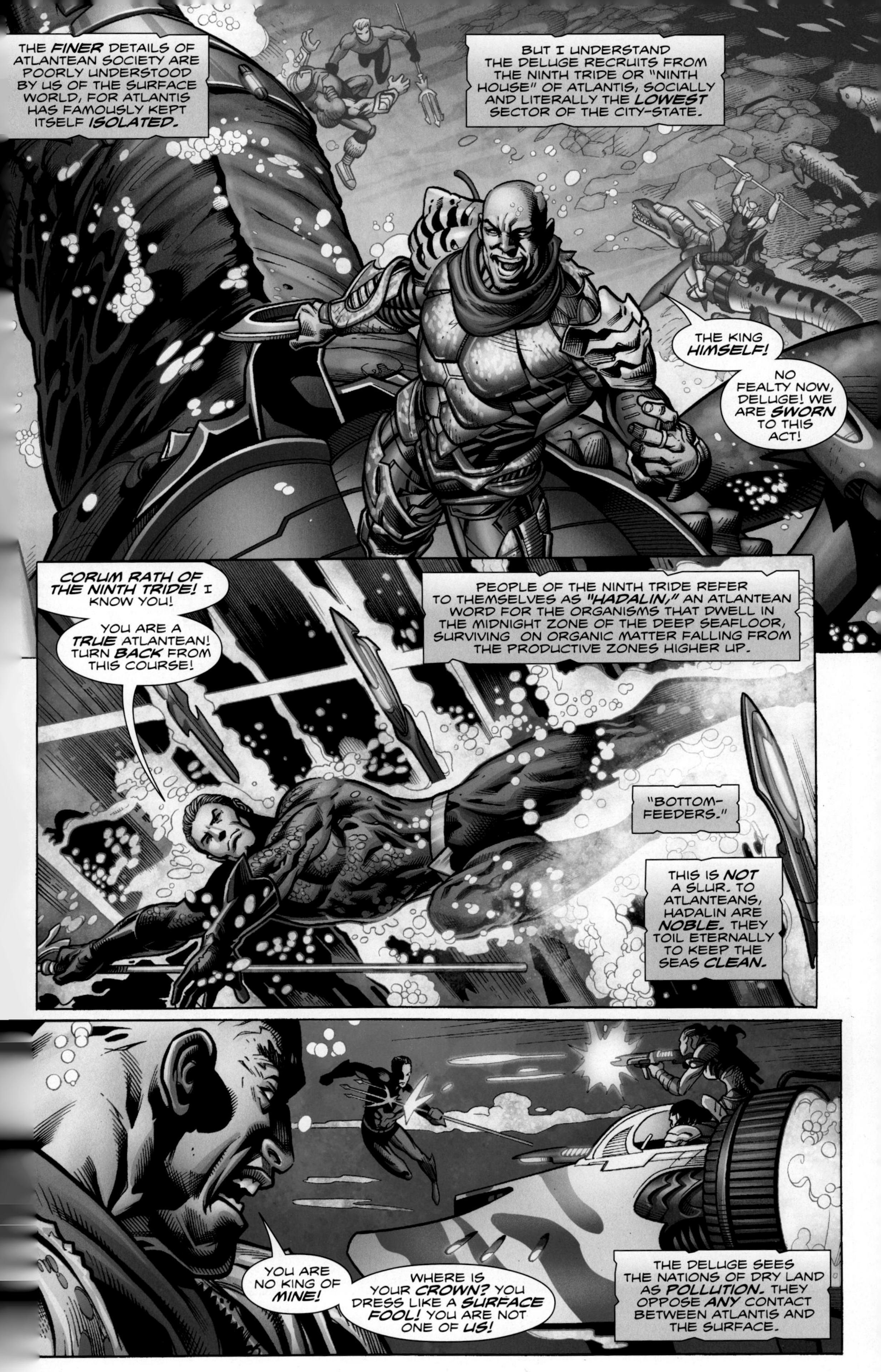
THE FINER DETAILS OF ATLANTEAN SOCIETY ARE POORLY UNDERSTOOD BY US OF THE SURFACE WORLD, FOR ATLANTIS HAS FAMOUSLY KEPT ITSELF ISOLATED.
BUT I UNDERSTAND THE DELUGE RECRUITS FROM THE NINTH TRIDE OR "NINTH HOUSE" OF ATLANTIS, SOCIALLY AND LITERALLY THE LOWEST SECTOR OF THE CITY-STATE.
THE KING HIMSELF!
NO FEALTY NOW, DELUGE! WE ARE SWORN TO THIS ACT!
CORUM RATH OF THE NINTH TRIDE! I KNOW YOU!
YOU ARE A TRUE ATLANTEAN! TURN BACK FROM THIS COURSE!
PEOPLE OF THE NINTH TRIDE REFER TO THEMSELVES AS "HADALIN," AN ATLANTEAN WORD FOR THE ORGANISMS THAT DWELL IN THE MIDNIGHT ZONE OF THE DEEP SEAFLOOR, SURVIVING ON ORGANIC MATTER FALLING FROM THE PRODUCTIVE ZONES HIGHER UP.
"BOTTOM-FEEDERS."
THIS IS NOT A SLUR. TO ATLANTEANS, HADALIN ARE NOBLE. THEY TOIL ETERNALLY TO KEEP THE SEAS CLEAN.
YOU ARE NO KING OF MINE!
WHERE IS YOUR CROWN? YOU DRESS LIKE A SURFACE FOOL! YOU ARE NOT ONE OF US!
THE DELUGE SEES THE NATIONS OF DRY LAND AS POLLUTION. THEY OPPOSE ANY CONTACT BETWEEN ATLANTIS AND THE SURFACE.

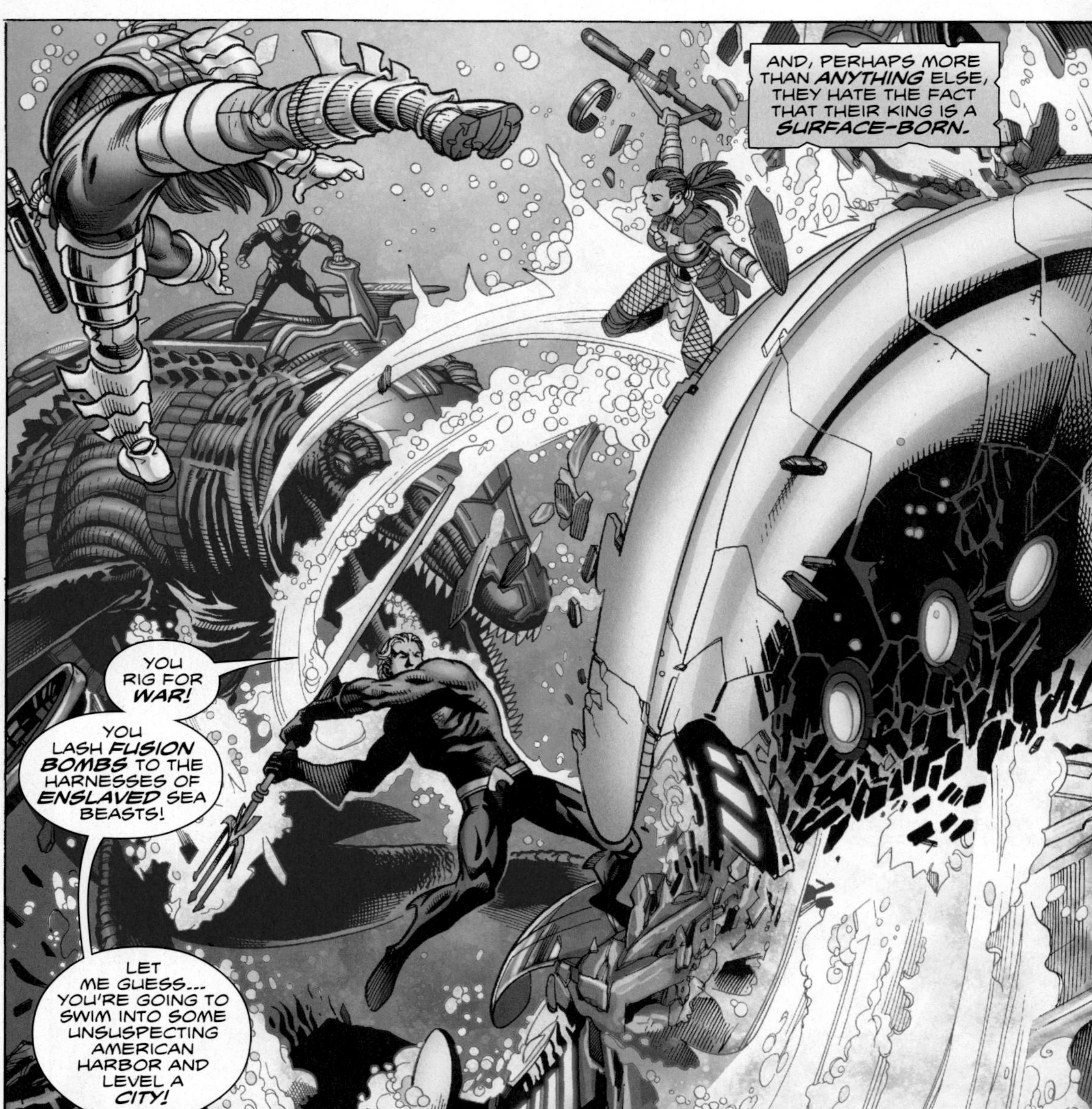
AND, PERHAPS MORE THAN ANYTHING ELSE, THEY HATE THE FACT THAT THEIR KING IS A SURFACE-BORN.
YOU RIG FOR WAR!
YOU LASH FUSION BOMBS TO THE HARNESSES OF ENSLAVED SEA BEASTS!
LET ME GUESS... YOU'RE GOING TO SWIM INTO SOME UNSUSPECTING AMERICAN HARBOR AND LEVEL A CITY!
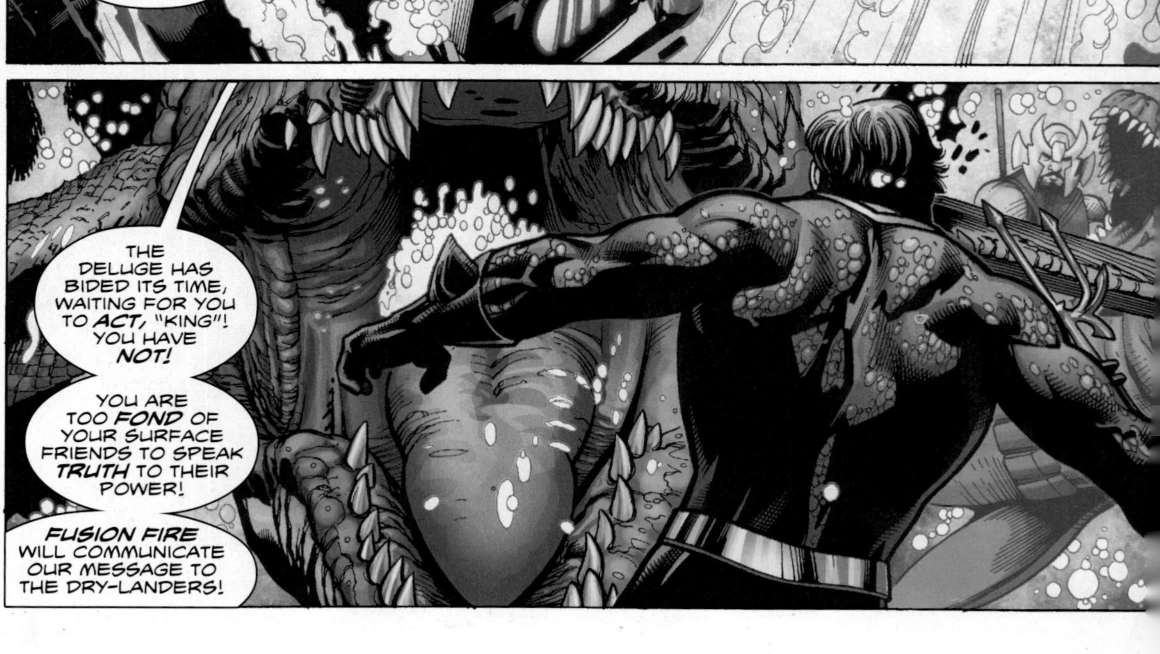
THE DELUGE HAS BIDED ITS TIME, WAITING FOR YOU TO ACT, "KING"! YOU HAVE NOT!
YOU ARE TOO FOND OF YOUR SURFACE FRIENDS TO SPEAK TRUTH TO THEIR POWER!
FUSION FIRE WILL COMMUNICATE OUR MESSAGE TO THE DRY-LANDERS!

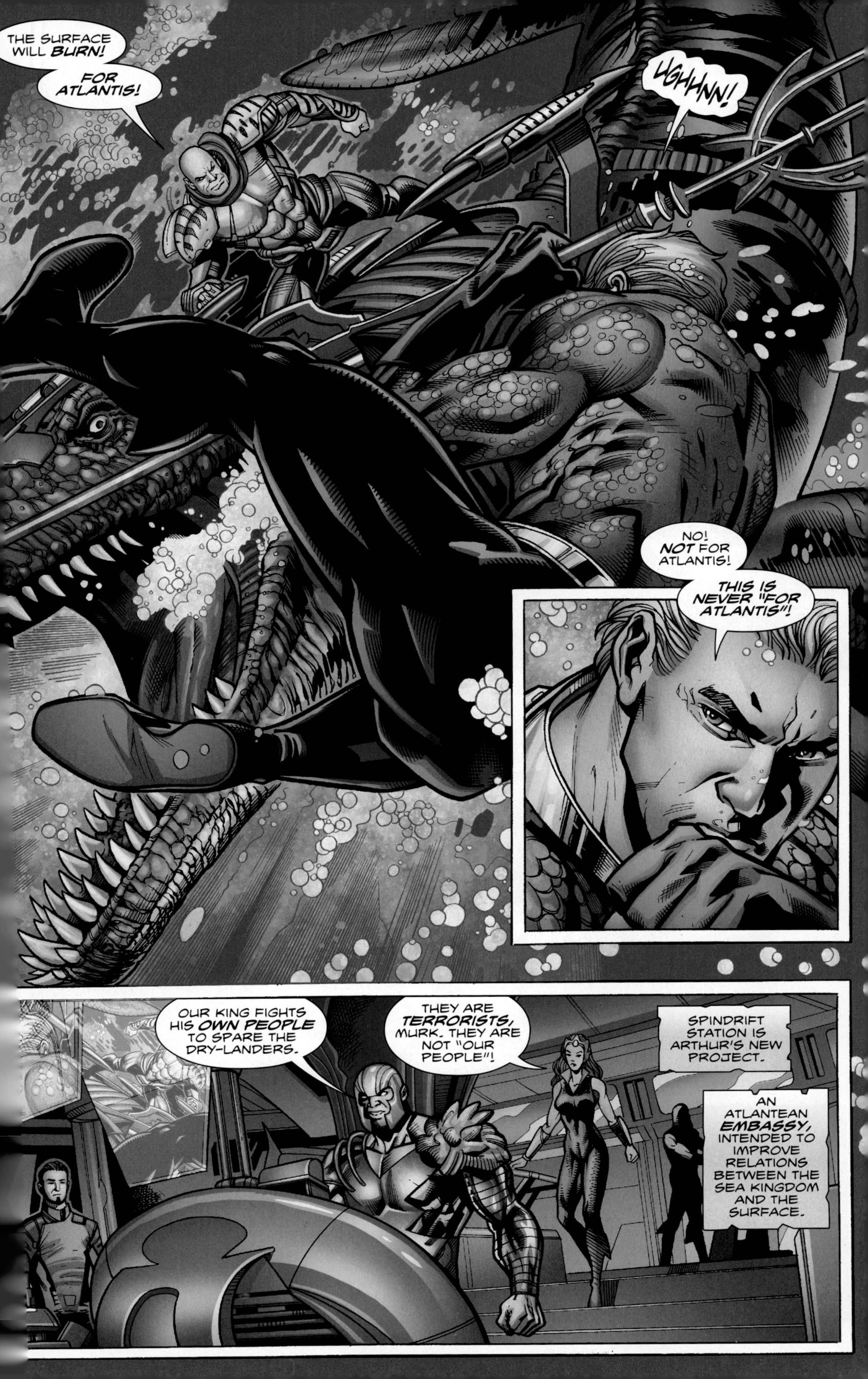
THE SURFACE WILL BURN!
FOR ATLANTIS!
UGHHNN!
NO! NOT FOR ATLANTIS!
THIS IS NEVER "FOR ATLANTIS"!
OUR KING FIGHTS HIS OWN PEOPLE TO SPARE THE DRY-LANDERS.
THEY ARE TERRORISTS, MURK. THEY ARE NOT "OUR PEOPLE"!
SPINDRIFT STATION IS ARTHUR'S NEW PROJECT.
AN ATLANTEAN EMBASSY, INTENDED TO IMPROVE RELATIONS BETWEEN THE SEA KINGDOM AND THE SURFACE.

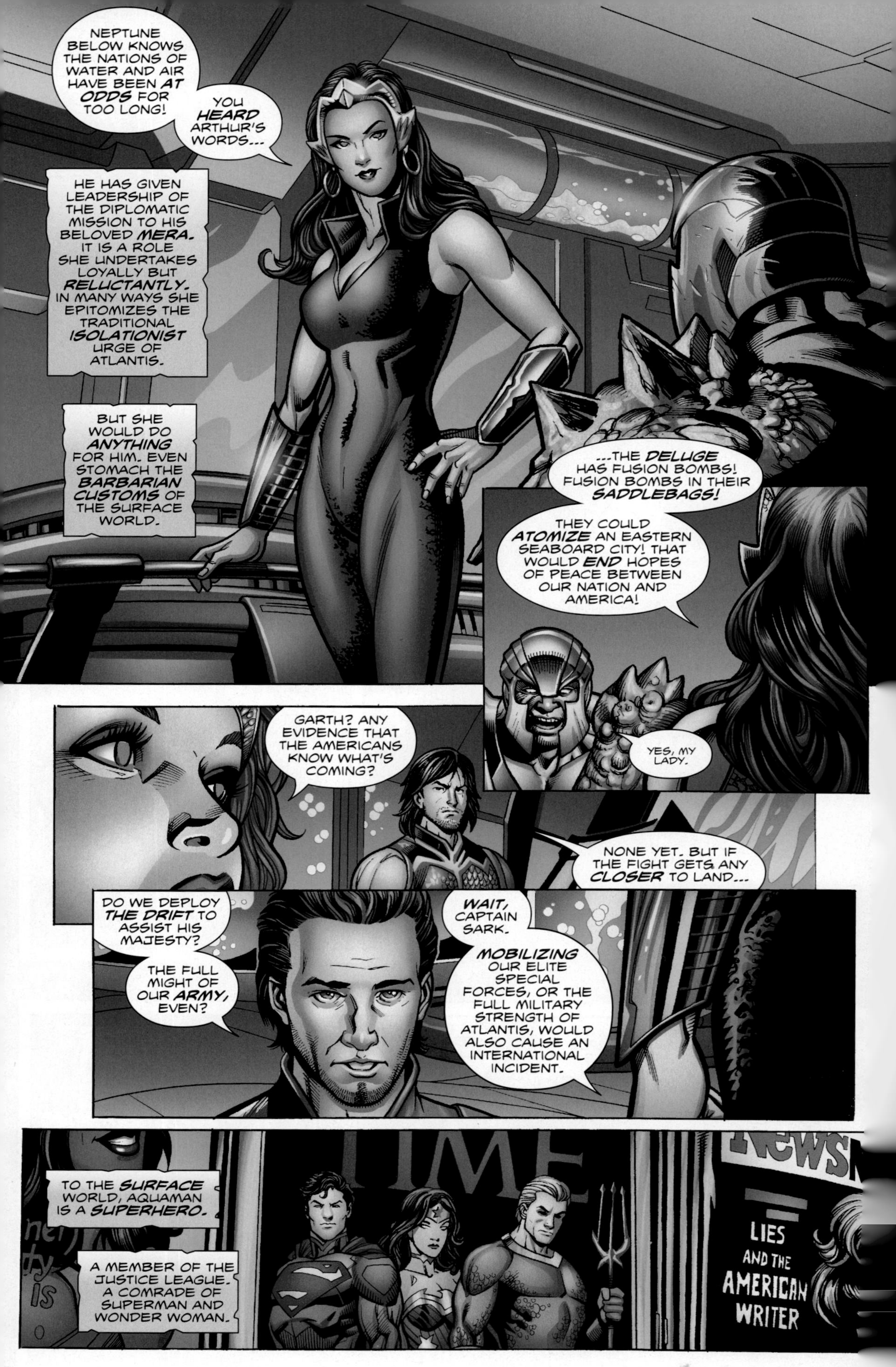
NEPTUNE BELOW KNOWS THE NATIONS OF WATER AND AIR HAVE BEEN AT ODDS FOR TOO LONG!
YOU HEARD ARTHUR'S WORDS...
HE HAS GIVEN LEADERSHIP OF THE DIPLOMATIC MISSION TO HIS BELOVED MERA. IT IS A ROLE SHE UNDERTAKES LOYALLY BUT RELUCTANTLY. IN MANY WAYS SHE EPITOMIZES THE TRADITIONAL ISOLATIONIST URGE OF ATLANTIS.
BUT SHE WOULD DO ANYTHING FOR HIM. EVEN STOMACH THE BARBARIAN CUSTOMS OF THE SURFACE WORLD.
...THE DELUGE HAS FUSION BOMBS! FUSION BOMBS IN THEIR SADDLEBAGS!
THEY COULD ATOMIZE AN EASTERN SEABOARD CITY! THAT WOULD END HOPES OF PEACE BETWEEN OUR NATION AND AMERICA!
YES, MY LADY.
GARTH? ANY EVIDENCE THAT THE AMERICANS KNOW WHAT'S COMING?
NONE YET. BUT IF THE FIGHT GETS ANY CLOSER TO LAND...
DO WE DEPLOY THE DRIFT TO ASSIST HIS MAJESTY?
THE FULL MIGHT OF OUR ARMY, EVEN?
WAIT, CAPTAIN SARK.
MOBILIZING OUR ELITE SPECIAL FORCES, OR THE FULL MILITARY STRENGTH OF ATLANTIS, WOULD ALSO CAUSE AN INTERNATIONAL INCIDENT.
TO THE SURFACE WORLD, AQUAMAN IS A SUPERHERO.
A MEMBER OF THE JUSTICE LEAGUE. A COMRADE OF SUPERMAN AND WONDER WOMAN.
TIME
LIES AND THE AMERICAN WRITER

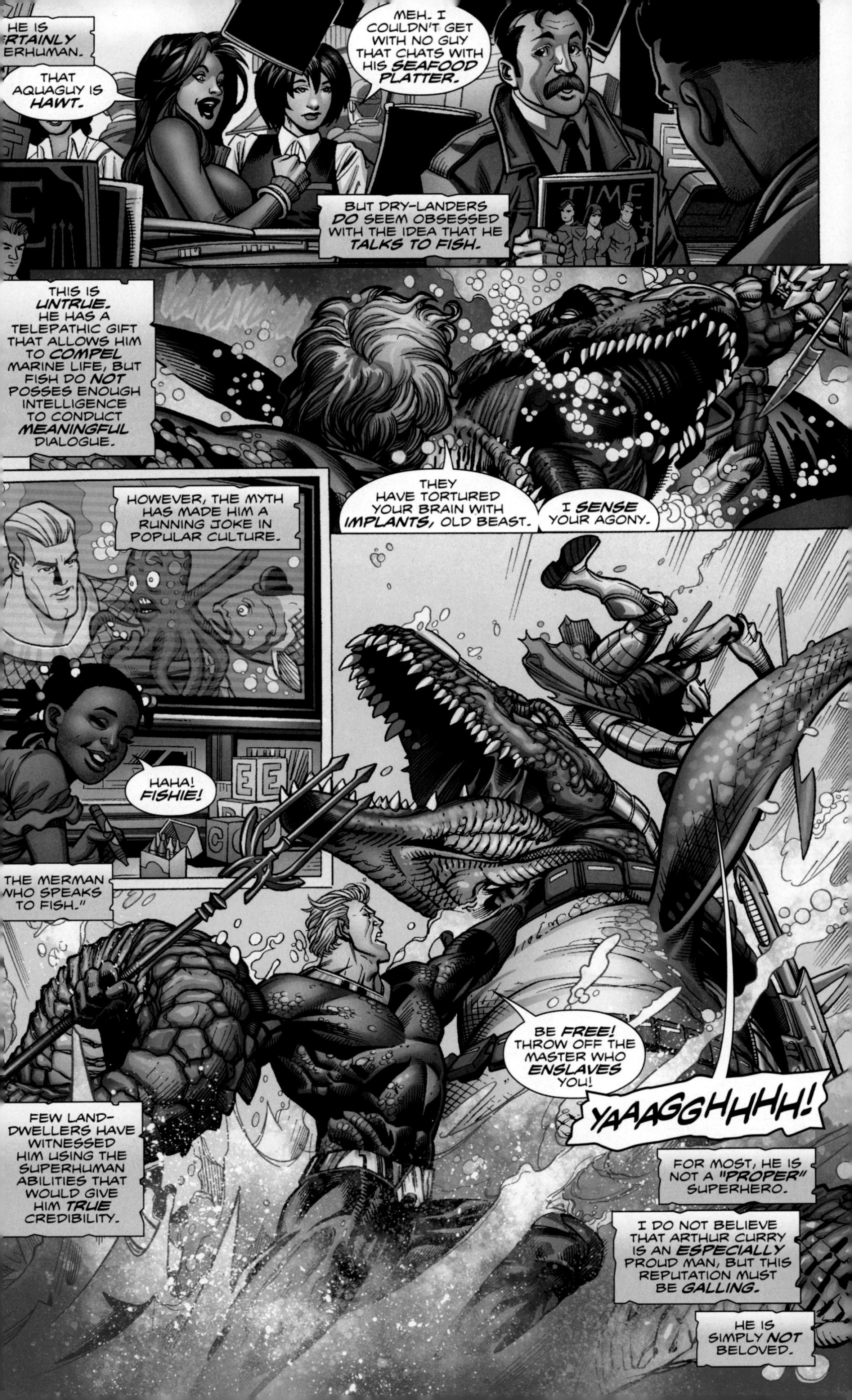
HE IS
RTAINLY
ERHUMAN.
THAT AQUAGUY IS HAWT.
MEH. I COULDN'T GET WITH NO GUY THAT CHATS WITH HIS SEAFOOD PLATTER.
BUT DRY-LANDERS DO SEEM OBSESSED WITH THE IDEA THAT HE TALKS TO FISH.
TIME
THIS IS UNTRUE. HE HAS A TELEPATHIC GIFT THAT ALLOWS HIM TO COMPEL MARINE LIFE, BUT FISH DO NOT POSSES ENOUGH INTELLIGENCE TO CONDUCT MEANINGFUL DIALOGUE.
THEY HAVE TORTURED YOUR BRAIN WITH IMPLANTS, OLD BEAST.
I SENSE YOUR AGONY.
HOWEVER, THE MYTH HAS MADE HIM A RUNNING JOKE IN POPULAR CULTURE.
HAHA! FISHIE!
THE MERMAN
WHO SPEAKS
TO FISH."
BE FREE! THROW OFF THE MASTER WHO ENSLAVES YOU!
YAAAGGHHHH!
FEW LAND-DWELLERS HAVE WITNESSED HIM USING THE SUPERHUMAN ABILITIES THAT WOULD GIVE HIM TRUE CREDIBILITY.
FOR MOST, HE IS NOT A "PROPER" SUPERHERO.
I DO NOT BELIEVE THAT ARTHUR CURRY IS AN ESPECIALLY PROUD MAN, BUT THIS REPUTATION MUST BE GALLING.
HE IS SIMPLY NOT BELOVED.

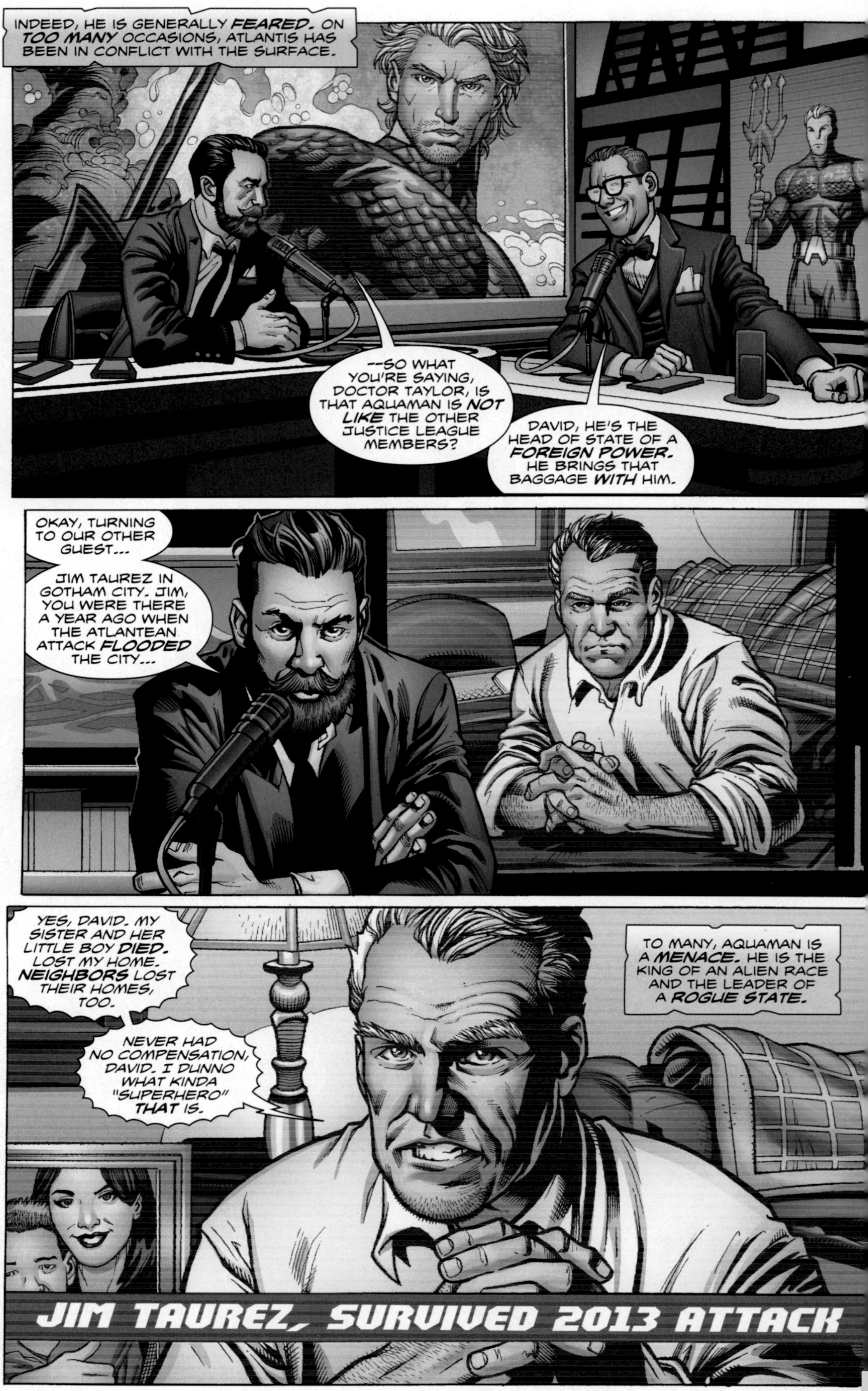
INDEED, HE IS GENERALLY FEARED. ON TOO MANY OCCASIONS, ATLANTIS HAS BEEN IN CONFLICT WITH THE SURFACE.
--SO WHAT YOU'RE SAYING, DOCTOR TAYLOR, IS THAT AQUAMAN IS NOT LIKE THE OTHER JUSTICE LEAGUE MEMBERS?
DAVID, HE'S THE HEAD OF STATE OF A FOREIGN POWER. HE BRINGS THAT BAGGAGE WITH HIM.
OKAY, TURNING TO OUR OTHER GUEST...
JIM TAUREZ IN GOTHAM CITY. JIM, YOU WERE THERE A YEAR AGO WHEN THE ATLANTEAN ATTACK FLOODED THE CITY...
YES, DAVID. MY SISTER AND HER LITTLE BOY DIED. LOST MY HOME. NEIGHBORS LOST THEIR HOMES, TOO.
NEVER HAD NO COMPENSATION, DAVID. I DUNNO WHAT KINDA "SUPERHERO" THAT IS.
TO MANY, AQUAMAN IS A MENACE. HE IS THE KING OF AN ALIEN RACE AND THE LEADER OF A ROGUE STATE.
JIM TAUREZ, SURVIVED 2013 ATTACK

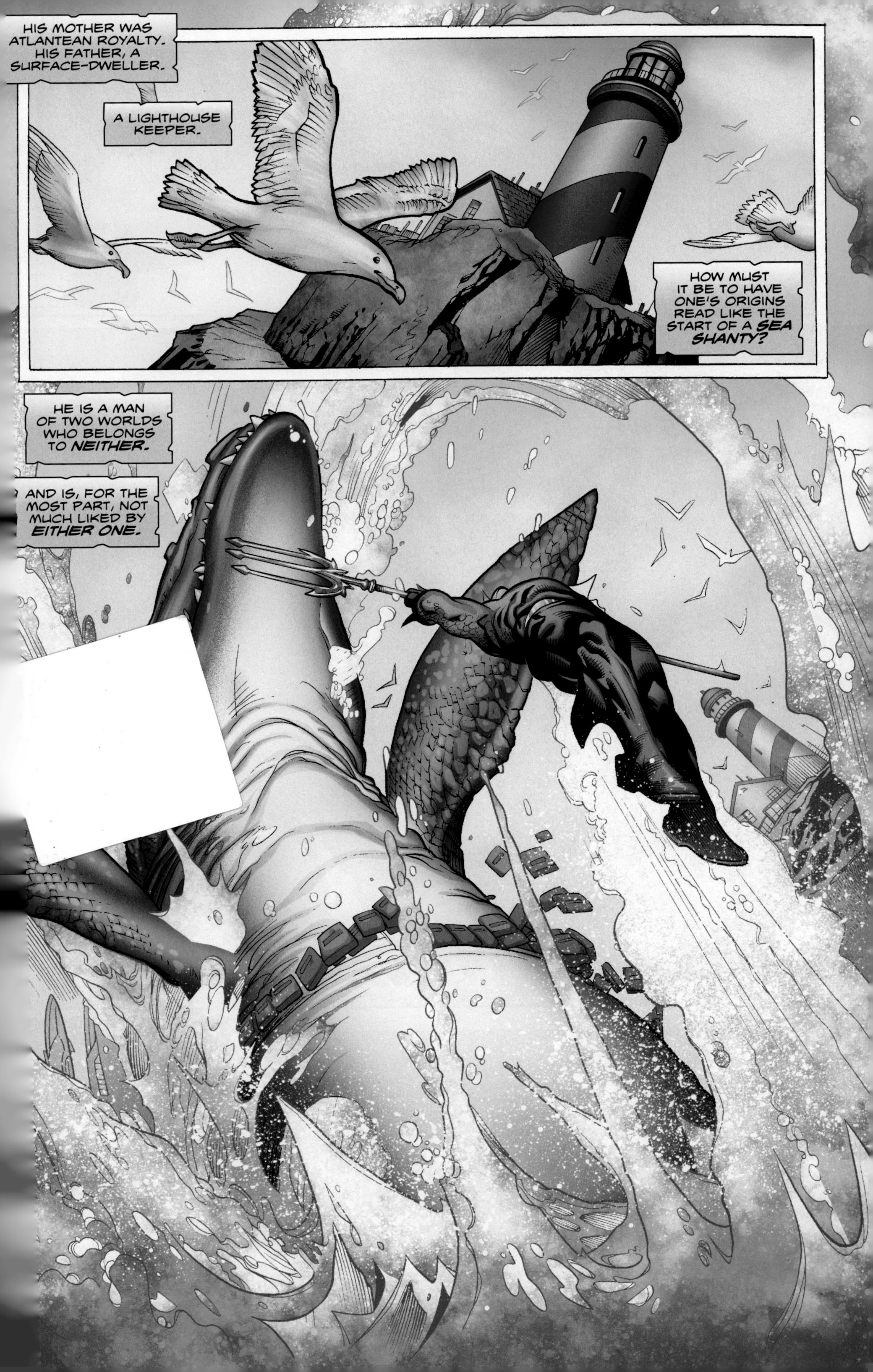
HIS MOTHER WAS ATLANTEAN ROYALTY. HIS FATHER, A SURFACE-DWELLER.
A LIGHTHOUSE KEEPER.
HOW MUST IT BE TO HAVE ONE'S ORIGINS READ LIKE THE START OF A *SEA SHANTY?*
HE IS A MAN OF TWO WORLDS WHO BELONGS TO *NEITHER.*
AND IS, FOR THE MOST PART, NOT MUCH LIKED BY *EITHER ONE.*

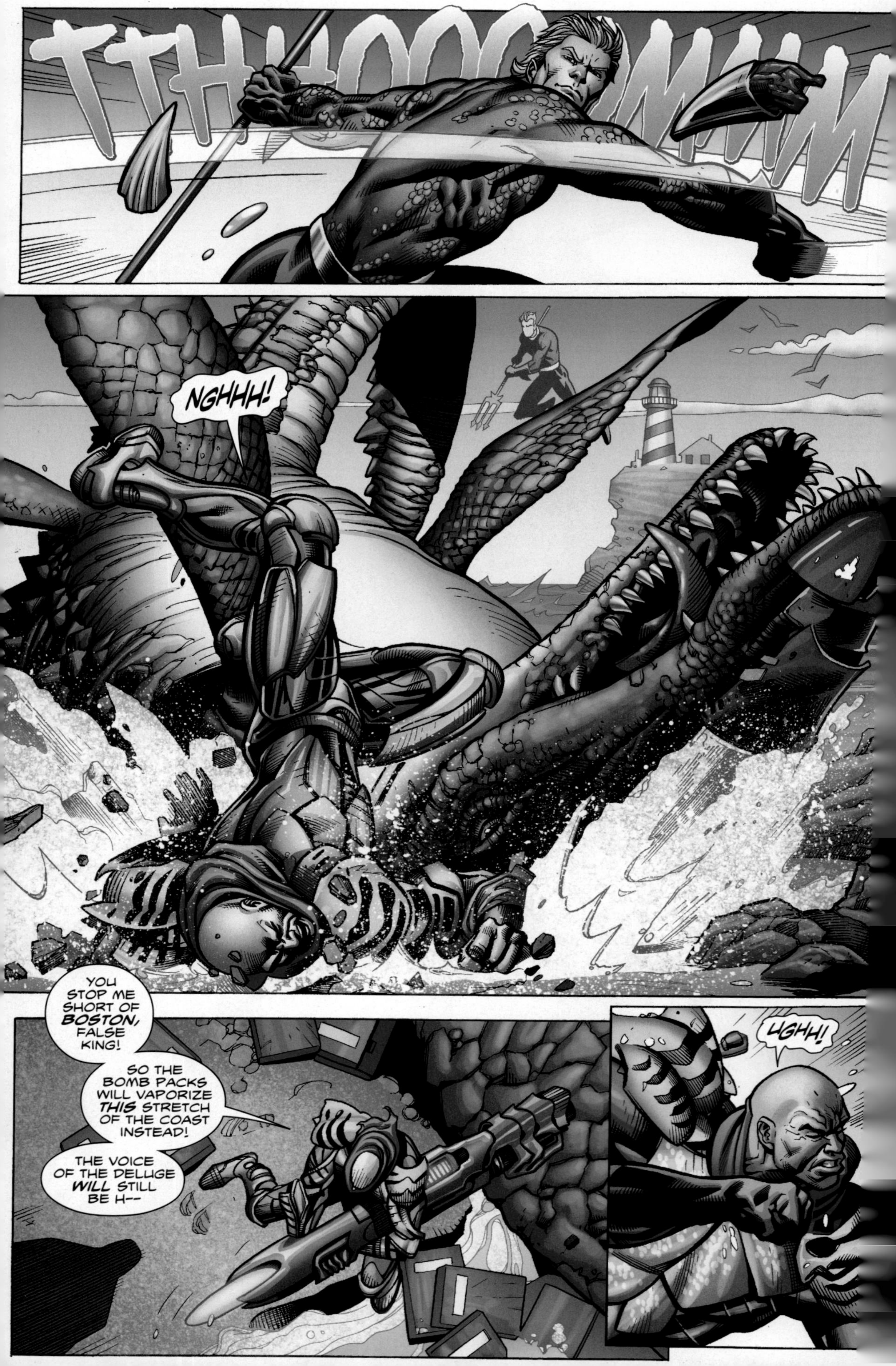
THHOOOMMM
NGHHH!
YOU STOP ME SHORT OF BOSTON, FALSE KING!
SO THE BOMB PACKS WILL VAPORIZE THIS STRETCH OF THE COAST INSTEAD!
THE VOICE OF THE DELUGE WILL STILL BE H--
UGHH!

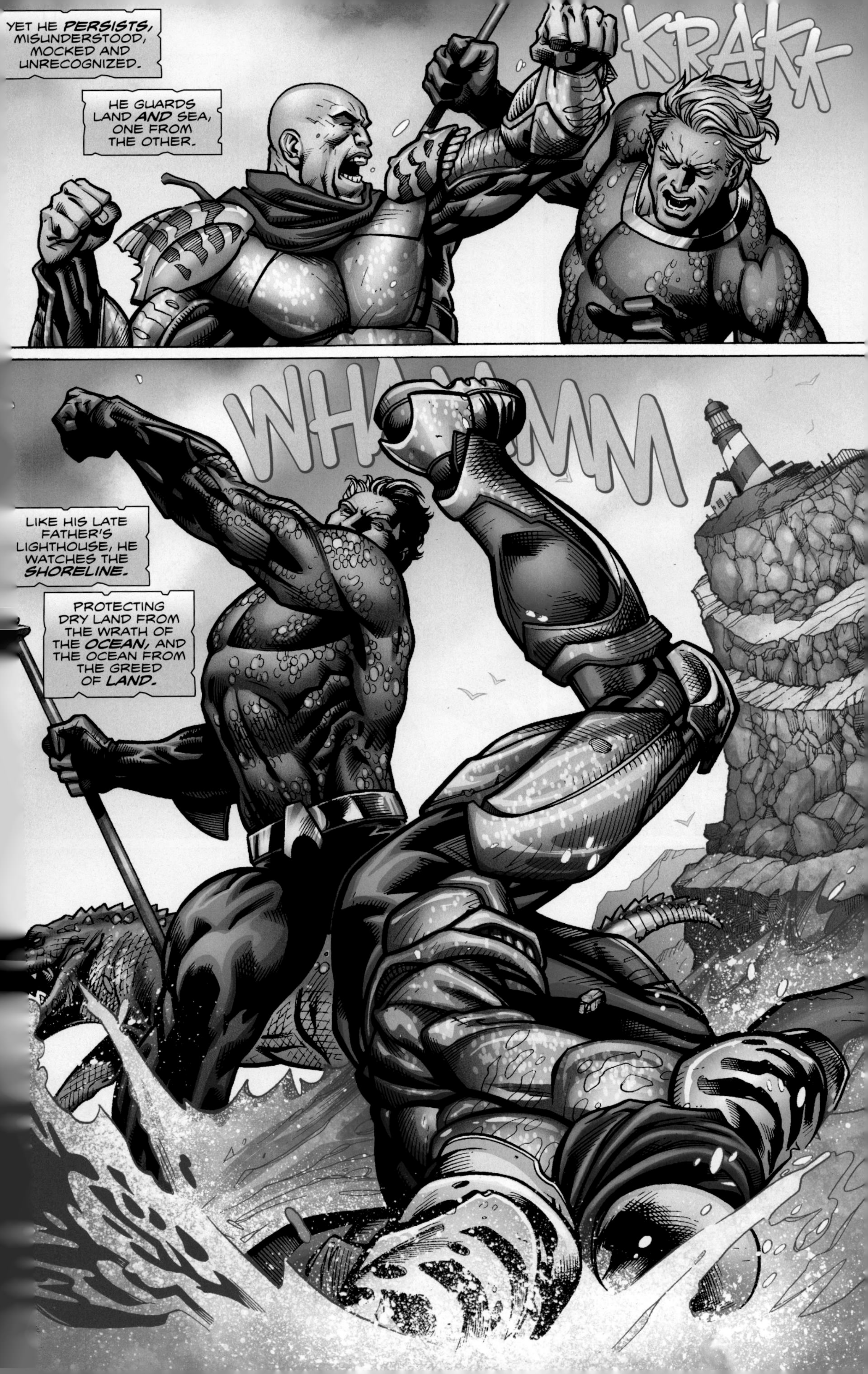

YET HE PERSISTS, MISUNDERSTOOD, MOCKED AND UNRECOGNIZED.
HE GUARDS LAND AND SEA, ONE FROM THE OTHER.
KRAKK
WHAMMM
LIKE HIS LATE FATHER'S LIGHTHOUSE, HE WATCHES THE SHORELINE.
PROTECTING DRY LAND FROM THE WRATH OF THE OCEAN, AND THE OCEAN FROM THE GREED OF LAND.

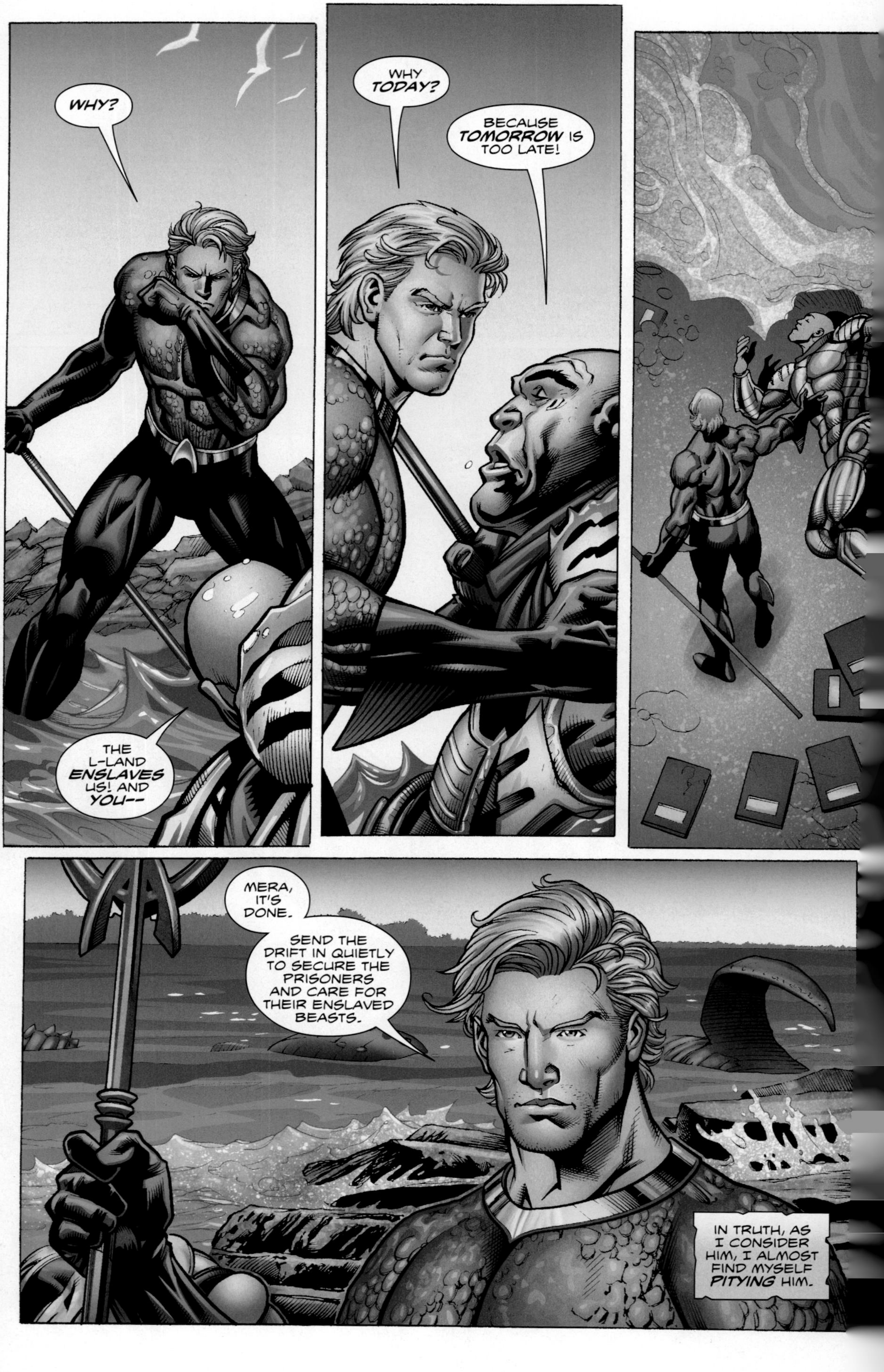
WHY?
THE L-LAND ENSLAVES US! AND YOU--
WHY TODAY?
BECAUSE TOMORROW IS TOO LATE!
MERA, IT'S DONE.
SEND THE DRIFT IN QUIETLY TO SECURE THE PRISONERS AND CARE FOR THEIR ENSLAVED BEASTS.
IN TRUTH, AS I CONSIDER HIM, I ALMOST FIND MYSELF PITYING HIM.

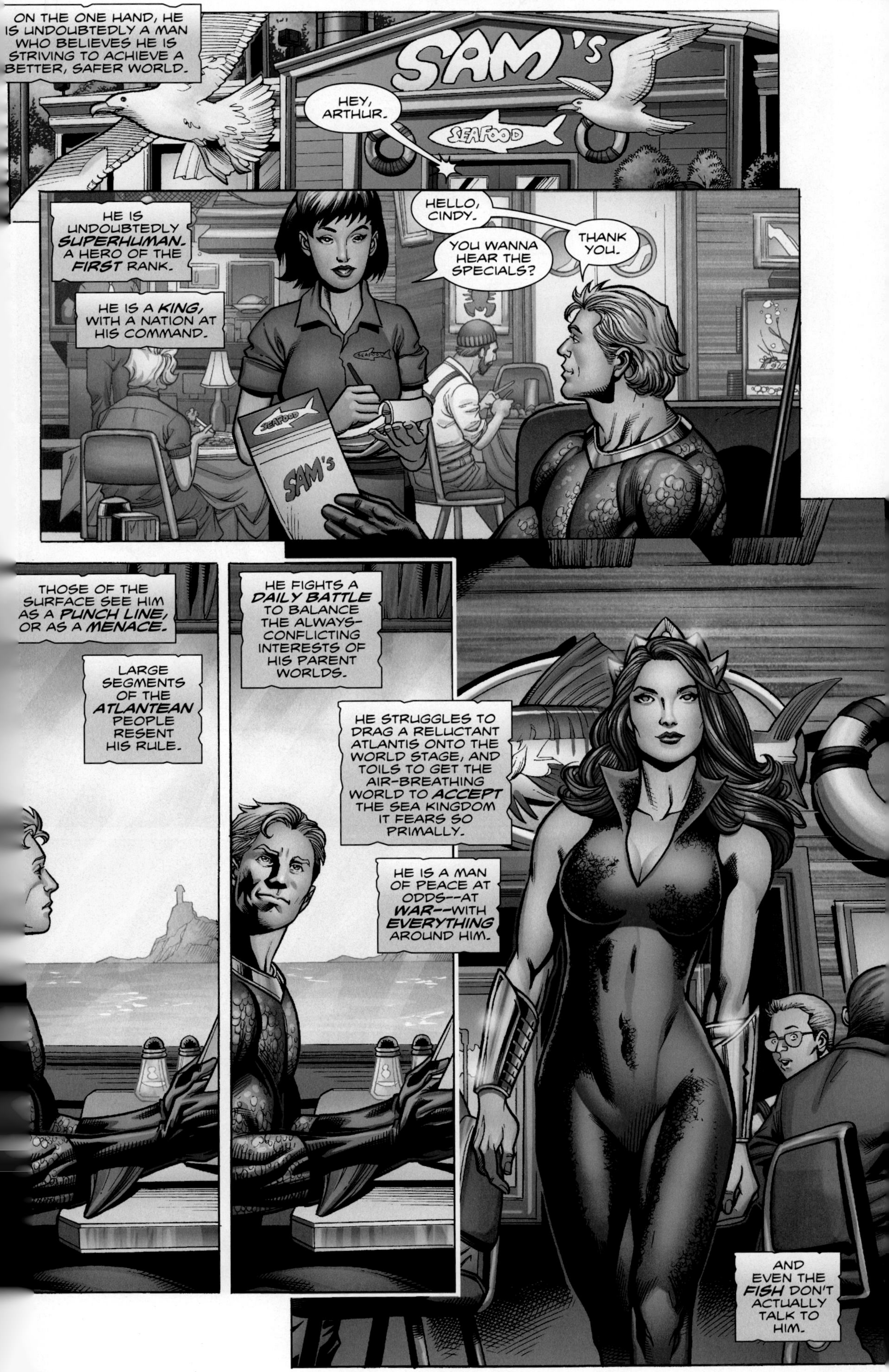
ON THE ONE HAND, HE IS UNDOUBTEDLY A MAN WHO BELIEVES HE IS STRIVING TO ACHIEVE A BETTER, SAFER WORLD.
SAM'S
HEY, ARTHUR.
SEAFOOD
HE IS UNDOUBTEDLY SUPERHUMAN. A HERO OF THE FIRST RANK.
HE IS A KING, WITH A NATION AT HIS COMMAND.
HELLO, CINDY.
YOU WANNA HEAR THE SPECIALS?
THANK YOU.
SEAFOOD
SAM'S
THOSE OF THE SURFACE SEE HIM AS A PUNCH LINE, OR AS A MENACE.
LARGE SEGMENTS OF THE ATLANTEAN PEOPLE RESENT HIS RULE.
HE FIGHTS A DAILY BATTLE TO BALANCE THE ALWAYS-CONFLICTING INTERESTS OF HIS PARENT WORLDS.
HE STRUGGLES TO DRAG A RELUCTANT ATLANTIS ONTO THE WORLD STAGE, AND TOILS TO GET THE AIR-BREATHING WORLD TO ACCEPT THE SEA KINGDOM IT FEARS SO PRIMALLY.
HE IS A MAN OF PEACE AT ODDS--AT WAR--WITH EVERYTHING AROUND HIM.
AND EVEN THE FISH DON'T ACTUALLY TALK TO HIM.

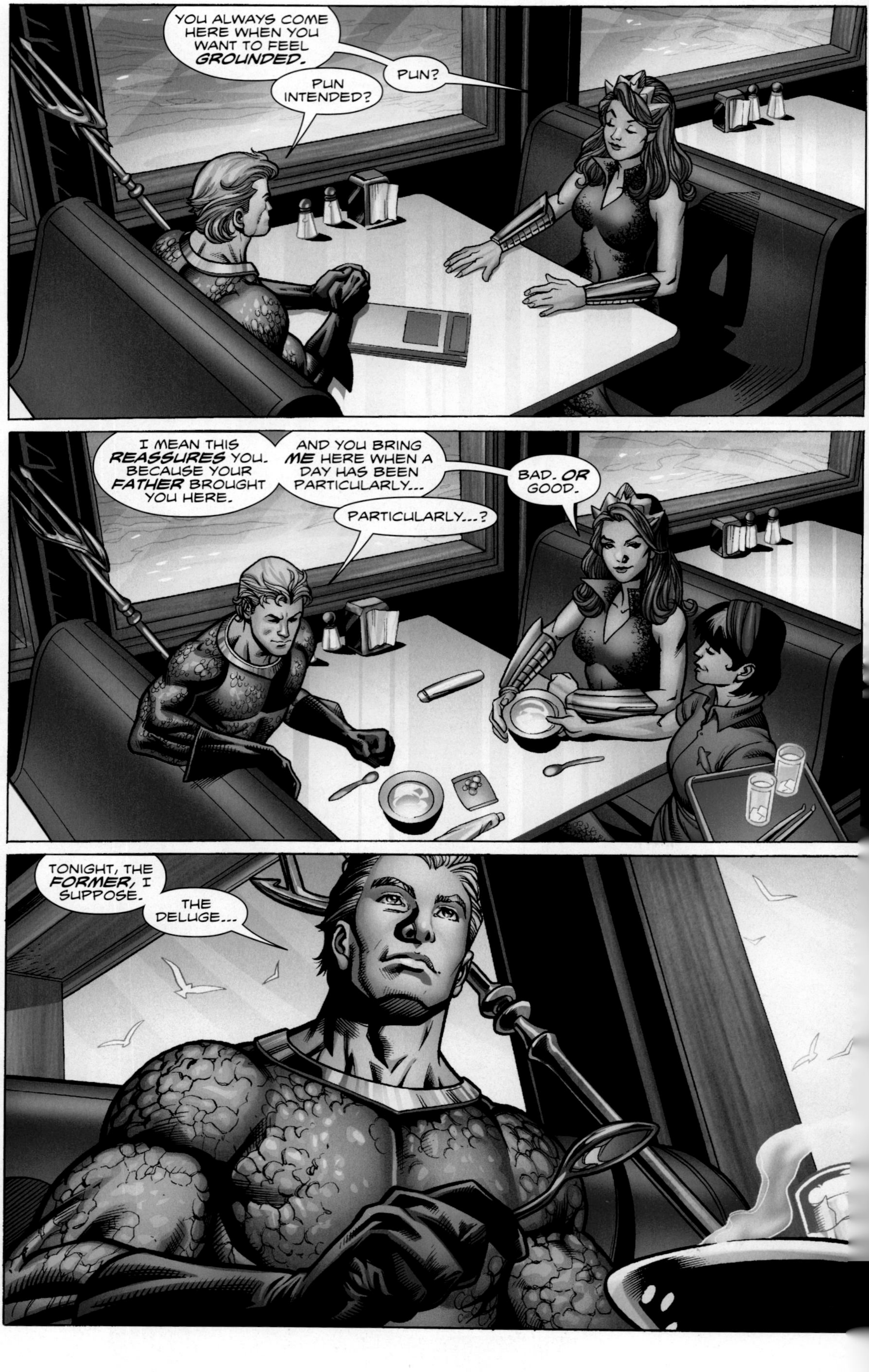
YOU ALWAYS COME HERE WHEN YOU WANT TO FEEL *GROUNDED.*
PUN?
PUN INTENDED?
I MEAN THIS *REASSURES* YOU. BECAUSE YOUR *FATHER* BROUGHT YOU HERE.
AND YOU BRING *ME* HERE WHEN A DAY HAS BEEN PARTICULARLY...
BAD. *OR* GOOD.
PARTICULARLY...?
TONIGHT, THE *FORMER,* I SUPPOSE.
THE DELUGE...

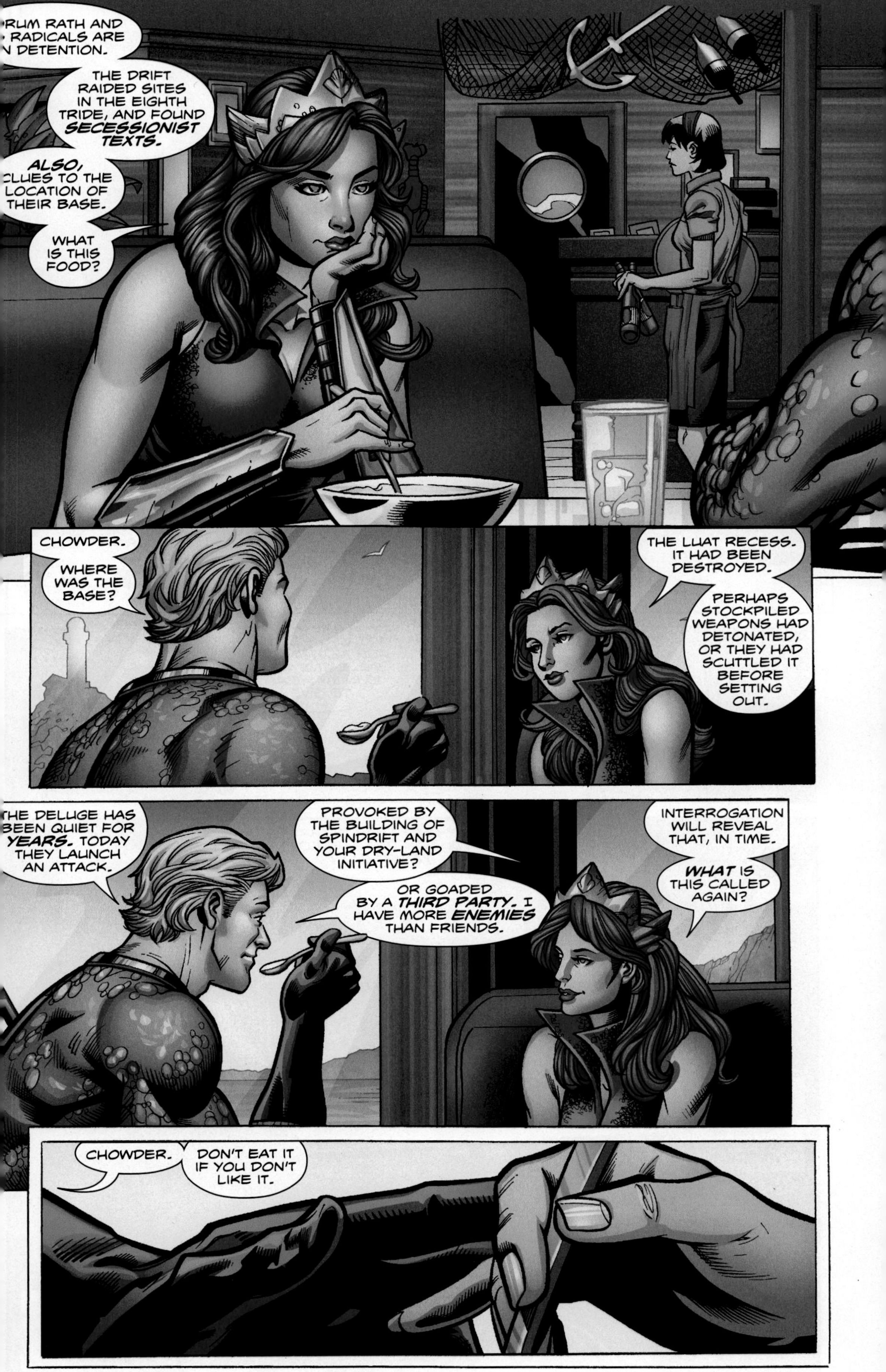

RUM RATH AND
RADICALS ARE
N DETENTION.
THE DRIFT RAIDED SITES IN THE EIGHTH TRIDE, AND FOUND SECESSIONIST TEXTS.
ALSO, CLUES TO THE LOCATION OF THEIR BASE.
WHAT IS THIS FOOD?
CHOWDER.
WHERE WAS THE BASE?
THE LUAT RECESS. IT HAD BEEN DESTROYED.
PERHAPS STOCKPILED WEAPONS HAD DETONATED, OR THEY HAD SCUTTLED IT BEFORE SETTING OUT.
THE DELUGE HAS BEEN QUIET FOR YEARS. TODAY THEY LAUNCH AN ATTACK.
PROVOKED BY THE BUILDING OF SPINDRIFT AND YOUR DRY-LAND INITIATIVE?
OR GOADED BY A THIRD PARTY. I HAVE MORE ENEMIES THAN FRIENDS.
INTERROGATION WILL REVEAL THAT, IN TIME.
WHAT IS THIS CALLED AGAIN?
CHOWDER.
DON'T EAT IT IF YOU DON'T LIKE IT.

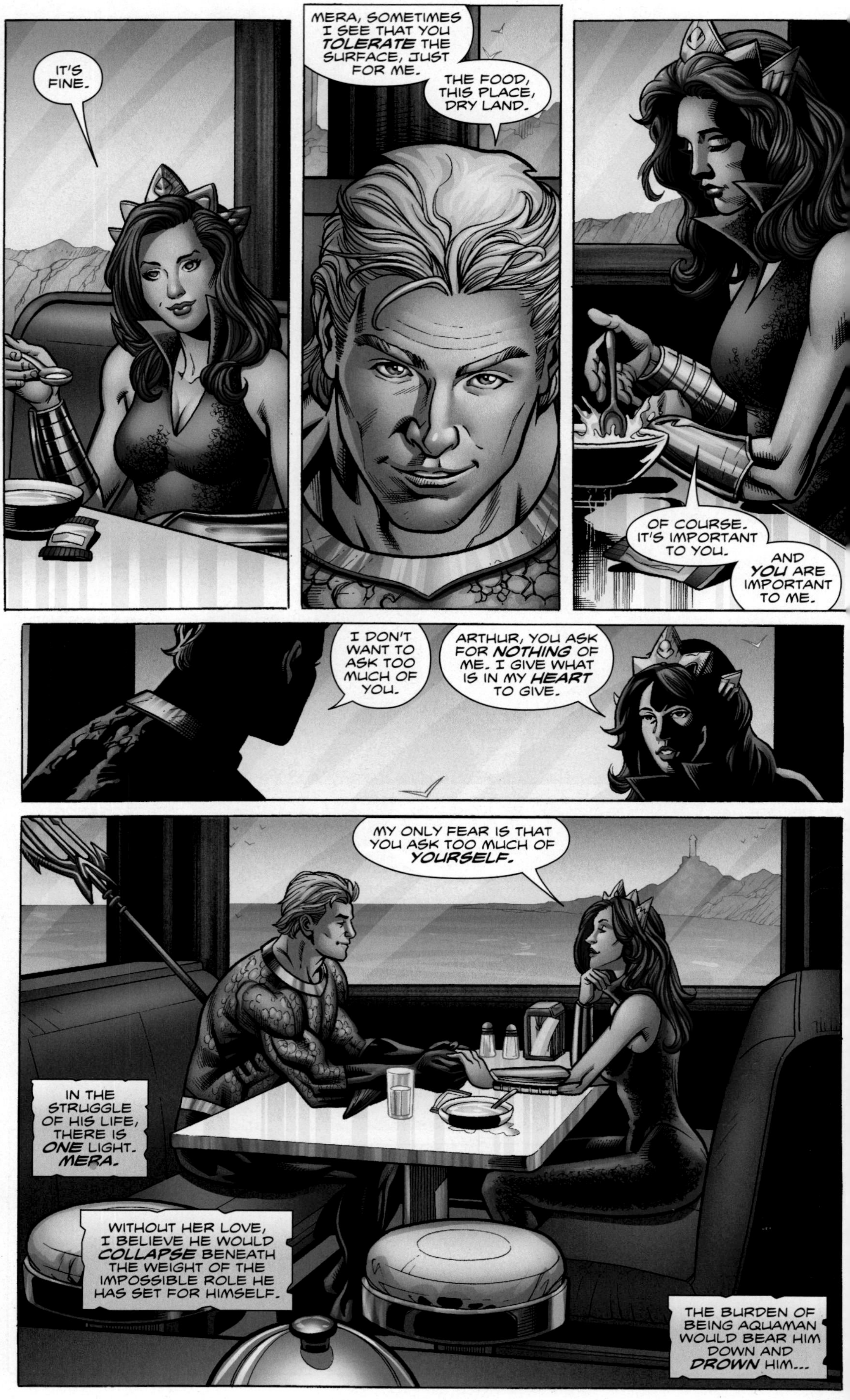
IT'S FINE.
MERA, SOMETIMES I SEE THAT YOU TOLERATE THE SURFACE, JUST FOR ME.
THE FOOD, THIS PLACE, DRY LAND.
OF COURSE. IT'S IMPORTANT TO YOU.
AND YOU ARE IMPORTANT TO ME.
I DON'T WANT TO ASK TOO MUCH OF YOU.
ARTHUR, YOU ASK FOR NOTHING OF ME. I GIVE WHAT IS IN MY HEART TO GIVE.
MY ONLY FEAR IS THAT YOU ASK TOO MUCH OF YOURSELF.
IN THE STRUGGLE OF HIS LIFE, THERE IS ONE LIGHT. MERA.
WITHOUT HER LOVE, I BELIEVE HE WOULD COLLAPSE BENEATH THE WEIGHT OF THE IMPOSSIBLE ROLE HE HAS SET FOR HIMSELF.
THE BURDEN OF BEING AQUAMAN WOULD BEAR HIM DOWN AND DROWN HIM...

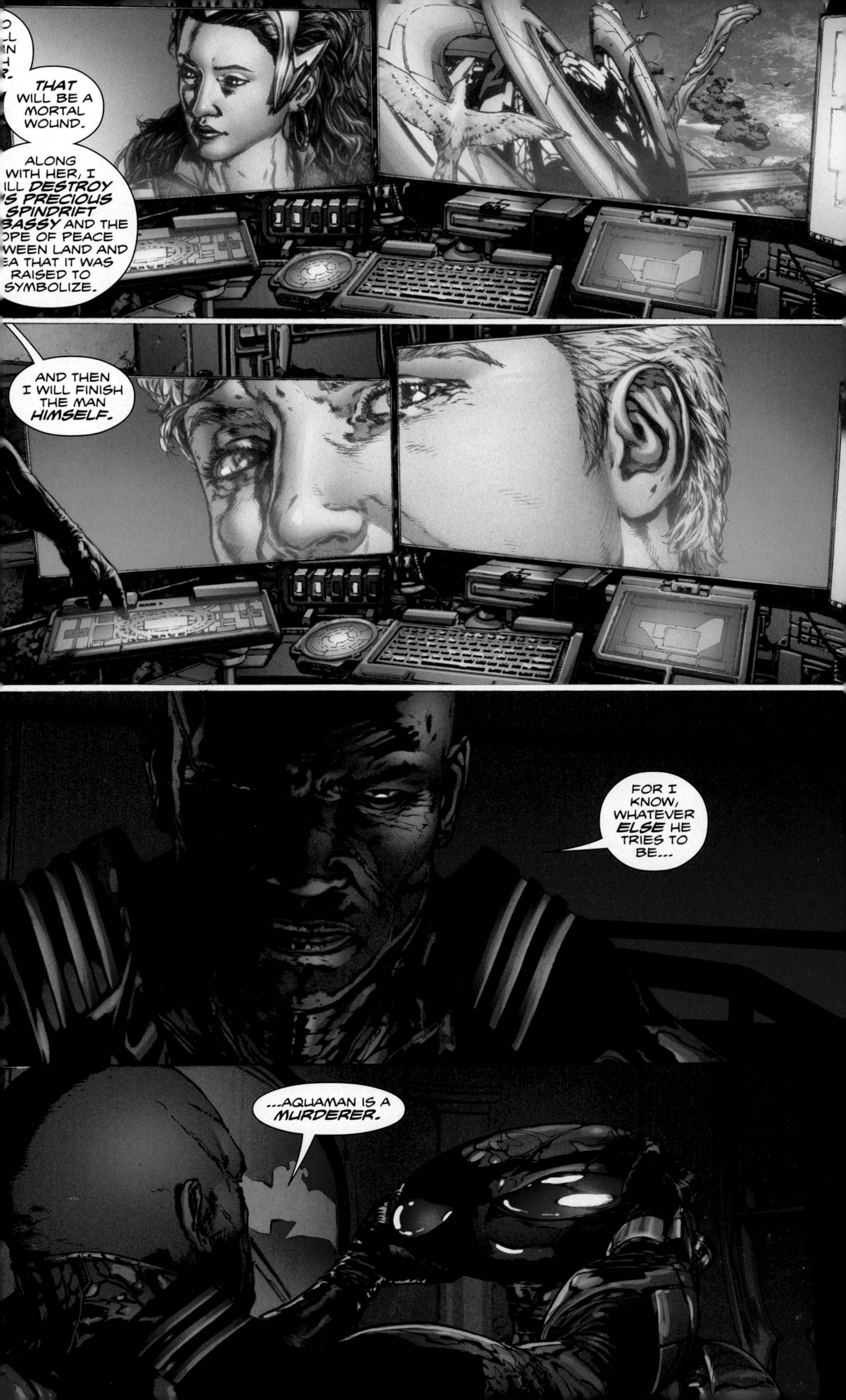
THAT WILL BE A MORTAL WOUND.
ALONG WITH HER, I ILL DESTROY 'S PRECIOUS SPINDRIFT BASSY AND THE OPE OF PEACE WEEN LAND AND A THAT IT WAS RAISED TO SYMBOLIZE.
AND THEN I WILL FINISH THE MAN HIMSELF.
FOR I KNOW, WHATEVER ELSE HE TRIES TO BE...
...AQUAMAN IS A MURDERER.

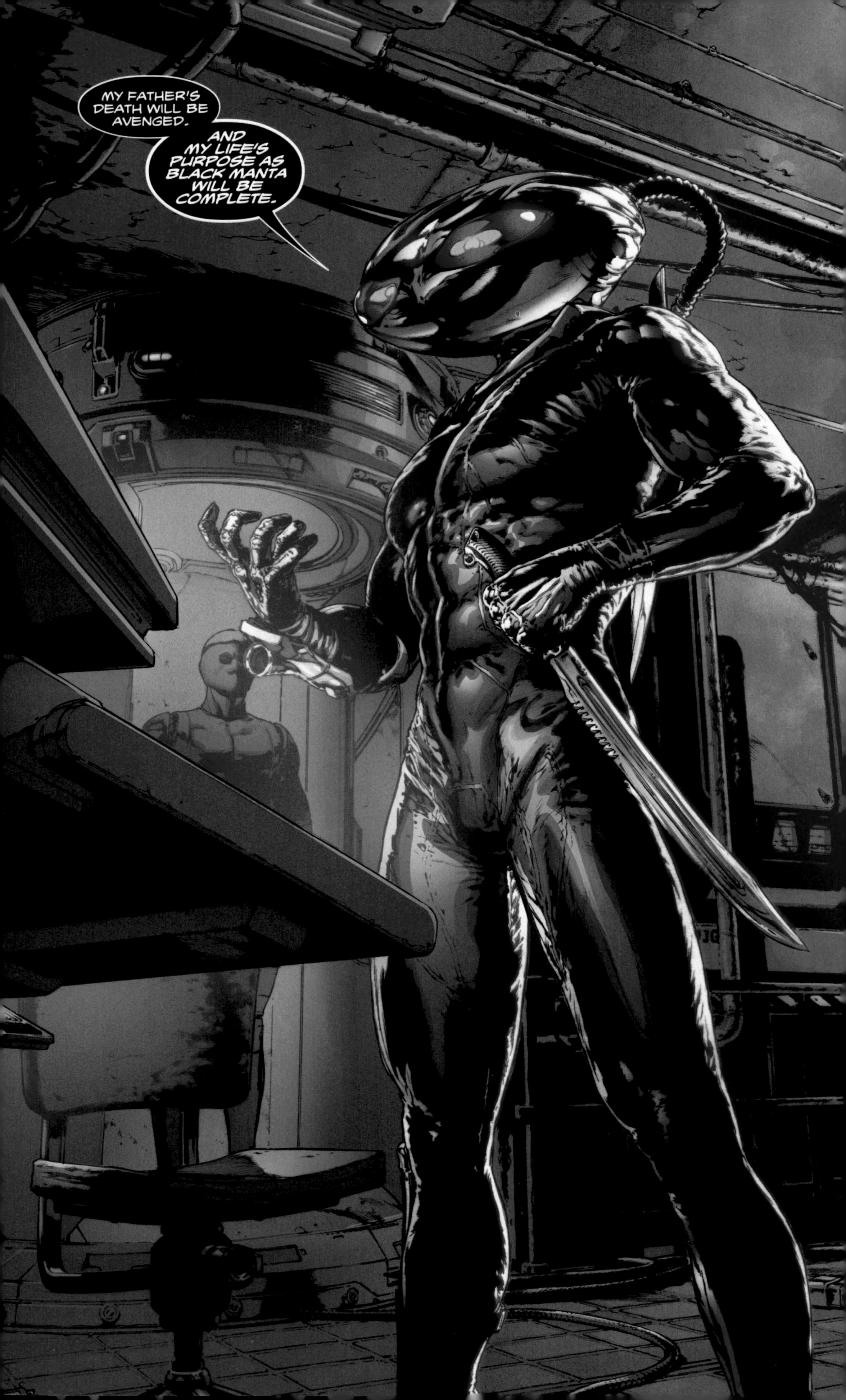
MY FATHER'S DEATH WILL BE AVENGED.
AND MY LIFE'S PURPOSE AS BLACK MANTA WILL BE COMPLETE.

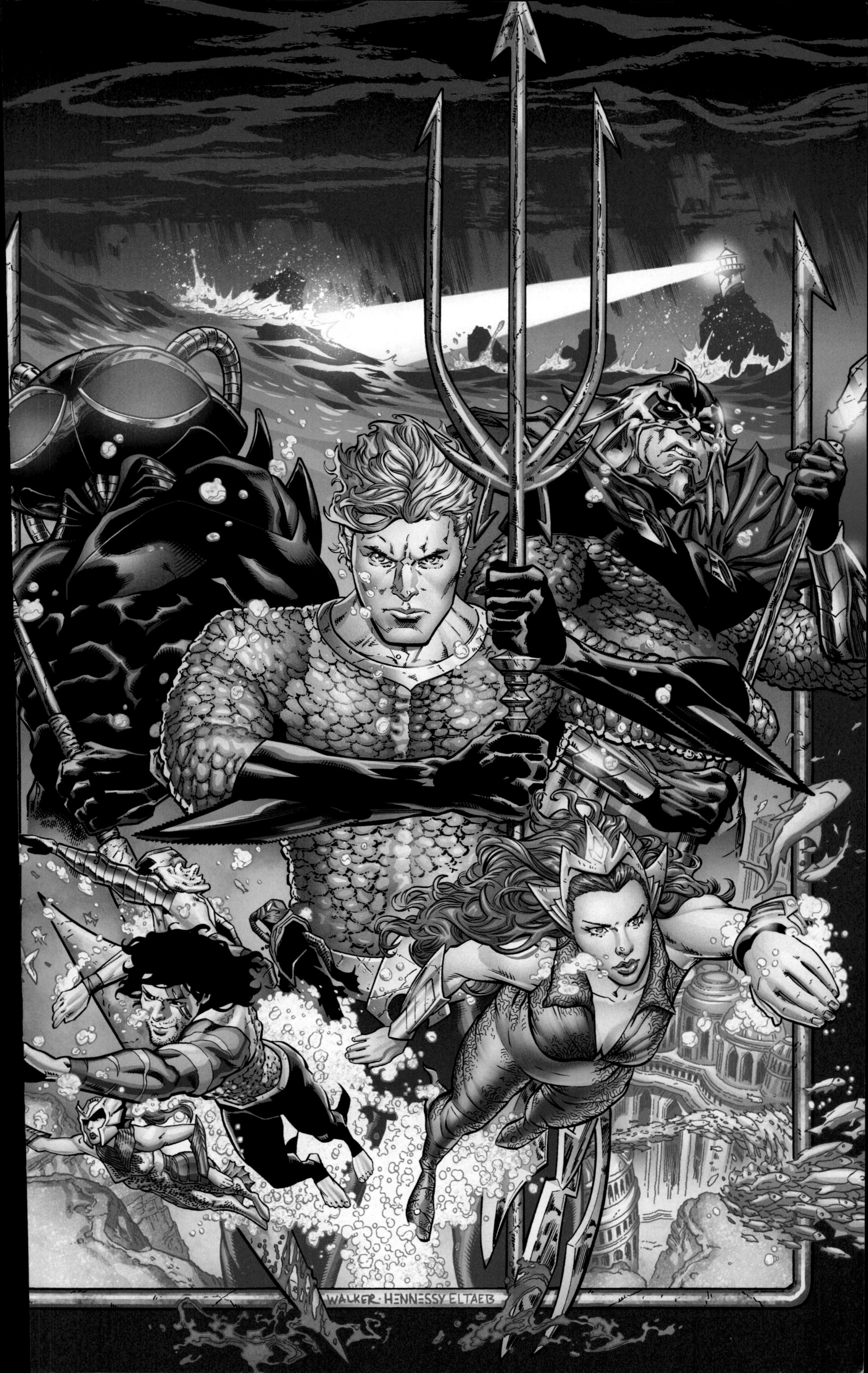
WALKER·HENNESSY ELTAEB

PART ONE: THE END OF FEAR

DAN ABNETT Writer * BRAD WALKER Penciller * ANDREW HENNESSY Inker * GABE ELTAEB Colorist * PAT BROSSEAU Letterer

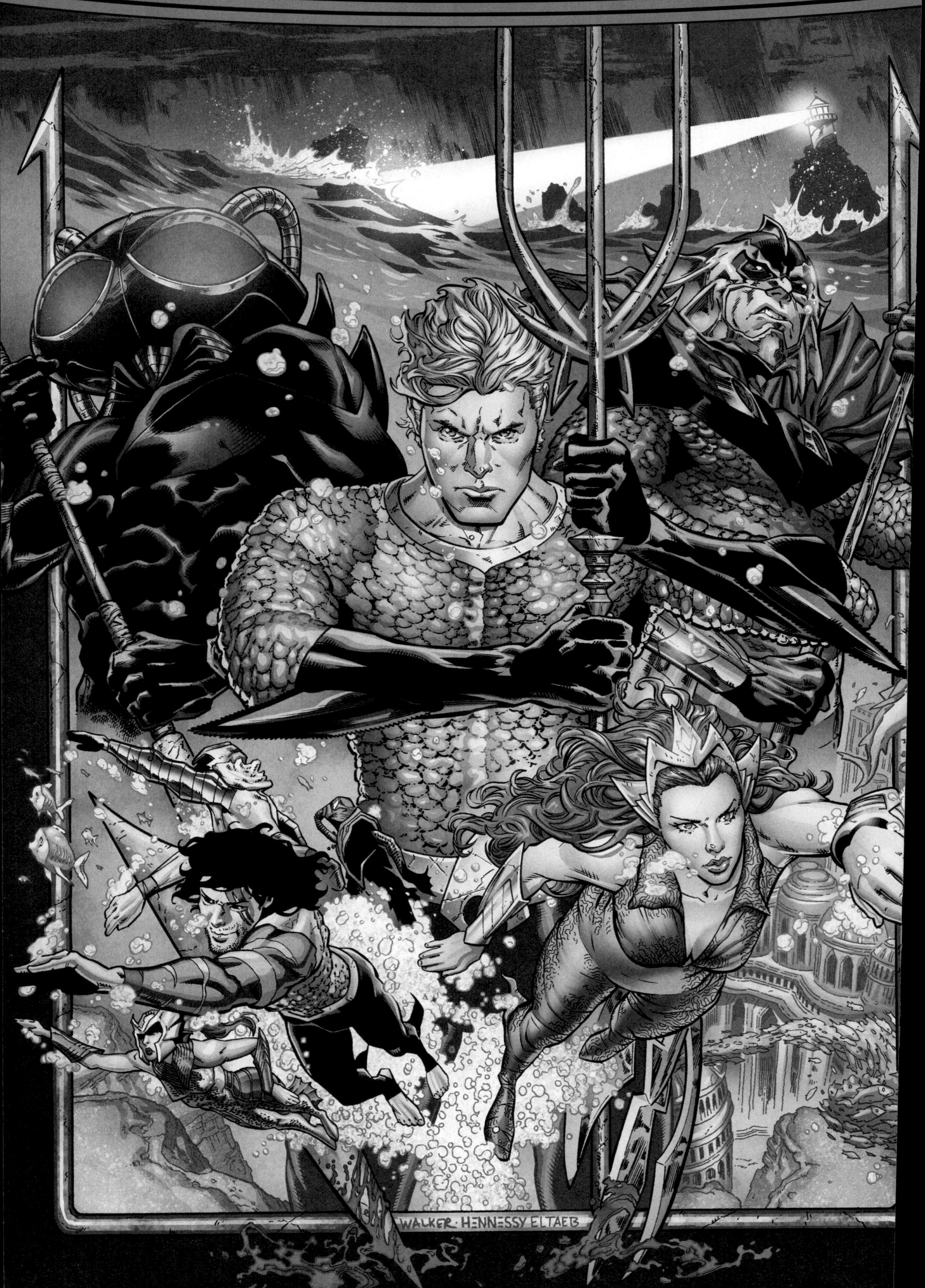
WALKER · HENNESSY ELTAEB

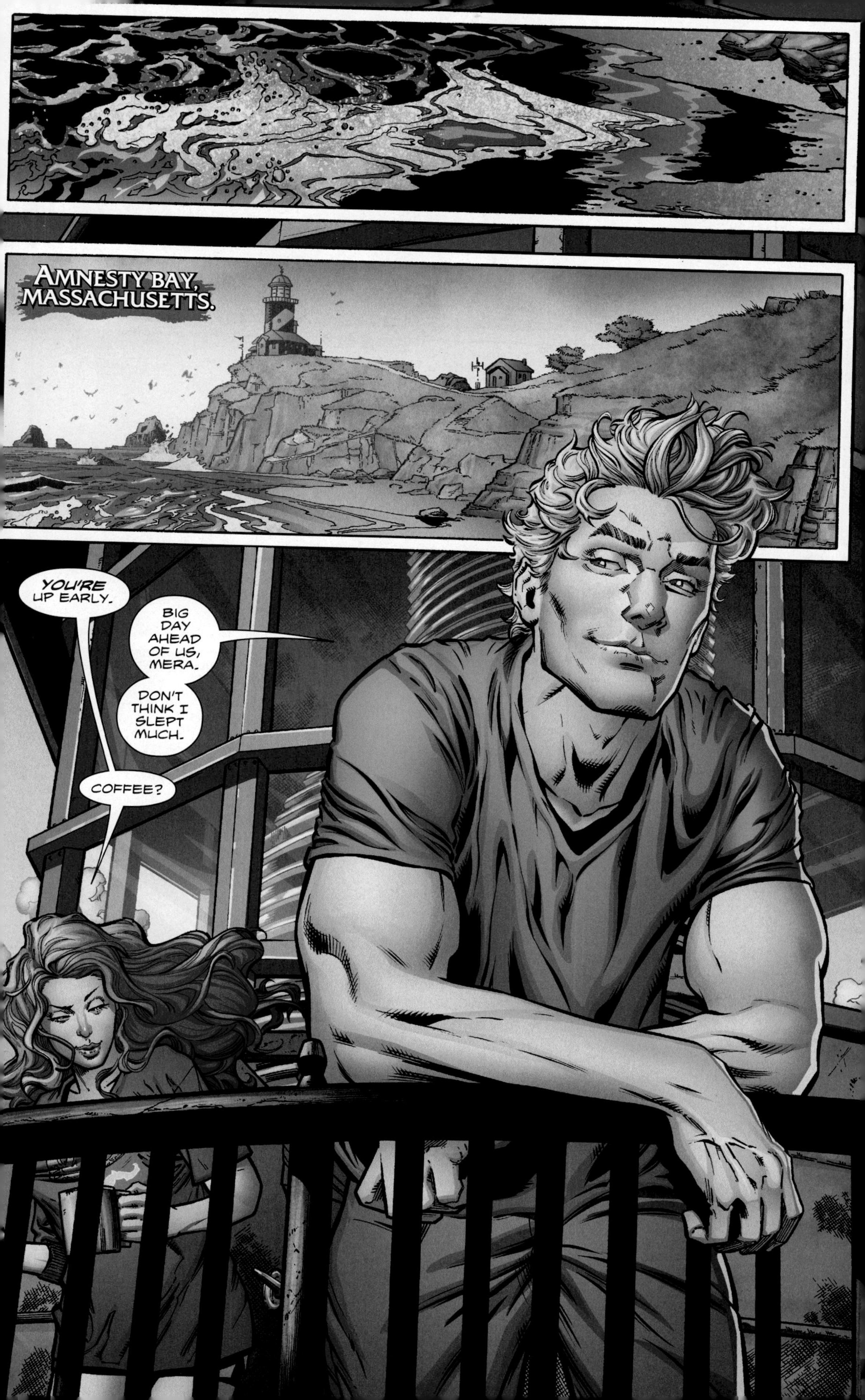
AMNESTY BAY, MASSACHUSETTS.
YOU'RE UP EARLY.
BIG DAY AHEAD OF US, MERA.
DON'T THINK I SLEPT MUCH.
COFFEE?

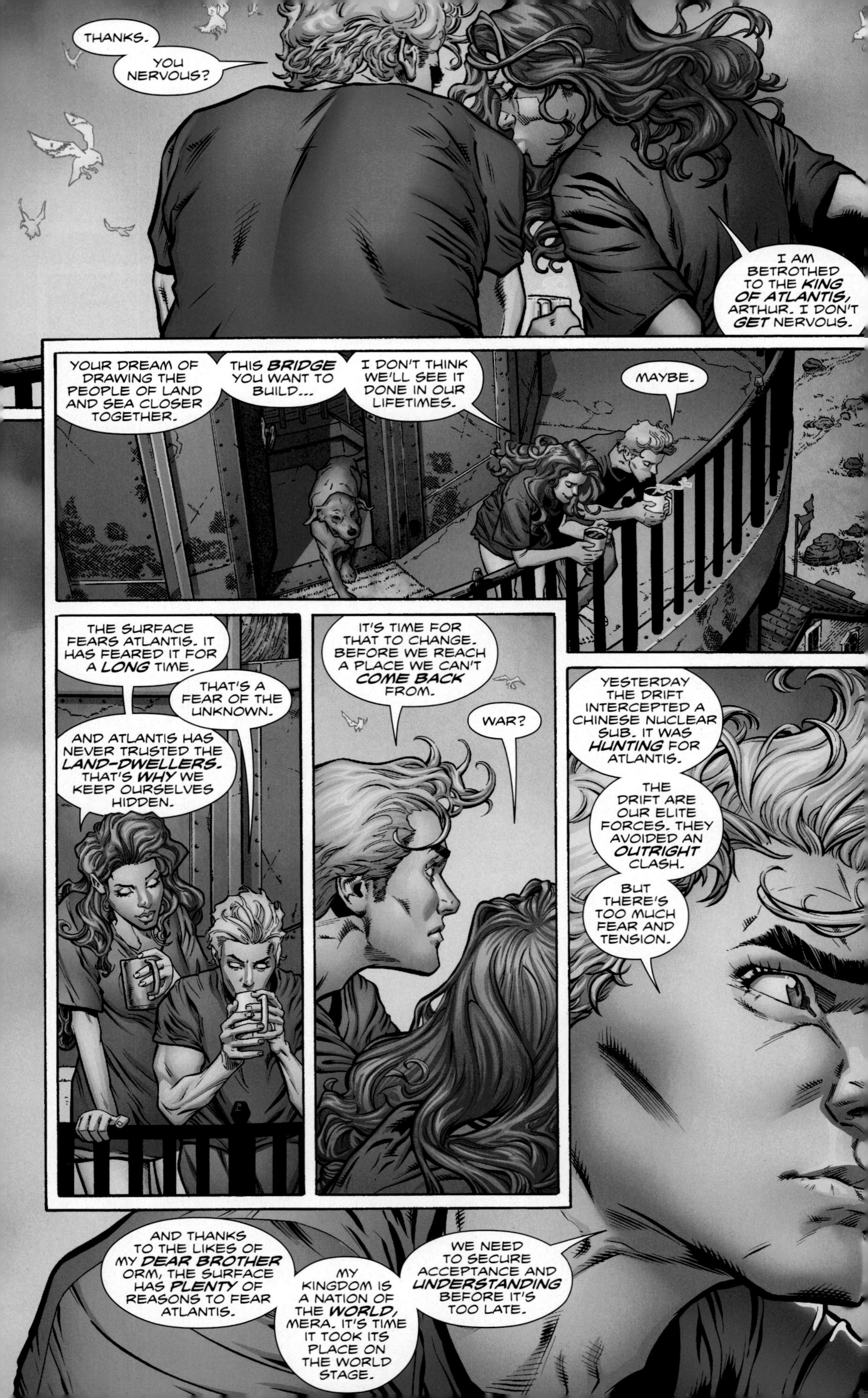

THANKS.
YOU NERVOUS?
I AM BETROTHED TO THE KING OF ATLANTIS, ARTHUR. I DON'T GET NERVOUS.
YOUR DREAM OF DRAWING THE PEOPLE OF LAND AND SEA CLOSER TOGETHER.
THIS BRIDGE YOU WANT TO BUILD...
I DON'T THINK WE'LL SEE IT DONE IN OUR LIFETIMES.
MAYBE.
THE SURFACE FEARS ATLANTIS. IT HAS FEARED IT FOR A LONG TIME.
THAT'S A FEAR OF THE UNKNOWN.
AND ATLANTIS HAS NEVER TRUSTED THE LAND-DWELLERS. THAT'S WHY WE KEEP OURSELVES HIDDEN.
IT'S TIME FOR THAT TO CHANGE. BEFORE WE REACH A PLACE WE CAN'T COME BACK FROM.
WAR?
YESTERDAY THE DRIFT INTERCEPTED A CHINESE NUCLEAR SUB. IT WAS HUNTING FOR ATLANTIS.
THE DRIFT ARE OUR ELITE FORCES. THEY AVOIDED AN OUTRIGHT CLASH.
BUT THERE'S TOO MUCH FEAR AND TENSION.
AND THANKS TO THE LIKES OF MY DEAR BROTHER ORM, THE SURFACE HAS PLENTY OF REASONS TO FEAR ATLANTIS.
MY KINGDOM IS A NATION OF THE WORLD, MERA. IT'S TIME IT TOOK ITS PLACE ON THE WORLD STAGE.
WE NEED TO SECURE ACCEPTANCE AND UNDERSTANDING BEFORE IT'S TOO LATE.

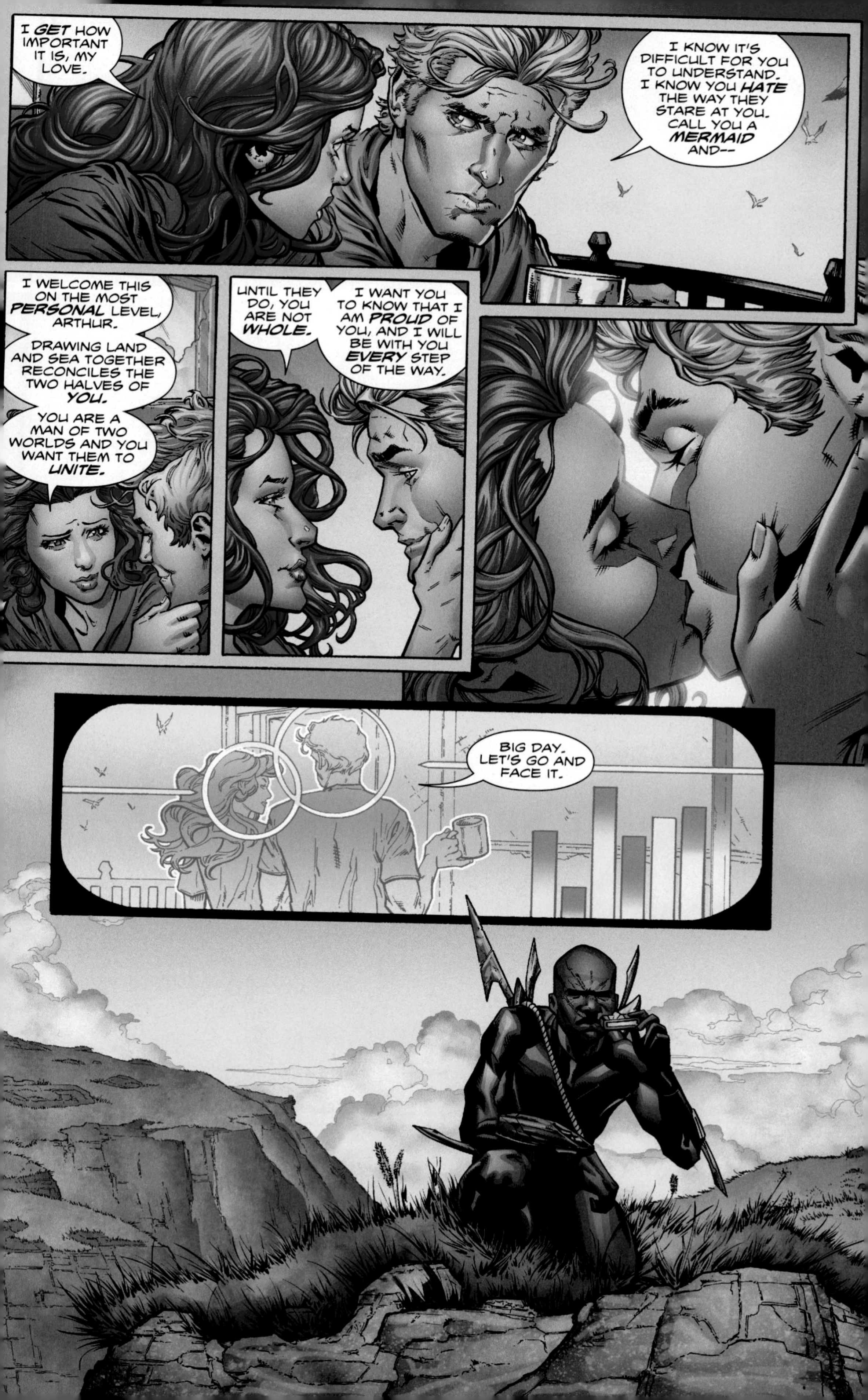
I GET HOW IMPORTANT IT IS, MY LOVE.
I KNOW IT'S DIFFICULT FOR YOU TO UNDERSTAND. I KNOW YOU HATE THE WAY THEY STARE AT YOU. CALL YOU A MERMAID AND--
I WELCOME THIS ON THE MOST PERSONAL LEVEL, ARTHUR.
DRAWING LAND AND SEA TOGETHER RECONCILES THE TWO HALVES OF YOU.
YOU ARE A MAN OF TWO WORLDS AND YOU WANT THEM TO UNITE.
UNTIL THEY DO, YOU ARE NOT WHOLE.
I WANT YOU TO KNOW THAT I AM PROUD OF YOU, AND I WILL BE WITH YOU EVERY STEP OF THE WAY.
BIG DAY. LET'S GO AND FACE IT.

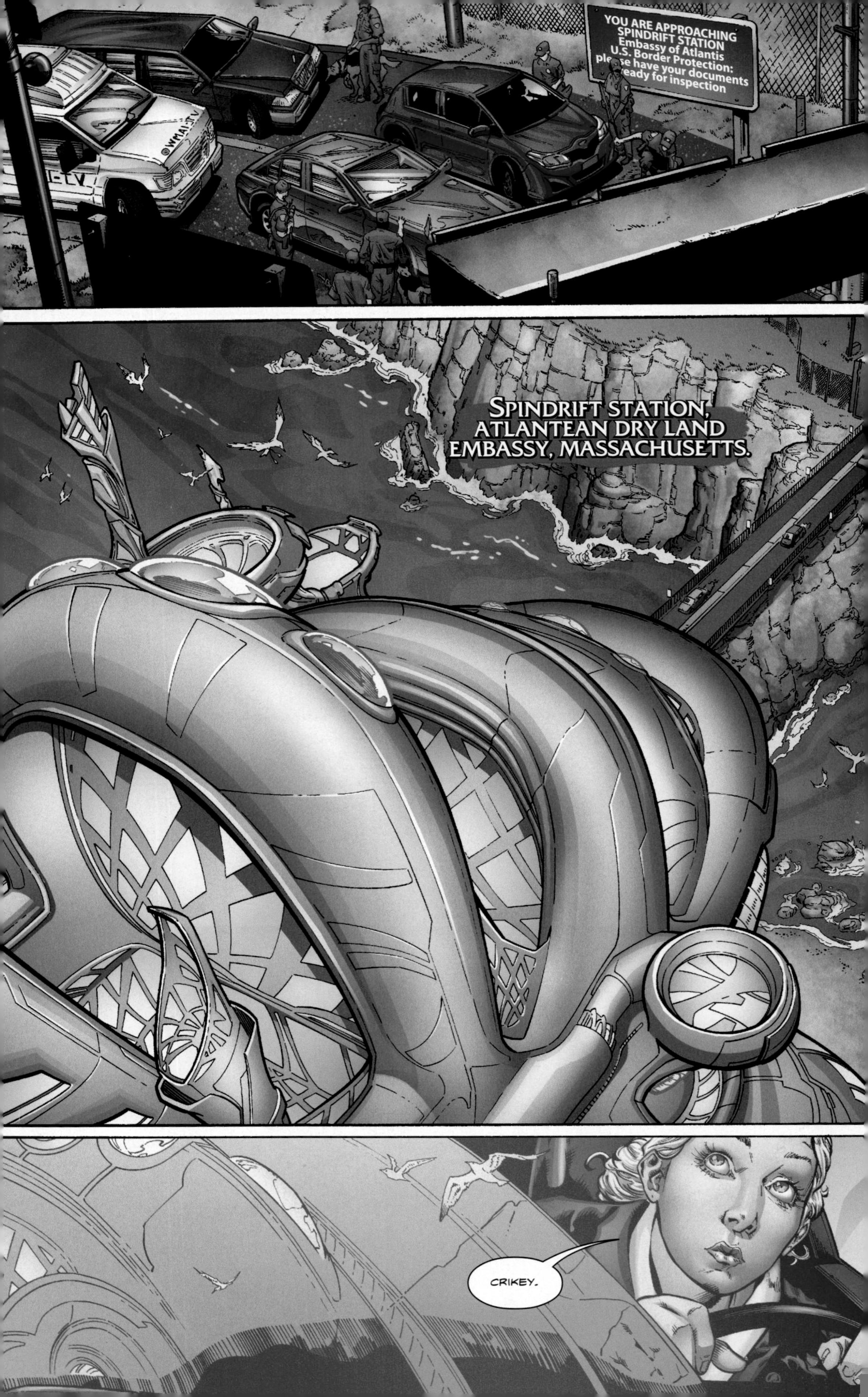
YOU ARE APPROACHING
SPINDRIFT STATION
Embassy of Atlantis
U.S. Border Protection:
ple se have your documents
eady for inspection
SPINDRIFT STATION, ATLANTEAN DRY LAND EMBASSY, MASSACHUSETTS.
CRIKEY.

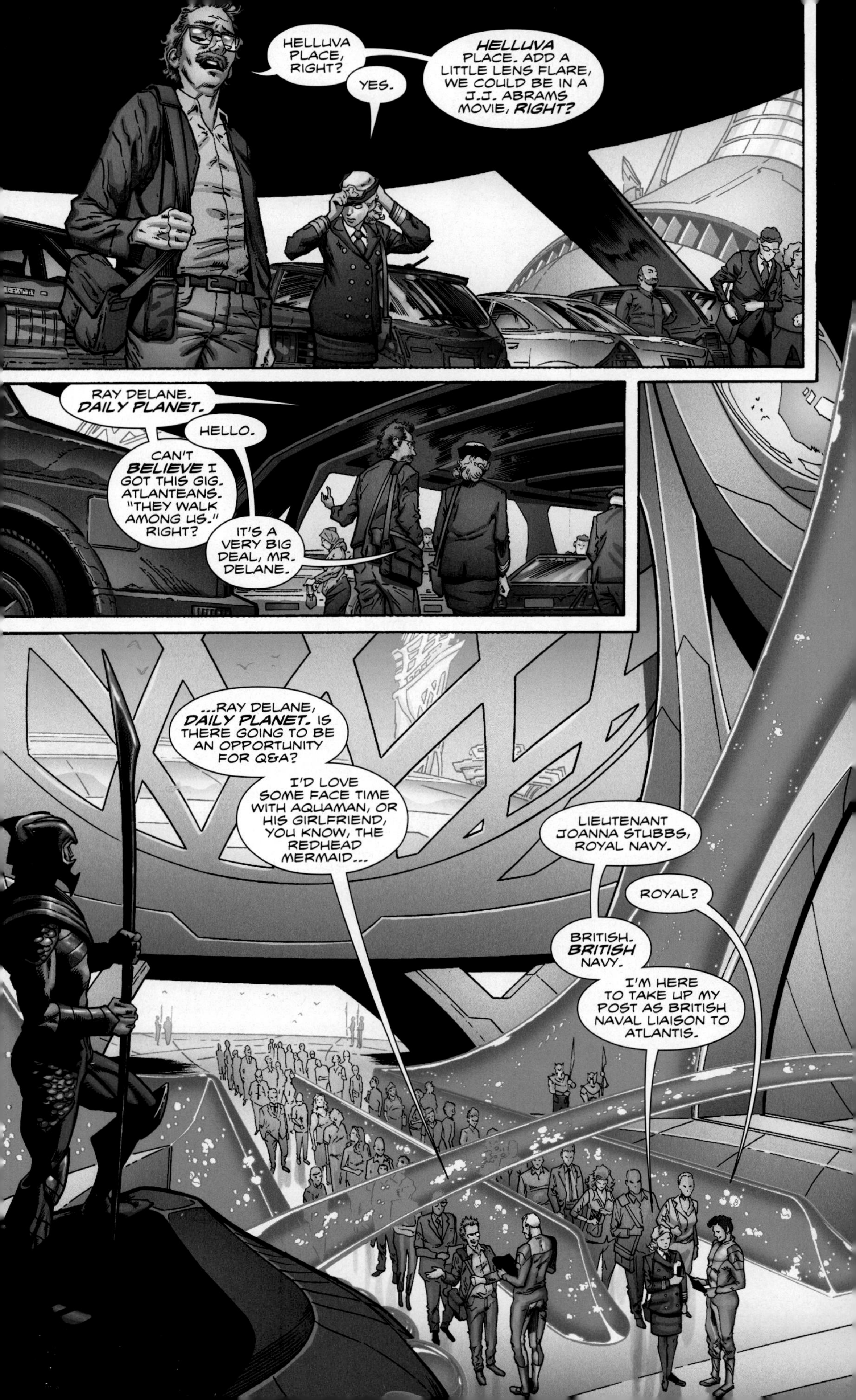
HELLUVA PLACE, RIGHT?
YES.
HELLUVA PLACE. ADD A LITTLE LENS FLARE, WE COULD BE IN A J.J. ABRAMS MOVIE, RIGHT?
RAY DELANE. DAILY PLANET.
HELLO.
CAN'T BELIEVE I GOT THIS GIG. ATLANTEANS. "THEY WALK AMONG US." RIGHT?
IT'S A VERY BIG DEAL, MR. DELANE.
...RAY DELANE, DAILY PLANET. IS THERE GOING TO BE AN OPPORTUNITY FOR Q&A?
I'D LOVE SOME FACE TIME WITH AQUAMAN, OR HIS GIRLFRIEND, YOU KNOW, THE REDHEAD MERMAID...
LIEUTENANT JOANNA STUBBS, ROYAL NAVY.
ROYAL?
BRITISH. BRITISH NAVY.
I'M HERE TO TAKE UP MY POST AS BRITISH NAVAL LIAISON TO ATLANTIS.

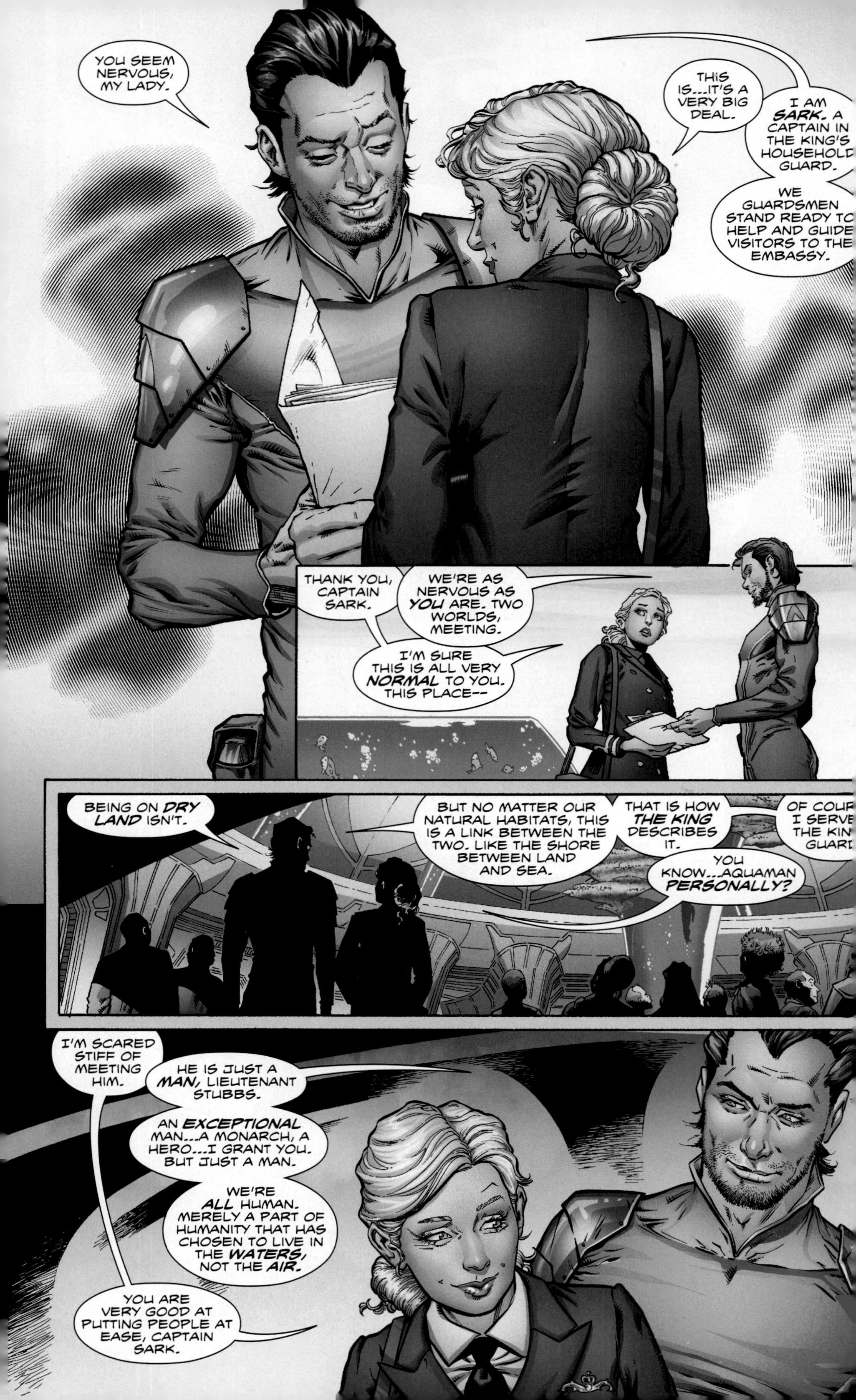
YOU SEEM NERVOUS, MY LADY.
THIS IS...IT'S A VERY BIG DEAL.
I AM SARK. A CAPTAIN IN THE KING'S HOUSEHOLD GUARD.
WE GUARDSMEN STAND READY TO HELP AND GUIDE VISITORS TO THE EMBASSY.
THANK YOU, CAPTAIN SARK.
WE'RE AS NERVOUS AS YOU ARE. TWO WORLDS, MEETING.
I'M SURE THIS IS ALL VERY NORMAL TO YOU. THIS PLACE--
BEING ON DRY LAND ISN'T.
BUT NO MATTER OUR NATURAL HABITATS, THIS IS A LINK BETWEEN THE TWO. LIKE THE SHORE BETWEEN LAND AND SEA.
THAT IS HOW THE KING DESCRIBES IT.
YOU KNOW...AQUAMAN PERSONALLY?
I'M SCARED STIFF OF MEETING HIM.
HE IS JUST A MAN, LIEUTENANT STUBBS.
AN EXCEPTIONAL MAN...A MONARCH, A HERO...I GRANT YOU. BUT JUST A MAN.
WE'RE ALL HUMAN. MERELY A PART OF HUMANITY THAT HAS CHOSEN TO LIVE IN THE WATERS, NOT THE AIR.
YOU ARE VERY GOOD AT PUTTING PEOPLE AT EASE, CAPTAIN SARK.

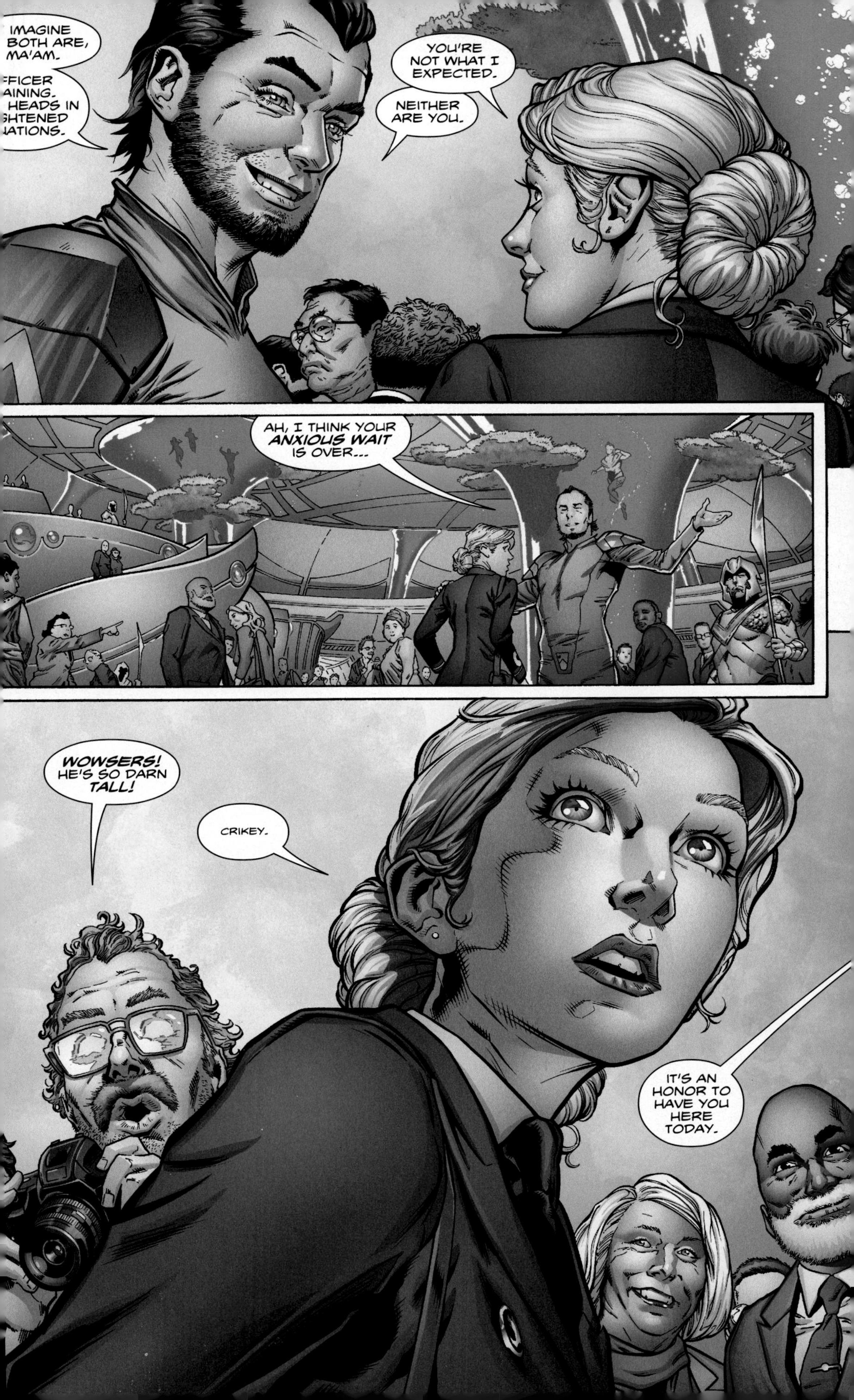

IMAGINE BOTH ARE, MA'AM.
FFICER AINING. HEADS IN GHTENED NATIONS.
YOU'RE NOT WHAT I EXPECTED.
NEITHER ARE YOU.
AH, I THINK YOUR ANXIOUS WAIT IS OVER...
WOWSERS! HE'S SO DARN TALL!
CRIKEY.
IT'S AN HONOR TO HAVE YOU HERE TODAY.

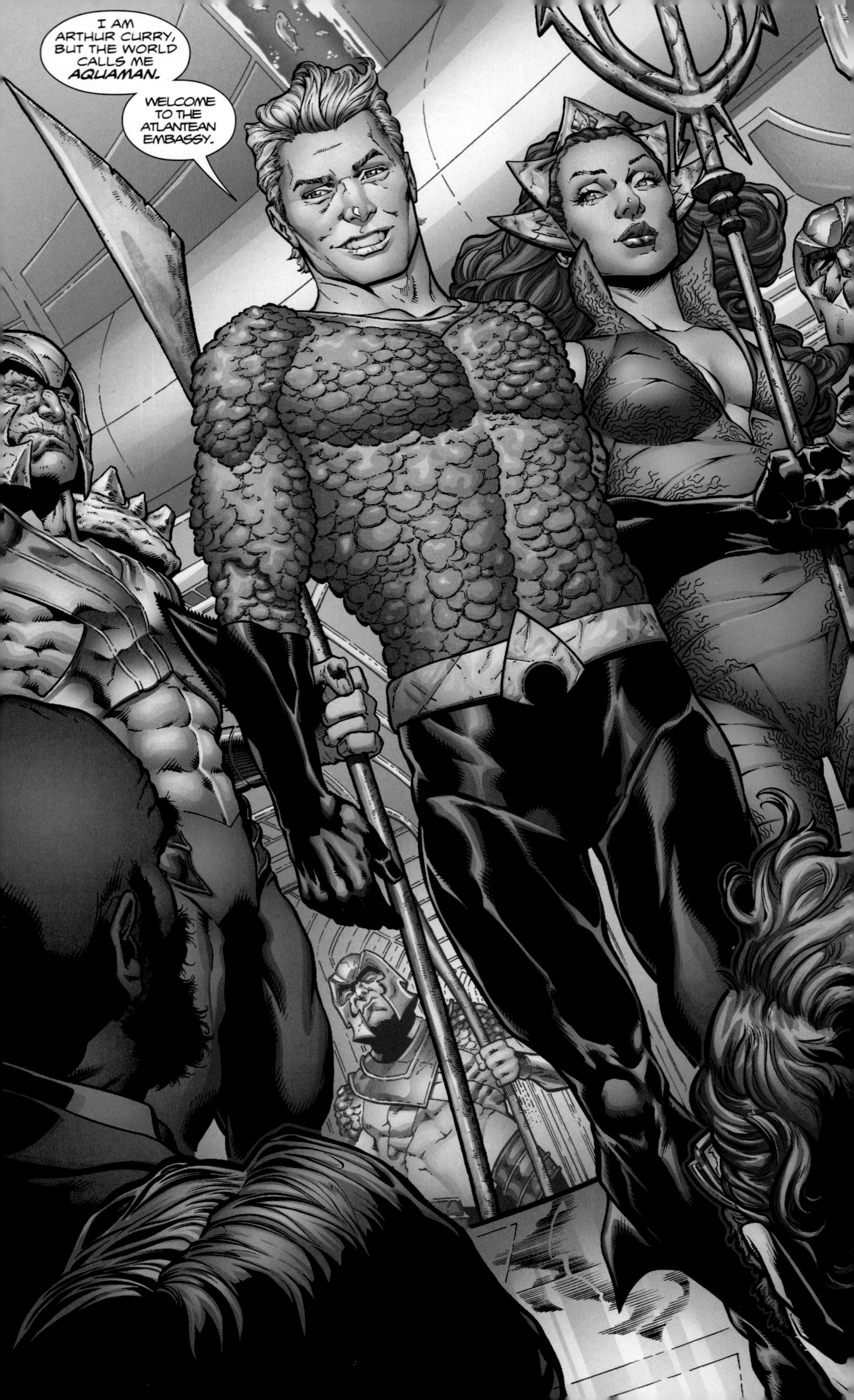
I AM ARTHUR CURRY, BUT THE WORLD CALLS ME AQUAMAN.
WELCOME TO THE ATLANTEAN EMBASSY.

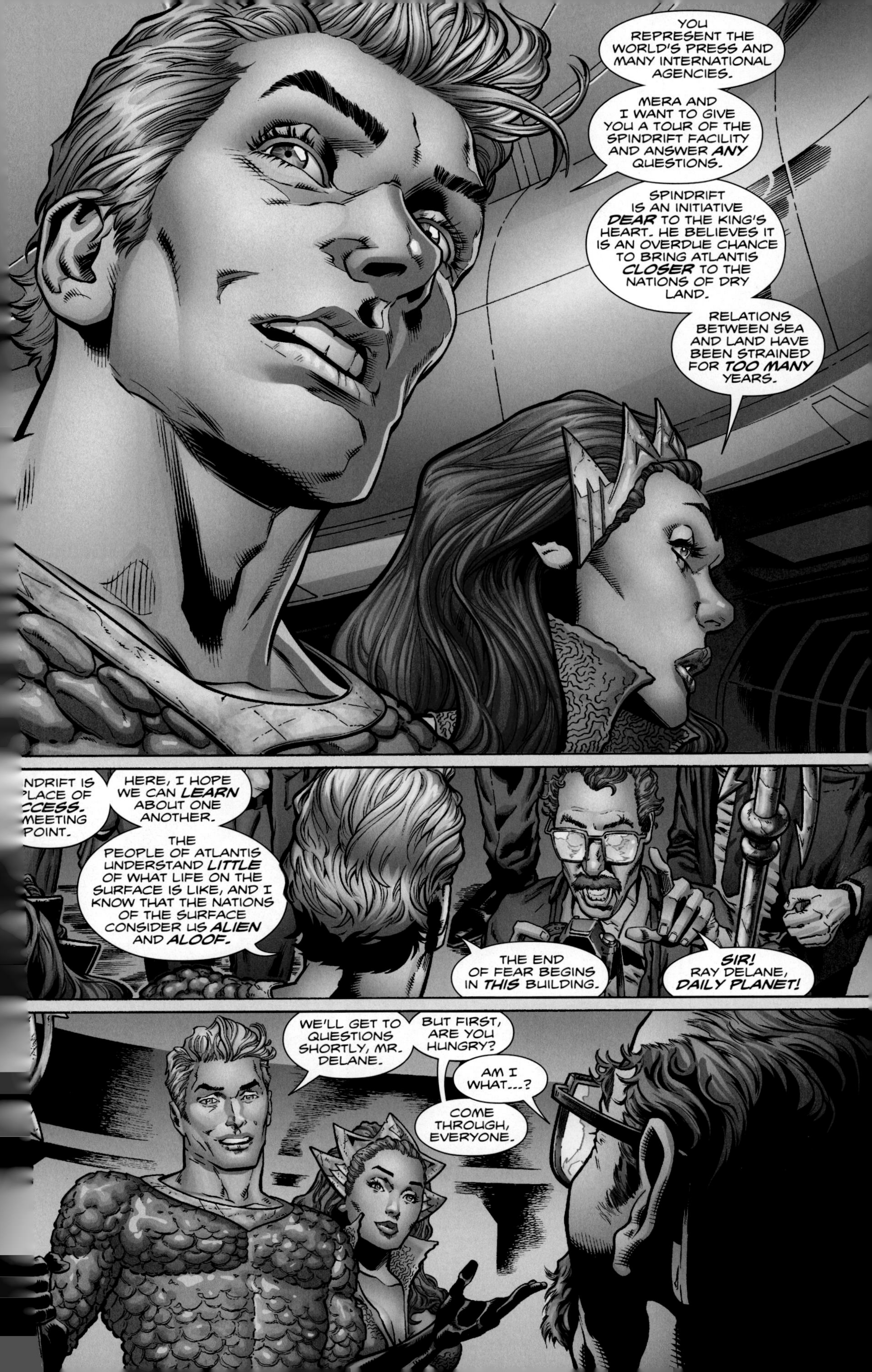
YOU REPRESENT THE WORLD'S PRESS AND MANY INTERNATIONAL AGENCIES.
MERA AND I WANT TO GIVE YOU A TOUR OF THE SPINDRIFT FACILITY AND ANSWER ANY QUESTIONS.
SPINDRIFT IS AN INITIATIVE DEAR TO THE KING'S HEART. HE BELIEVES IT IS AN OVERDUE CHANCE TO BRING ATLANTIS CLOSER TO THE NATIONS OF DRY LAND.
RELATIONS BETWEEN SEA AND LAND HAVE BEEN STRAINED FOR TOO MANY YEARS.
NDRIFT IS PLACE OF CCESS. MEETING POINT.
HERE, I HOPE WE CAN LEARN ABOUT ONE ANOTHER.
THE PEOPLE OF ATLANTIS UNDERSTAND LITTLE OF WHAT LIFE ON THE SURFACE IS LIKE, AND I KNOW THAT THE NATIONS OF THE SURFACE CONSIDER US ALIEN AND ALOOF.
THE END OF FEAR BEGINS IN THIS BUILDING.
SIR! RAY DELANE, DAILY PLANET!
WE'LL GET TO QUESTIONS SHORTLY, MR. DELANE.
BUT FIRST, ARE YOU HUNGRY?
AM I WHAT...?
COME THROUGH, EVERYONE.

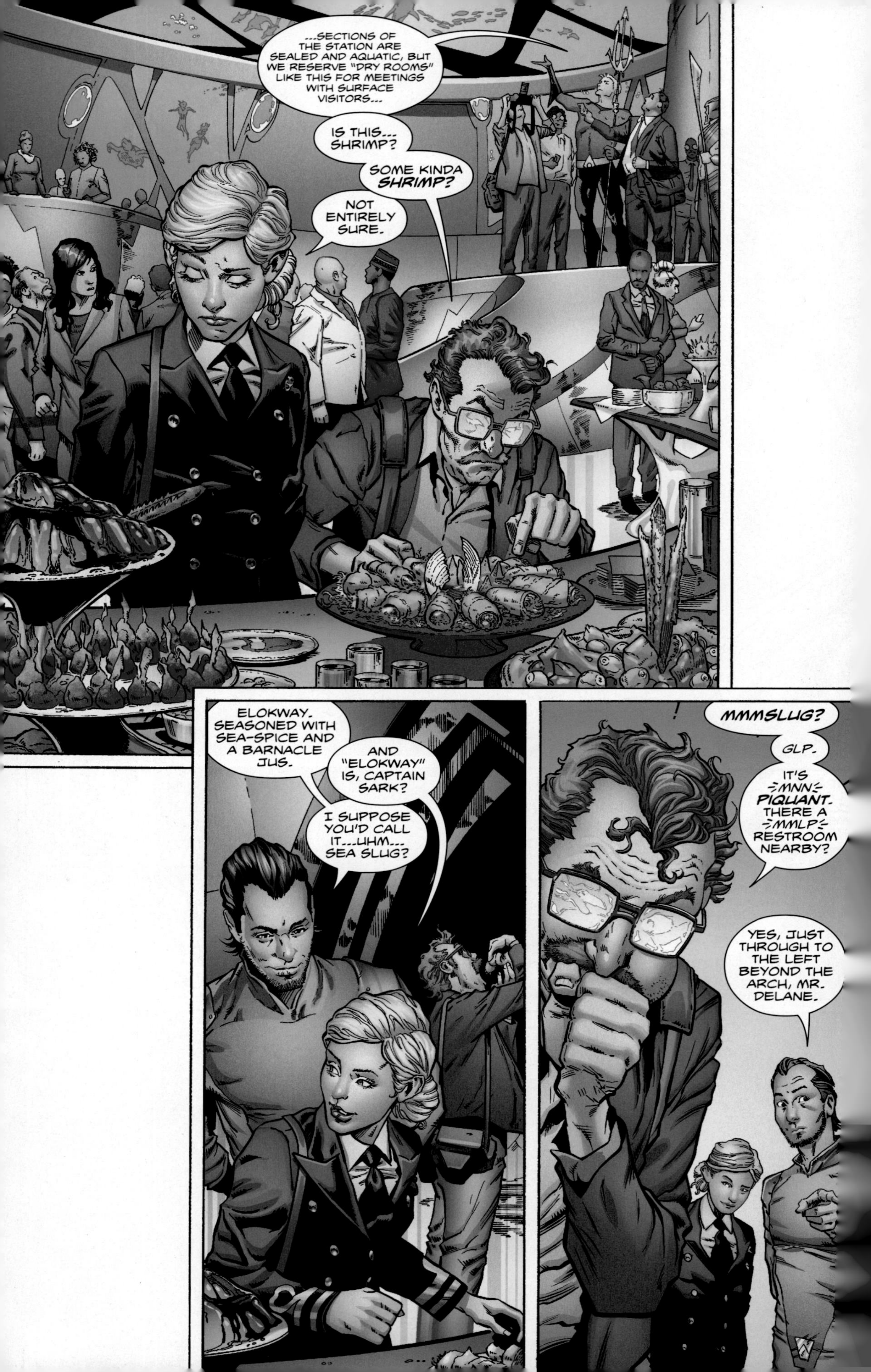
...SECTIONS OF THE STATION ARE SEALED AND AQUATIC, BUT WE RESERVE "DRY ROOMS" LIKE THIS FOR MEETINGS WITH SURFACE VISITORS...
IS THIS... SHRIMP?
SOME KINDA SHRIMP?
NOT ENTIRELY SURE.
ELOKWAY. SEASONED WITH SEA-SPICE AND A BARNACLE JUS.
AND "ELOKWAY" IS, CAPTAIN SARK?
I SUPPOSE YOU'D CALL IT...UHM... SEA SLUG?
MMMSLUG?
GLP.
IT'S MNN PIQUANT. THERE A MMLP RESTROOM NEARBY?
YES, JUST THROUGH TO THE LEFT BEYOND THE ARCH, MR. DELANE.

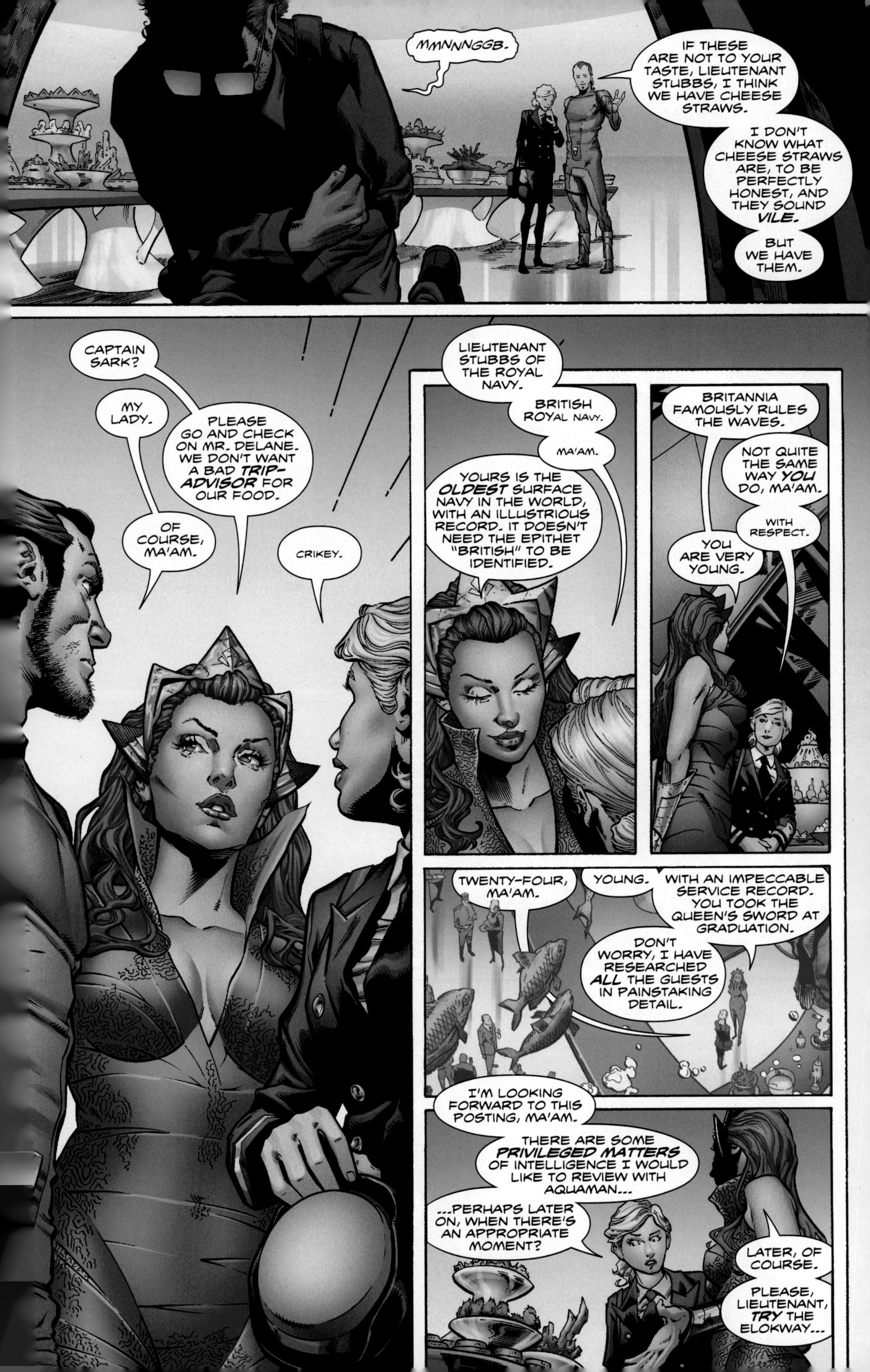

MMNNNGGB.
IF THESE ARE NOT TO YOUR TASTE, LIEUTENANT STUBBS, I THINK WE HAVE CHEESE STRAWS.
I DON'T KNOW WHAT CHEESE STRAWS ARE, TO BE PERFECTLY HONEST, AND THEY SOUND VILE.
BUT WE HAVE THEM.
CAPTAIN SARK?
MY LADY.
PLEASE GO AND CHECK ON MR. DELANE. WE DON'T WANT A BAD TRIP-ADVISOR FOR OUR FOOD.
OF COURSE, MA'AM.
CRIKEY.
LIEUTENANT STUBBS OF THE ROYAL NAVY.
BRITISH ROYAL NAVY.
MA'AM.
YOURS IS THE OLDEST SURFACE NAVY IN THE WORLD, WITH AN ILLUSTRIOUS RECORD. IT DOESN'T NEED THE EPITHET "BRITISH" TO BE IDENTIFIED.
BRITANNIA FAMOUSLY RULES THE WAVES.
NOT QUITE THE SAME WAY YOU DO, MA'AM.
WITH RESPECT.
YOU ARE VERY YOUNG.
TWENTY-FOUR, MA'AM.
YOUNG.
WITH AN IMPECCABLE SERVICE RECORD. YOU TOOK THE QUEEN'S SWORD AT GRADUATION.
DON'T WORRY, I HAVE RESEARCHED ALL THE GUESTS IN PAINSTAKING DETAIL.
I'M LOOKING FORWARD TO THIS POSTING, MA'AM.
THERE ARE SOME PRIVILEGED MATTERS OF INTELLIGENCE I WOULD LIKE TO REVIEW WITH AQUAMAN...
...PERHAPS LATER ON, WHEN THERE'S AN APPROPRIATE MOMENT?
LATER, OF COURSE.
PLEASE, LIEUTENANT, TRY THE ELOKWAY...

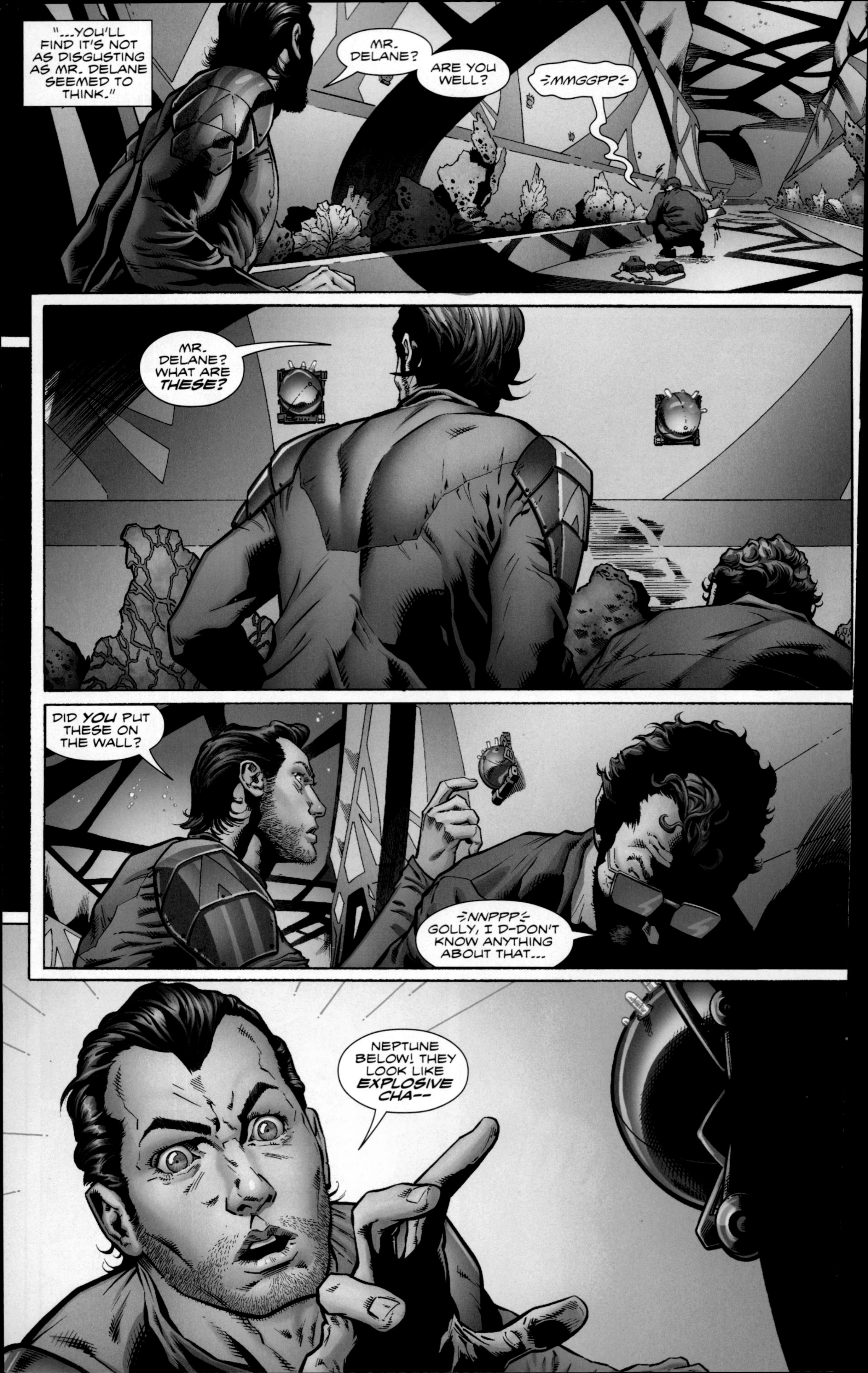

"...YOU'LL FIND IT'S NOT AS DISGUSTING AS MR. DELANE SEEMED TO THINK."
MR. DELANE?
ARE YOU WELL?
=MMGGPP=
MR. DELANE? WHAT ARE *THESE?*
DID *YOU* PUT THESE ON THE WALL?
=NNPPP= GOLLY, I D-DON'T KNOW ANYTHING ABOUT THAT...
NEPTUNE BELOW! THEY LOOK LIKE *EXPLOSIVE CHA--*

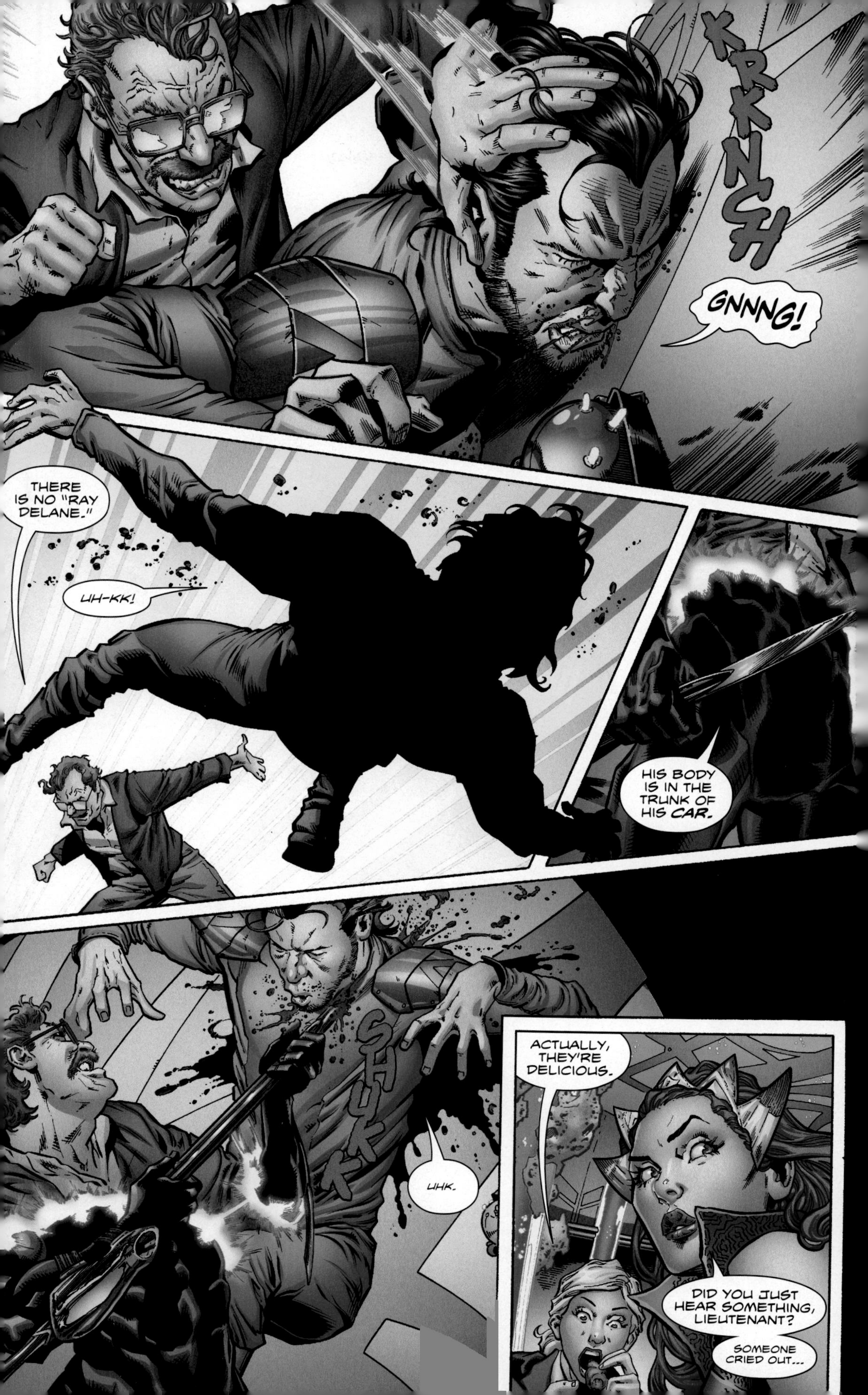
KRKNCH
GNNNG!
THERE IS NO "RAY DELANE."
UH-KK!
HIS BODY IS IN THE TRUNK OF HIS *CAR*.
SHUKK
UHK.
ACTUALLY, THEY'RE DELICIOUS.
DID YOU JUST HEAR SOMETHING, LIEUTENANT?
SOMEONE CRIED OUT...

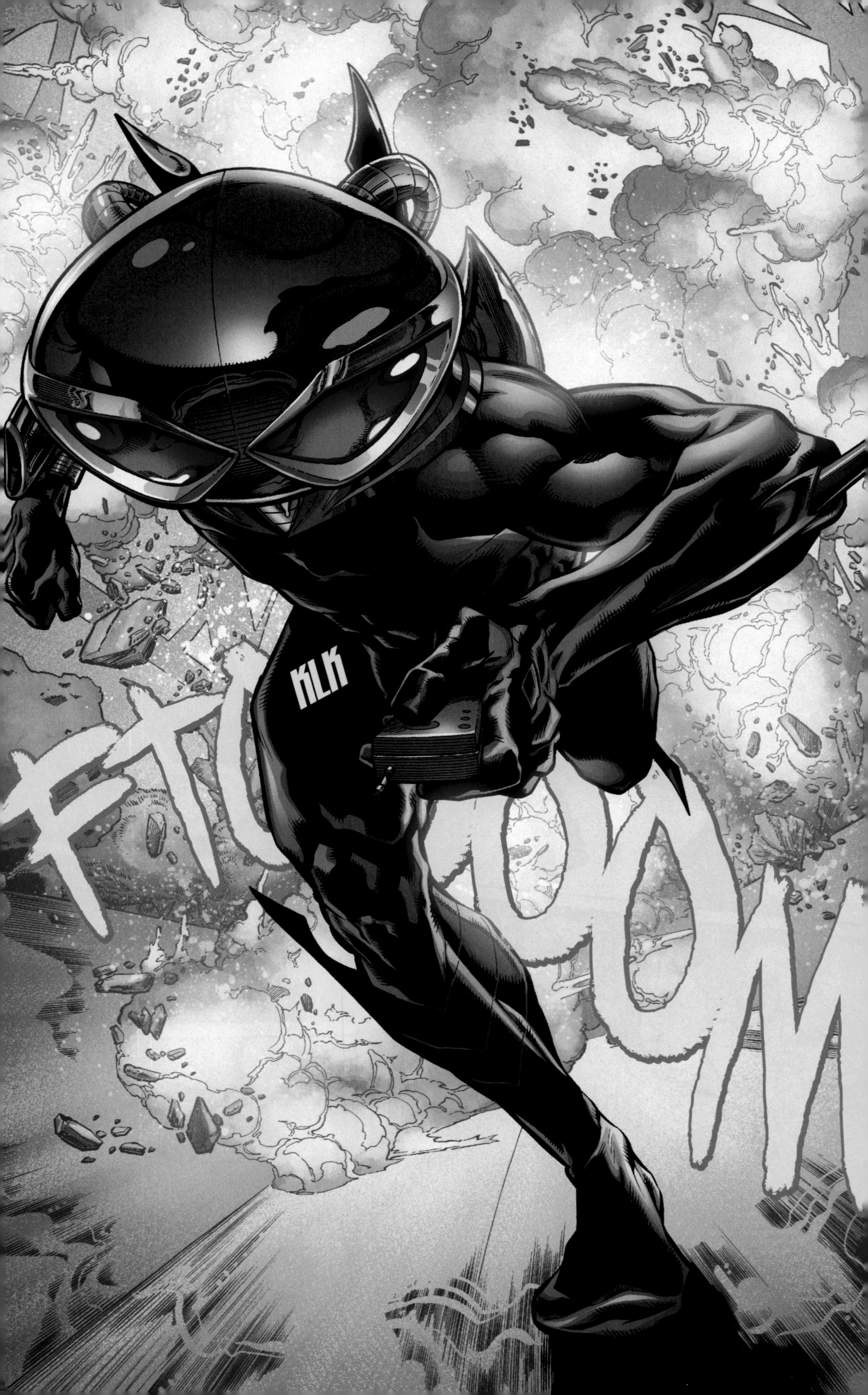
KLK

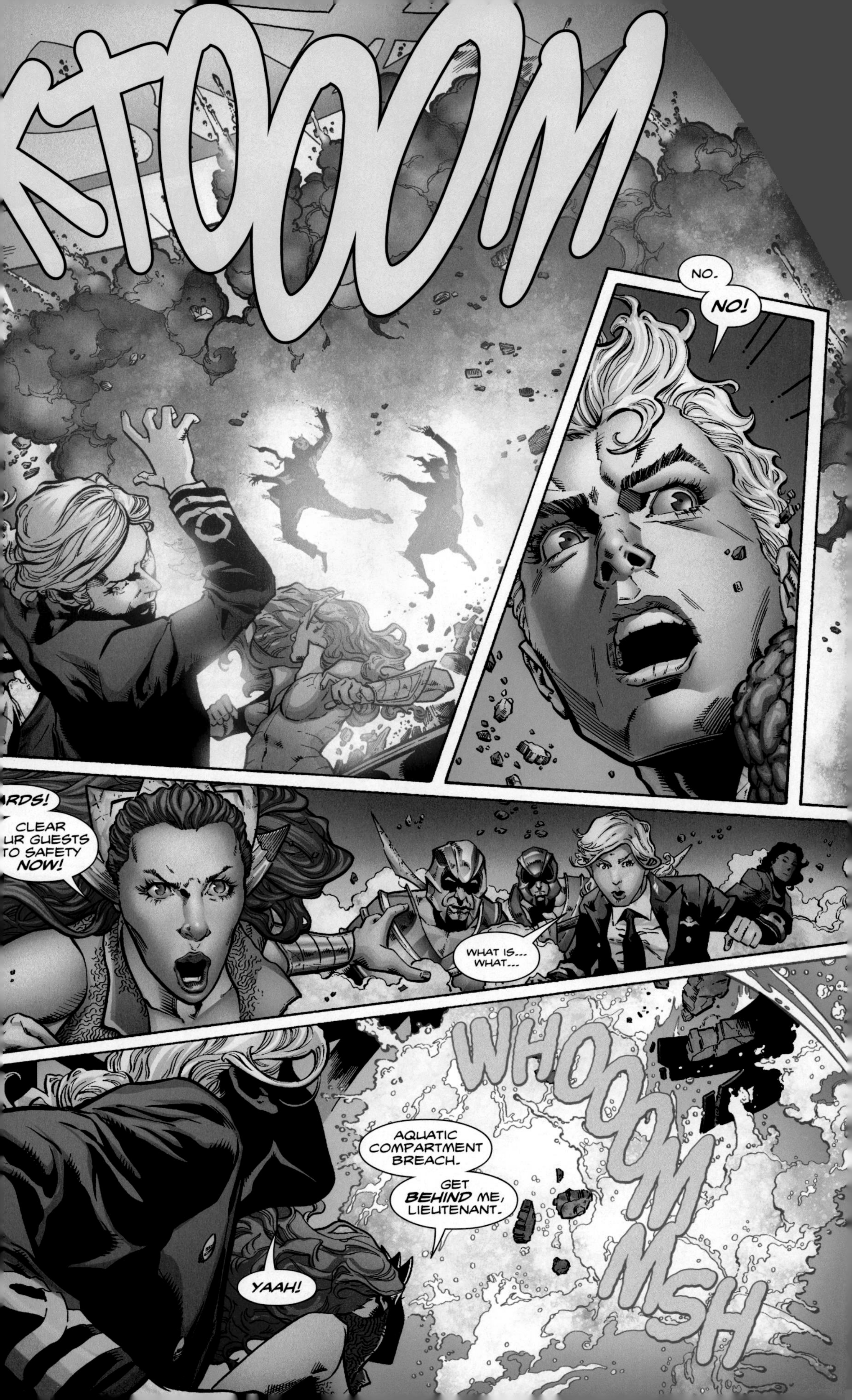
KTOOOM
NO.
NO!
ARDS!
CLEAR
UR GUESTS
TO SAFETY
NOW!
WHAT IS...
WHAT...
WHOOOOMMSH
AQUATIC COMPARTMENT BREACH.
GET BEHIND ME, LIEUTENANT.
YAAH!

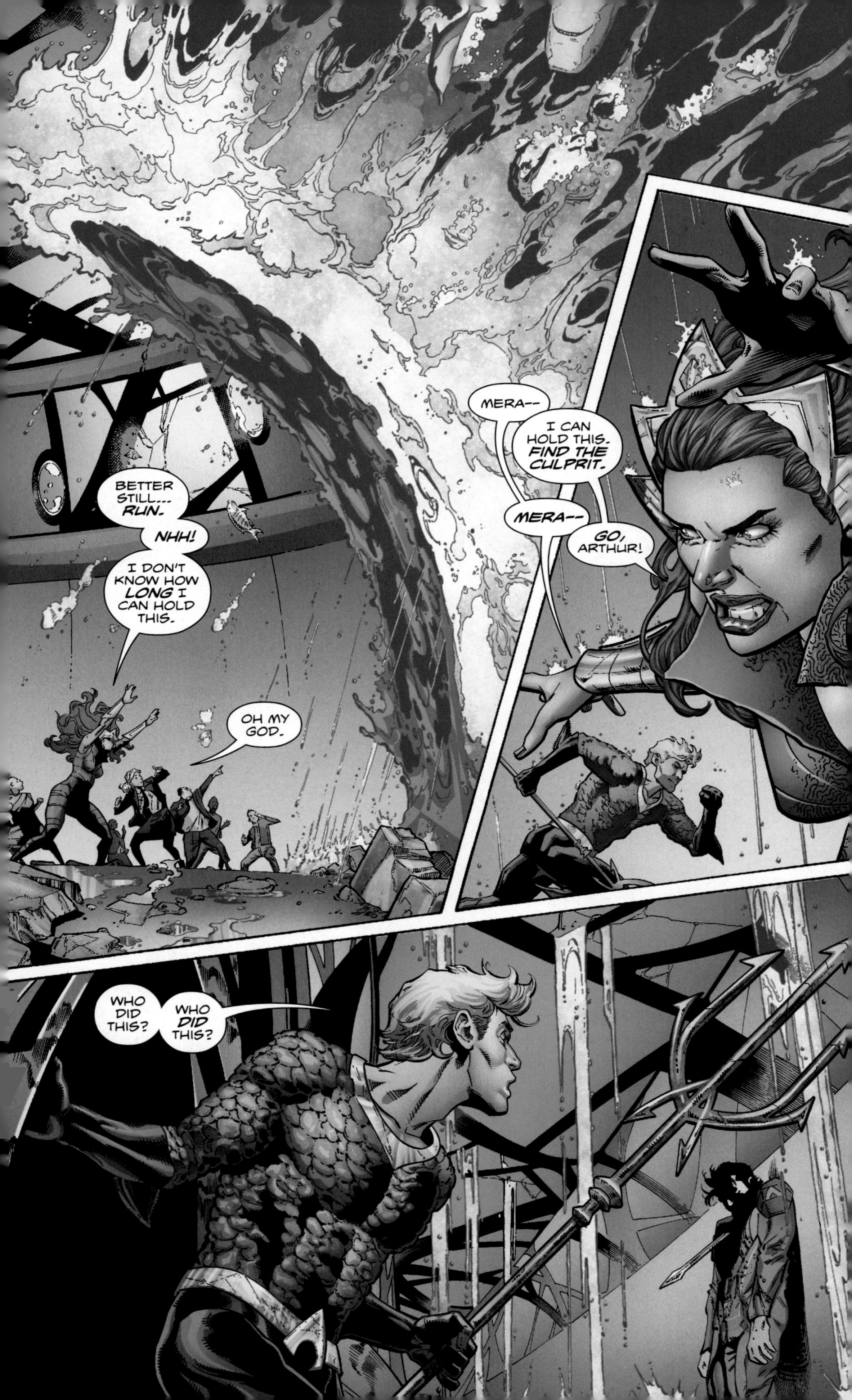
BETTER STILL... RUN.
NHH!
I DON'T KNOW HOW LONG I CAN HOLD THIS.
OH MY GOD.
MERA--
I CAN HOLD THIS. FIND THE CULPRIT.
MERA--
GO, ARTHUR!
WHO DID THIS?
WHO DID THIS?

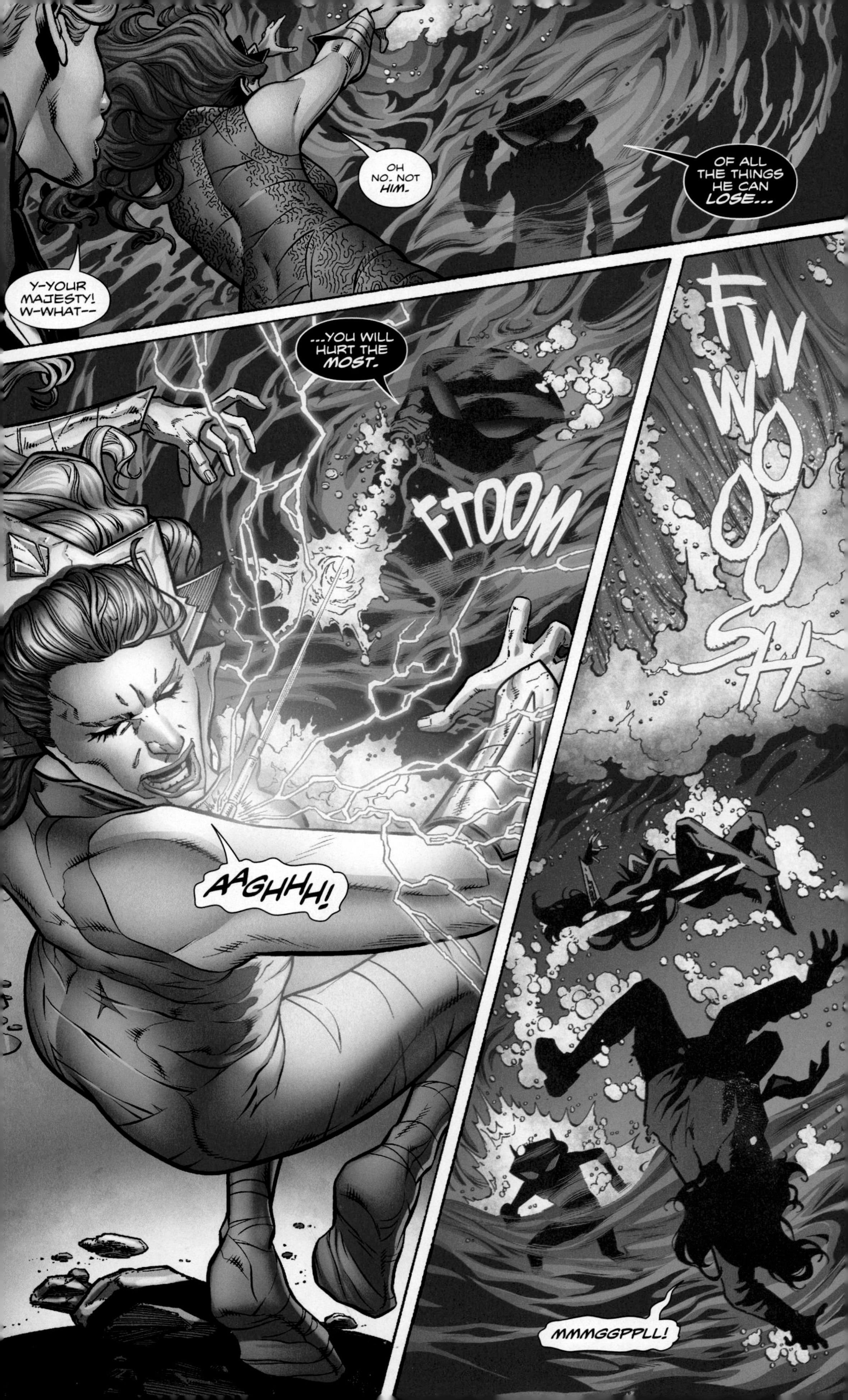
OH NO. NOT HIM.
OF ALL THE THINGS HE CAN LOSE...
Y-YOUR MAJESTY! W-WHAT--
...YOU WILL HURT THE MOST.
FTOOM
AAGHHH!
FWOOOSH
MMMGGPPLL!

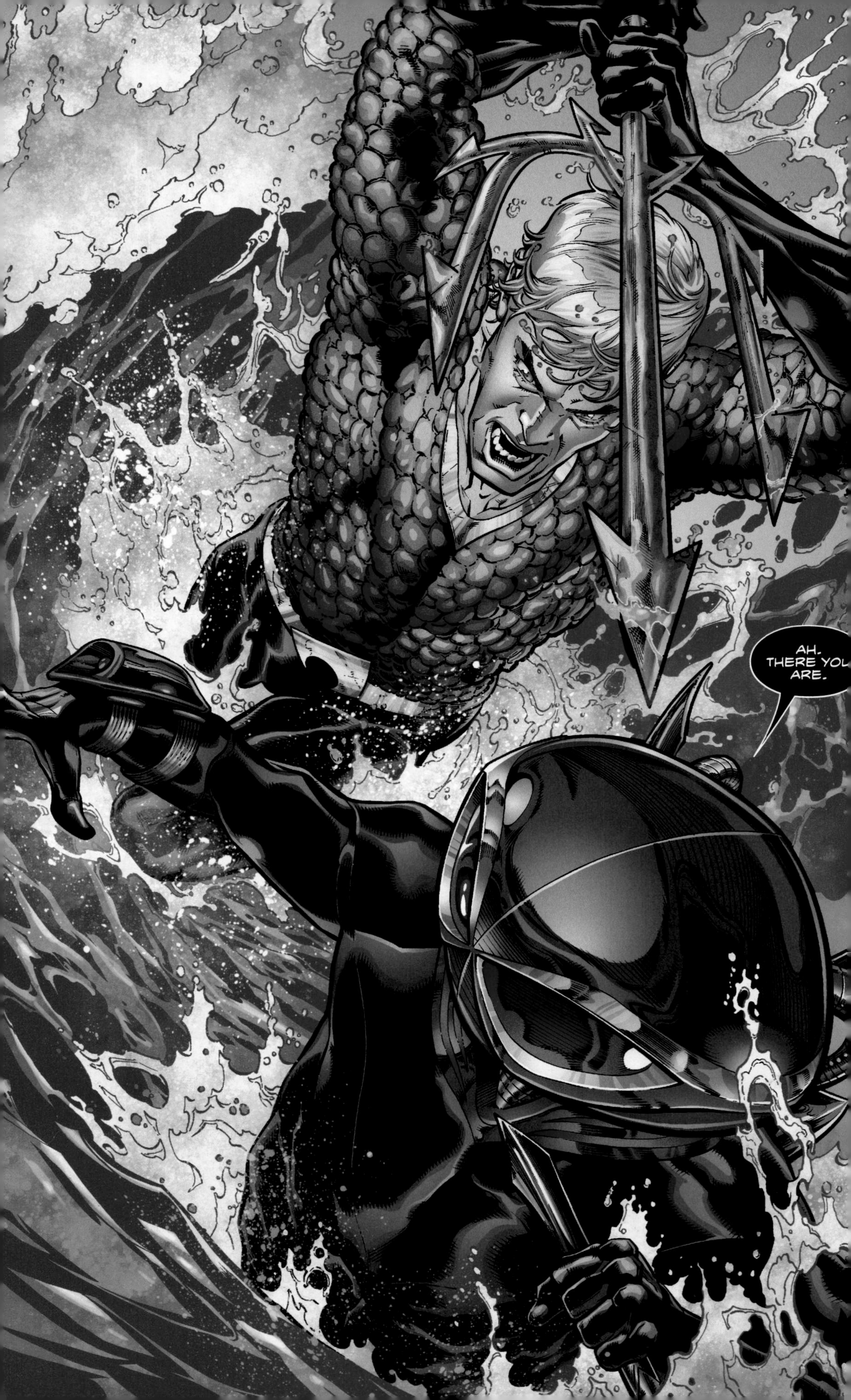
AH. THERE YOU ARE.

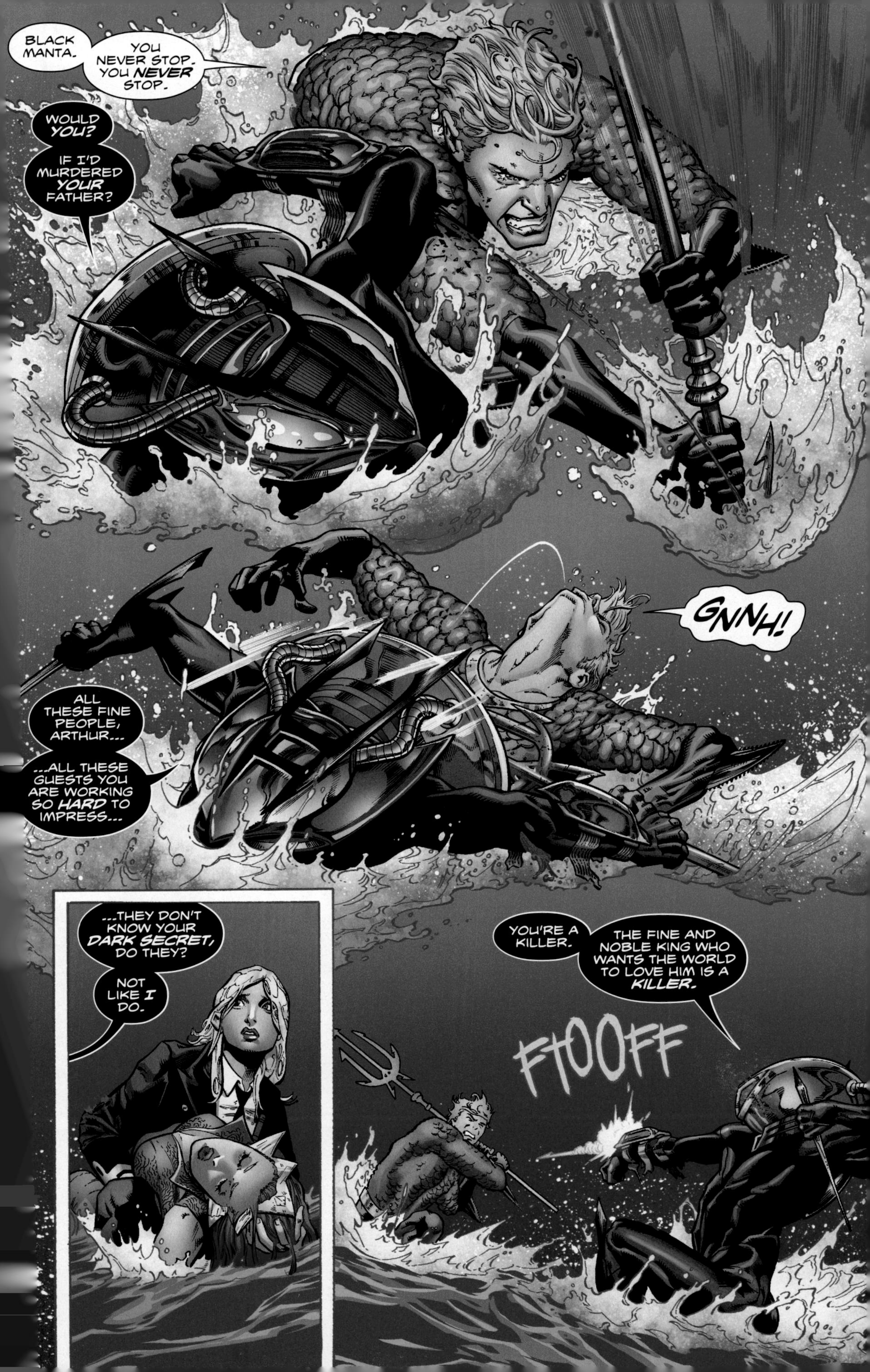
BLACK MANTA.
YOU NEVER STOP. YOU NEVER STOP.
WOULD YOU?
IF I'D MURDERED YOUR FATHER?
GNNH!
ALL THESE FINE PEOPLE, ARTHUR...
...ALL THESE GUESTS YOU ARE WORKING SO HARD TO IMPRESS...
...THEY DON'T KNOW YOUR DARK SECRET, DO THEY?
NOT LIKE I DO.
YOU'RE A KILLER.
THE FINE AND NOBLE KING WHO WANTS THE WORLD TO LOVE HIM IS A KILLER.
FTOOFF

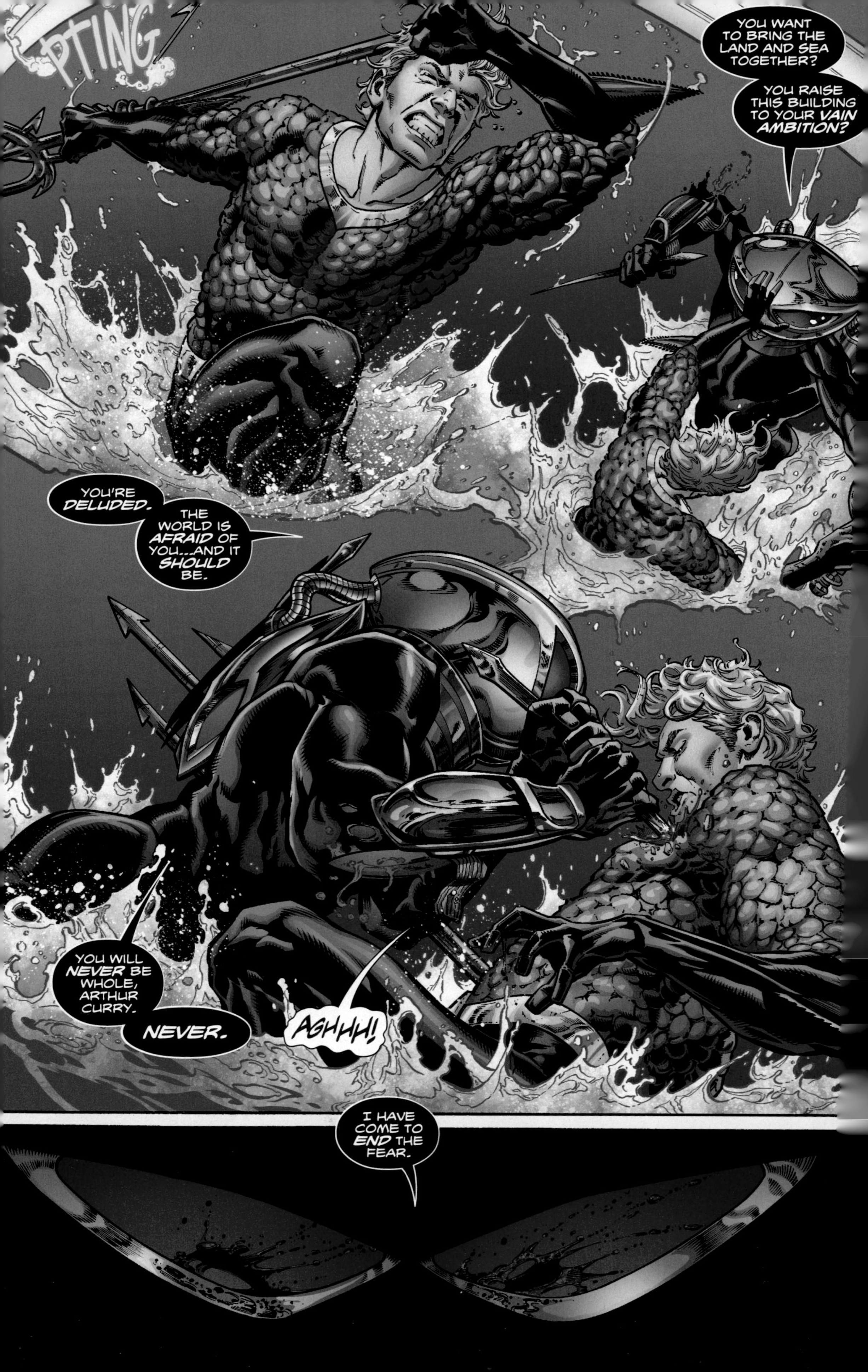

PTING
YOU WANT TO BRING THE LAND AND SEA TOGETHER?
YOU RAISE THIS BUILDING TO YOUR VAIN AMBITION?
YOU'RE DELUDED.
THE WORLD IS AFRAID OF YOU...AND IT SHOULD BE.
YOU WILL NEVER BE WHOLE, ARTHUR CURRY.
NEVER.
AGHHH!
I HAVE COME TO END THE FEAR.

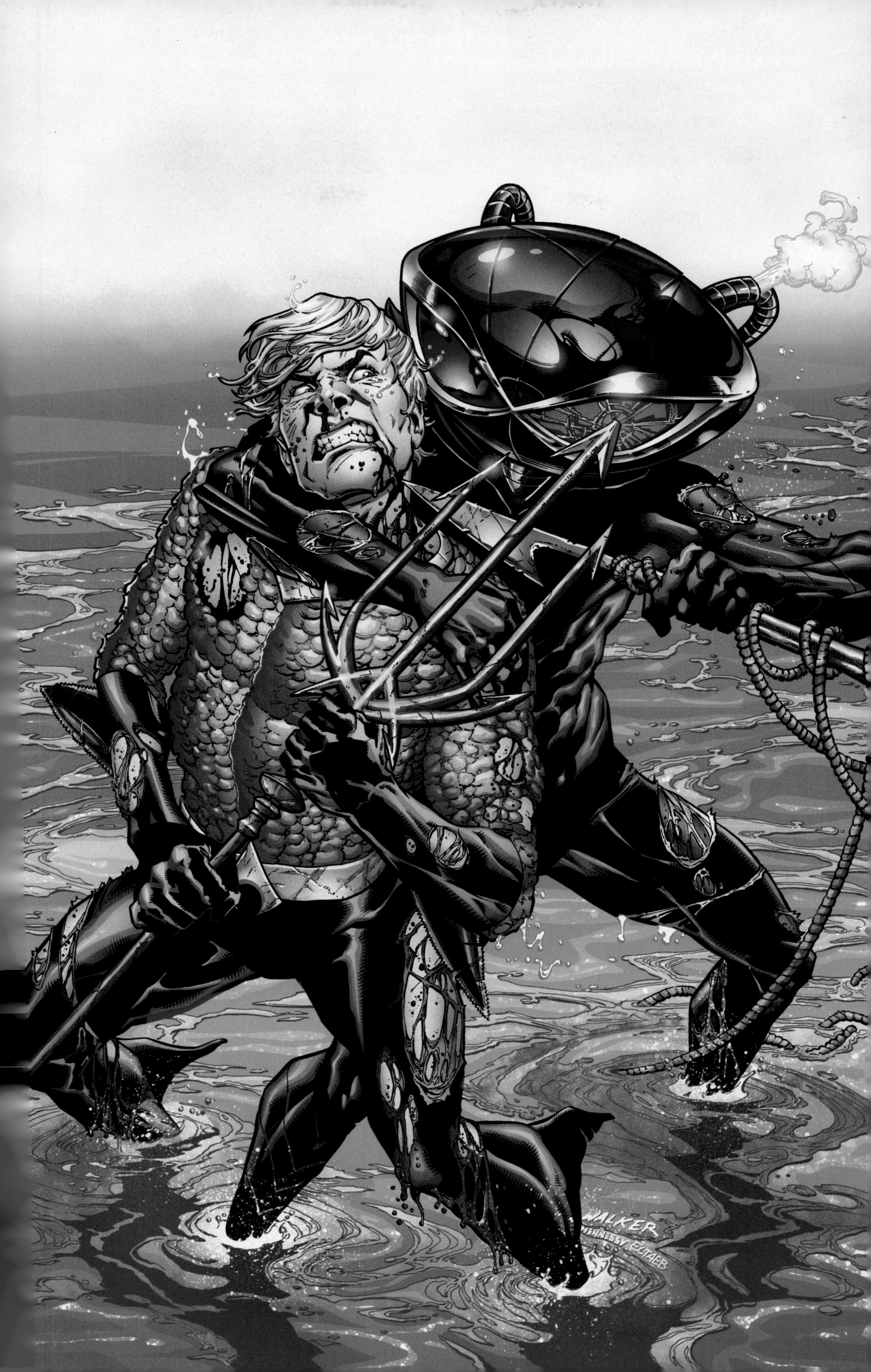
WALKER
HENNESSY ELTAEB

PART TWO: FULL CIRCLE

DAN ABNETT Writer * SCOT EATON Penciller * WAYNE FAUCHER Inker * GABE ELTAEB Colorist * PAT BROSSEAU Letterer

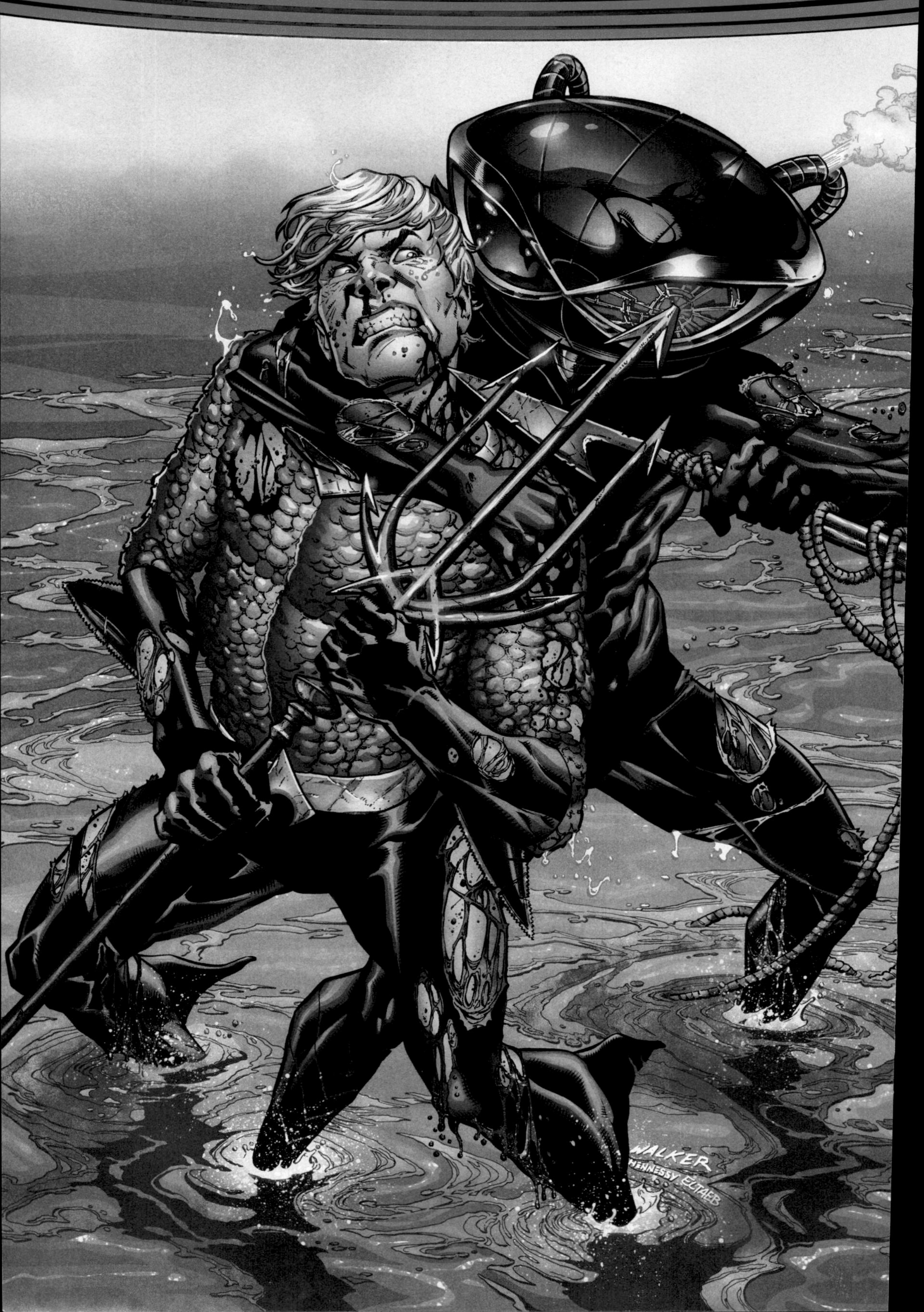
WALKER
HENNESSY ELTAEB

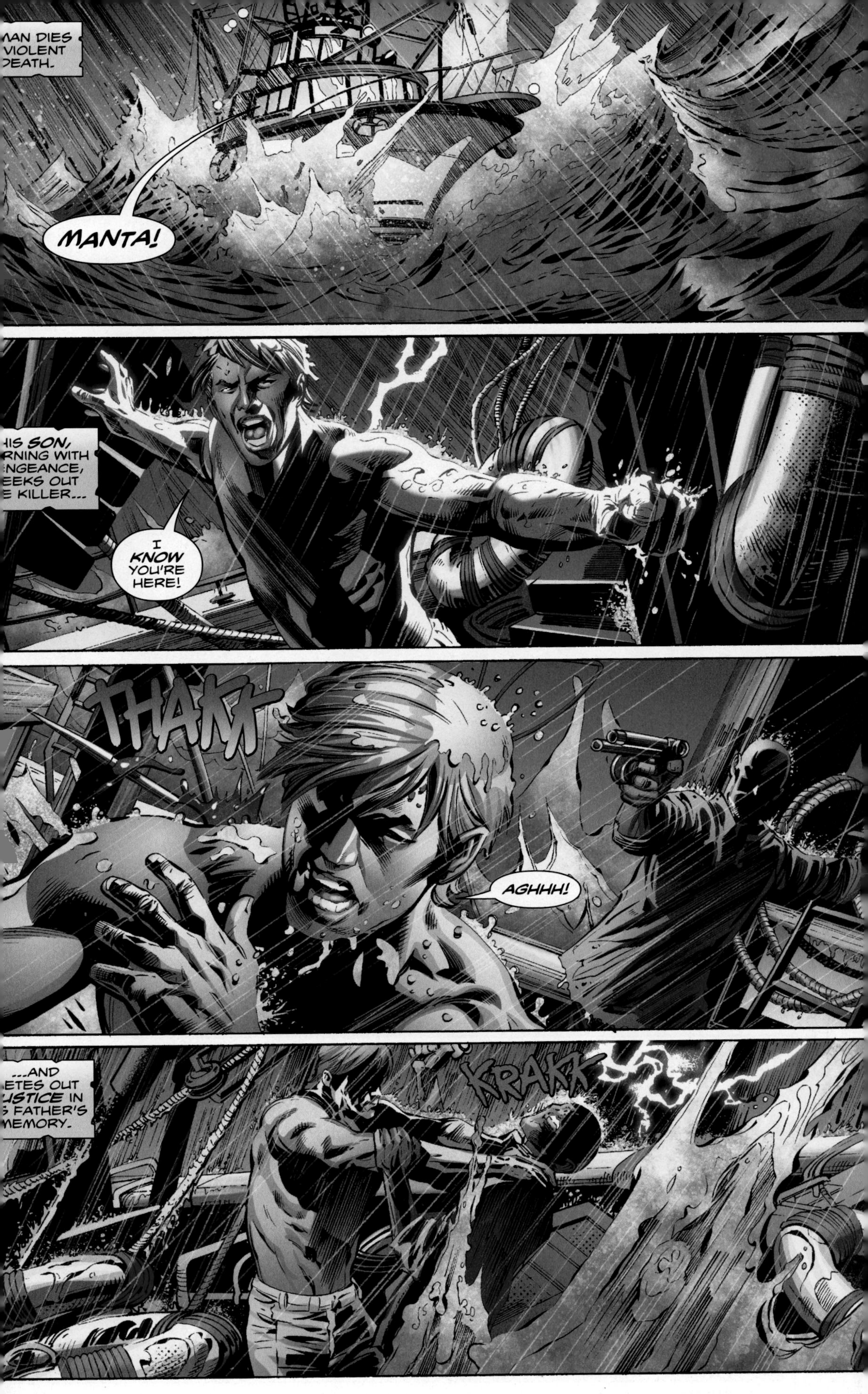
MAN DIES
VIOLENT
DEATH.
MANTA!
HIS SON,
RNING WITH
NGEANCE,
EEKS OUT
E KILLER...
I KNOW YOU'RE HERE!
THAKK
AGHHH!
...AND
ETES OUT
USTICE IN
FATHER'S
MEMORY.
KRAKK

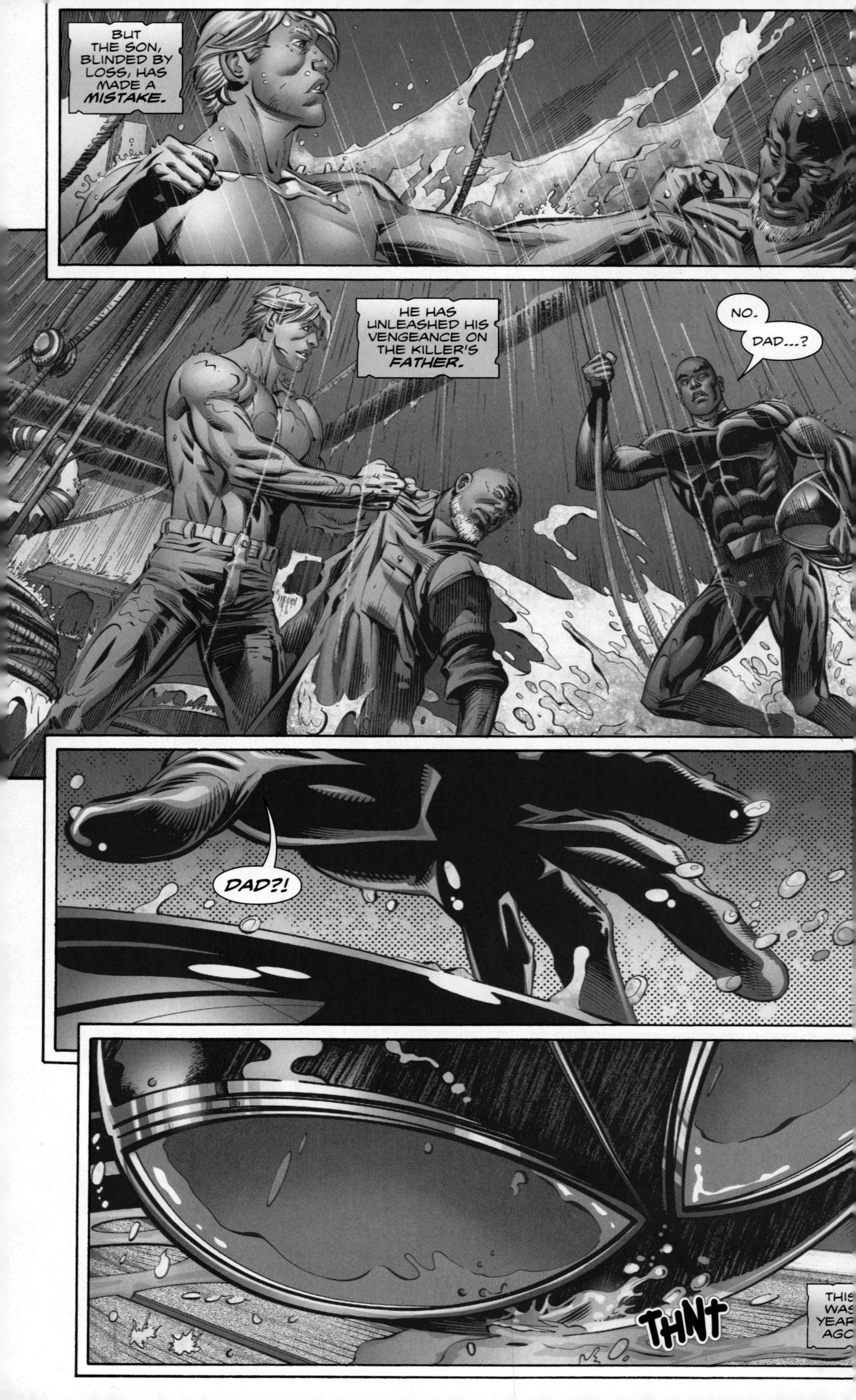

BUT THE SON, BLINDED BY LOSS, HAS MADE A MISTAKE.
HE HAS UNLEASHED HIS VENGEANCE ON THE KILLER'S FATHER.
NO.
DAD...?
DAD?!
THNT

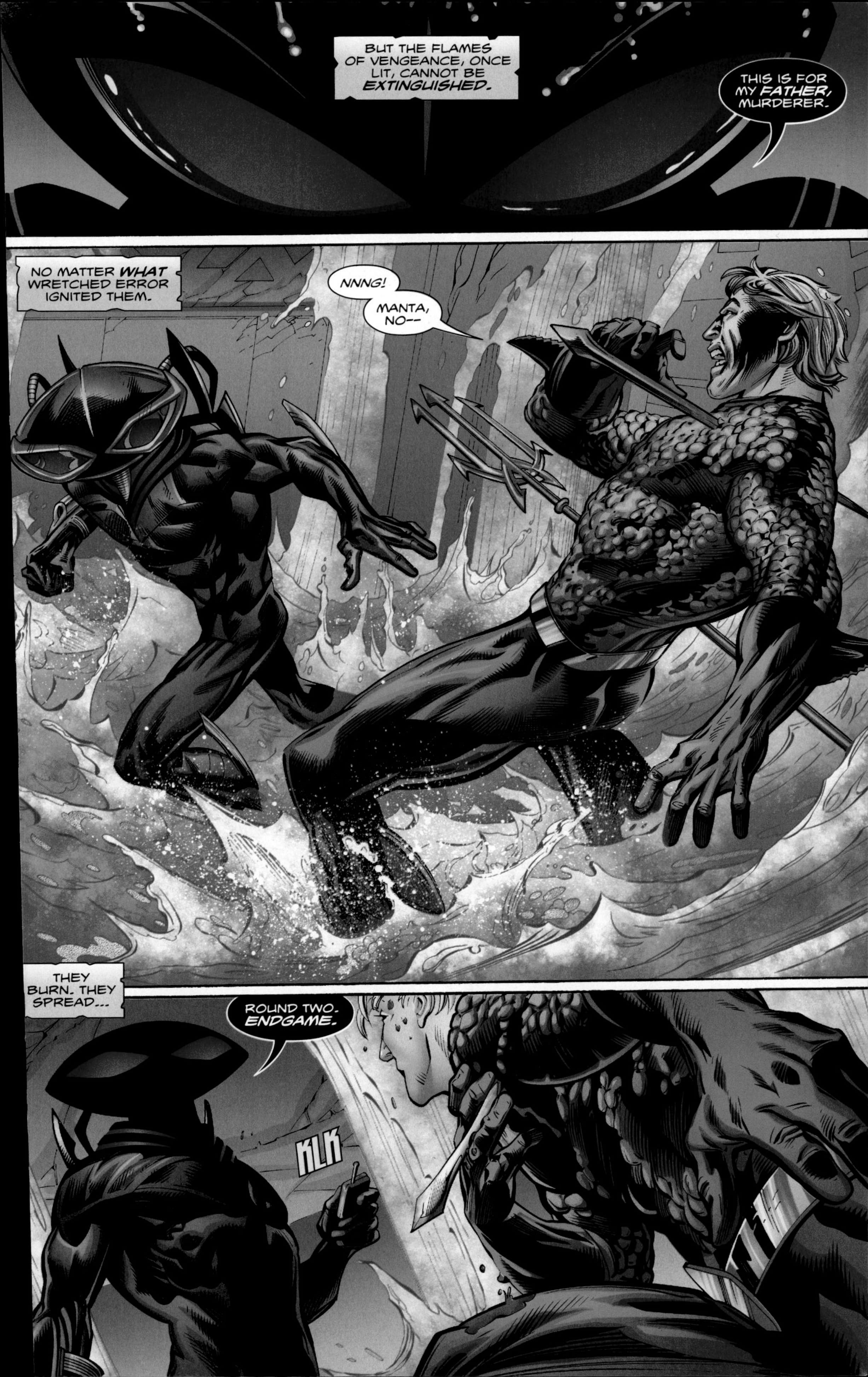

BUT THE FLAMES OF VENGEANCE, ONCE LIT, CANNOT BE EXTINGUISHED.
THIS IS FOR MY FATHER, MURDERER.
NO MATTER WHAT WRETCHED ERROR IGNITED THEM.
NNNG!
MANTA, NO--
THEY BURN. THEY SPREAD...
ROUND TWO. ENDGAME.
KLK

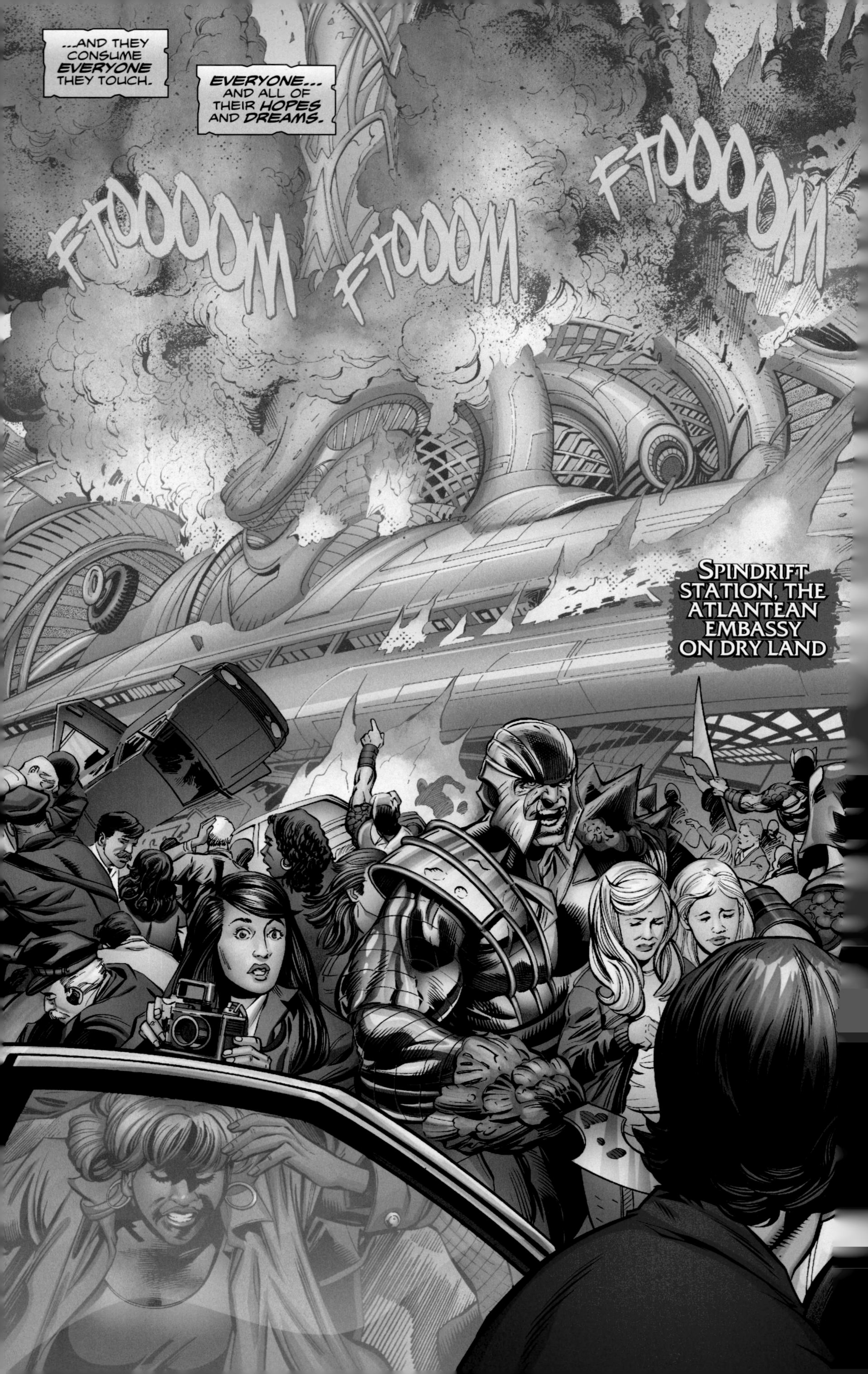
...AND THEY CONSUME EVERYONE THEY TOUCH.
EVERYONE... AND ALL OF THEIR HOPES AND DREAMS.
FTOOOOM
FTOOOM
FTOOOOOM
SPINDRIFT STATION, THE ATLANTEAN EMBASSY ON DRY LAND

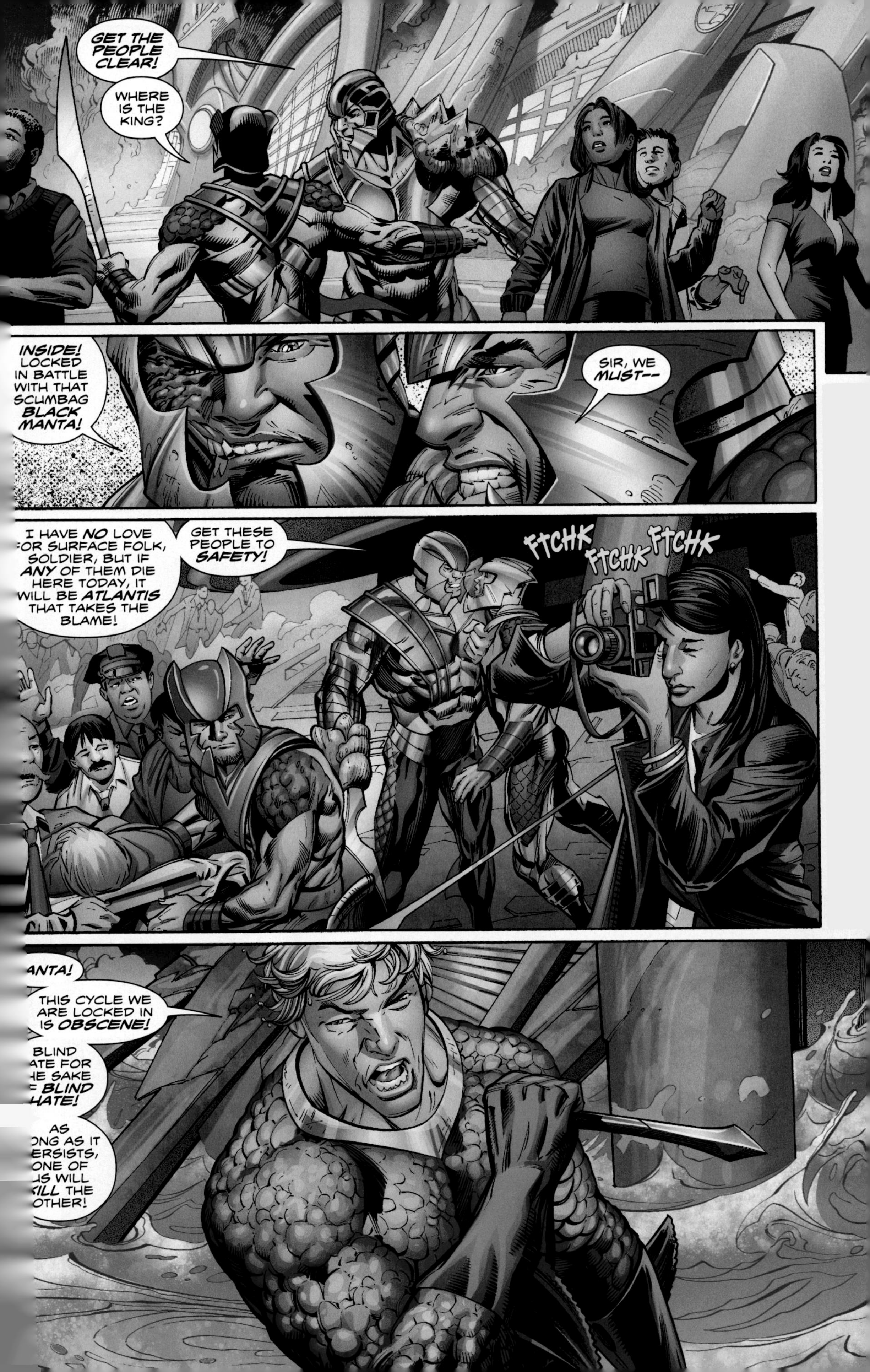
GET THE PEOPLE CLEAR!
WHERE IS THE KING?
INSIDE! LOCKED IN BATTLE WITH THAT SCUMBAG BLACK MANTA!
SIR, WE MUST--
I HAVE NO LOVE FOR SURFACE FOLK, SOLDIER, BUT IF ANY OF THEM DIE HERE TODAY, IT WILL BE ATLANTIS THAT TAKES THE BLAME!
GET THESE PEOPLE TO SAFETY!
FTCHK
FTCHK
FTCHK
ANTA!
THIS CYCLE WE ARE LOCKED IN IS OBSCENE!
BLIND ATE FOR HE SAKE F BLIND HATE!
AS ONG AS IT ERSISTS, ONE OF US WILL KILL THE OTHER!

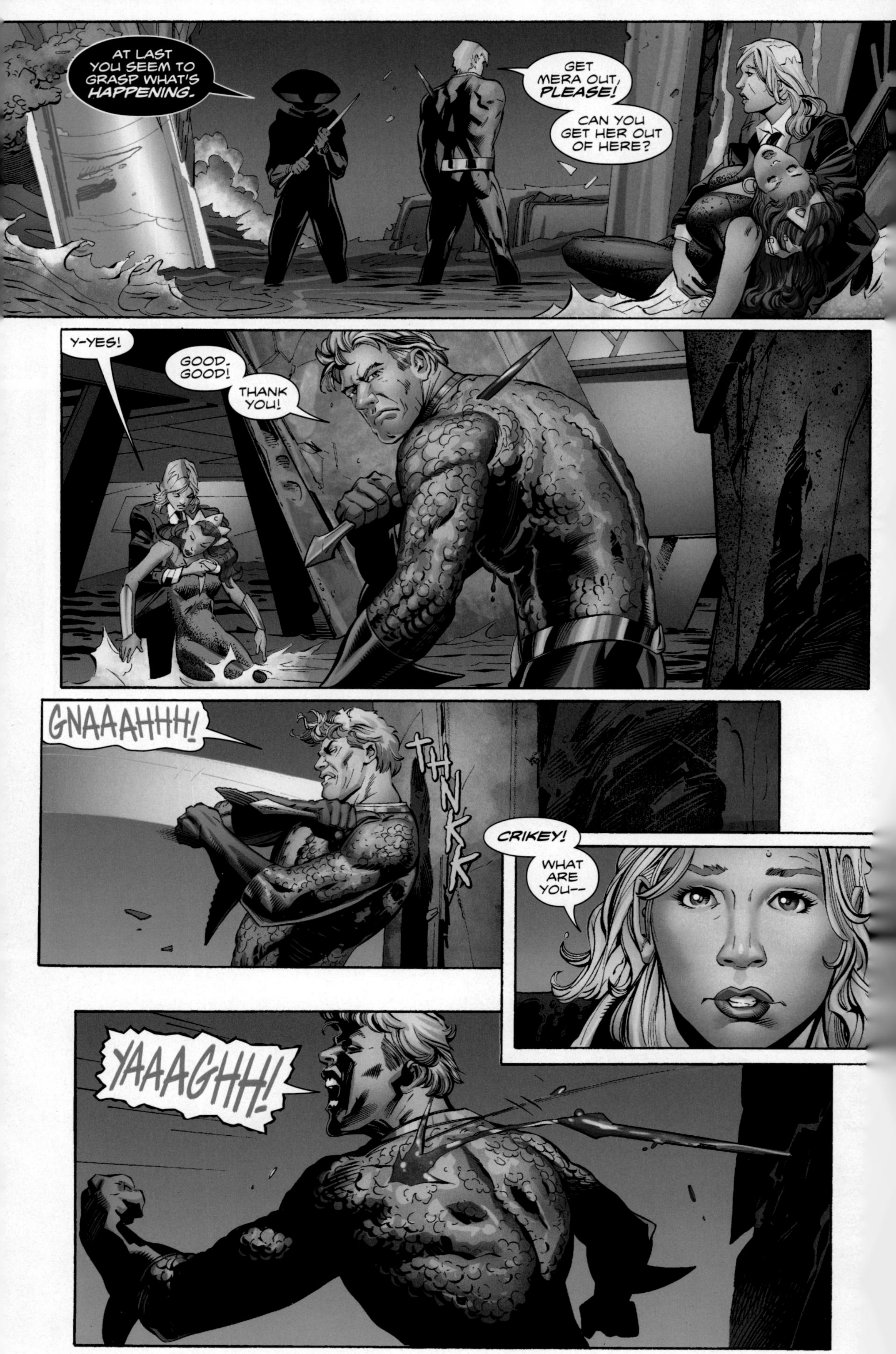
AT LAST YOU SEEM TO GRASP WHAT'S HAPPENING.
GET MERA OUT, PLEASE!
CAN YOU GET HER OUT OF HERE?
Y-YES!
GOOD. GOOD!
THANK YOU!
GNAAAHHH!
THNKK
CRIKEY!
WHAT ARE YOU--
YAAAGHH!

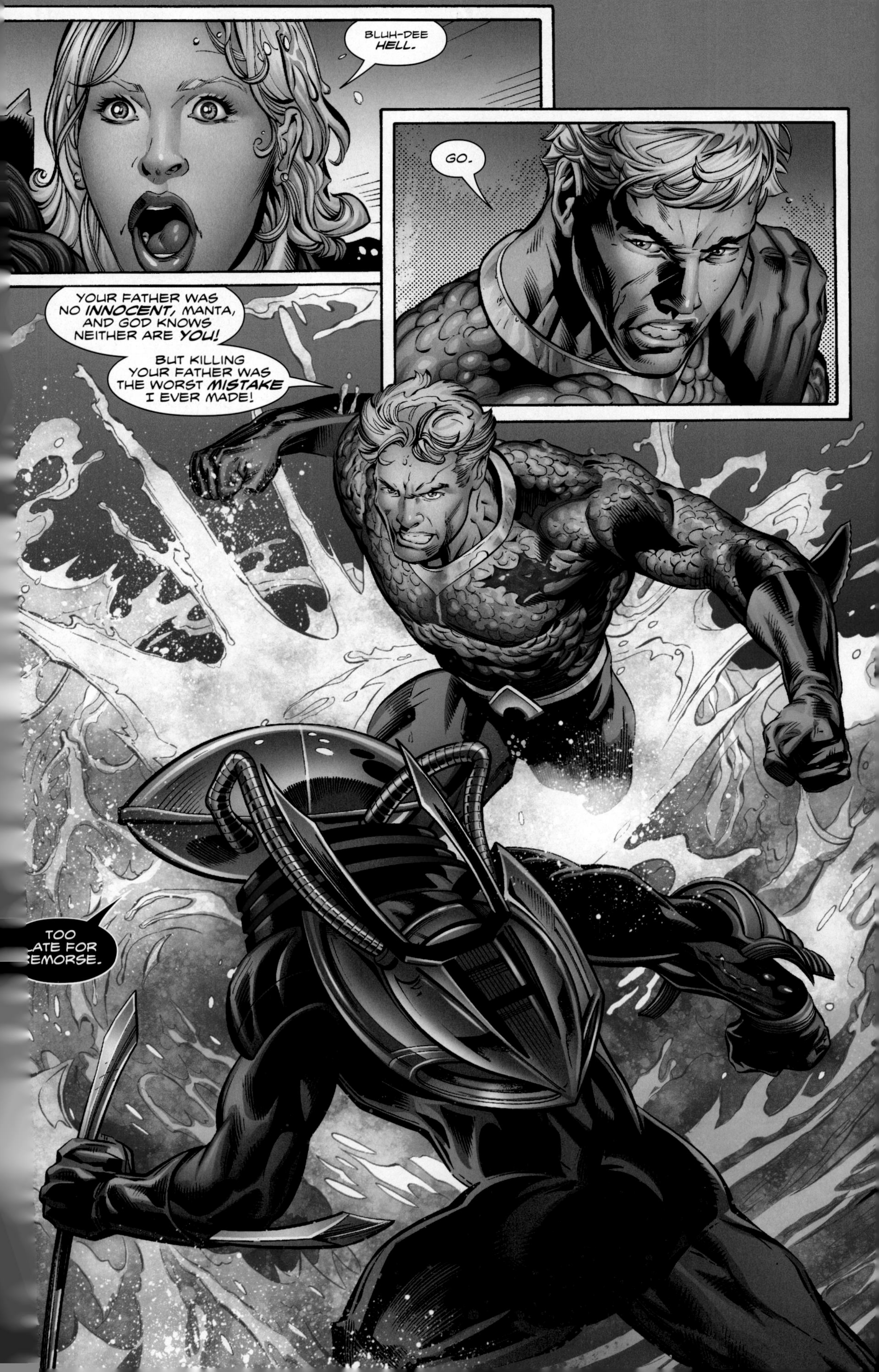
BLUH-DEE HELL.
GO.
YOUR FATHER WAS NO INNOCENT, MANTA, AND GOD KNOWS NEITHER ARE YOU!
BUT KILLING YOUR FATHER WAS THE WORST MISTAKE I EVER MADE!
TOO LATE FOR REMORSE.

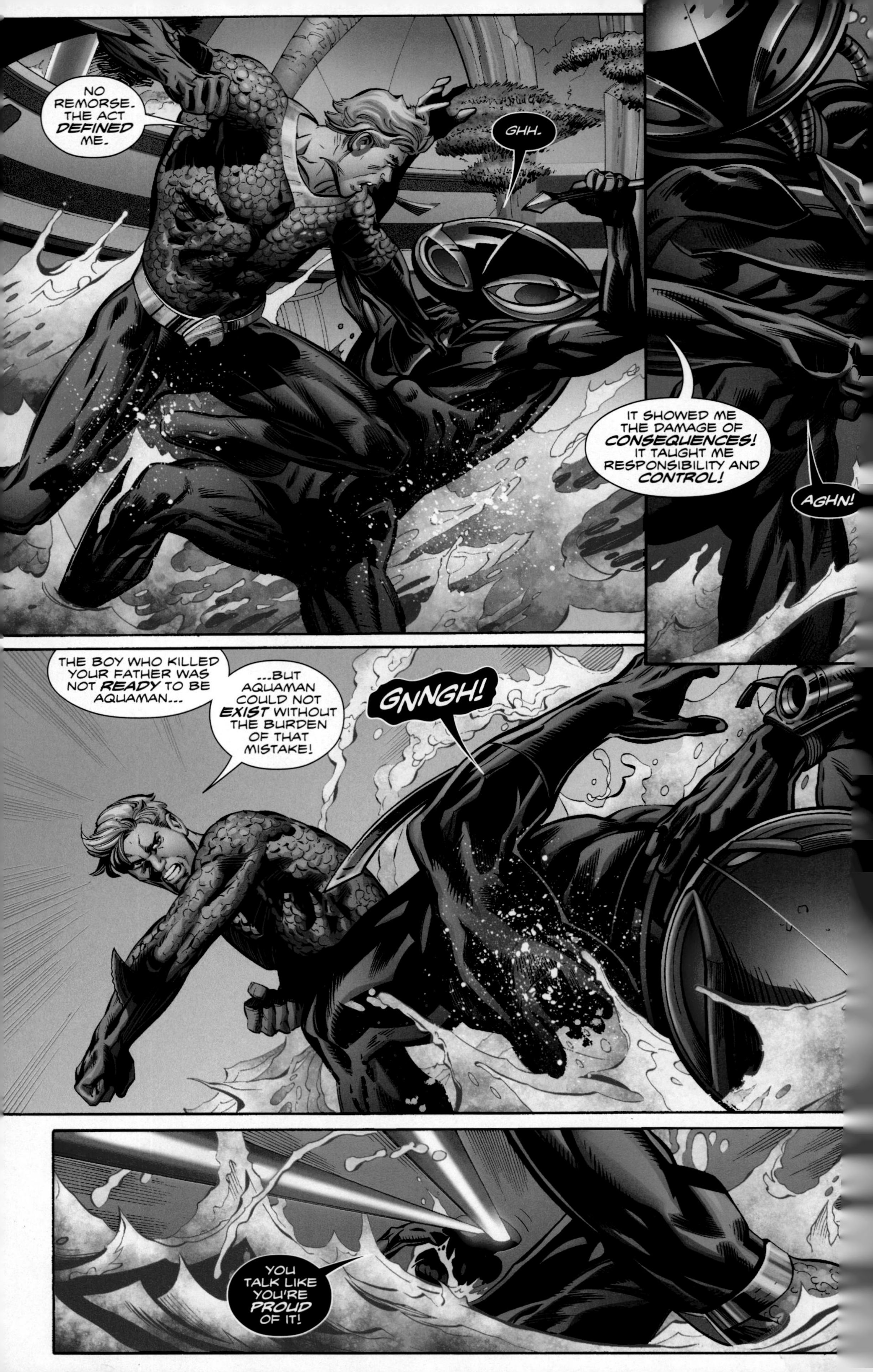
NO REMORSE. THE ACT DEFINED ME.
GHH.
IT SHOWED ME THE DAMAGE OF CONSEQUENCES! IT TAUGHT ME RESPONSIBILITY AND CONTROL!
AGHN!
THE BOY WHO KILLED YOUR FATHER WAS NOT READY TO BE AQUAMAN...
...BUT AQUAMAN COULD NOT EXIST WITHOUT THE BURDEN OF THAT MISTAKE!
GNNGH!
YOU TALK LIKE YOU'RE PROUD OF IT!

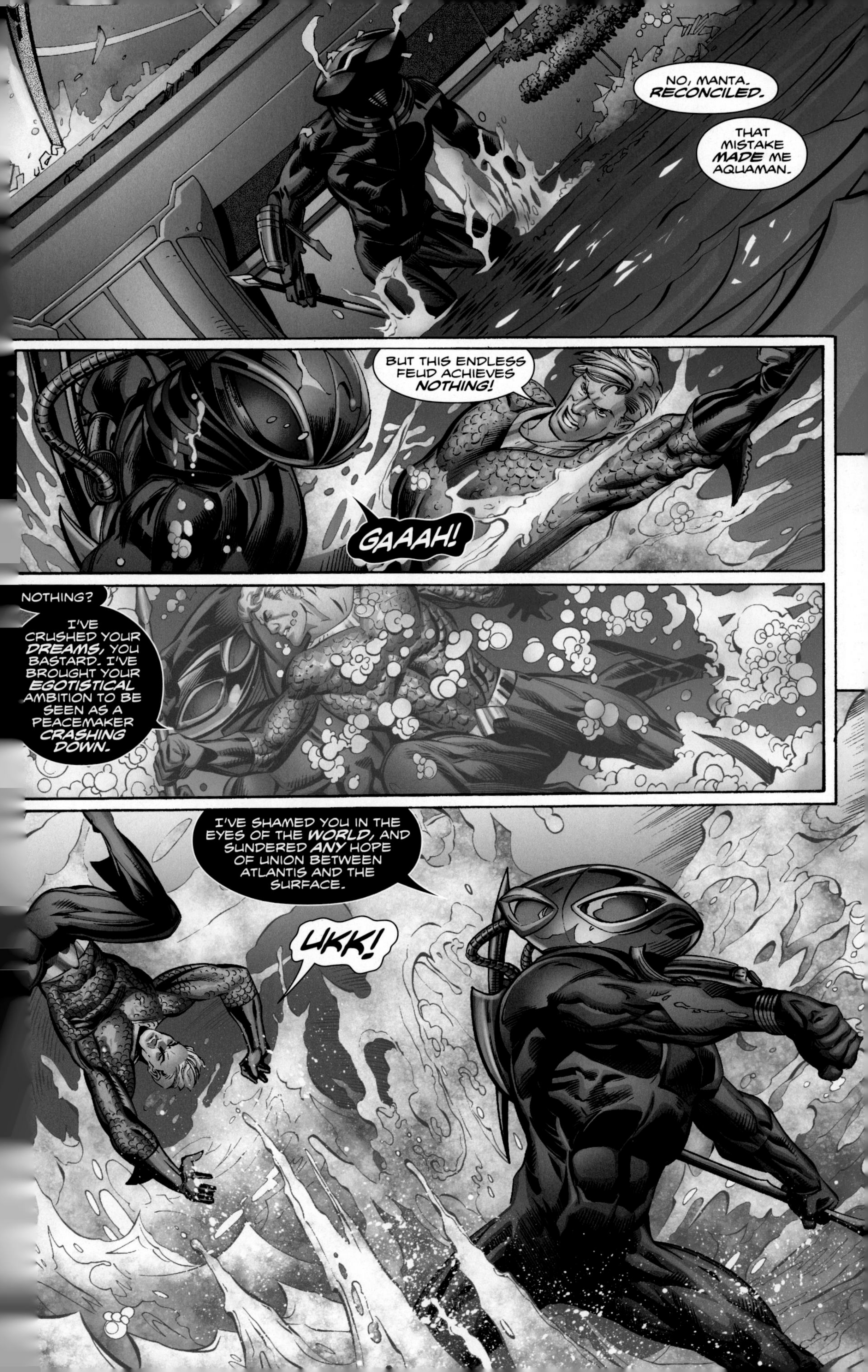
NO, MANTA. RECONCILED.
THAT MISTAKE MADE ME AQUAMAN.
BUT THIS ENDLESS FEUD ACHIEVES NOTHING!
GAAAH!
NOTHING?
I'VE CRUSHED YOUR DREAMS, YOU BASTARD. I'VE BROUGHT YOUR EGOTISTICAL AMBITION TO BE SEEN AS A PEACEMAKER CRASHING DOWN.
I'VE SHAMED YOU IN THE EYES OF THE WORLD, AND SUNDERED ANY HOPE OF UNION BETWEEN ATLANTIS AND THE SURFACE.
UKK!

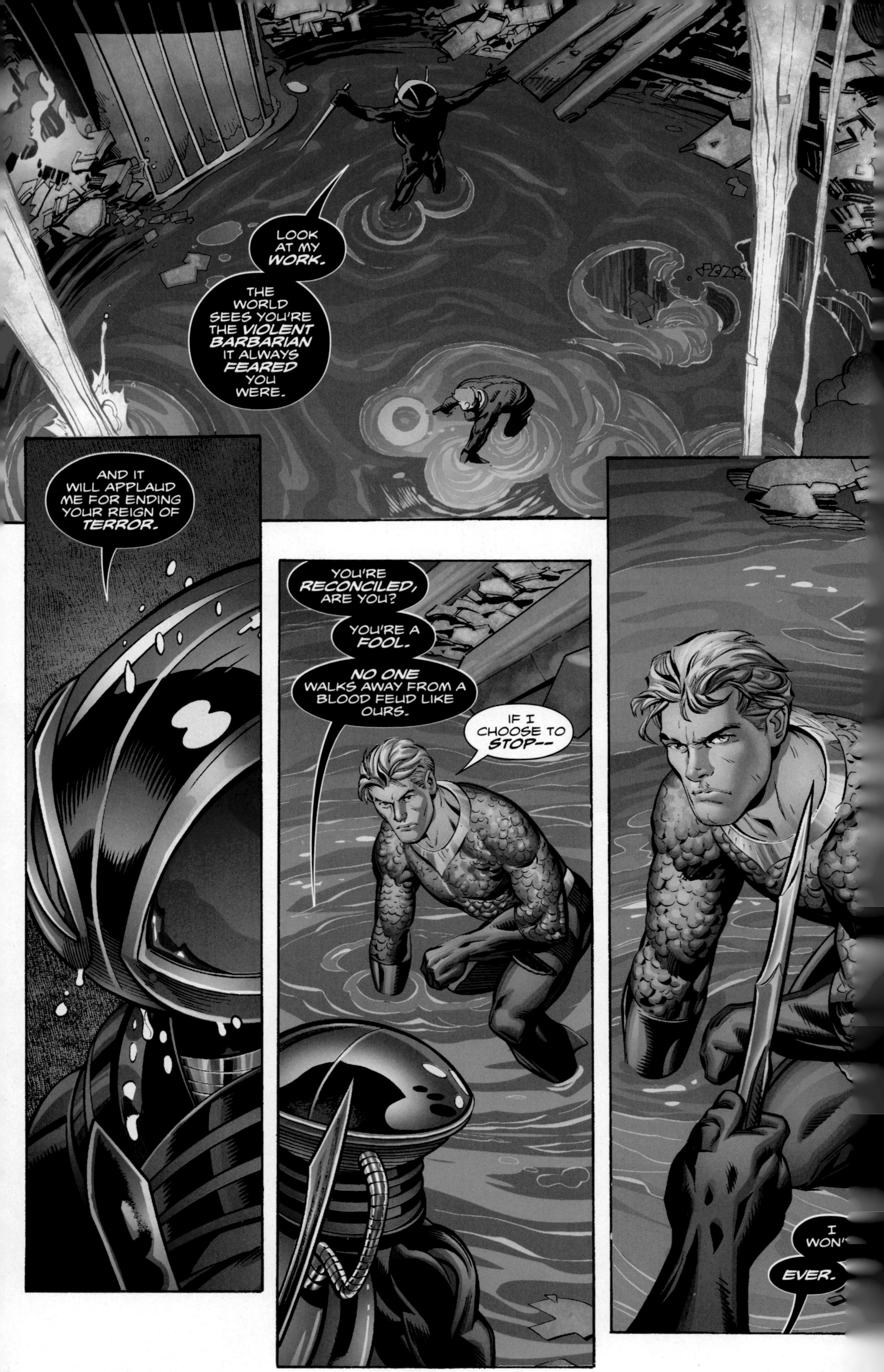
LOOK AT MY WORK.
THE WORLD SEES YOU'RE THE VIOLENT BARBARIAN IT ALWAYS FEARED YOU WERE.
AND IT WILL APPLAUD ME FOR ENDING YOUR REIGN OF TERROR.
YOU'RE RECONCILED, ARE YOU?
YOU'RE A FOOL.
NO ONE WALKS AWAY FROM A BLOOD FEUD LIKE OURS.
IF I CHOOSE TO STOP--
EVER.

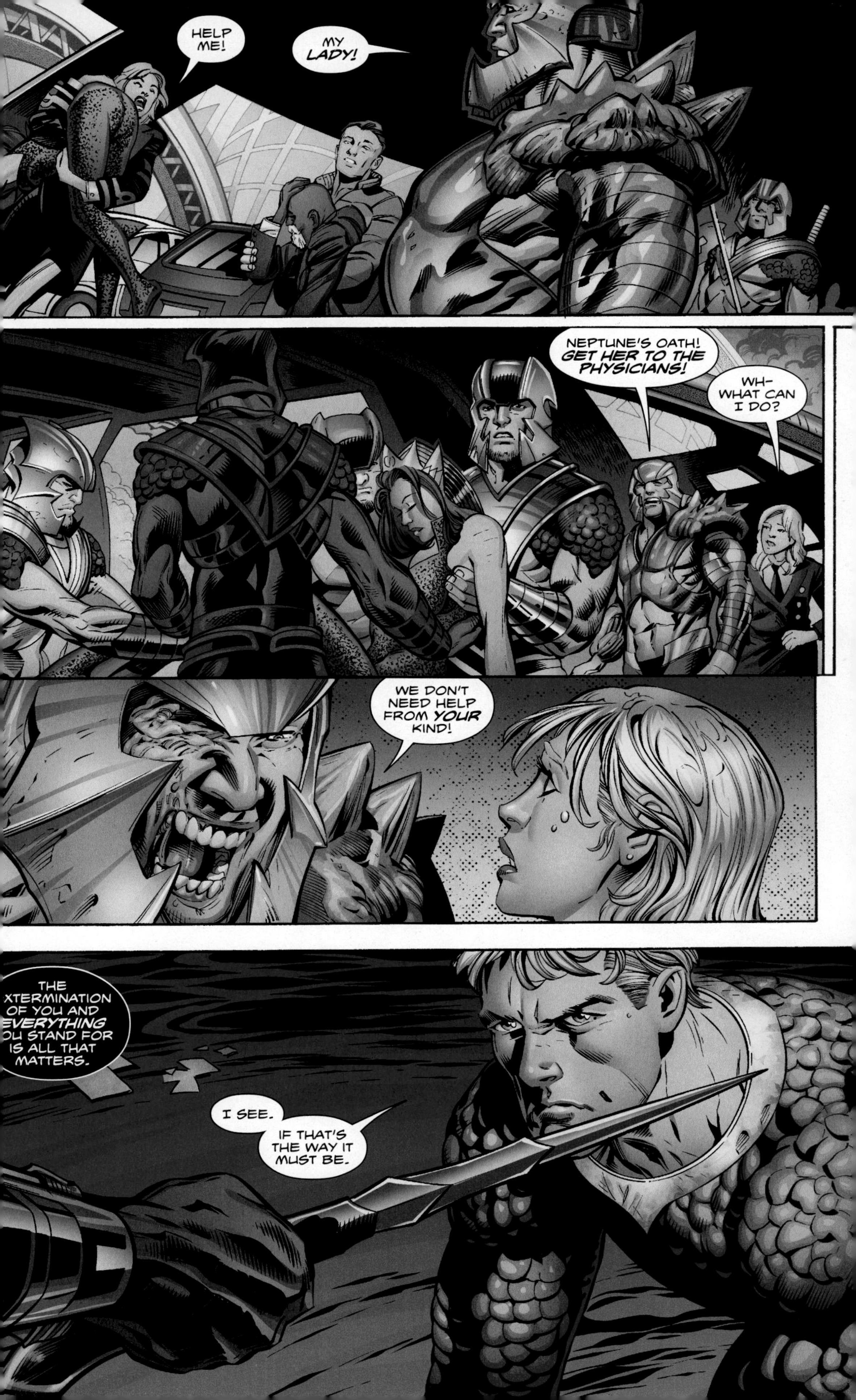
HELP ME!
MY LADY!
NEPTUNE'S OATH! GET HER TO THE PHYSICIANS!
WH- WHAT CAN I DO?
WE DON'T NEED HELP FROM YOUR KIND!
THE XTERMINATION OF YOU AND EVERYTHING OU STAND FOR IS ALL THAT MATTERS.
I SEE.
IF THAT'S THE WAY IT MUST BE.

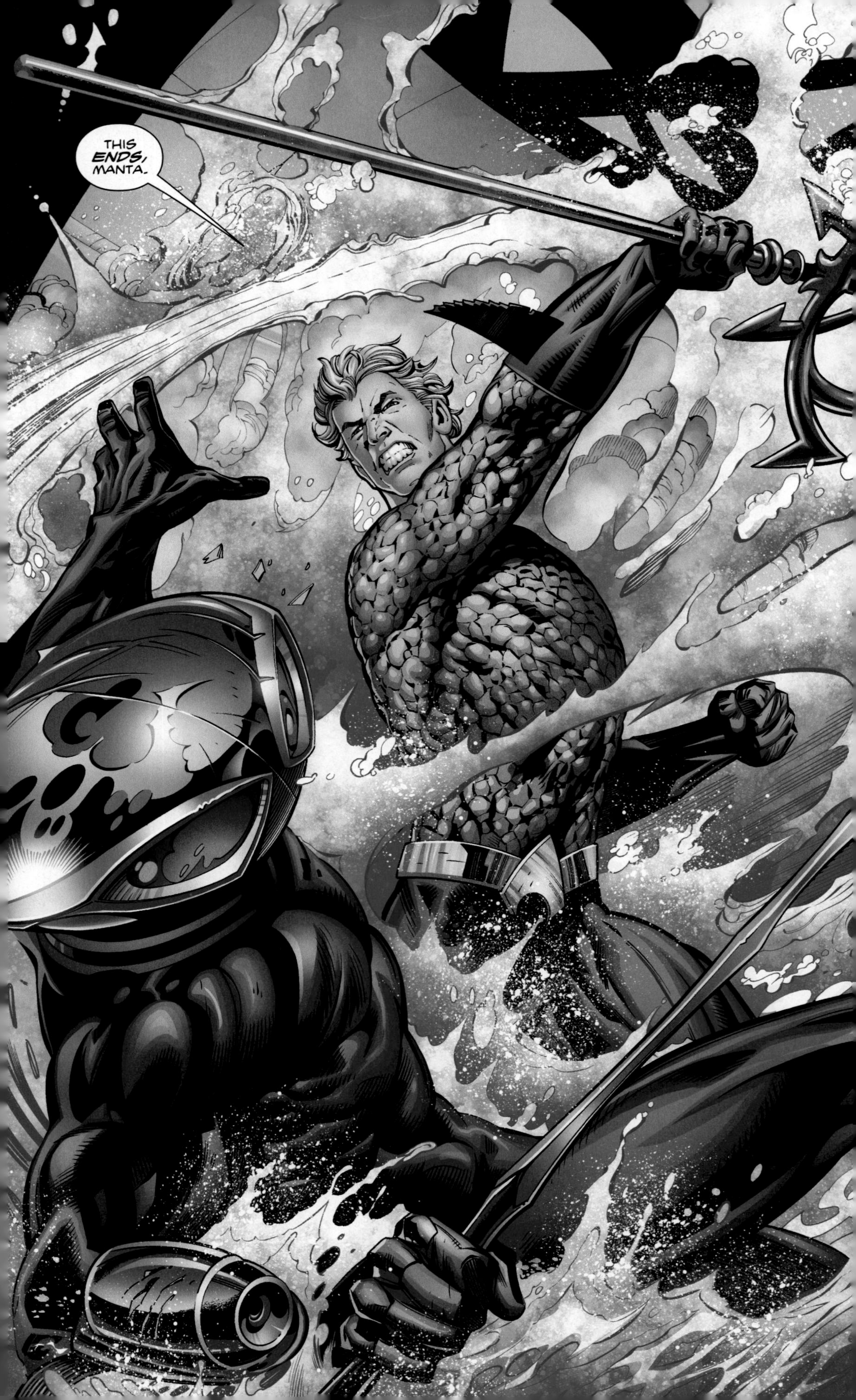
THIS ENDS, MANTA.

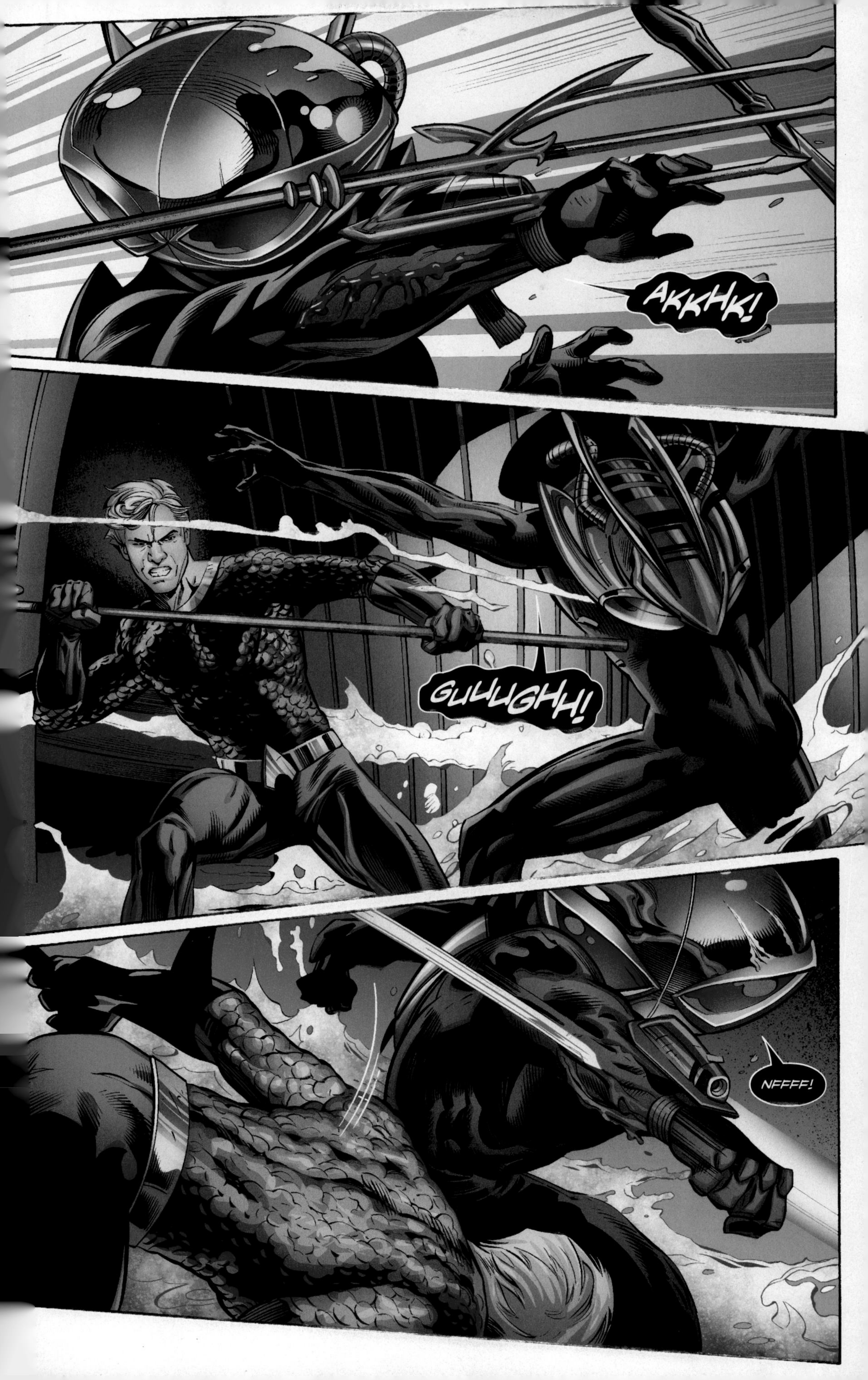
AKKHK!
GUUUGHH!
NFFFF!

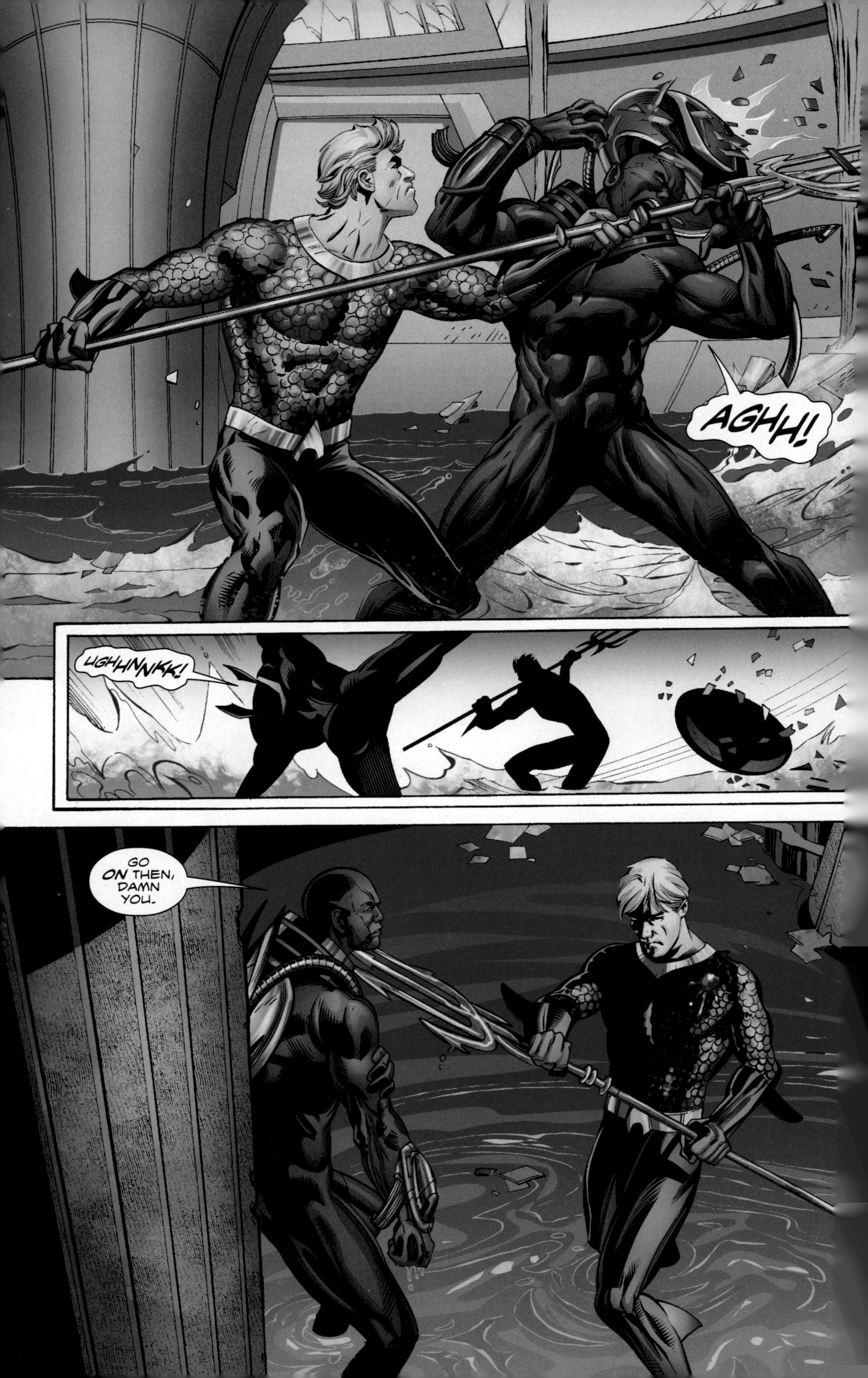
AGHH!
UGHHNNKK!
GO ON THEN, DAMN YOU.

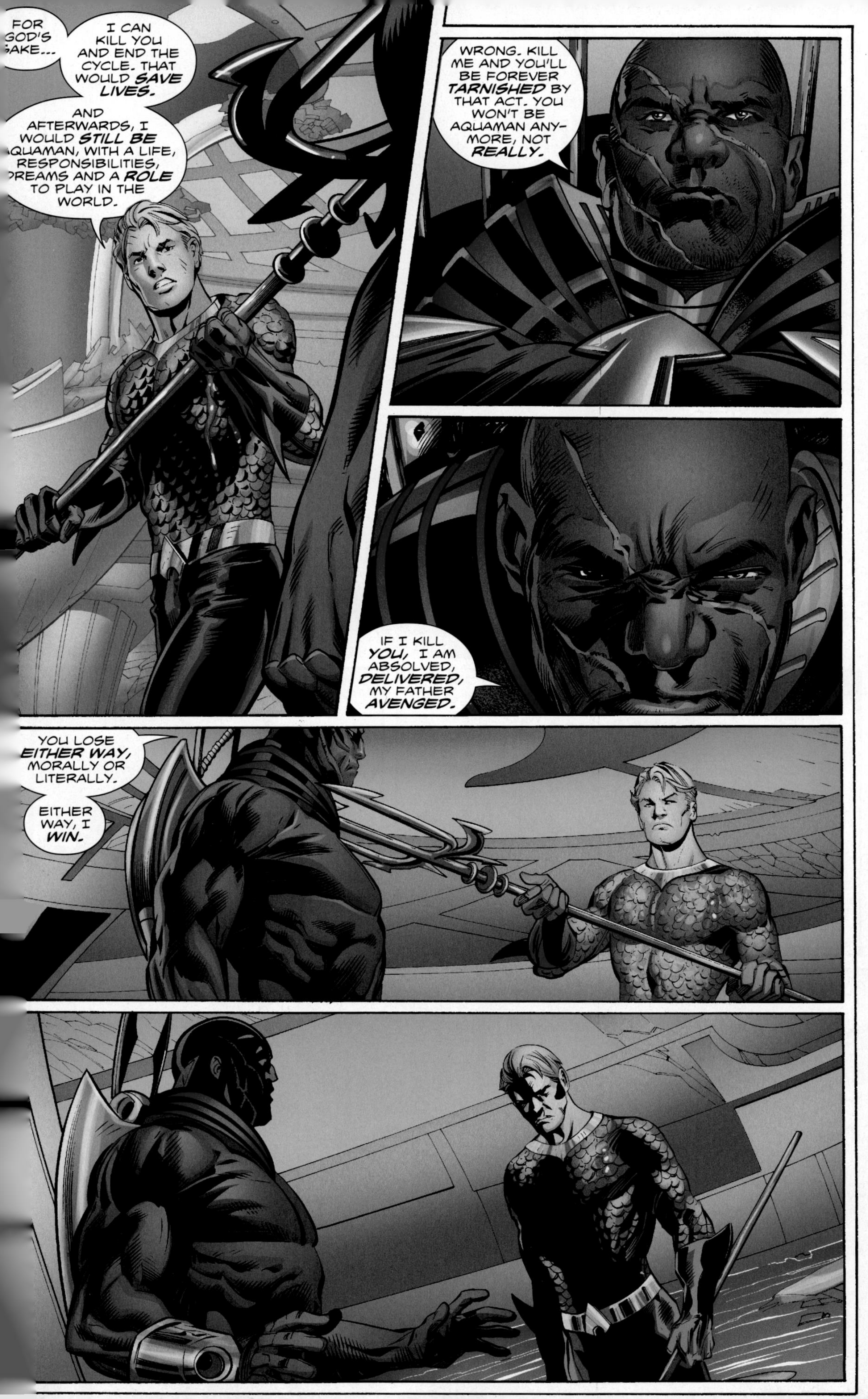
FOR GOD'S SAKE...
I CAN KILL YOU AND END THE CYCLE. THAT WOULD SAVE LIVES.
AND AFTERWARDS, I WOULD STILL BE AQUAMAN, WITH A LIFE, RESPONSIBILITIES, DREAMS AND A ROLE TO PLAY IN THE WORLD.
WRONG. KILL ME AND YOU'LL BE FOREVER TARNISHED BY THAT ACT. YOU WON'T BE AQUAMAN ANY-MORE, NOT REALLY.
IF I KILL YOU, I AM ABSOLVED, DELIVERED, MY FATHER AVENGED.
YOU LOSE EITHER WAY, MORALLY OR LITERALLY.
EITHER WAY, I WIN.

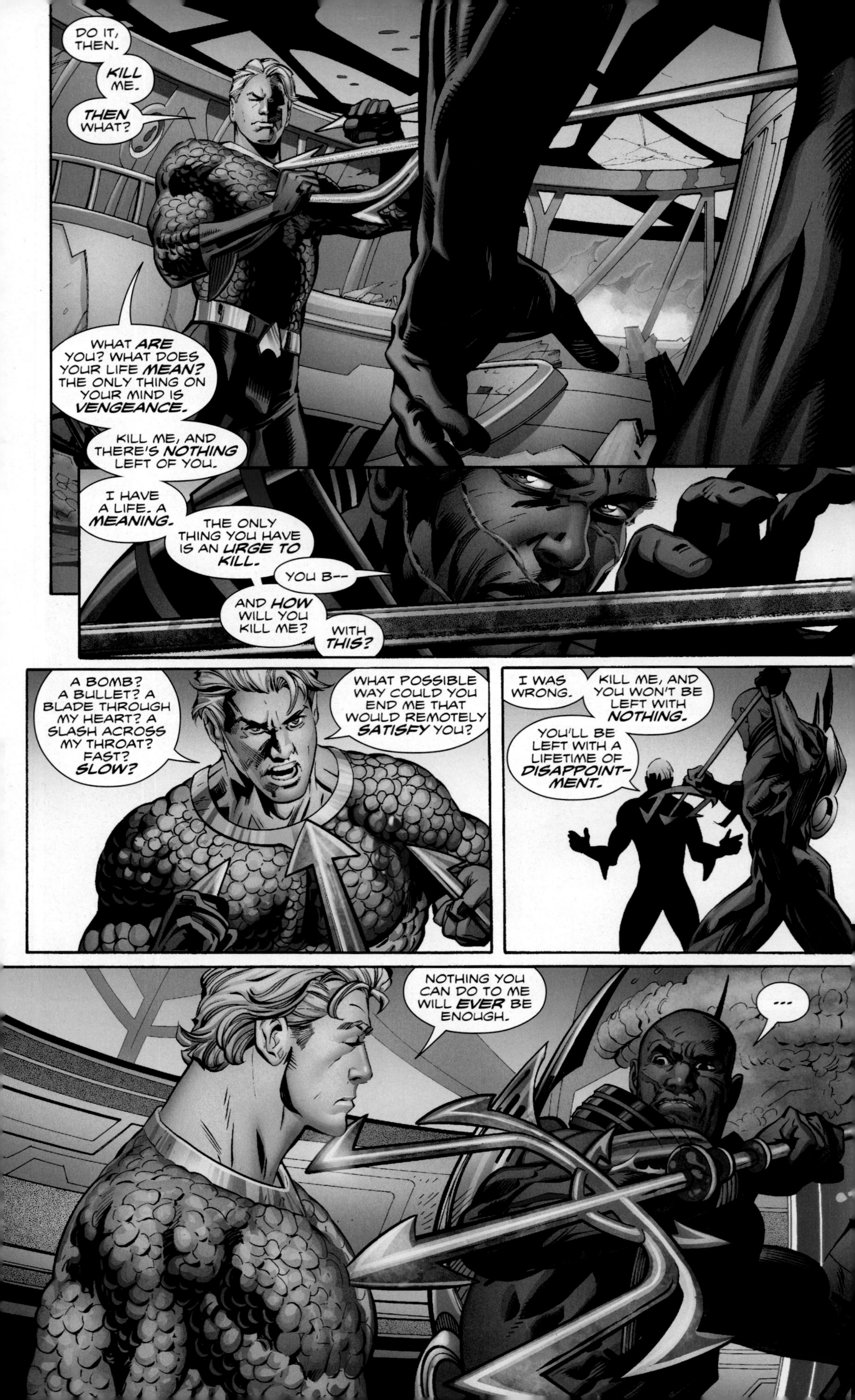
DO IT, THEN.
KILL ME.
THEN WHAT?
WHAT ARE YOU? WHAT DOES YOUR LIFE MEAN? THE ONLY THING ON YOUR MIND IS VENGEANCE.
KILL ME, AND THERE'S NOTHING LEFT OF YOU.
I HAVE A LIFE. A MEANING.
THE ONLY THING YOU HAVE IS AN URGE TO KILL.
YOU B--
AND HOW WILL YOU KILL ME?
WITH THIS?
A BOMB? A BULLET? A BLADE THROUGH MY HEART? A SLASH ACROSS MY THROAT? FAST? SLOW?
WHAT POSSIBLE WAY COULD YOU END ME THAT WOULD REMOTELY SATISFY YOU?
I WAS WRONG.
KILL ME, AND YOU WON'T BE LEFT WITH NOTHING.
YOU'LL BE LEFT WITH A LIFETIME OF DISAPPOINTMENT.
NOTHING YOU CAN DO TO ME WILL EVER BE ENOUGH.
...

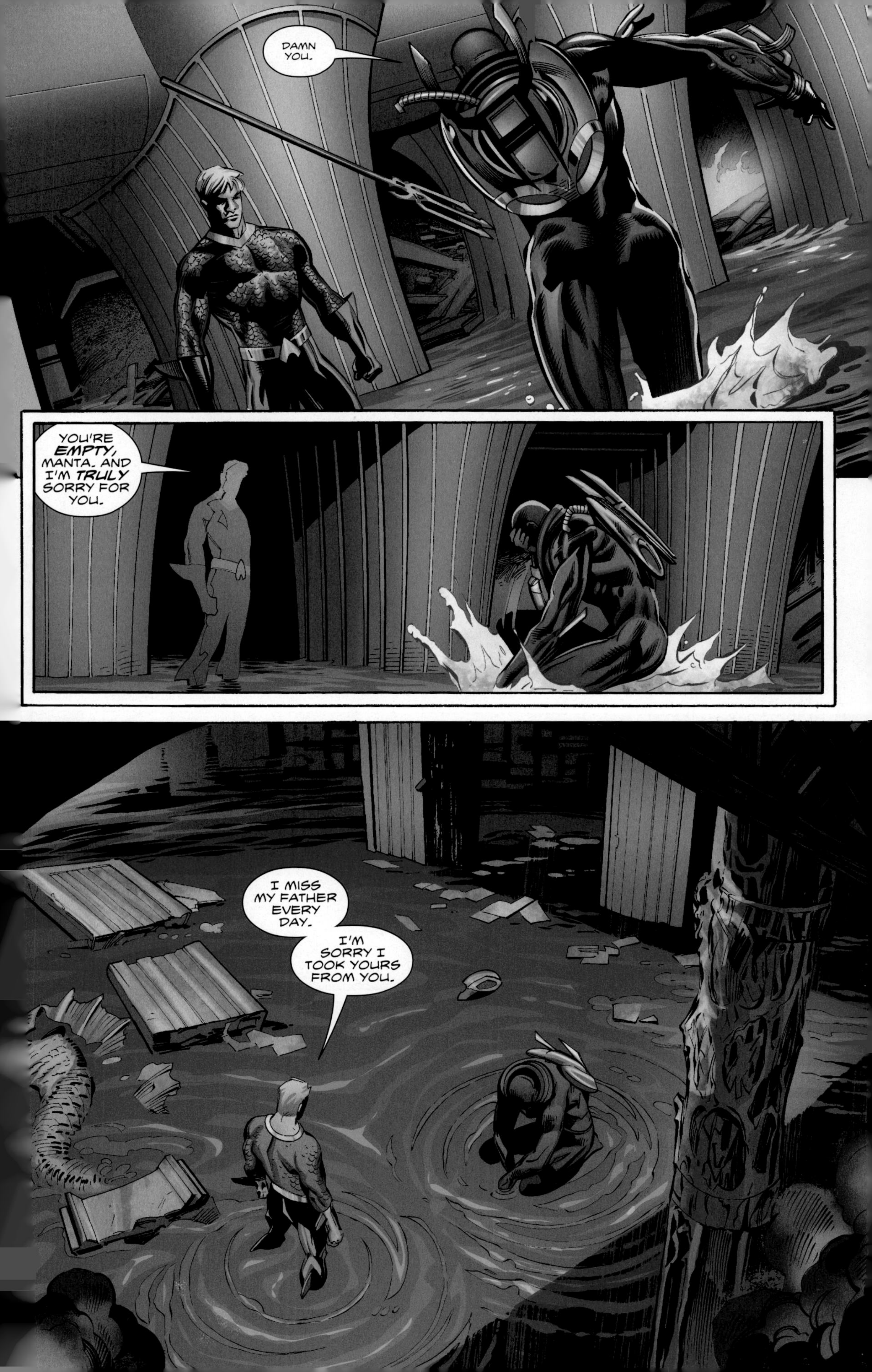
DAMN YOU.
YOU'RE **EMPTY**, MANTA. AND I'M **TRULY** SORRY FOR YOU.
I MISS MY FATHER EVERY DAY.
I'M SORRY I TOOK YOURS FROM YOU.

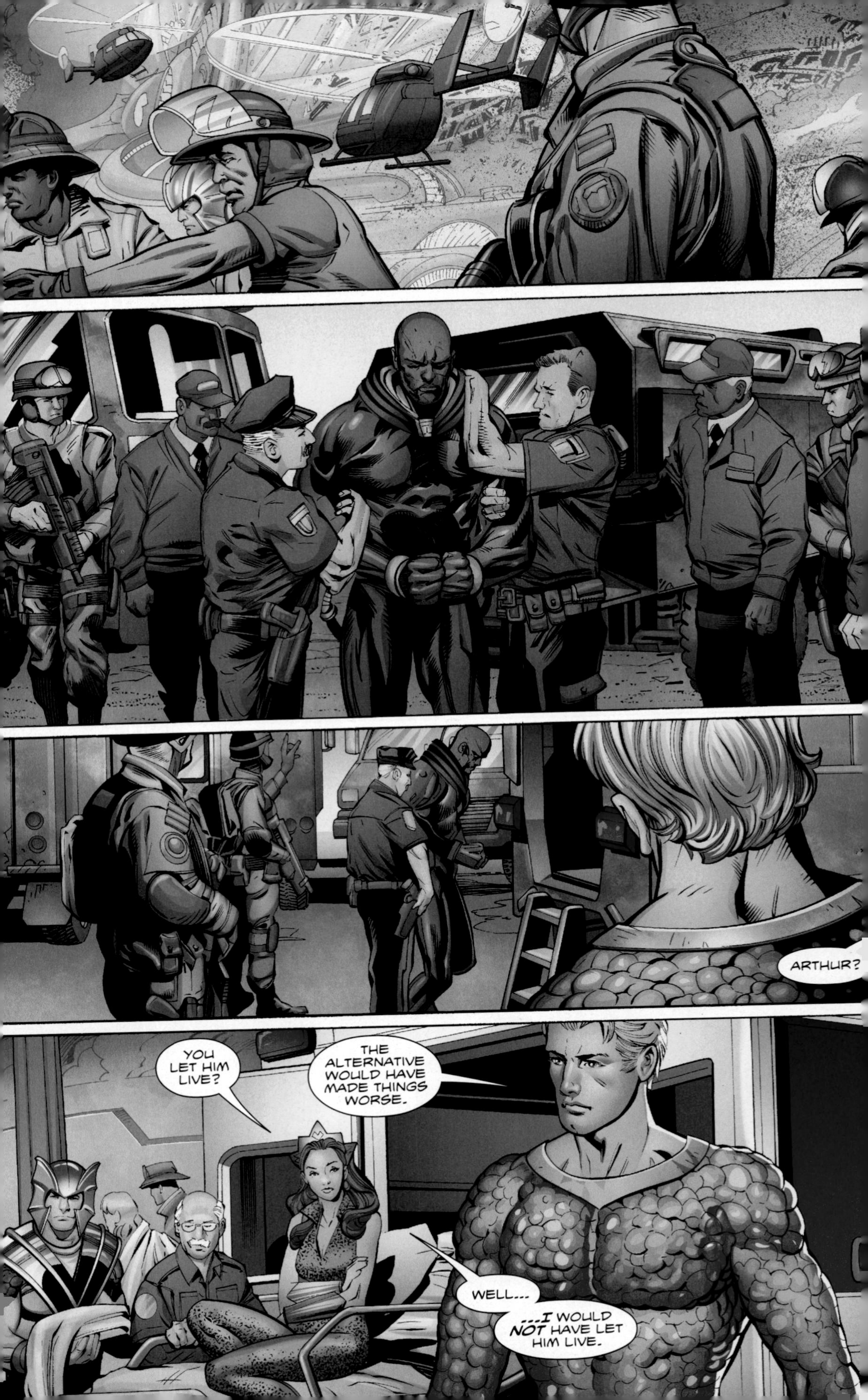
ARTHUR?
YOU LET HIM LIVE?
THE ALTERNATIVE WOULD HAVE MADE THINGS WORSE.
WELL...
...I WOULD NOT HAVE LET HIM LIVE.

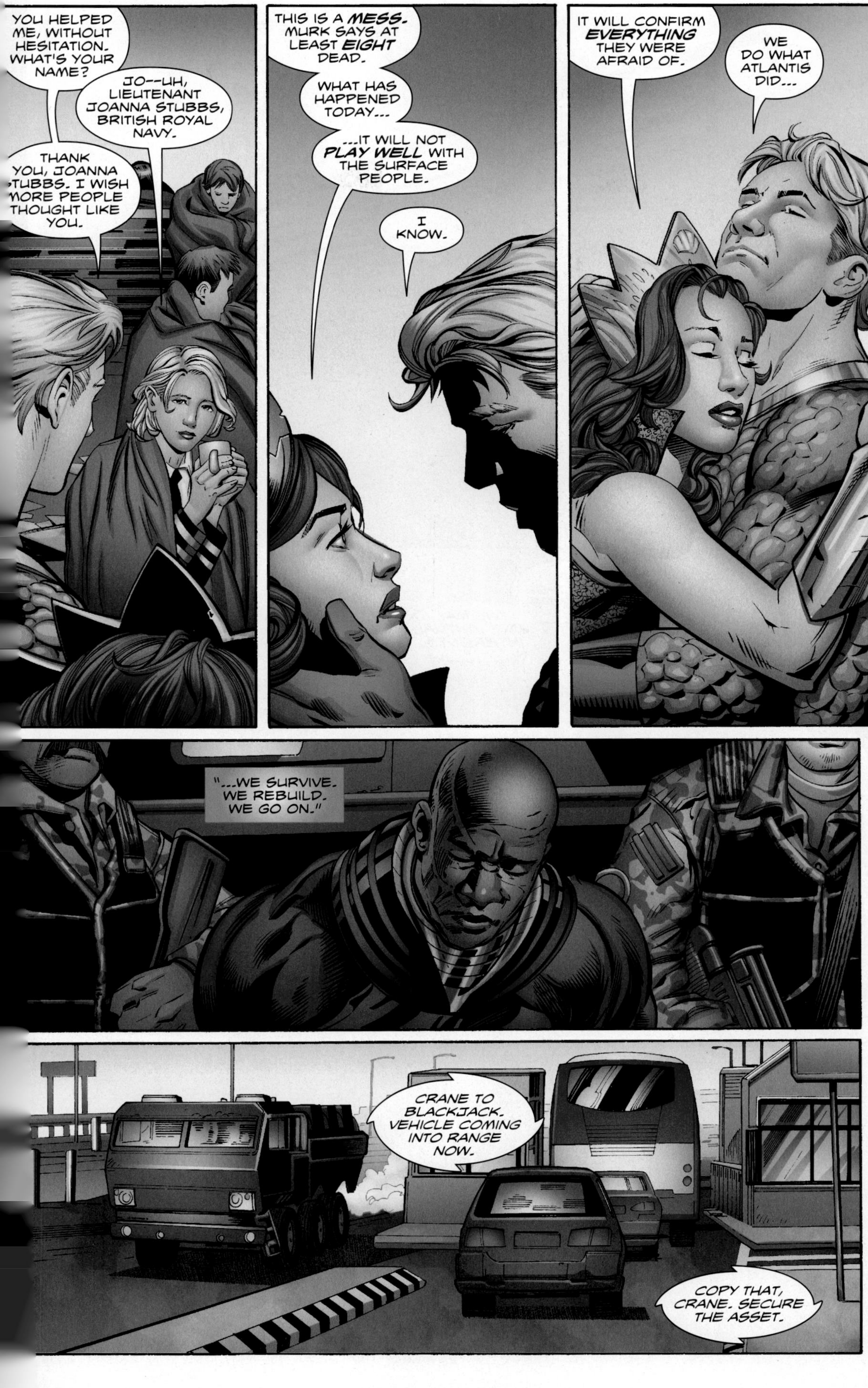
YOU HELPED ME, WITHOUT HESITATION. WHAT'S YOUR NAME?
JO--UH, LIEUTENANT JOANNA STUBBS, BRITISH ROYAL NAVY.
THANK YOU, JOANNA STUBBS. I WISH MORE PEOPLE THOUGHT LIKE YOU.
THIS IS A MESS. MURK SAYS AT LEAST EIGHT DEAD.
WHAT HAS HAPPENED TODAY...
...IT WILL NOT PLAY WELL WITH THE SURFACE PEOPLE.
I KNOW.
IT WILL CONFIRM EVERYTHING THEY WERE AFRAID OF.
WE DO WHAT ATLANTIS DID...
"...WE SURVIVE. WE REBUILD. WE GO ON."
CRANE TO BLACKJACK. VEHICLE COMING INTO RANGE NOW.
COPY THAT, CRANE. SECURE THE ASSET.

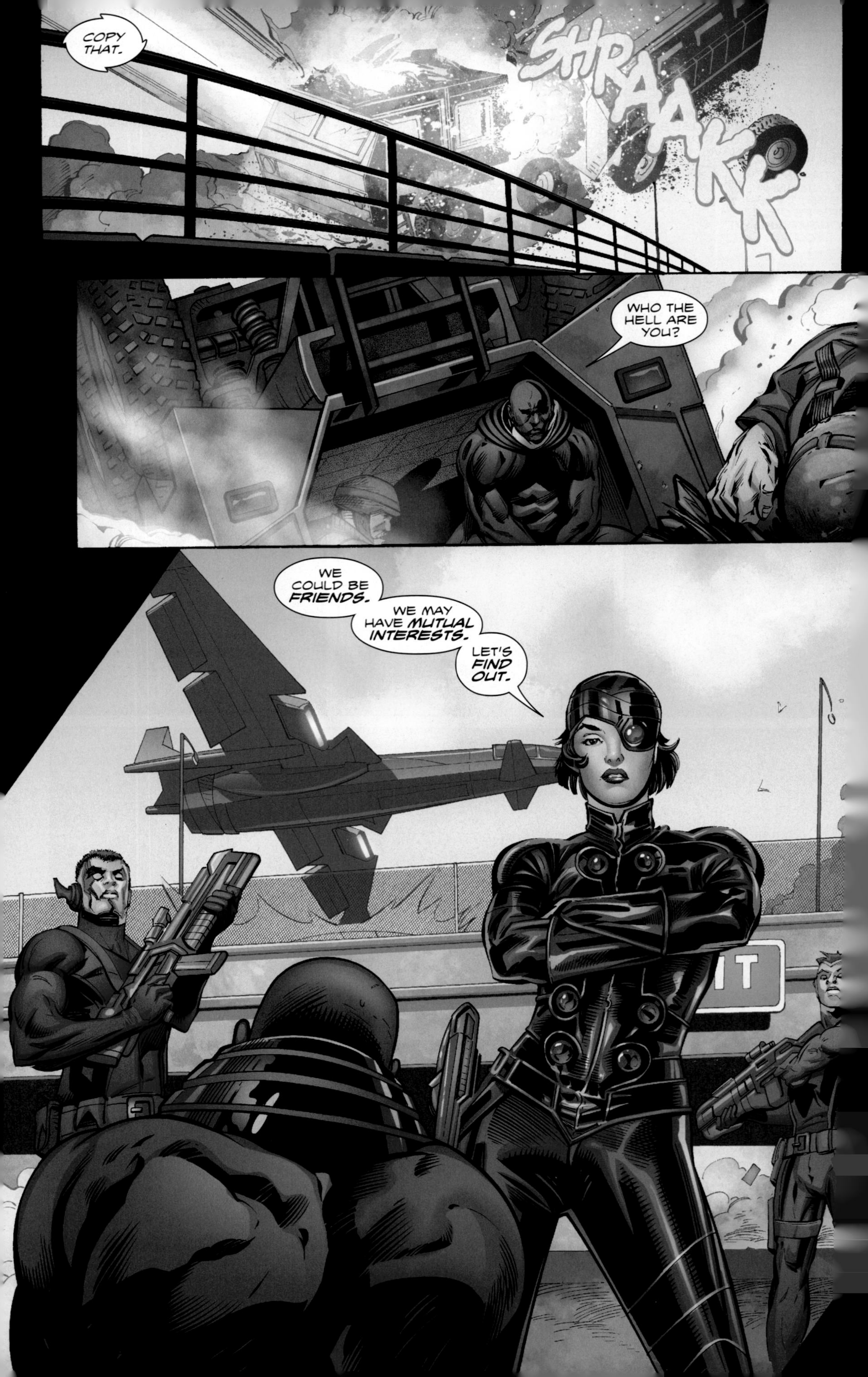
COPY THAT.
SHRAAKK
WHO THE HELL ARE YOU?
WE COULD BE FRIENDS.
WE MAY HAVE MUTUAL INTERESTS.
LET'S FIND OUT.

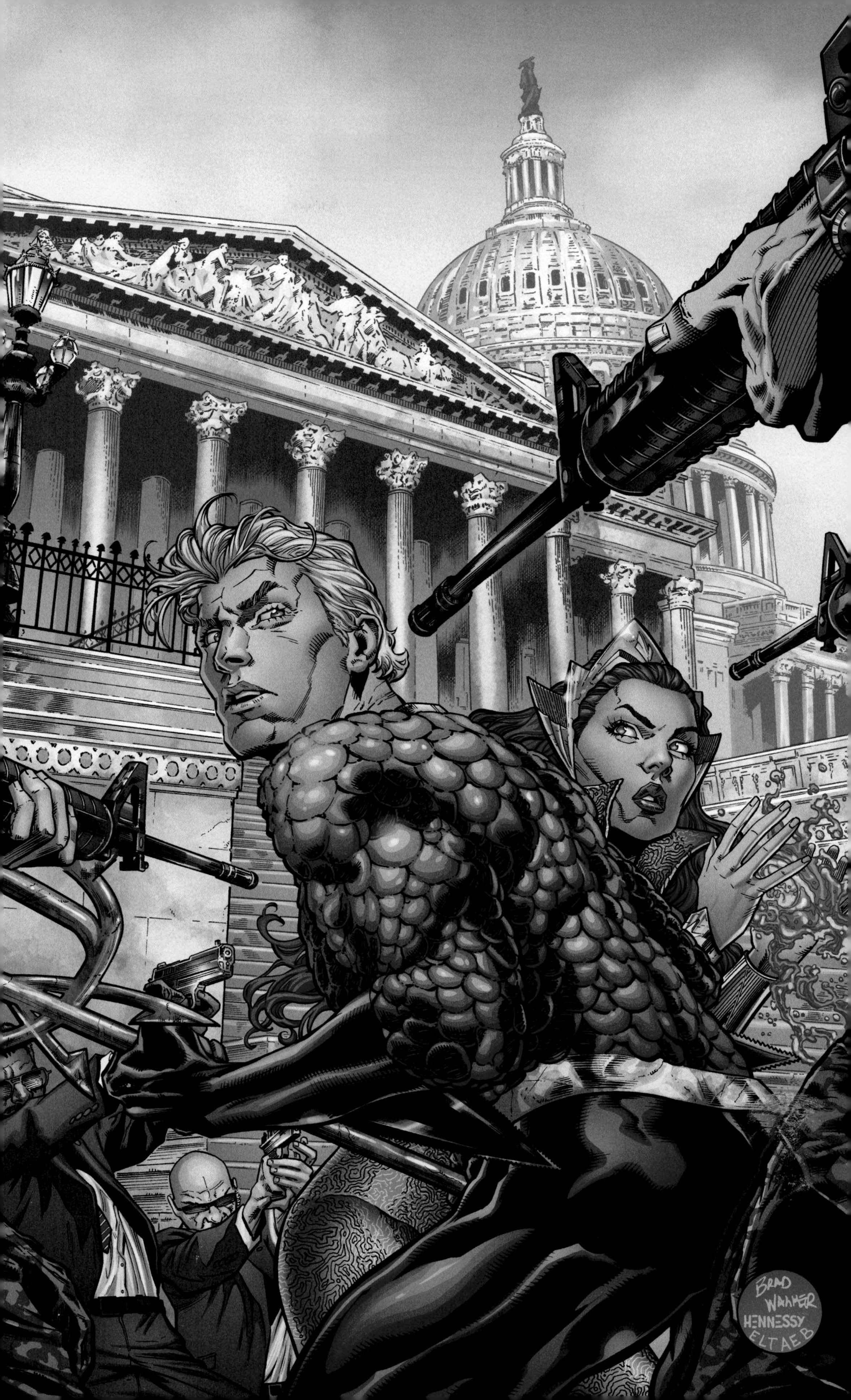
BRAD
HENNESSY
ELTAEB

PART THREE: CAPITOL CRIMES

DAN ABNETT Writer * PHILIPPE BRIONES Artist * GABE ELTAEB Colorist * PAT BROSSEAU Letterer

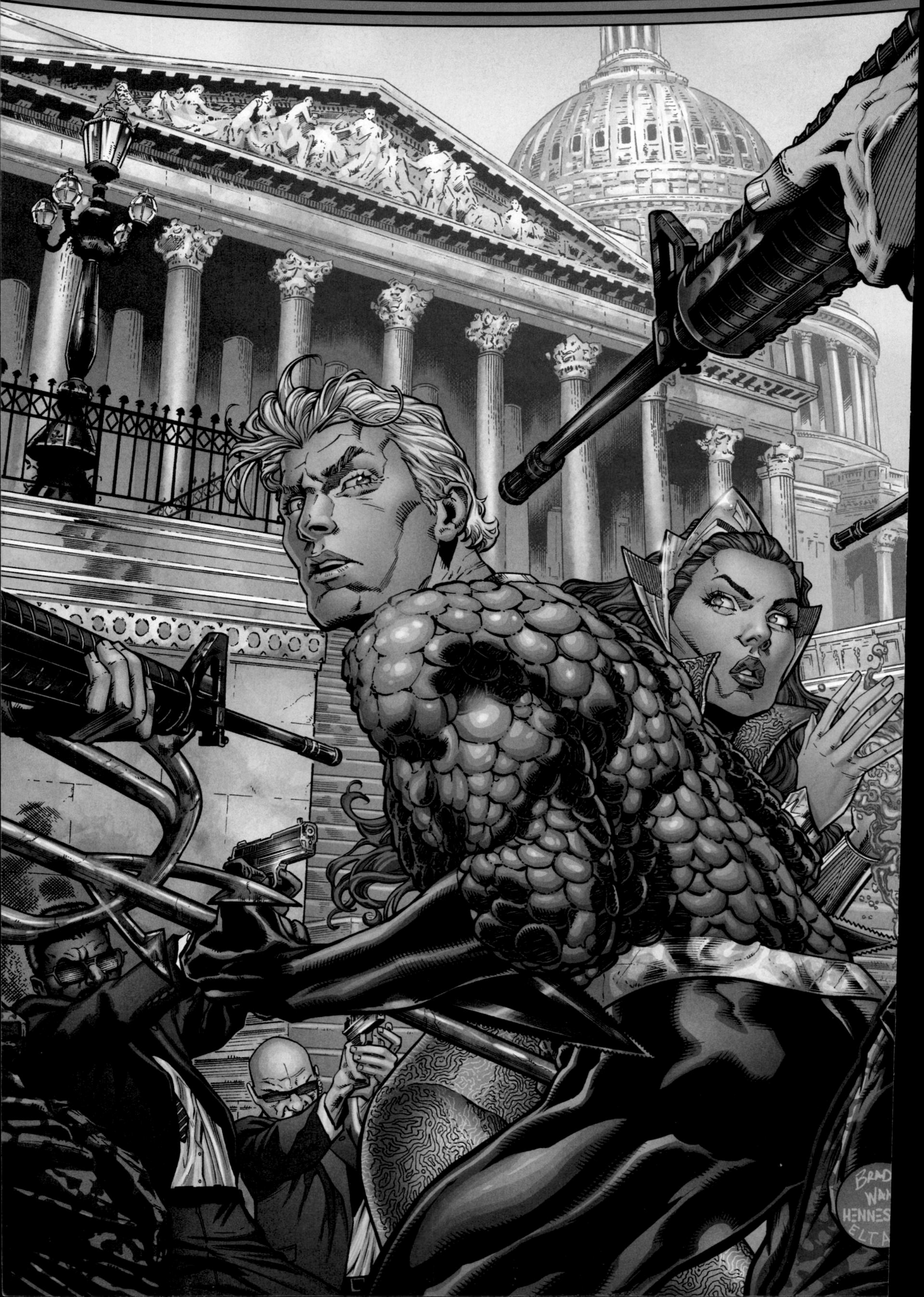

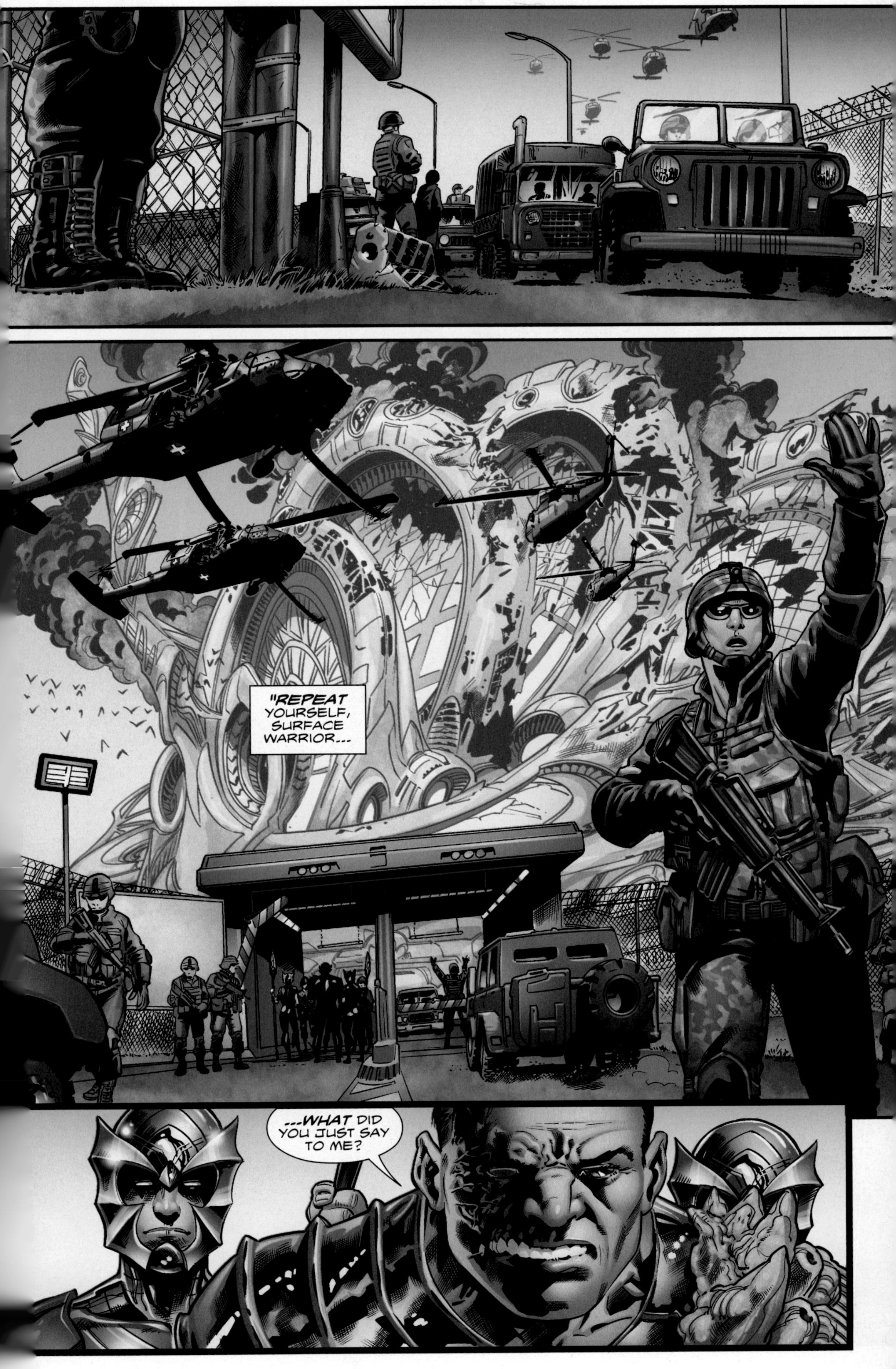
"REPEAT YOURSELF, SURFACE WARRIOR...
...WHAT DID YOU JUST SAY TO ME?

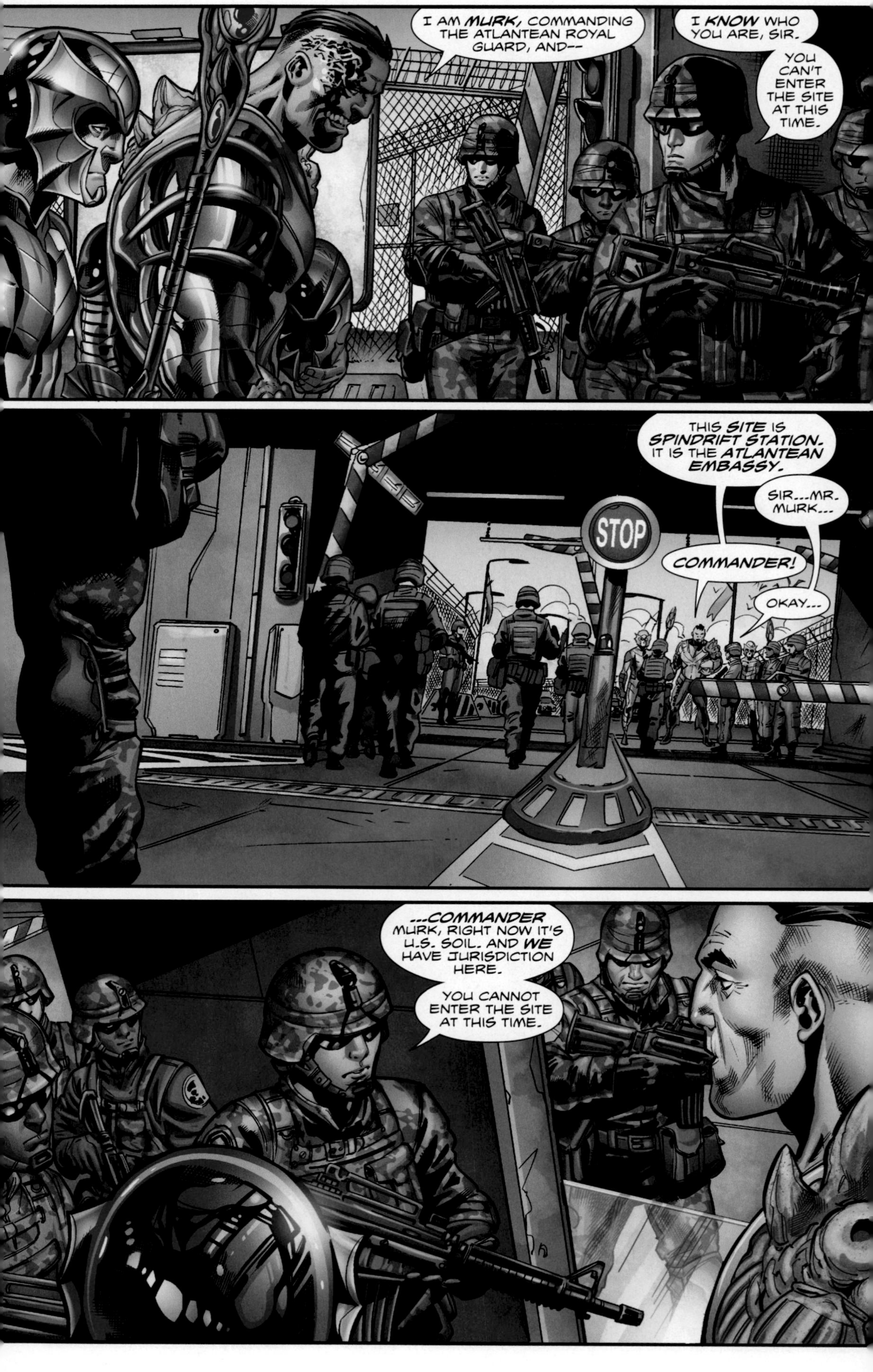
I AM MURK, COMMANDING THE ATLANTEAN ROYAL GUARD, AND--
I KNOW WHO YOU ARE, SIR.
YOU CAN'T ENTER THE SITE AT THIS TIME.
THIS SITE IS SPINDRIFT STATION. IT IS THE ATLANTEAN EMBASSY.
SIR...MR. MURK...
COMMANDER!
OKAY...
STOP
...COMMANDER MURK, RIGHT NOW IT'S U.S. SOIL. AND WE HAVE JURISDICTION HERE.
YOU CANNOT ENTER THE SITE AT THIS TIME.

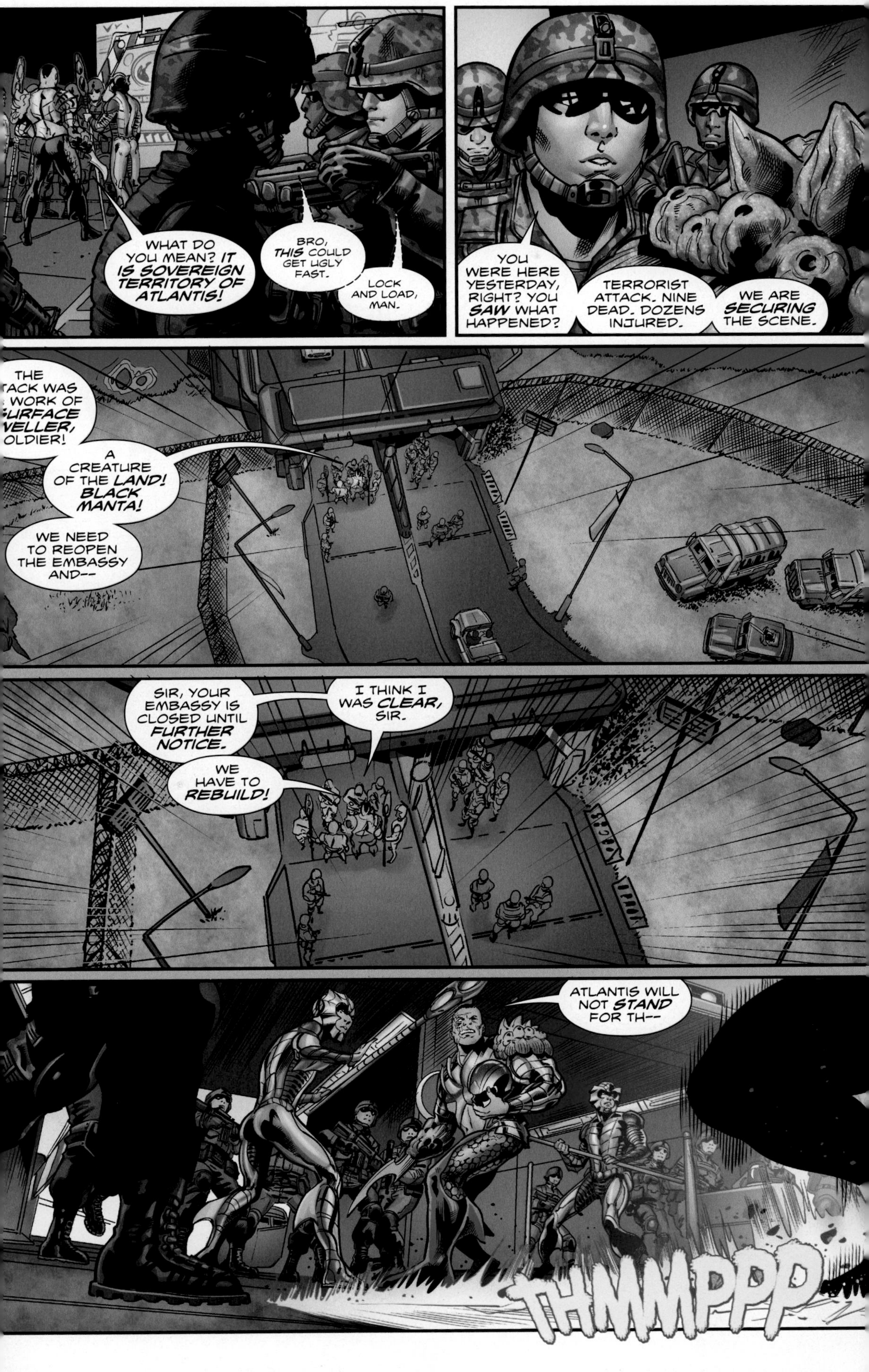
WHAT DO YOU MEAN? IT IS SOVEREIGN TERRITORY OF ATLANTIS!
BRO, THIS COULD GET UGLY FAST.
LOCK AND LOAD, MAN.
YOU WERE HERE YESTERDAY, RIGHT? YOU SAW WHAT HAPPENED?
TERRORIST ATTACK. NINE DEAD. DOZENS INJURED.
WE ARE SECURING THE SCENE.
THE ...TACK WAS ... WORK OF ...URFACE ...WELLER, ...OLDIER!
A CREATURE OF THE LAND! BLACK MANTA!
WE NEED TO REOPEN THE EMBASSY AND--
SIR, YOUR EMBASSY IS CLOSED UNTIL FURTHER NOTICE.
I THINK I WAS CLEAR, SIR.
WE HAVE TO REBUILD!
ATLANTIS WILL NOT STAND FOR TH--
THMMPPP

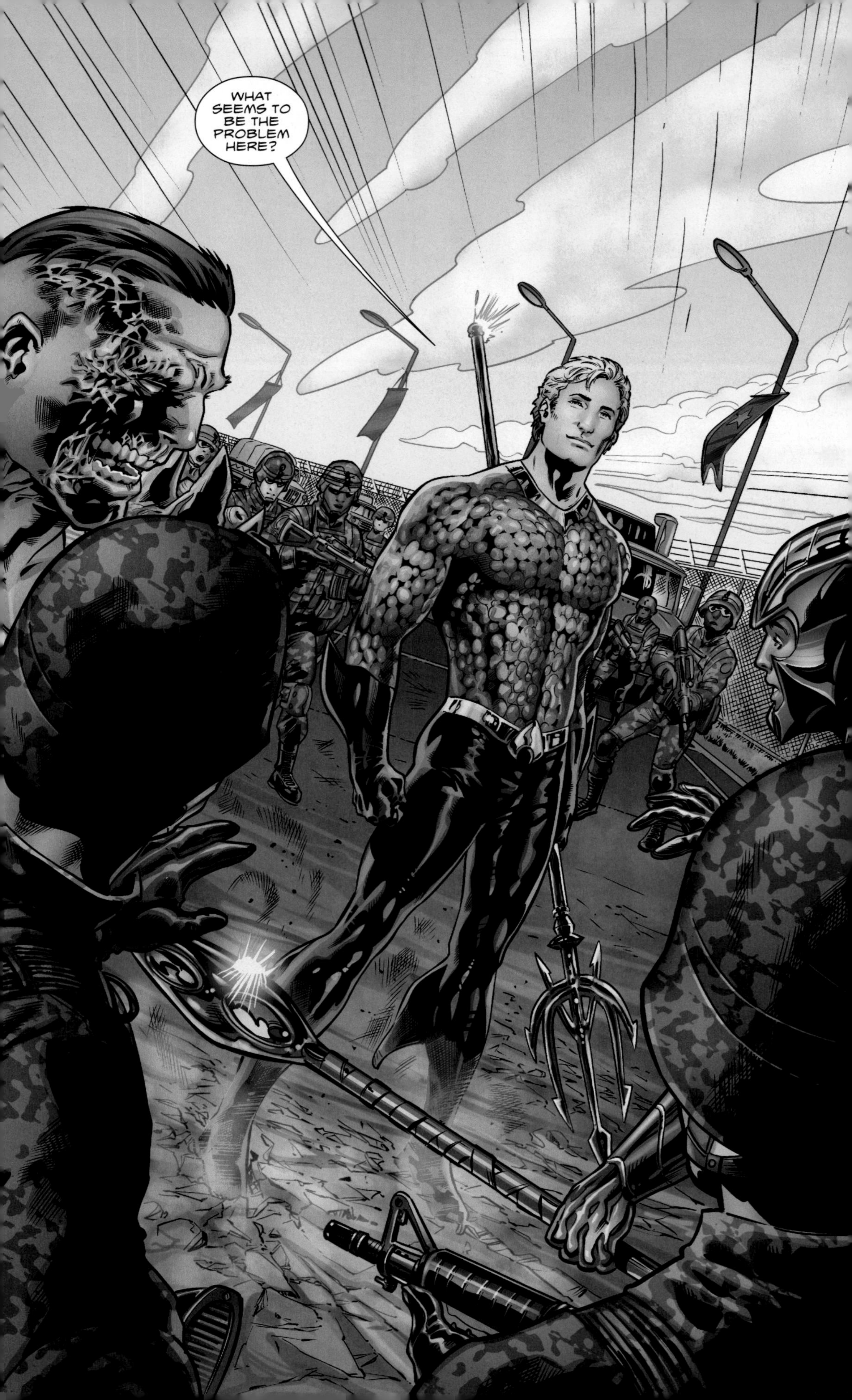
WHAT SEEMS TO BE THE PROBLEM HERE?

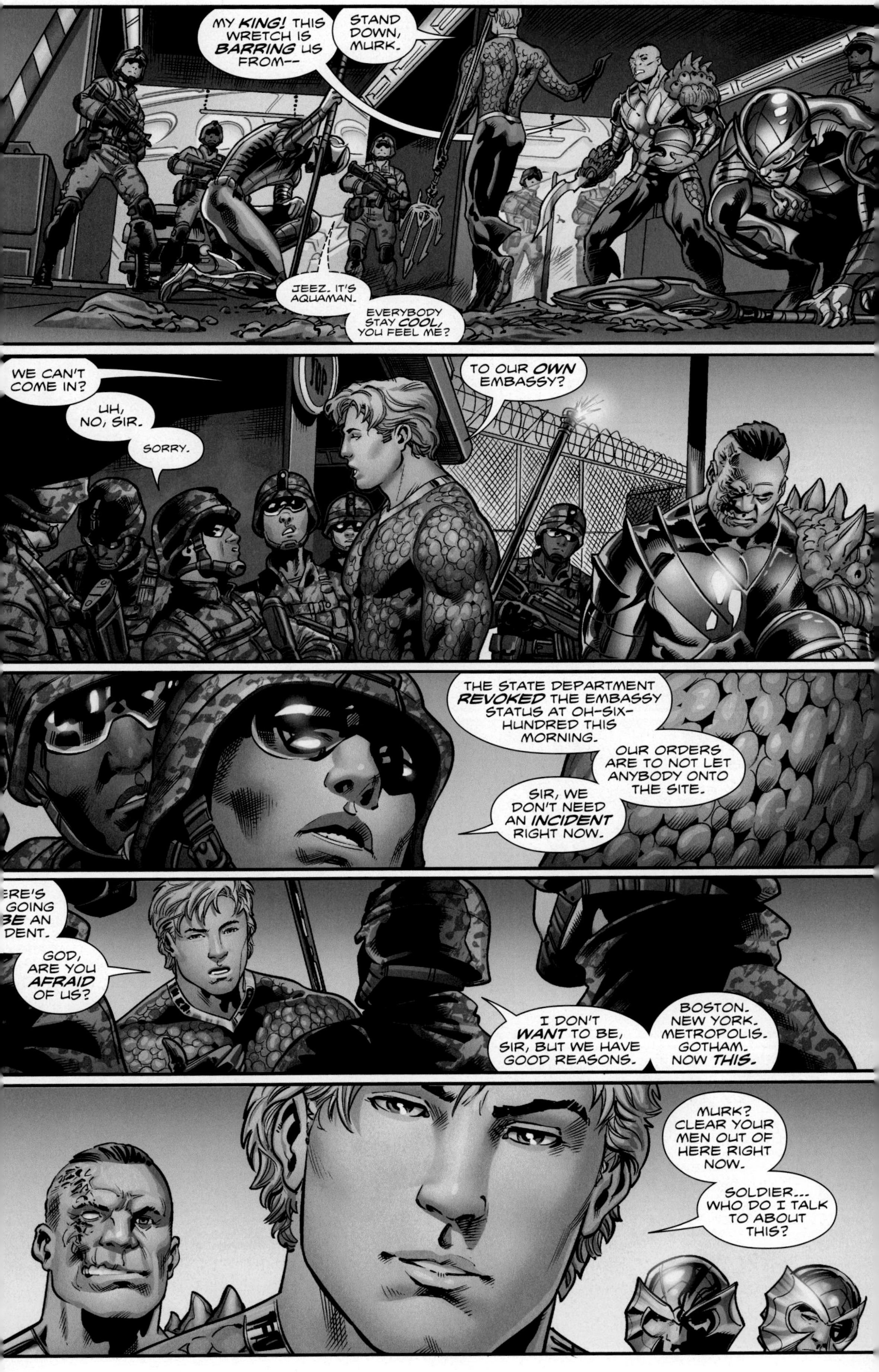

MY KING! THIS WRETCH IS BARRING US FROM--
STAND DOWN, MURK.
JEEZ. IT'S AQUAMAN.
EVERYBODY STAY COOL, YOU FEEL ME?
WE CAN'T COME IN?
TO OUR OWN EMBASSY?
UH, NO, SIR.
SORRY.
THE STATE DEPARTMENT REVOKED THE EMBASSY STATUS AT OH-SIX-HUNDRED THIS MORNING.
OUR ORDERS ARE TO NOT LET ANYBODY ONTO THE SITE.
SIR, WE DON'T NEED AN INCIDENT RIGHT NOW.
GOD, ARE YOU AFRAID OF US?
I DON'T WANT TO BE, SIR, BUT WE HAVE GOOD REASONS.
BOSTON. NEW YORK. METROPOLIS. GOTHAM. NOW THIS.
MURK? CLEAR YOUR MEN OUT OF HERE RIGHT NOW.
SOLDIER... WHO DO I TALK TO ABOUT THIS?

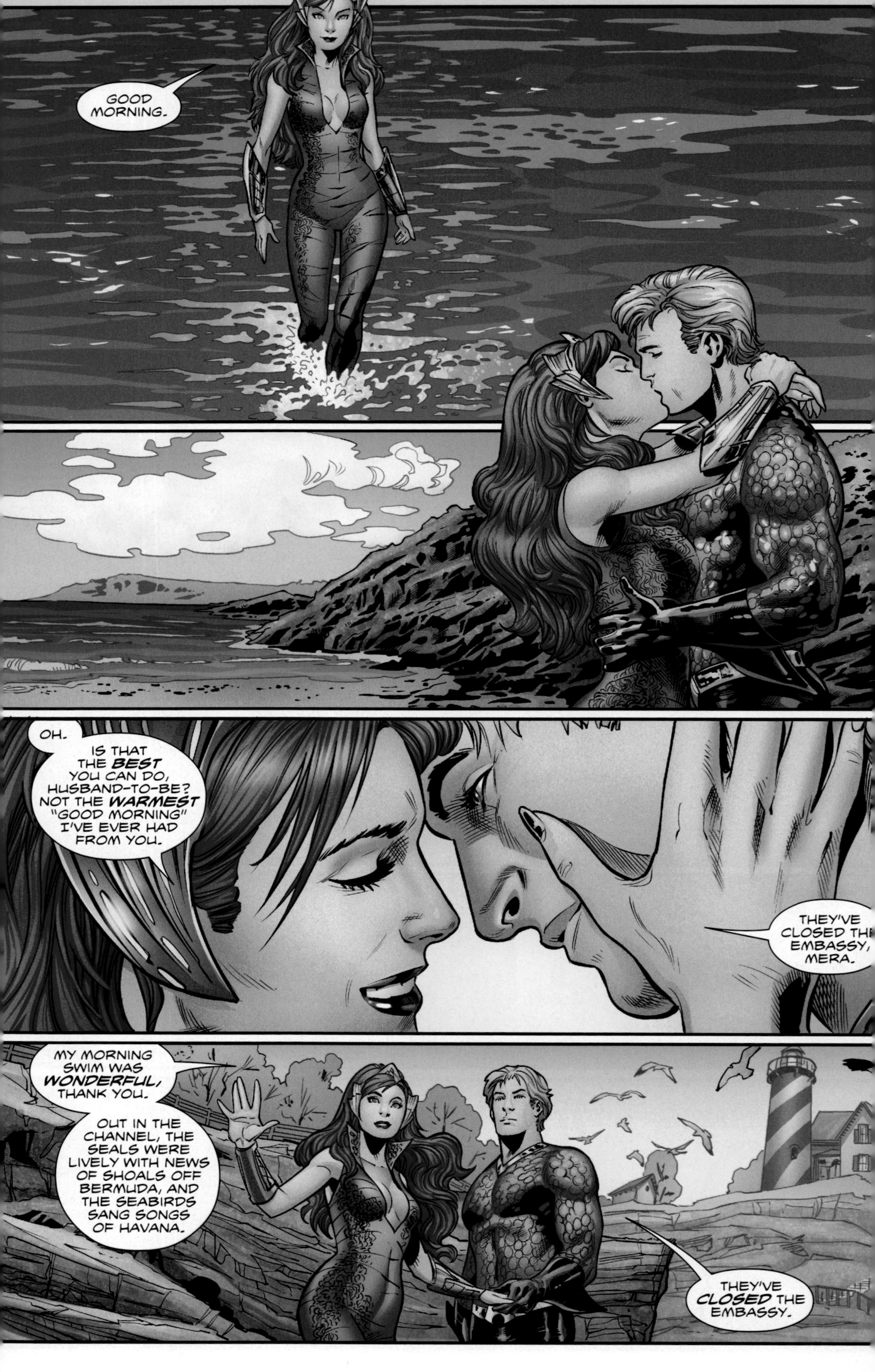
GOOD MORNING.
OH.
IS THAT THE BEST YOU CAN DO, HUSBAND-TO-BE? NOT THE WARMEST "GOOD MORNING" I'VE EVER HAD FROM YOU.
THEY'VE CLOSED THE EMBASSY, MERA.
MY MORNING SWIM WAS WONDERFUL, THANK YOU.
OUT IN THE CHANNEL, THE SEALS WERE LIVELY WITH NEWS OF SHOALS OFF BERMUDA, AND THE SEABIRDS SANG SONGS OF HAVANA.
THEY'VE CLOSED THE EMBASSY.

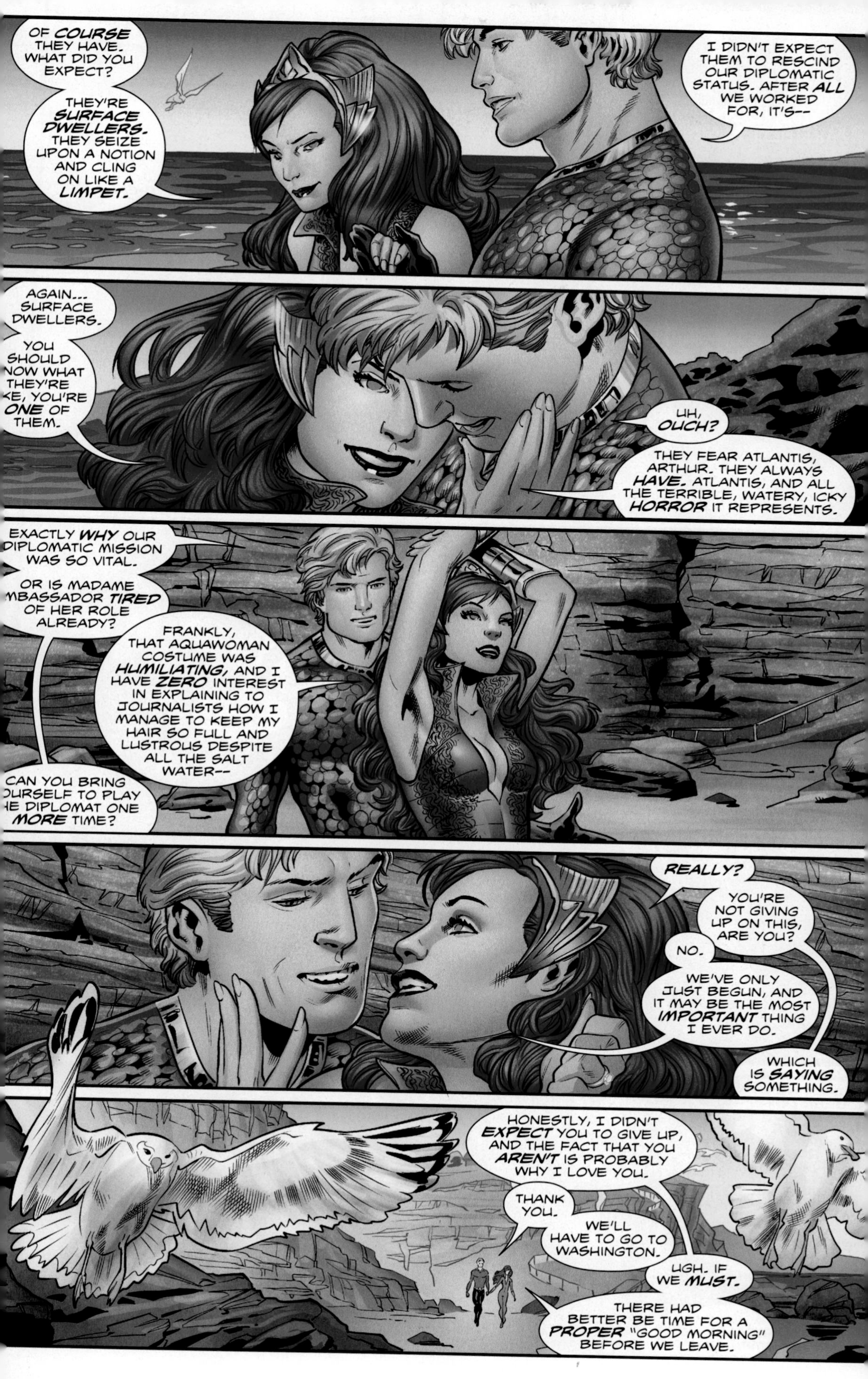

OF COURSE THEY HAVE. WHAT DID YOU EXPECT?
THEY'RE SURFACE DWELLERS. THEY SEIZE UPON A NOTION AND CLING ON LIKE A LIMPET.
I DIDN'T EXPECT THEM TO RESCIND OUR DIPLOMATIC STATUS. AFTER ALL WE WORKED FOR, IT'S--
AGAIN... SURFACE DWELLERS.
YOU SHOULD NOW WHAT THEY'RE KE, YOU'RE ONE OF THEM.
UH, OUCH?
THEY FEAR ATLANTIS, ARTHUR. THEY ALWAYS HAVE. ATLANTIS, AND ALL THE TERRIBLE, WATERY, ICKY HORROR IT REPRESENTS.
EXACTLY WHY OUR DIPLOMATIC MISSION WAS SO VITAL.
OR IS MADAME MBASSADOR TIRED OF HER ROLE ALREADY?
FRANKLY, THAT AQUAWOMAN COSTUME WAS HUMILIATING, AND I HAVE ZERO INTEREST IN EXPLAINING TO JOURNALISTS HOW I MANAGE TO KEEP MY HAIR SO FULL AND LUSTROUS DESPITE ALL THE SALT WATER--
CAN YOU BRING OURSELF TO PLAY HE DIPLOMAT ONE MORE TIME?
REALLY?
YOU'RE NOT GIVING UP ON THIS, ARE YOU?
NO.
WE'VE ONLY JUST BEGUN, AND IT MAY BE THE MOST IMPORTANT THING I EVER DO.
WHICH IS SAYING SOMETHING.
HONESTLY, I DIDN'T EXPECT YOU TO GIVE UP, AND THE FACT THAT YOU AREN'T IS PROBABLY WHY I LOVE YOU.
THANK YOU.
WE'LL HAVE TO GO TO WASHINGTON.
UGH. IF WE MUST.
THERE HAD BETTER BE TIME FOR A PROPER "GOOD MORNING" BEFORE WE LEAVE.

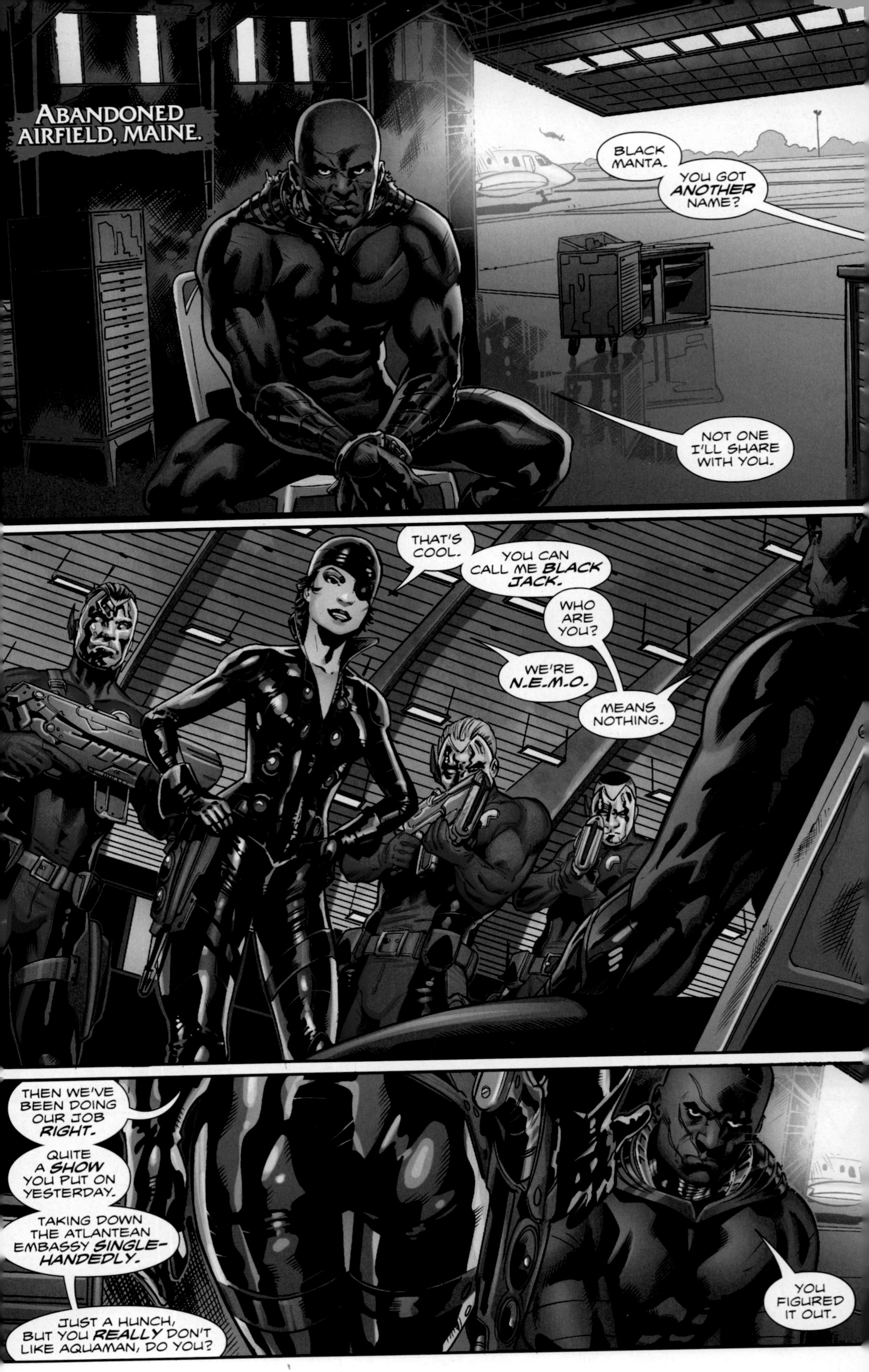

ABANDONED AIRFIELD, MAINE.
BLACK MANTA.
YOU GOT *ANOTHER* NAME?
NOT ONE I'LL SHARE WITH YOU.
THAT'S COOL.
YOU CAN CALL ME *BLACK JACK.*
WHO ARE YOU?
WE'RE *N.E.M.O.*
MEANS NOTHING.
THEN WE'VE BEEN DOING OUR JOB *RIGHT.*
QUITE A *SHOW* YOU PUT ON YESTERDAY.
TAKING DOWN THE ATLANTEAN EMBASSY *SINGLE-HANDEDLY.*
JUST A HUNCH, BUT YOU *REALLY* DON'T LIKE AQUAMAN, DO YOU?
YOU FIGURED IT OUT.

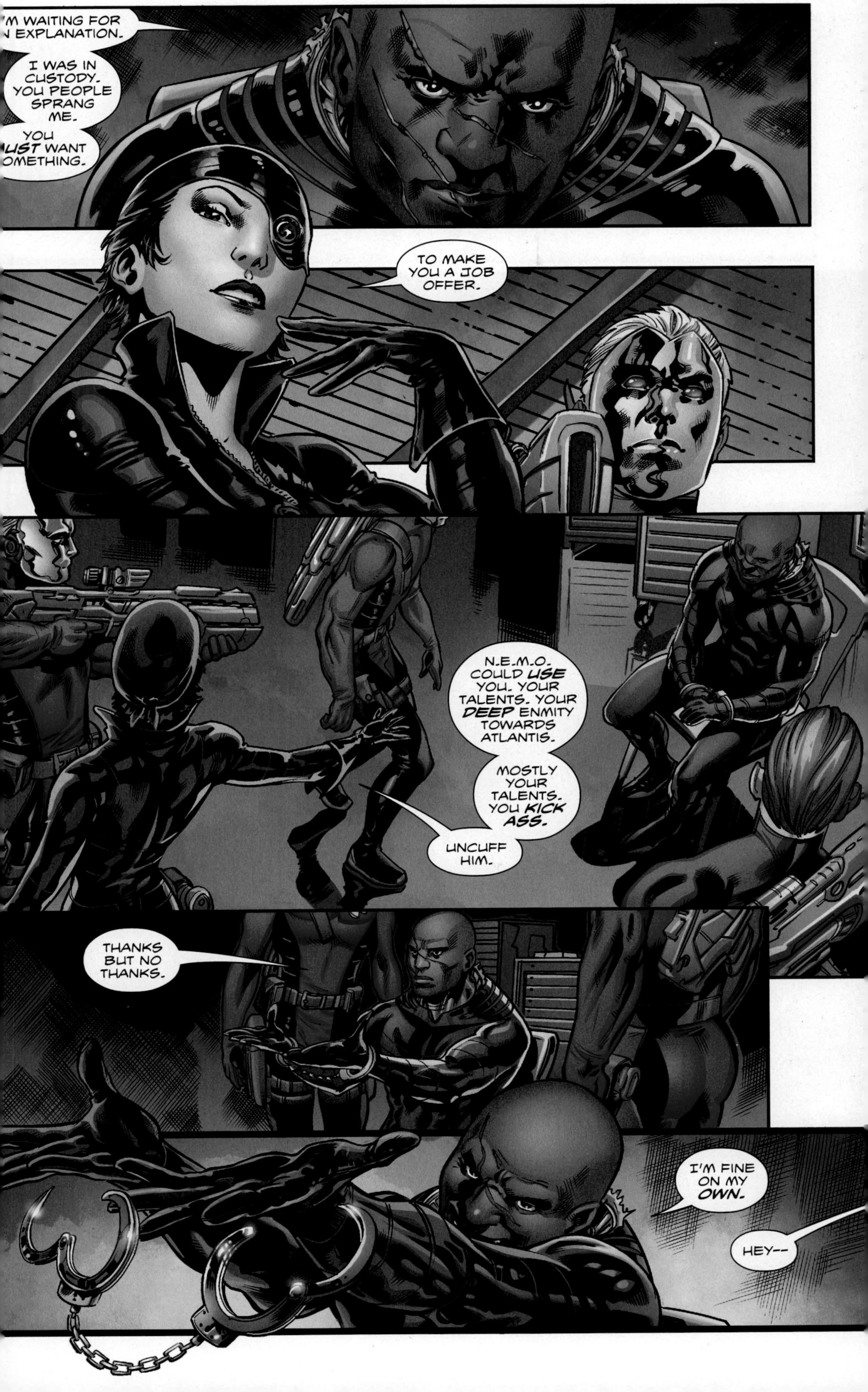
'M WAITING FOR
N EXPLANATION.
I WAS IN CUSTODY. YOU PEOPLE SPRANG ME.
YOU UST WANT OMETHING.
TO MAKE YOU A JOB OFFER.
N.E.M.O. COULD USE YOU. YOUR TALENTS. YOUR DEEP ENMITY TOWARDS ATLANTIS.
MOSTLY YOUR TALENTS. YOU KICK ASS.
UNCUFF HIM.
THANKS BUT NO THANKS.
I'M FINE ON MY OWN.
HEY--

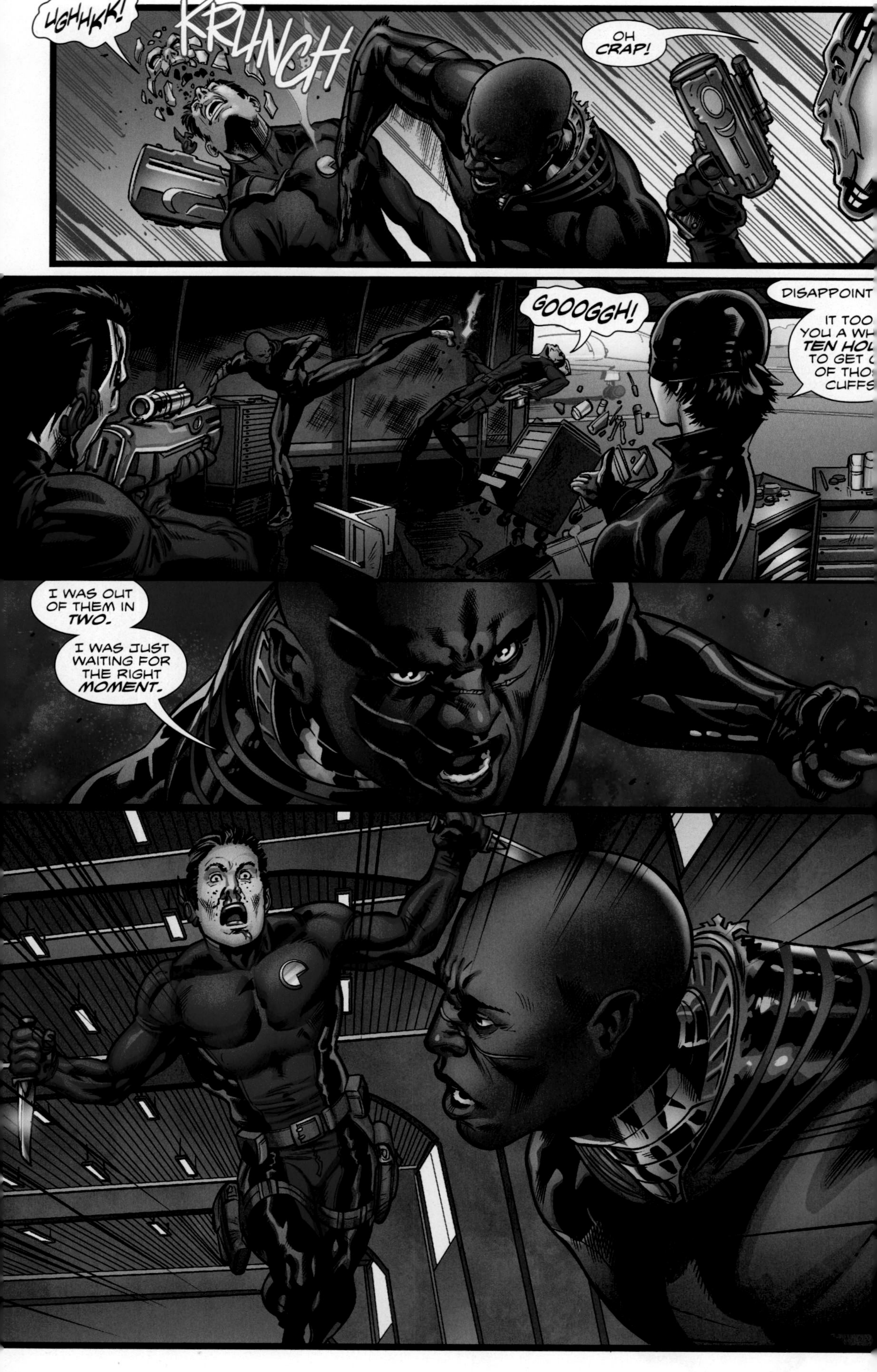
UGHHKK!
KRUNCH
OH CRAP!
GOOOGGH!
DISAPPOINT
IT TOO
YOU A WH
TEN HOL
TO GET
OF THOS
CUFFS
I WAS OUT OF THEM IN TWO.
I WAS JUST WAITING FOR THE RIGHT MOMENT.

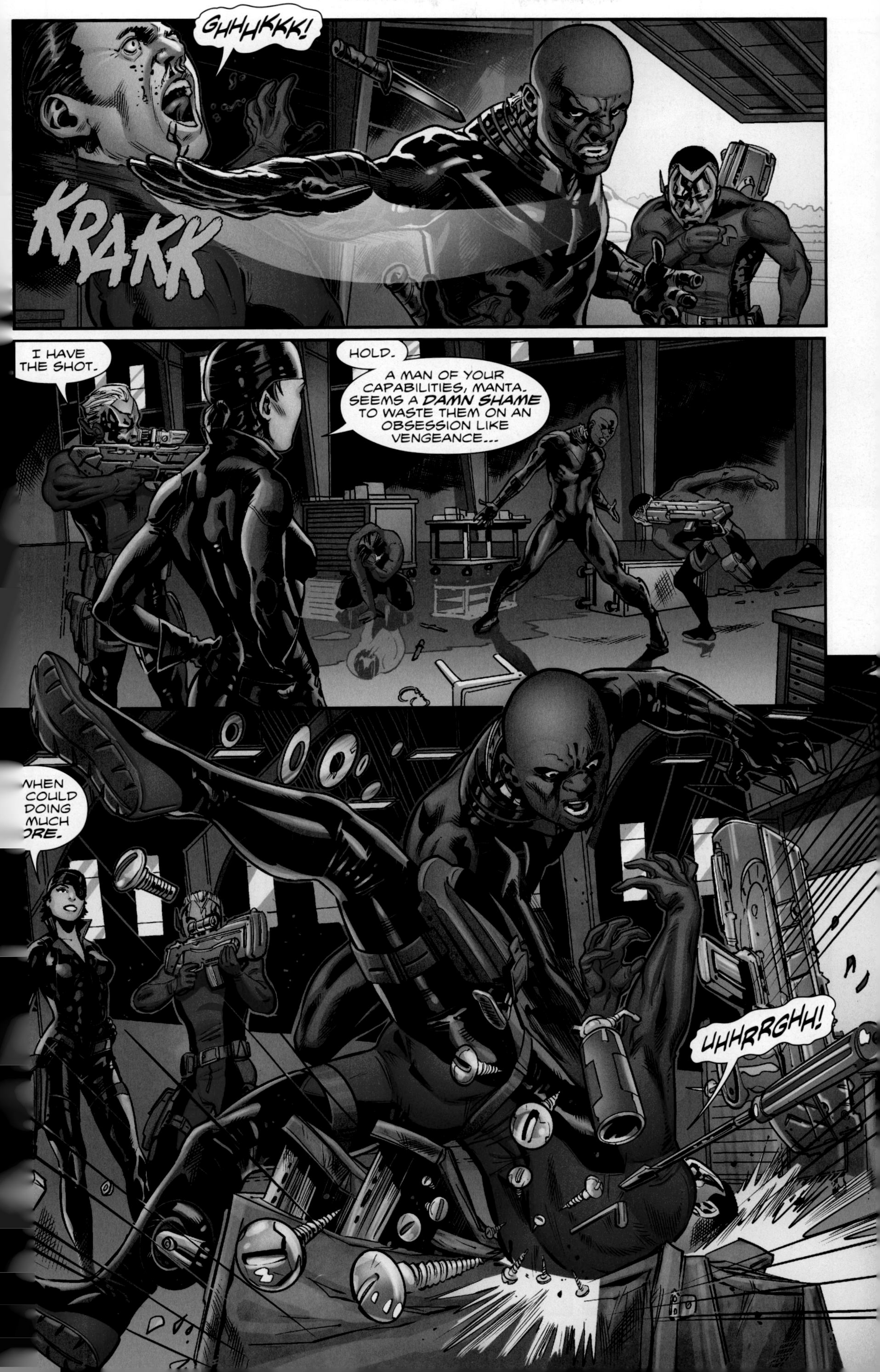
GHHHKKK!
KRAKK
I HAVE THE SHOT.
HOLD.
A MAN OF YOUR CAPABILITIES, MANTA. SEEMS A DAMN SHAME TO WASTE THEM ON AN OBSESSION LIKE VENGEANCE...
WHEN COULD DOING MUCH ORE.
UHHRRGHH!

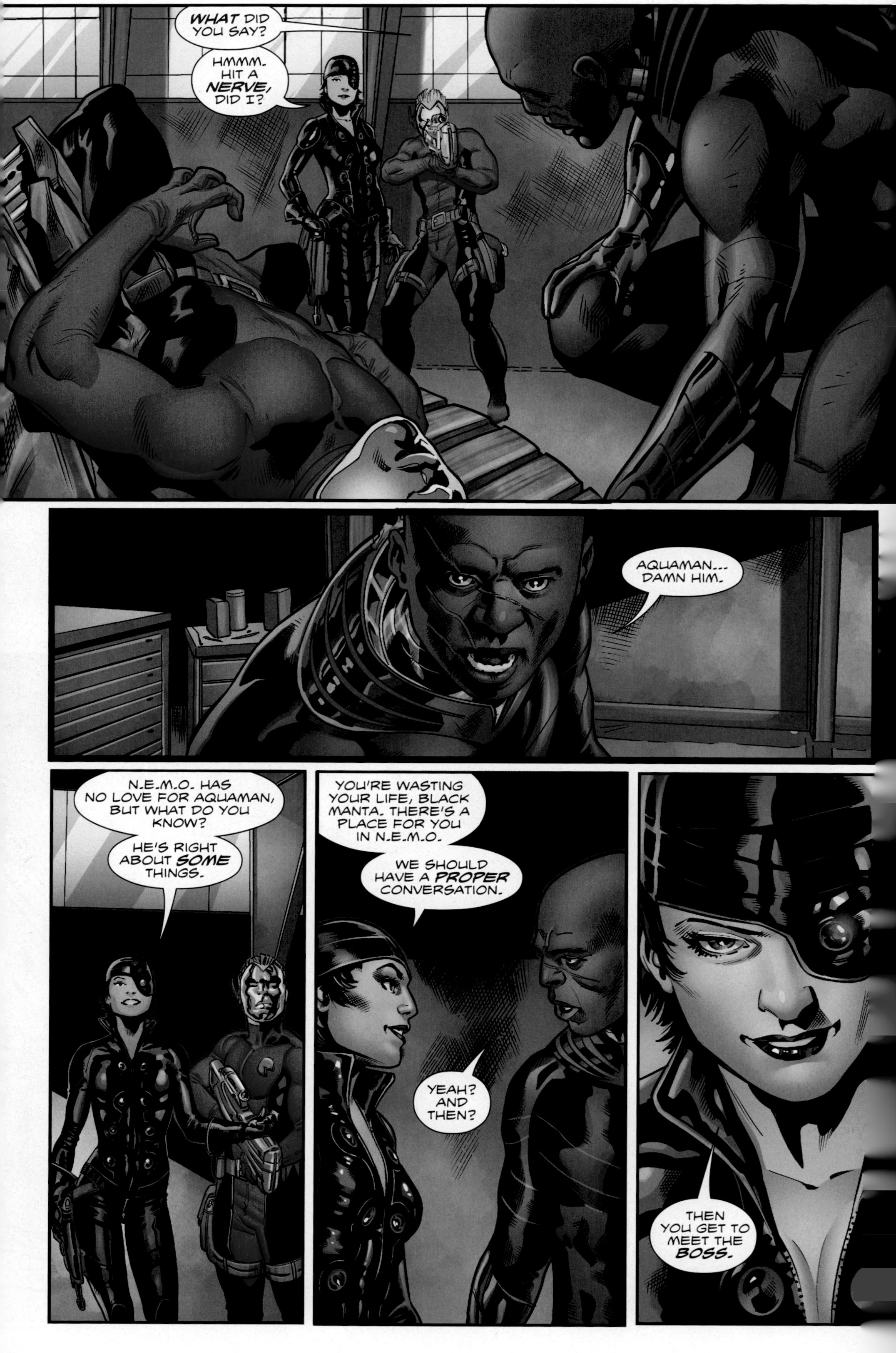
WHAT DID YOU SAY?
HMMM. HIT A NERVE, DID I?
AQUAMAN... DAMN HIM.
N.E.M.O. HAS NO LOVE FOR AQUAMAN, BUT WHAT DO YOU KNOW?
HE'S RIGHT ABOUT SOME THINGS.
YOU'RE WASTING YOUR LIFE, BLACK MANTA. THERE'S A PLACE FOR YOU IN N.E.M.O.
WE SHOULD HAVE A PROPER CONVERSATION.
YEAH? AND THEN?
THEN YOU GET TO MEET THE BOSS.

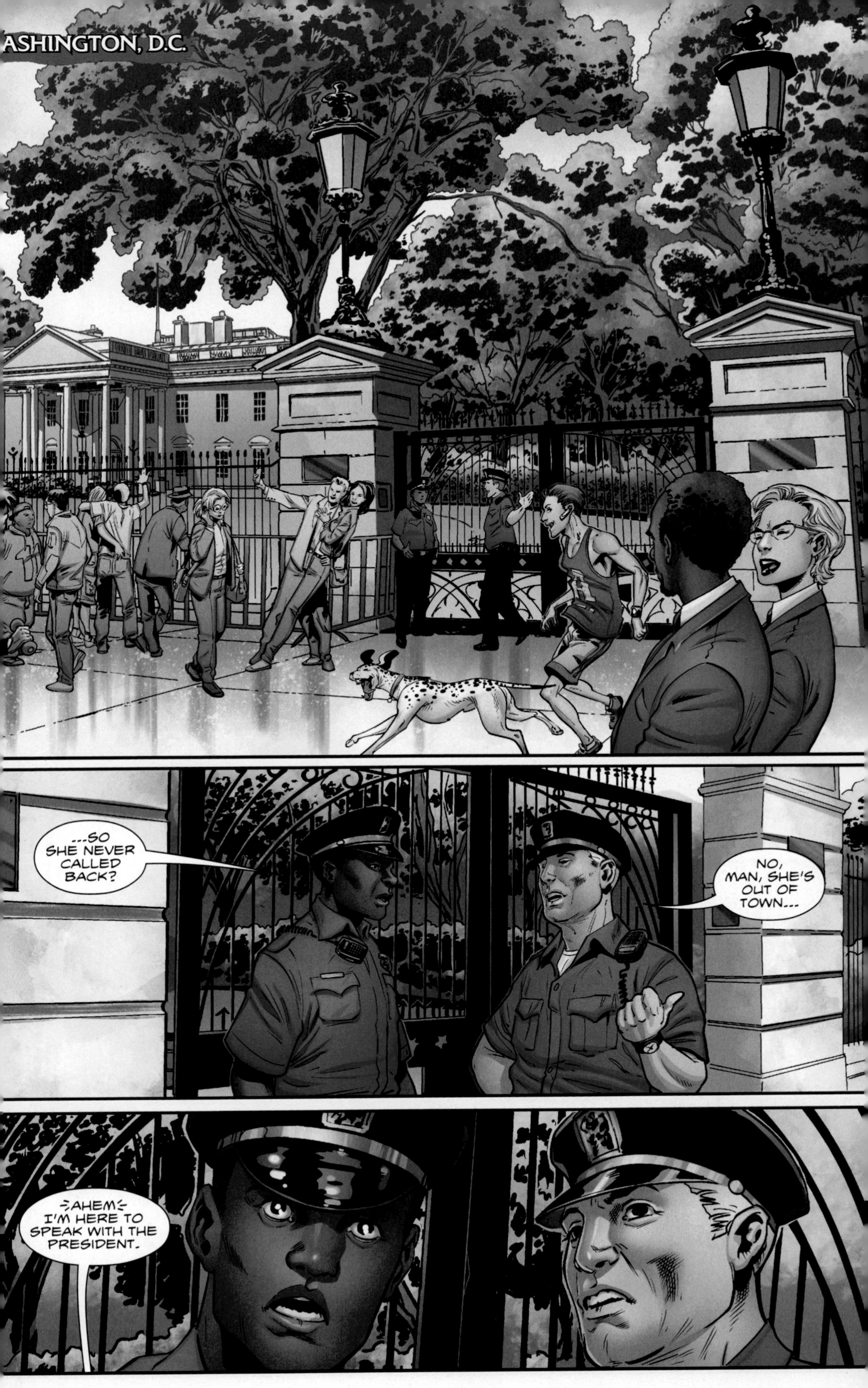
ASHINGTON, D.C.
...SO SHE NEVER CALLED BACK?
NO, MAN, SHE'S OUT OF TOWN...
AHEM
I'M HERE TO SPEAK WITH THE PRESIDENT.

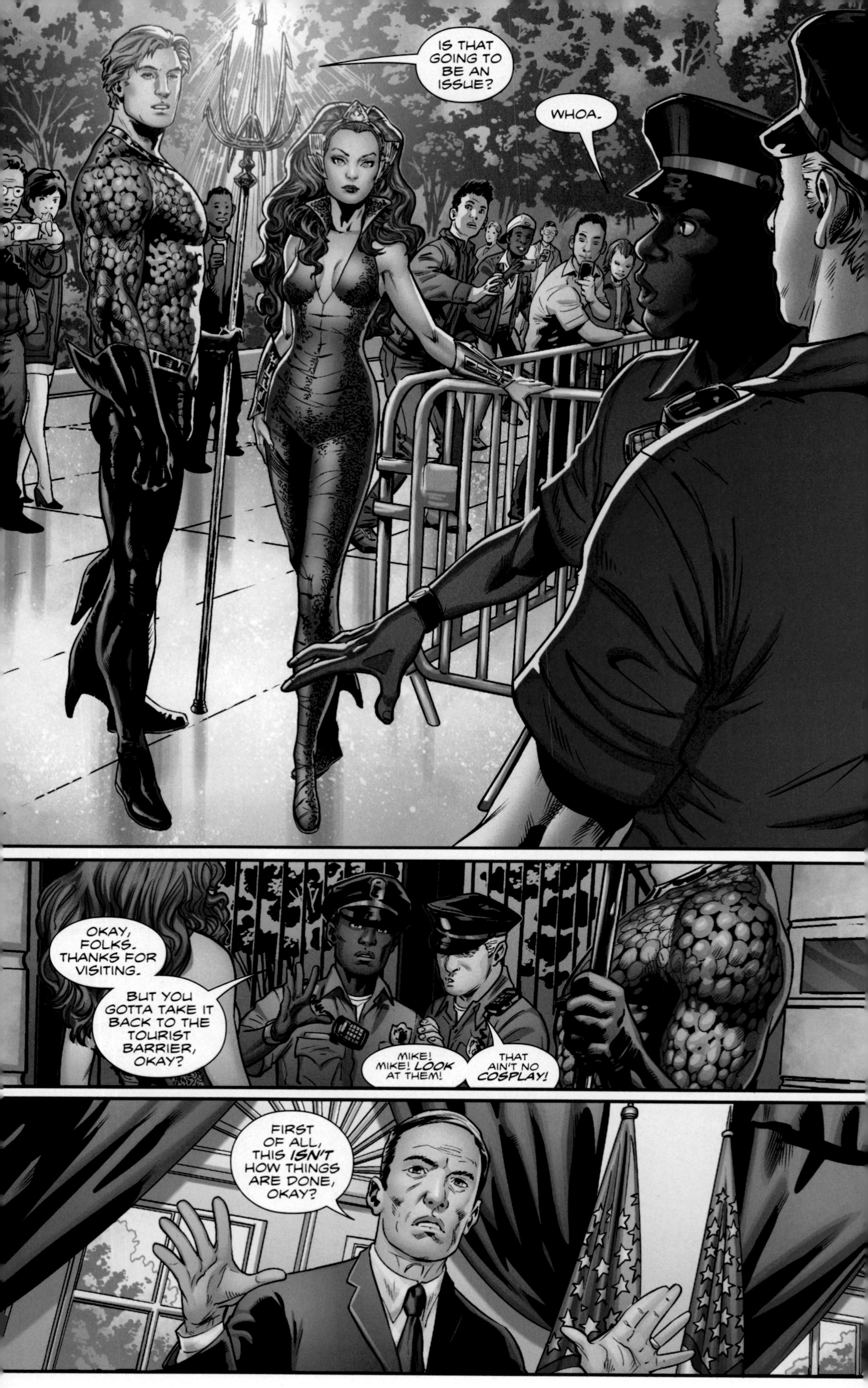
IS THAT GOING TO BE AN ISSUE?
WHOA.
OKAY, FOLKS. THANKS FOR VISITING.
BUT YOU GOTTA TAKE IT BACK TO THE TOURIST BARRIER, OKAY?
MIKE! MIKE! LOOK AT THEM!
THAT AIN'T NO COSPLAY!
FIRST OF ALL, THIS ISN'T HOW THINGS ARE DONE, OKAY?

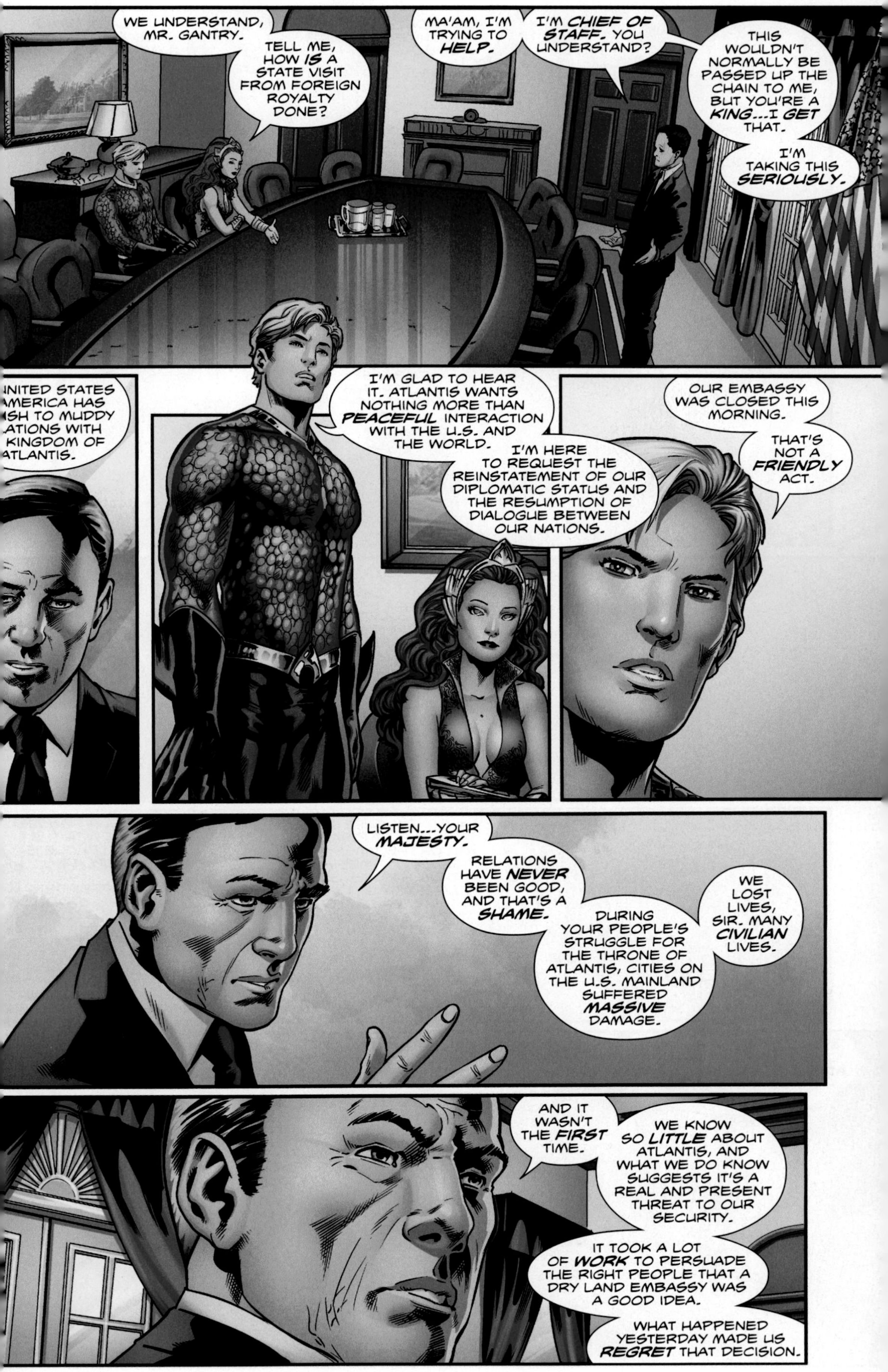
WE UNDERSTAND, MR. GANTRY.
TELL ME, HOW IS A STATE VISIT FROM FOREIGN ROYALTY DONE?
MA'AM, I'M TRYING TO HELP.
I'M CHIEF OF STAFF. YOU UNDERSTAND?
THIS WOULDN'T NORMALLY BE PASSED UP THE CHAIN TO ME, BUT YOU'RE A KING...I GET THAT.
I'M TAKING THIS SERIOUSLY.
NITED STATES MERICA HAS SH TO MUDDY ATIONS WITH KINGDOM OF TLANTIS.
I'M GLAD TO HEAR IT. ATLANTIS WANTS NOTHING MORE THAN PEACEFUL INTERACTION WITH THE U.S. AND THE WORLD.
I'M HERE TO REQUEST THE REINSTATEMENT OF OUR DIPLOMATIC STATUS AND THE RESUMPTION OF DIALOGUE BETWEEN OUR NATIONS.
OUR EMBASSY WAS CLOSED THIS MORNING.
THAT'S NOT A FRIENDLY ACT.
LISTEN...YOUR MAJESTY.
RELATIONS HAVE NEVER BEEN GOOD, AND THAT'S A SHAME.
DURING YOUR PEOPLE'S STRUGGLE FOR THE THRONE OF ATLANTIS, CITIES ON THE U.S. MAINLAND SUFFERED MASSIVE DAMAGE.
WE LOST LIVES, SIR. MANY CIVILIAN LIVES.
AND IT WASN'T THE FIRST TIME.
WE KNOW SO LITTLE ABOUT ATLANTIS, AND WHAT WE DO KNOW SUGGESTS IT'S A REAL AND PRESENT THREAT TO OUR SECURITY.
IT TOOK A LOT OF WORK TO PERSUADE THE RIGHT PEOPLE THAT A DRY LAND EMBASSY WAS A GOOD IDEA.
WHAT HAPPENED YESTERDAY MADE US REGRET THAT DECISION.

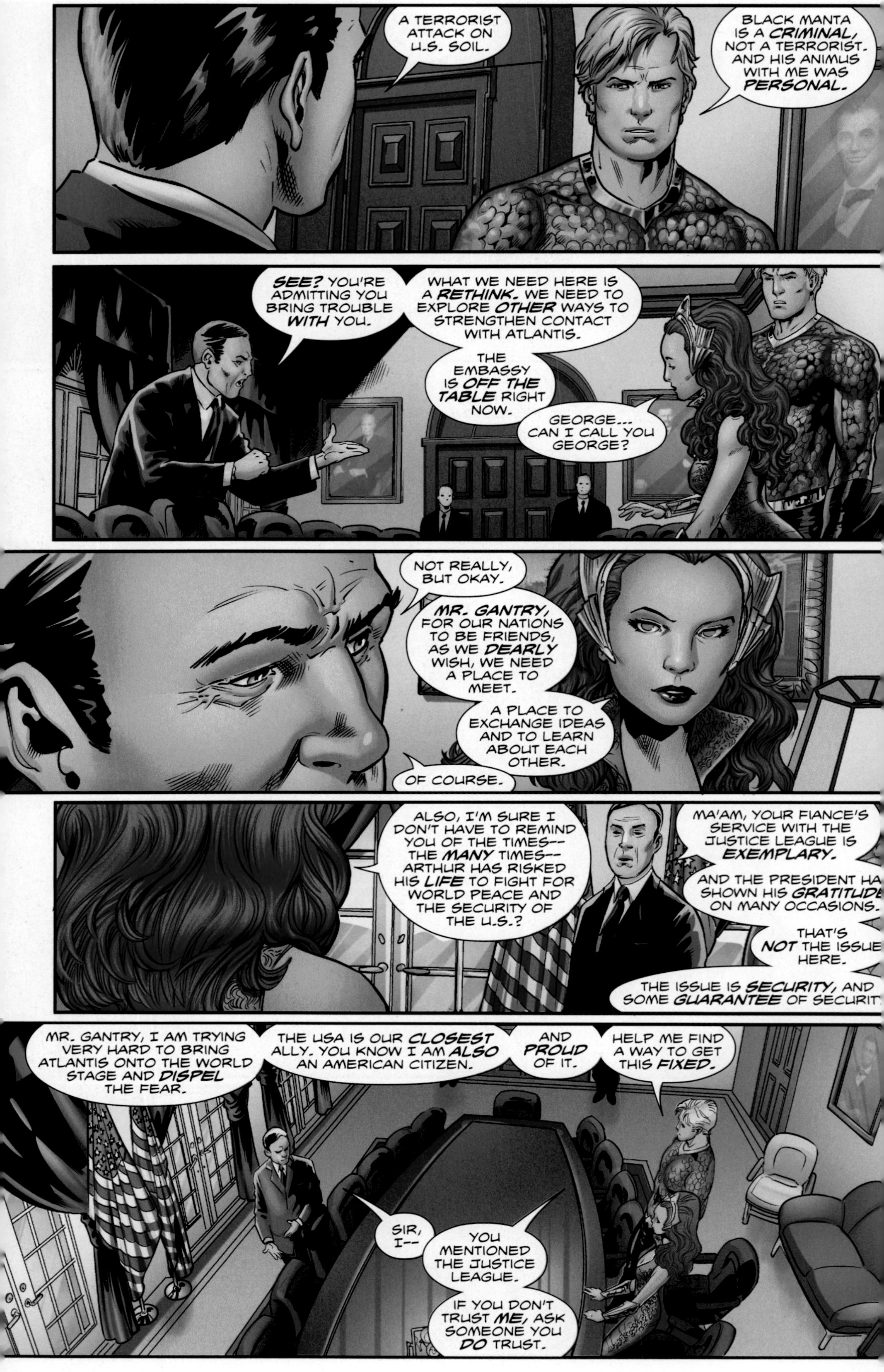

A TERRORIST ATTACK ON U.S. SOIL.
BLACK MANTA IS A CRIMINAL, NOT A TERRORIST. AND HIS ANIMUS WITH ME WAS PERSONAL.
SEE? YOU'RE ADMITTING YOU BRING TROUBLE WITH YOU.
WHAT WE NEED HERE IS A RETHINK. WE NEED TO EXPLORE OTHER WAYS TO STRENGTHEN CONTACT WITH ATLANTIS.
THE EMBASSY IS OFF THE TABLE RIGHT NOW.
GEORGE... CAN I CALL YOU GEORGE?
NOT REALLY, BUT OKAY.
MR. GANTRY, FOR OUR NATIONS TO BE FRIENDS, AS WE DEARLY WISH, WE NEED A PLACE TO MEET.
A PLACE TO EXCHANGE IDEAS AND TO LEARN ABOUT EACH OTHER.
OF COURSE.
ALSO, I'M SURE I DON'T HAVE TO REMIND YOU OF THE TIMES-- THE MANY TIMES-- ARTHUR HAS RISKED HIS LIFE TO FIGHT FOR WORLD PEACE AND THE SECURITY OF THE U.S.?
MA'AM, YOUR FIANCE'S SERVICE WITH THE JUSTICE LEAGUE IS EXEMPLARY.
AND THE PRESIDENT HA SHOWN HIS GRATITUDE ON MANY OCCASIONS.
THAT'S NOT THE ISSUE HERE.
THE ISSUE IS SECURITY, AND SOME GUARANTEE OF SECURIT
MR. GANTRY, I AM TRYING VERY HARD TO BRING ATLANTIS ONTO THE WORLD STAGE AND DISPEL THE FEAR.
THE USA IS OUR CLOSEST ALLY. YOU KNOW I AM ALSO AN AMERICAN CITIZEN.
AND PROUD OF IT.
HELP ME FIND A WAY TO GET THIS FIXED.
SIR, I--
YOU MENTIONED THE JUSTICE LEAGUE.
IF YOU DON'T TRUST ME, ASK SOMEONE YOU DO TRUST.

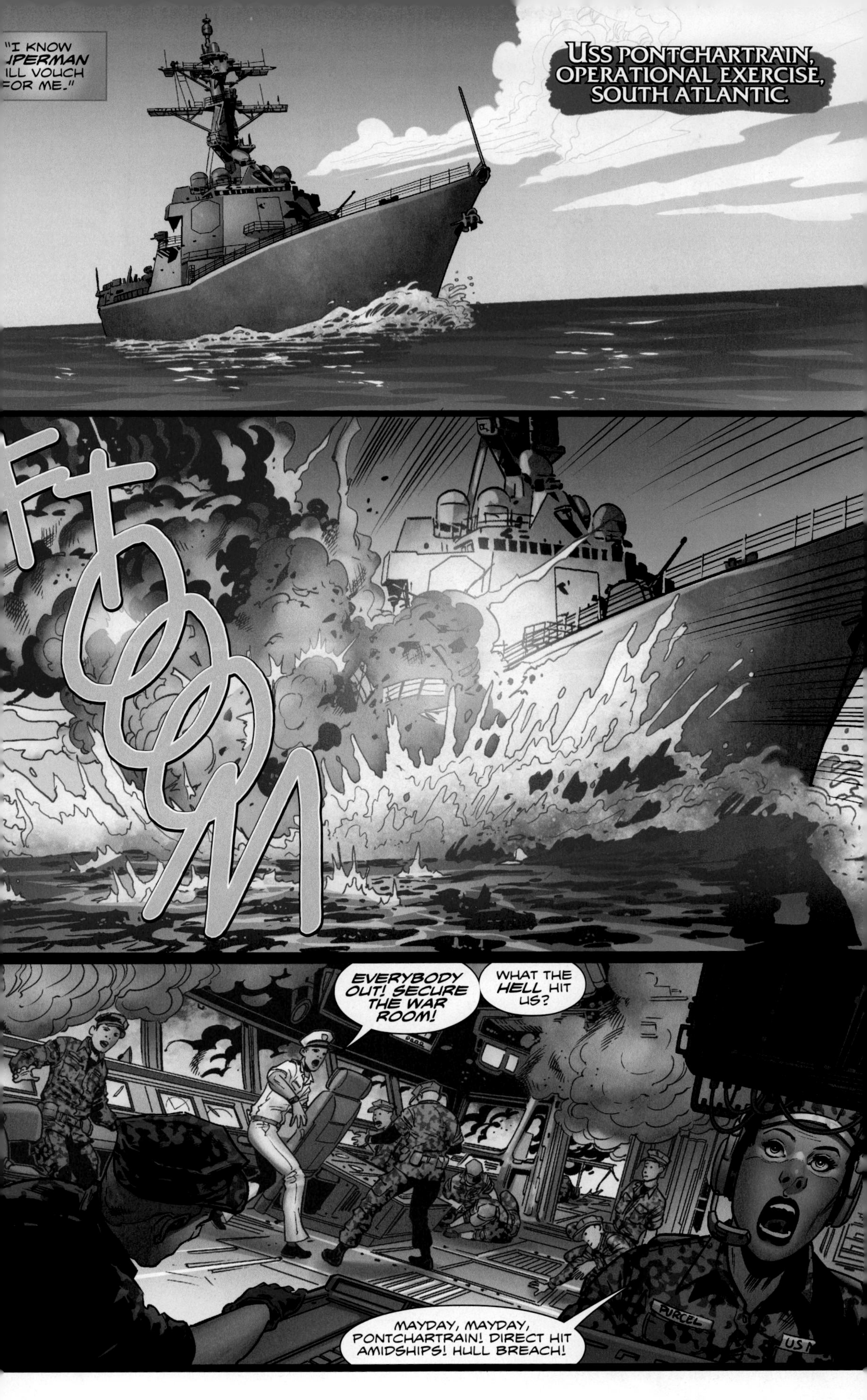
"I KNOW UPERMAN ILL VOUCH FOR ME."
USS PONTCHARTRAIN, OPERATIONAL EXERCISE, SOUTH ATLANTIC.
FFTOOOOM
EVERYBODY OUT! SECURE THE WAR ROOM!
WHAT THE HELL HIT US?
PURCEL
MAYDAY, MAYDAY, PONTCHARTRAIN! DIRECT HIT AMIDSHIPS! HULL BREACH!

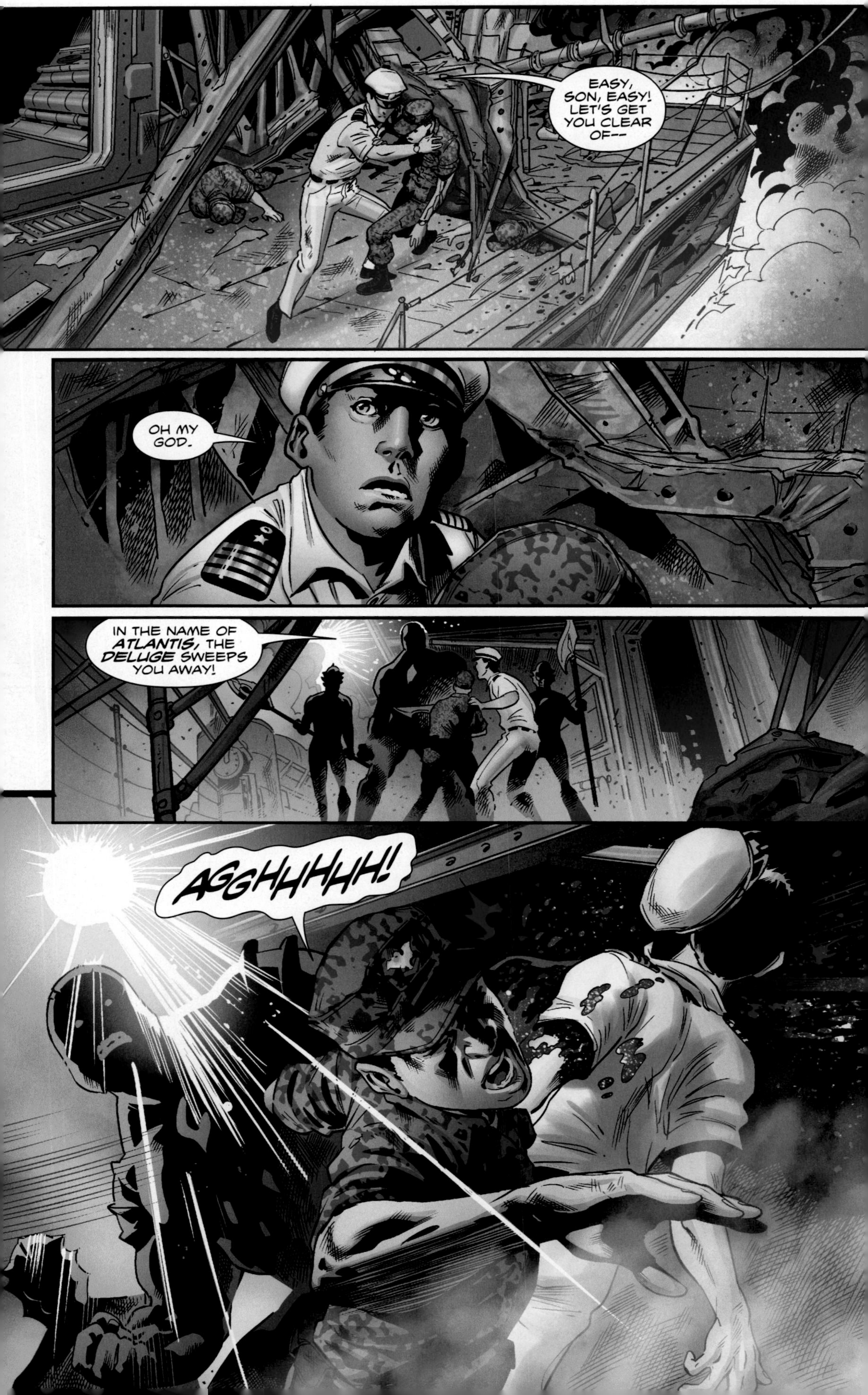
EASY, SON, EASY! LET'S GET YOU CLEAR OF--
OH MY GOD.
IN THE NAME OF *ATLANTIS*, THE *DELUGE* SWEEPS YOU AWAY!
AGGHHHHH!

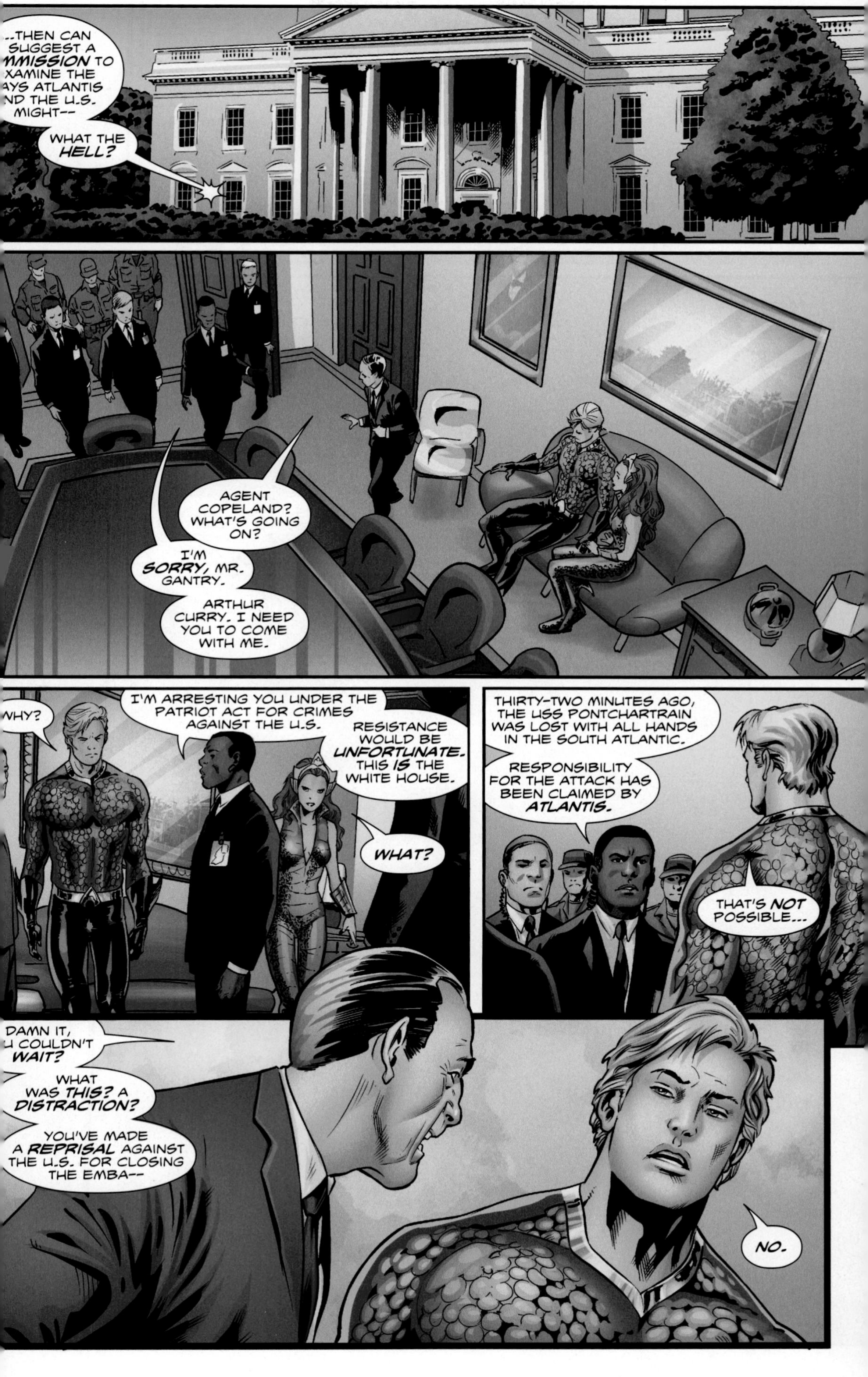

...THEN CAN SUGGEST A MMISSION TO XAMINE THE AYS ATLANTIS ND THE U.S. MIGHT--
WHAT THE HELL?
AGENT COPELAND? WHAT'S GOING ON?
I'M SORRY, MR. GANTRY.
ARTHUR CURRY. I NEED YOU TO COME WITH ME.
WHY?
I'M ARRESTING YOU UNDER THE PATRIOT ACT FOR CRIMES AGAINST THE U.S.
RESISTANCE WOULD BE UNFORTUNATE. THIS IS THE WHITE HOUSE.
WHAT?
THIRTY-TWO MINUTES AGO, THE USS PONTCHARTRAIN WAS LOST WITH ALL HANDS IN THE SOUTH ATLANTIC.
RESPONSIBILITY FOR THE ATTACK HAS BEEN CLAIMED BY ATLANTIS.
THAT'S NOT POSSIBLE...
DAMN IT, U COULDN'T WAIT?
WHAT WAS THIS? A DISTRACTION?
YOU'VE MADE A REPRISAL AGAINST THE U.S. FOR CLOSING THE EMBA--
NO.

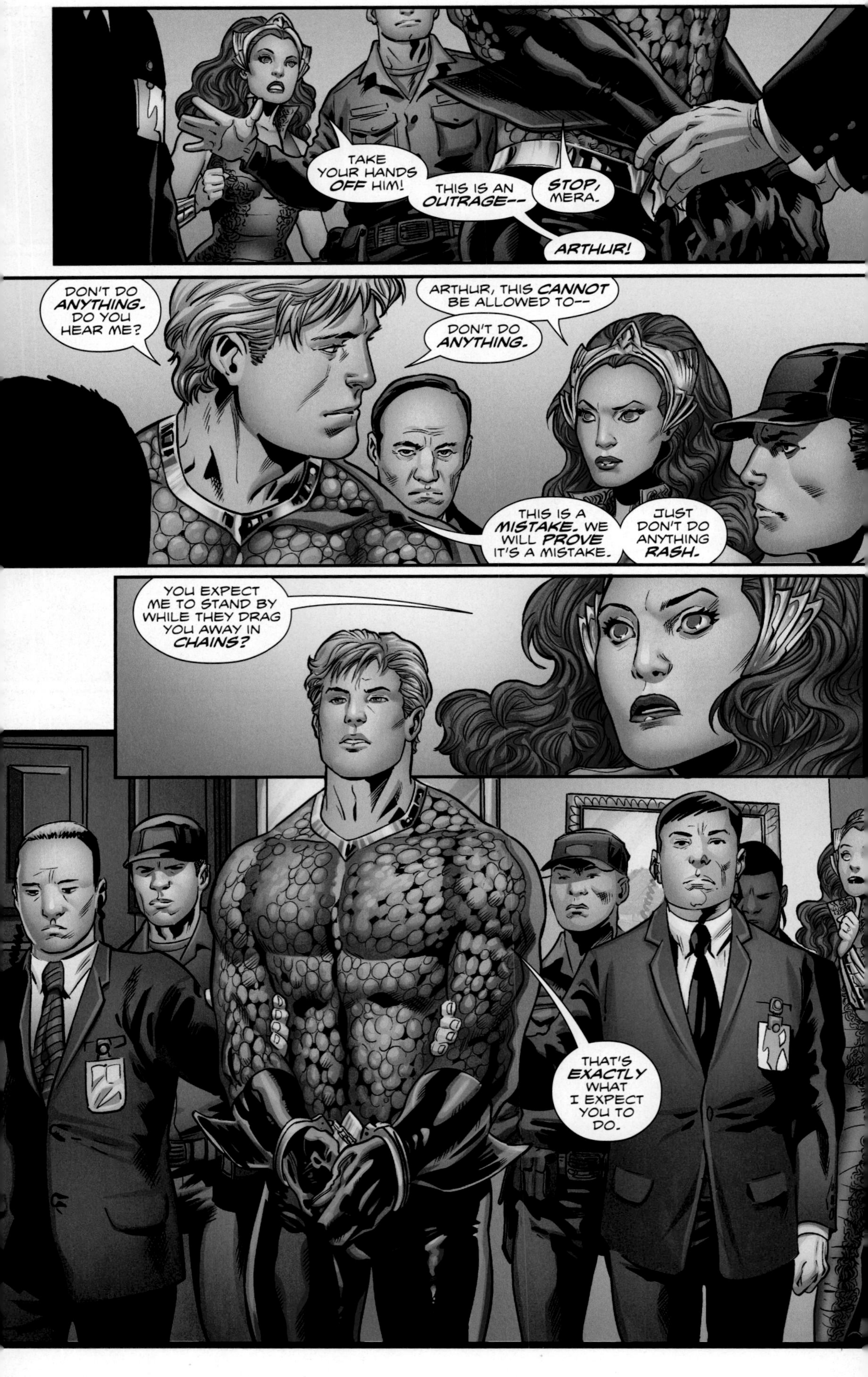
TAKE YOUR HANDS OFF HIM!
THIS IS AN OUTRAGE--
STOP, MERA.
ARTHUR!
DON'T DO ANYTHING. DO YOU HEAR ME?
ARTHUR, THIS CANNOT BE ALLOWED TO--
DON'T DO ANYTHING.
THIS IS A MISTAKE. WE WILL PROVE IT'S A MISTAKE.
JUST DON'T DO ANYTHING RASH.
YOU EXPECT ME TO STAND BY WHILE THEY DRAG YOU AWAY IN CHAINS?
THAT'S EXACTLY WHAT I EXPECT YOU TO DO.

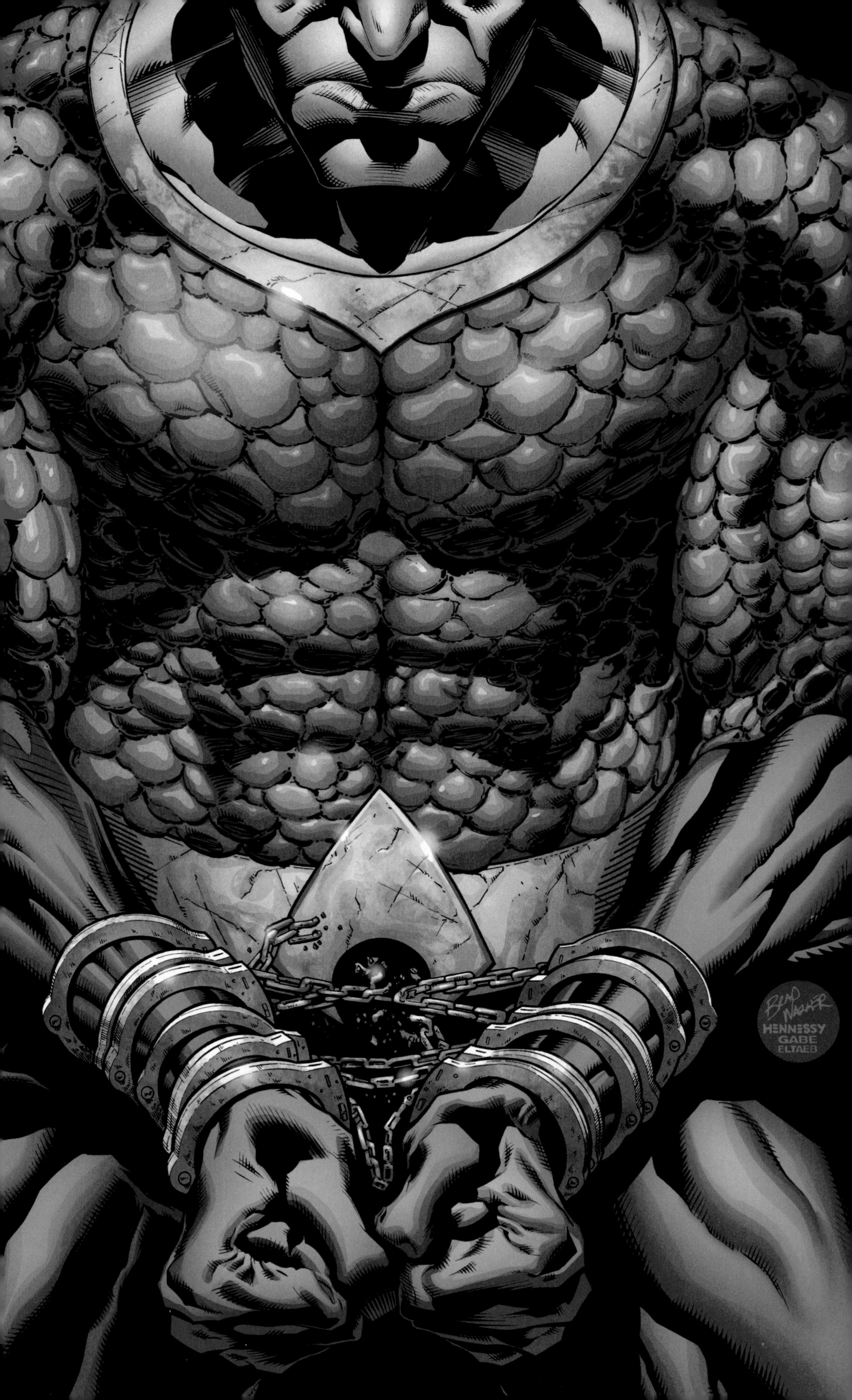
BRAD WALKER
HENNESSY
GABE
ELTAEB

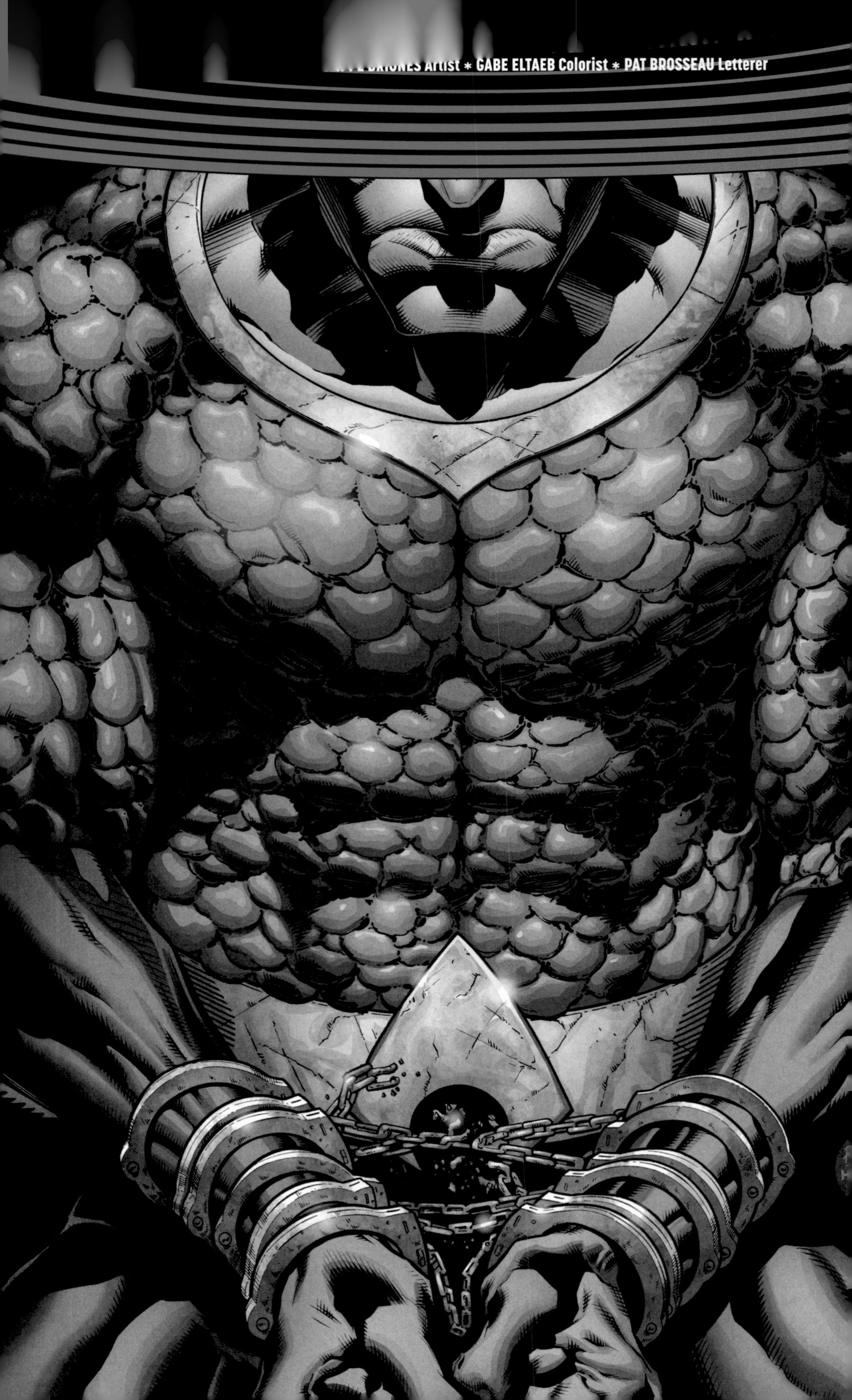
BRIONES Artist * GABE ELTAEB Colorist * PAT BROSSEAU Letterer

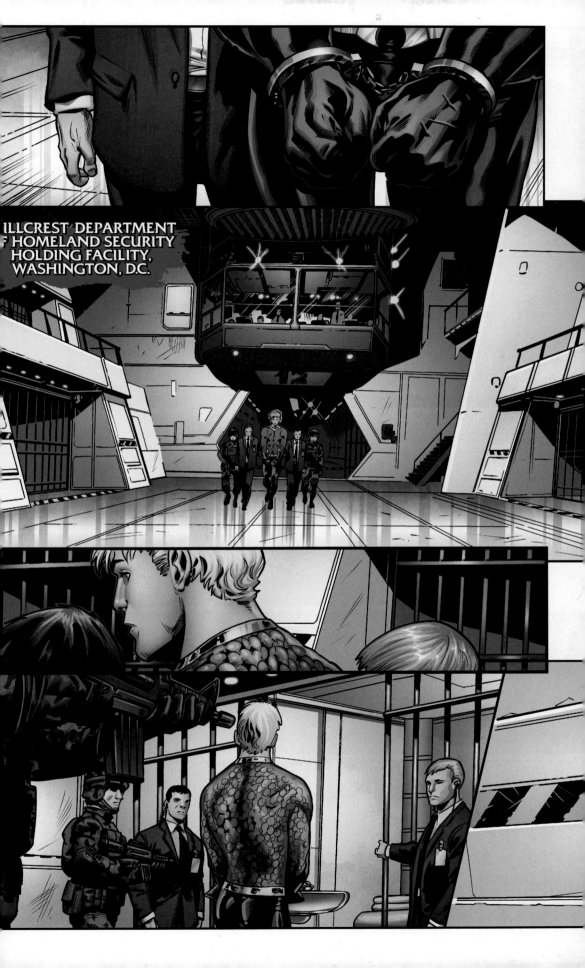

ILLCREST DEPARTMENT
F HOMELAND SECURITY
HOLDING FACILITY,
WASHINGTON, D.C.

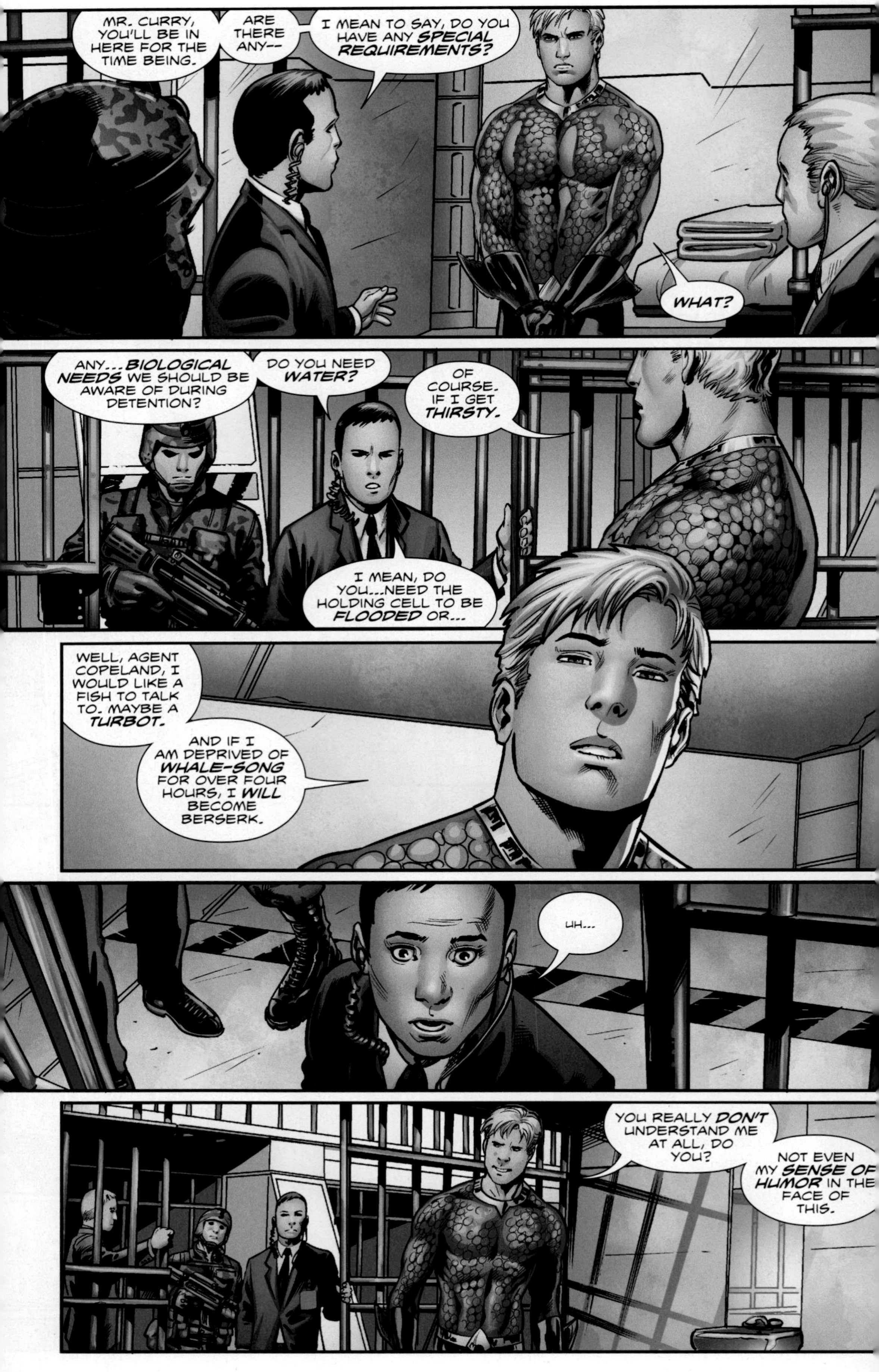
MR. CURRY, YOU'LL BE IN HERE FOR THE TIME BEING.
ARE THERE ANY--
I MEAN TO SAY, DO YOU HAVE ANY SPECIAL REQUIREMENTS?
WHAT?
ANY... BIOLOGICAL NEEDS WE SHOULD BE AWARE OF DURING DETENTION?
DO YOU NEED WATER?
OF COURSE. IF I GET THIRSTY.
I MEAN, DO YOU...NEED THE HOLDING CELL TO BE FLOODED OR...
WELL, AGENT COPELAND, I WOULD LIKE A FISH TO TALK TO. MAYBE A TURBOT.
AND IF I AM DEPRIVED OF WHALE-SONG FOR OVER FOUR HOURS, I WILL BECOME BERSERK.
UH...
YOU REALLY DON'T UNDERSTAND ME AT ALL, DO YOU?
NOT EVEN MY SENSE OF HUMOR IN THE FACE OF THIS.

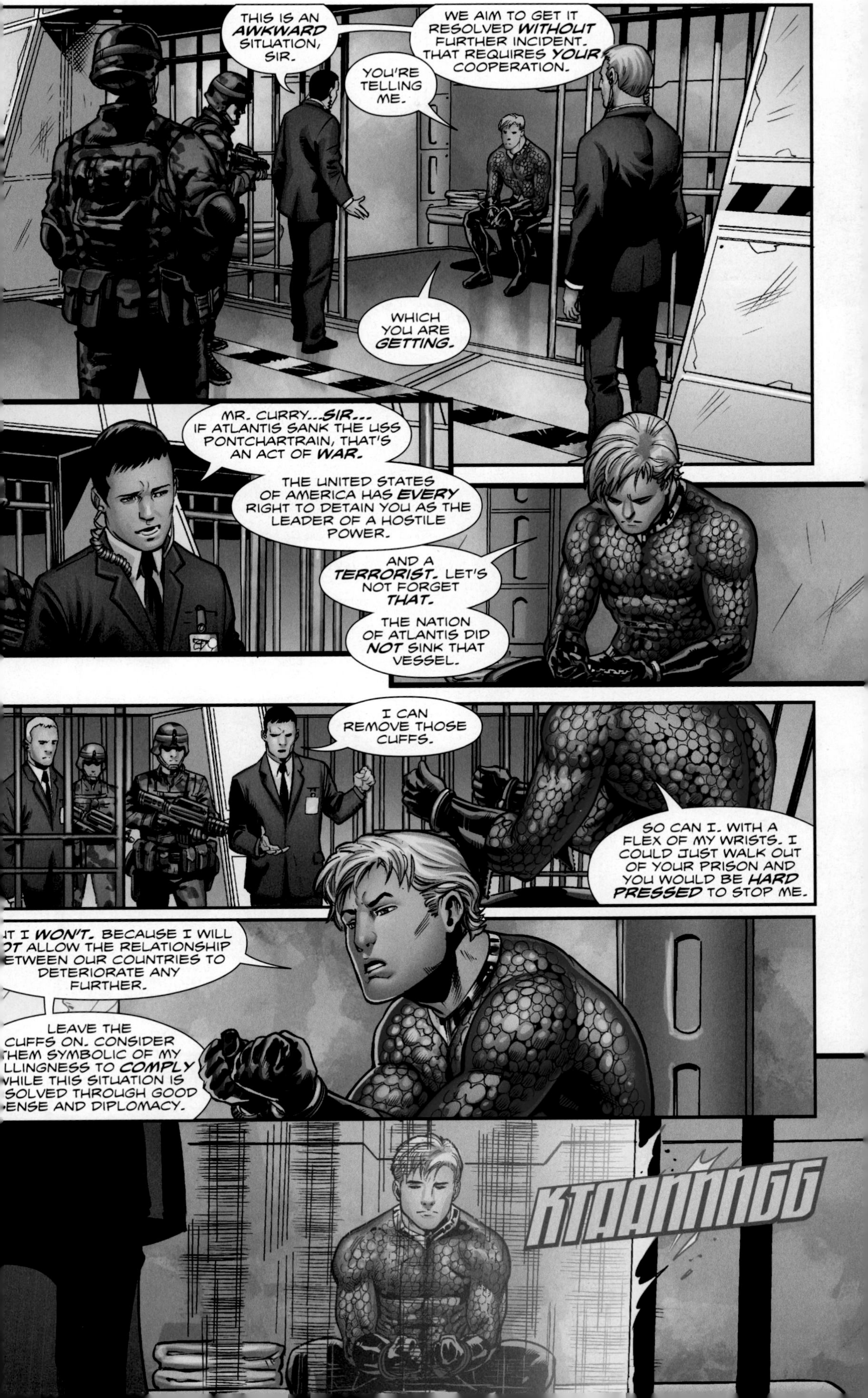
THIS IS AN AWKWARD SITUATION, SIR.
WE AIM TO GET IT RESOLVED WITHOUT FURTHER INCIDENT. THAT REQUIRES YOUR COOPERATION.
YOU'RE TELLING ME.
WHICH YOU ARE GETTING.
MR. CURRY...SIR... IF ATLANTIS SANK THE USS PONTCHARTRAIN, THAT'S AN ACT OF WAR.
THE UNITED STATES OF AMERICA HAS EVERY RIGHT TO DETAIN YOU AS THE LEADER OF A HOSTILE POWER.
AND A TERRORIST. LET'S NOT FORGET THAT.
THE NATION OF ATLANTIS DID NOT SINK THAT VESSEL.
I CAN REMOVE THOSE CUFFS.
SO CAN I. WITH A FLEX OF MY WRISTS. I COULD JUST WALK OUT OF YOUR PRISON AND YOU WOULD BE HARD PRESSED TO STOP ME.
IT I WON'T. BECAUSE I WILL OT ALLOW THE RELATIONSHIP ETWEEN OUR COUNTRIES TO DETERIORATE ANY FURTHER.
LEAVE THE CUFFS ON. CONSIDER THEM SYMBOLIC OF MY LLINGNESS TO COMPLY WHILE THIS SITUATION IS SOLVED THROUGH GOOD ENSE AND DIPLOMACY.
KTAANNNGG

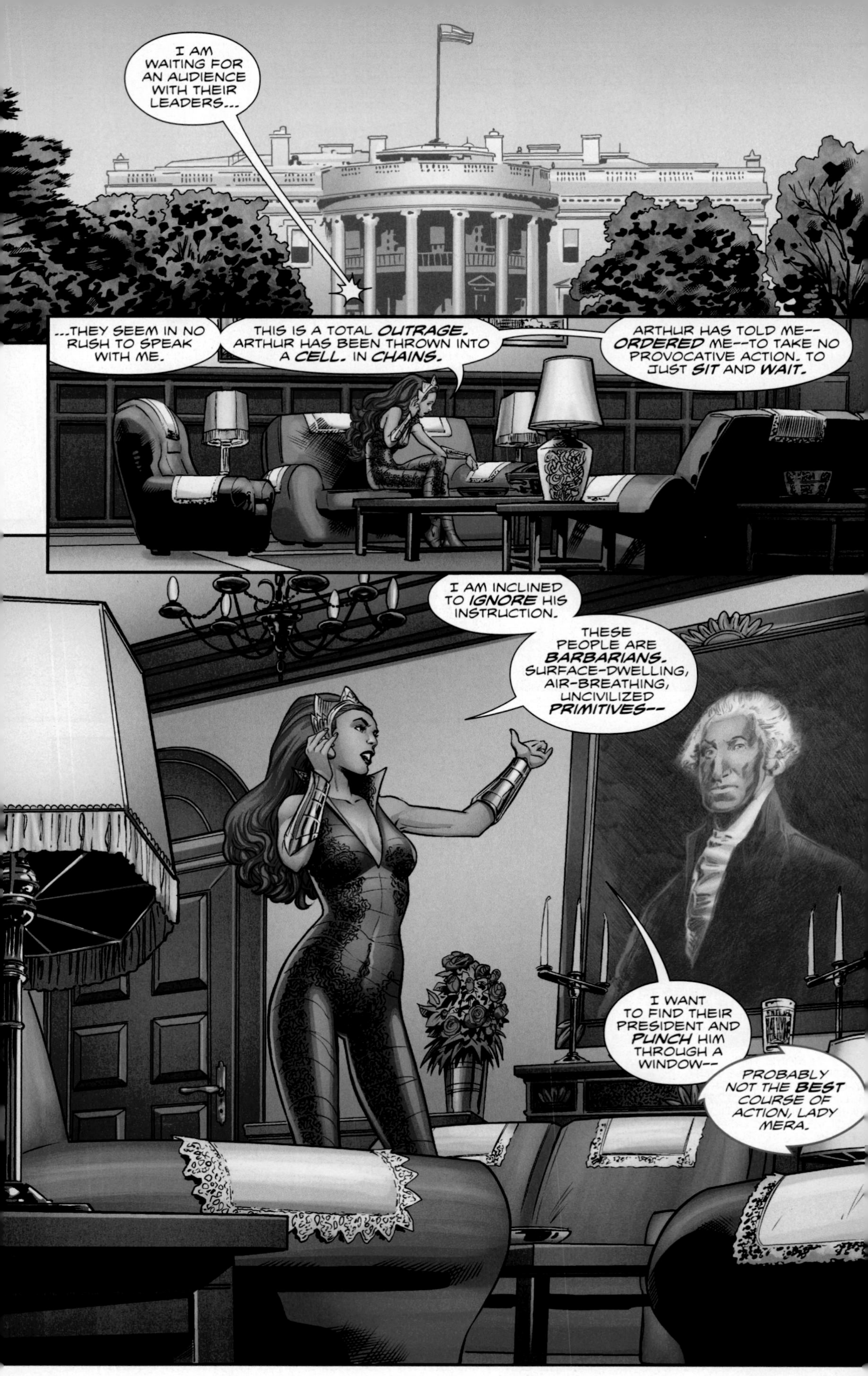
I AM WAITING FOR AN AUDIENCE WITH THEIR LEADERS...
...THEY SEEM IN NO RUSH TO SPEAK WITH ME.
THIS IS A TOTAL OUTRAGE. ARTHUR HAS BEEN THROWN INTO A CELL. IN CHAINS.
ARTHUR HAS TOLD ME-- ORDERED ME--TO TAKE NO PROVOCATIVE ACTION. TO JUST SIT AND WAIT.
I AM INCLINED TO IGNORE HIS INSTRUCTION.
THESE PEOPLE ARE BARBARIANS. SURFACE-DWELLING, AIR-BREATHING, UNCIVILIZED PRIMITIVES--
I WANT TO FIND THEIR PRESIDENT AND PUNCH HIM THROUGH A WINDOW--
PROBABLY NOT THE BEST COURSE OF ACTION, LADY MERA.

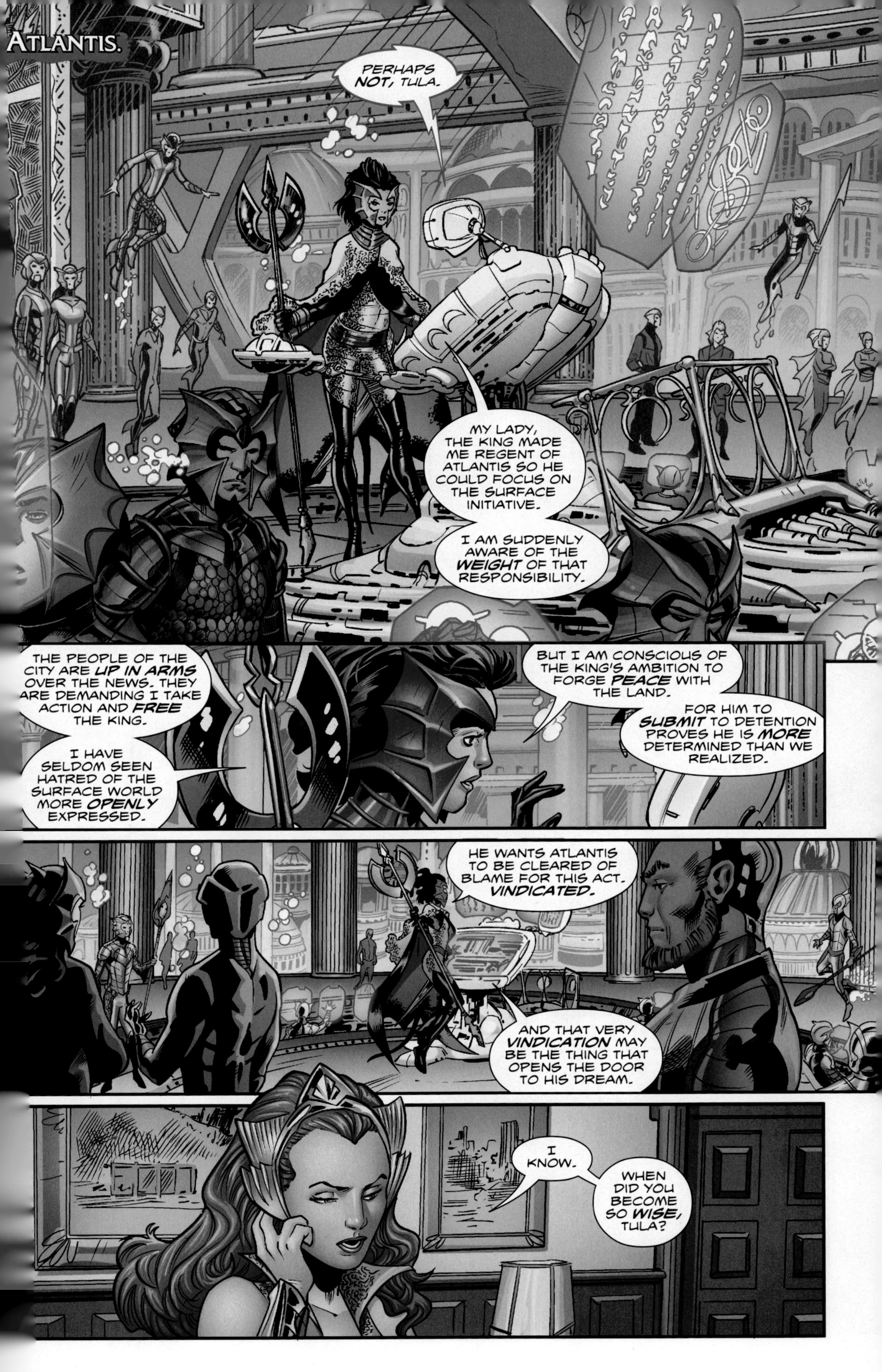
ATLANTIS.
PERHAPS NOT, TULA.
MY LADY, THE KING MADE ME REGENT OF ATLANTIS SO HE COULD FOCUS ON THE SURFACE INITIATIVE.
I AM SUDDENLY AWARE OF THE WEIGHT OF THAT RESPONSIBILITY.
THE PEOPLE OF THE CITY ARE UP IN ARMS OVER THE NEWS. THEY ARE DEMANDING I TAKE ACTION AND FREE THE KING.
I HAVE SELDOM SEEN HATRED OF THE SURFACE WORLD MORE OPENLY EXPRESSED.
BUT I AM CONSCIOUS OF THE KING'S AMBITION TO FORGE PEACE WITH THE LAND.
FOR HIM TO SUBMIT TO DETENTION PROVES HE IS MORE DETERMINED THAN WE REALIZED.
HE WANTS ATLANTIS TO BE CLEARED OF BLAME FOR THIS ACT. VINDICATED.
AND THAT VERY VINDICATION MAY BE THE THING THAT OPENS THE DOOR TO HIS DREAM.
I KNOW.
WHEN DID YOU BECOME SO WISE, TULA?

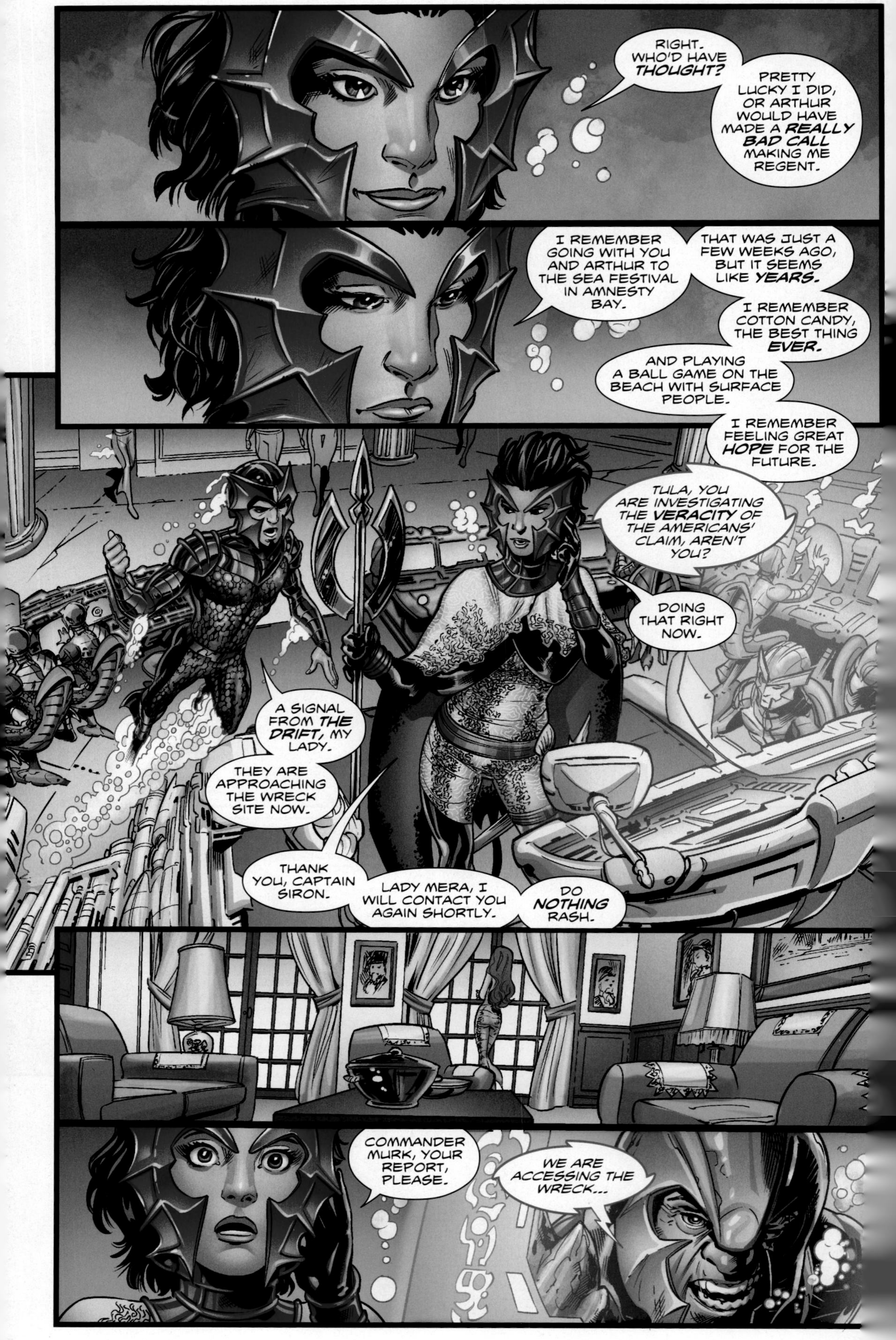

RIGHT. WHO'D HAVE THOUGHT?
PRETTY LUCKY I DID, OR ARTHUR WOULD HAVE MADE A REALLY BAD CALL MAKING ME REGENT.
I REMEMBER GOING WITH YOU AND ARTHUR TO THE SEA FESTIVAL IN AMNESTY BAY.
THAT WAS JUST A FEW WEEKS AGO, BUT IT SEEMS LIKE YEARS.
I REMEMBER COTTON CANDY, THE BEST THING EVER.
AND PLAYING A BALL GAME ON THE BEACH WITH SURFACE PEOPLE.
I REMEMBER FEELING GREAT HOPE FOR THE FUTURE.
TULA, YOU ARE INVESTIGATING THE VERACITY OF THE AMERICANS' CLAIM, AREN'T YOU?
DOING THAT RIGHT NOW.
A SIGNAL FROM THE DRIFT, MY LADY.
THEY ARE APPROACHING THE WRECK SITE NOW.
THANK YOU, CAPTAIN SIRON.
LADY MERA, I WILL CONTACT YOU AGAIN SHORTLY.
DO NOTHING RASH.
COMMANDER MURK, YOUR REPORT, PLEASE.
WE ARE ACCESSING THE WRECK...

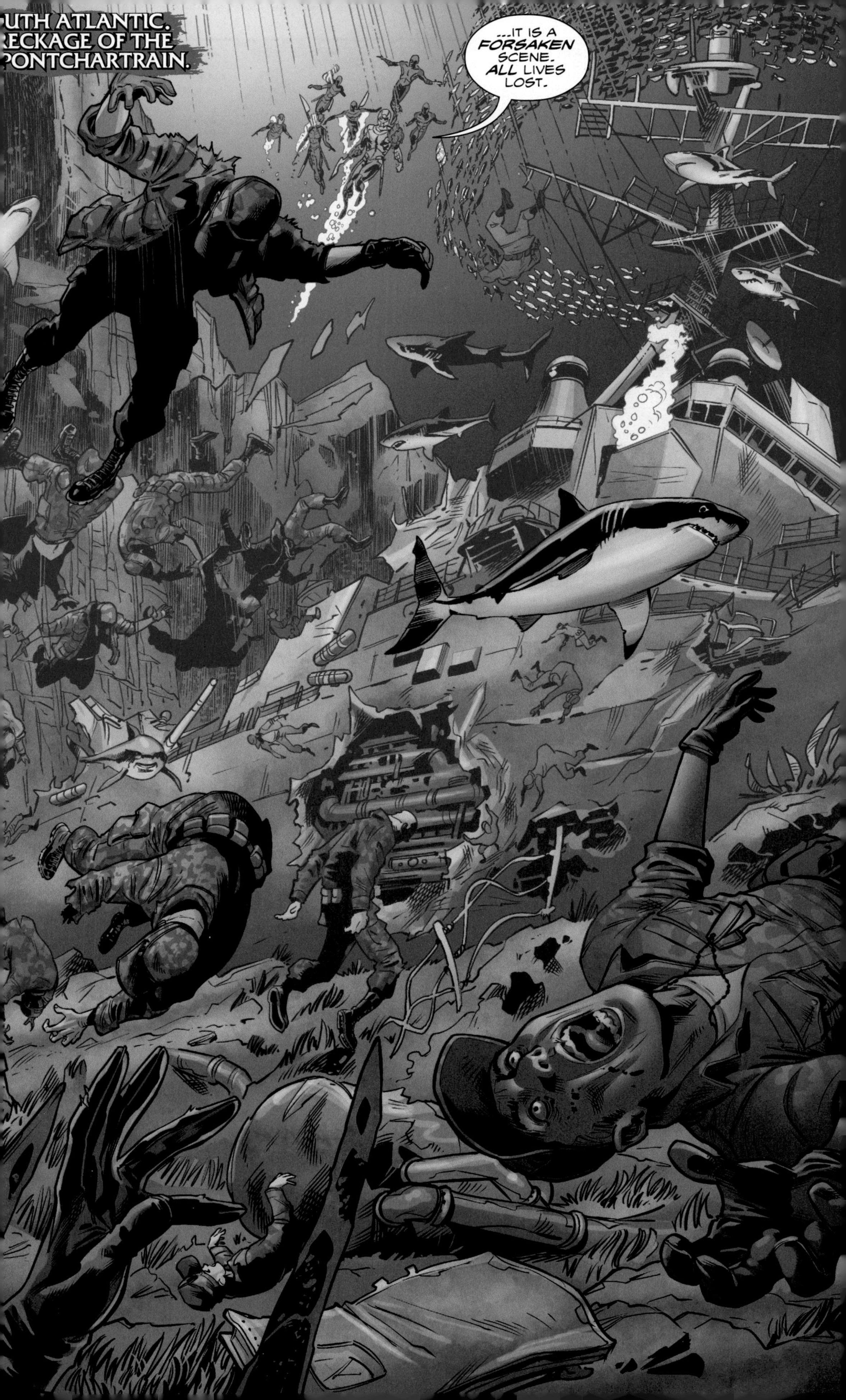
UTH ATLANTIC.
RECKAGE OF THE
PONTCHARTRAIN.
...IT IS A FORSAKEN SCENE. ALL LIVES LOST.

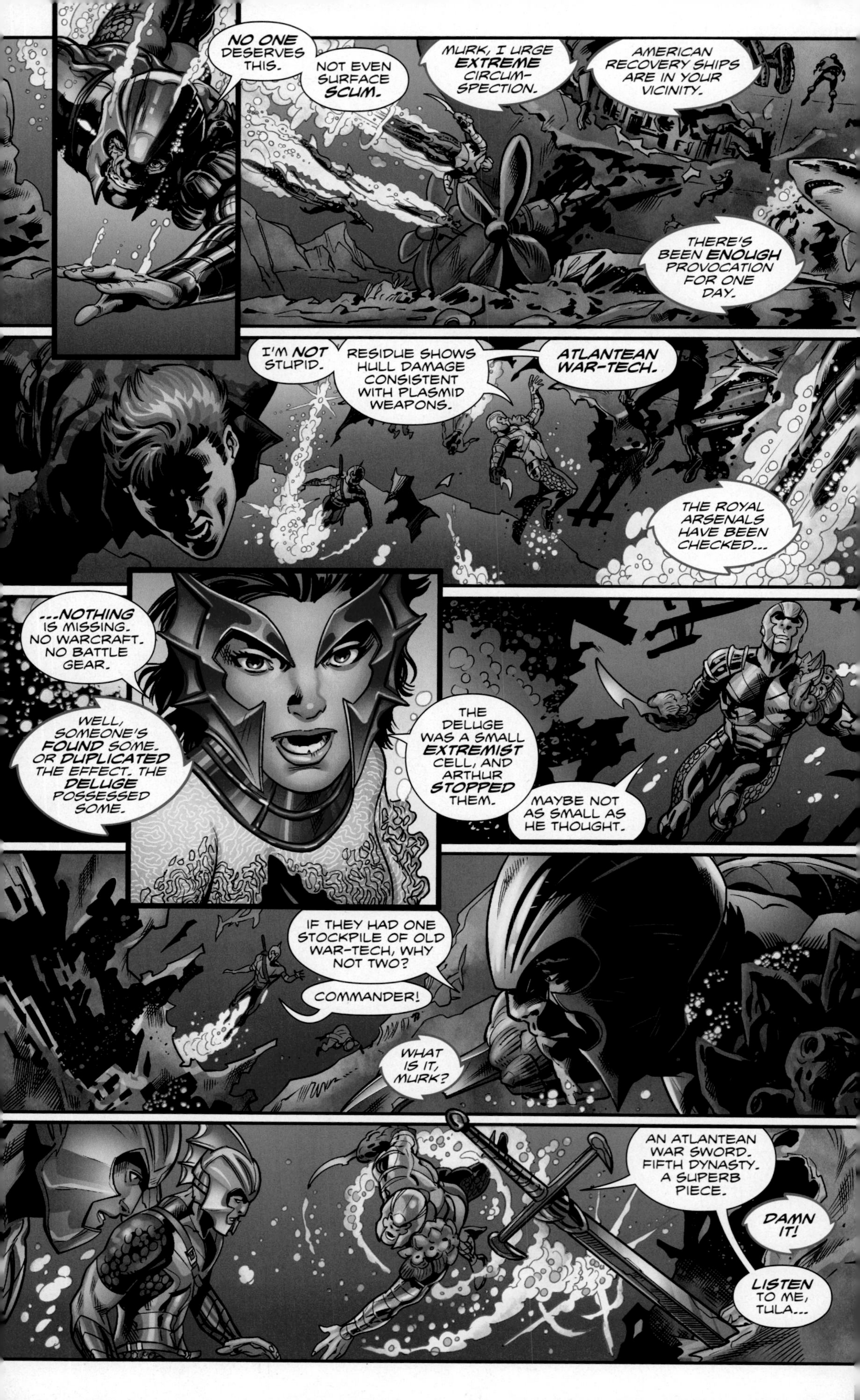
NO ONE DESERVES THIS.
NOT EVEN SURFACE SCUM.
MURK, I URGE EXTREME CIRCUM-SPECTION.
AMERICAN RECOVERY SHIPS ARE IN YOUR VICINITY.
THERE'S BEEN ENOUGH PROVOCATION FOR ONE DAY.
I'M NOT STUPID.
RESIDUE SHOWS HULL DAMAGE CONSISTENT WITH PLASMID WEAPONS.
ATLANTEAN WAR-TECH.
THE ROYAL ARSENALS HAVE BEEN CHECKED...
...NOTHING IS MISSING. NO WARCRAFT. NO BATTLE GEAR.
WELL, SOMEONE'S FOUND SOME. OR DUPLICATED THE EFFECT. THE DELUGE POSSESSED SOME.
THE DELUGE WAS A SMALL EXTREMIST CELL, AND ARTHUR STOPPED THEM.
MAYBE NOT AS SMALL AS HE THOUGHT.
IF THEY HAD ONE STOCKPILE OF OLD WAR-TECH, WHY NOT TWO?
COMMANDER!
WHAT IS IT, MURK?
AN ATLANTEAN WAR SWORD. FIFTH DYNASTY. A SUPERB PIECE.
DAMN IT!
LISTEN TO ME, TULA...

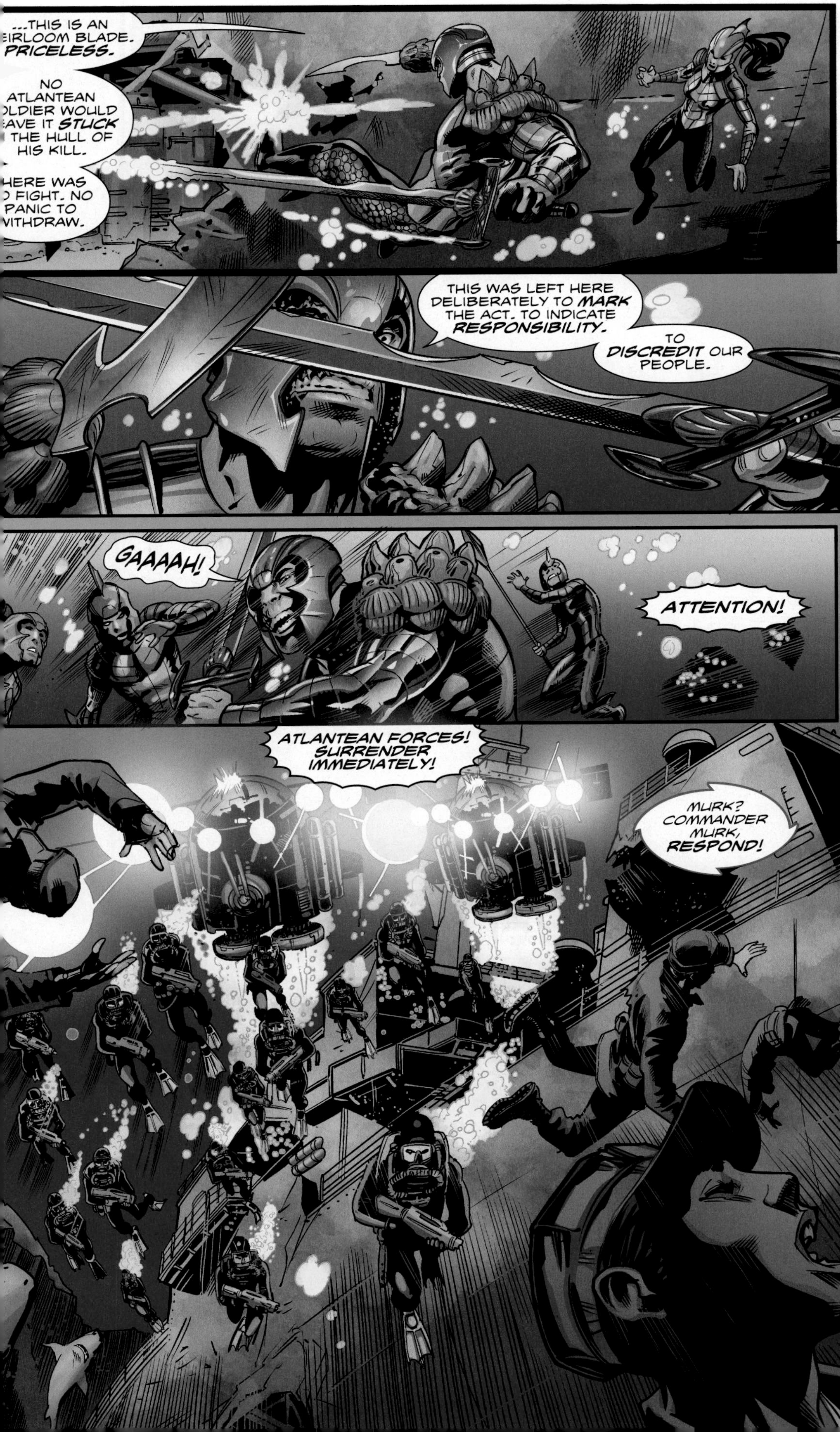
...THIS IS AN
EIRLOOM BLADE.
PRICELESS.
NO ATLANTEAN OLDIER WOULD EAVE IT STUCK THE HULL OF HIS KILL.
HERE WAS O FIGHT. NO PANIC TO WITHDRAW.
THIS WAS LEFT HERE DELIBERATELY TO MARK THE ACT. TO INDICATE RESPONSIBILITY.
TO DISCREDIT OUR PEOPLE.
GAAAAH!
ATTENTION!
ATLANTEAN FORCES! SURRENDER IMMEDIATELY!
MURK? COMMANDER MURK, RESPOND!

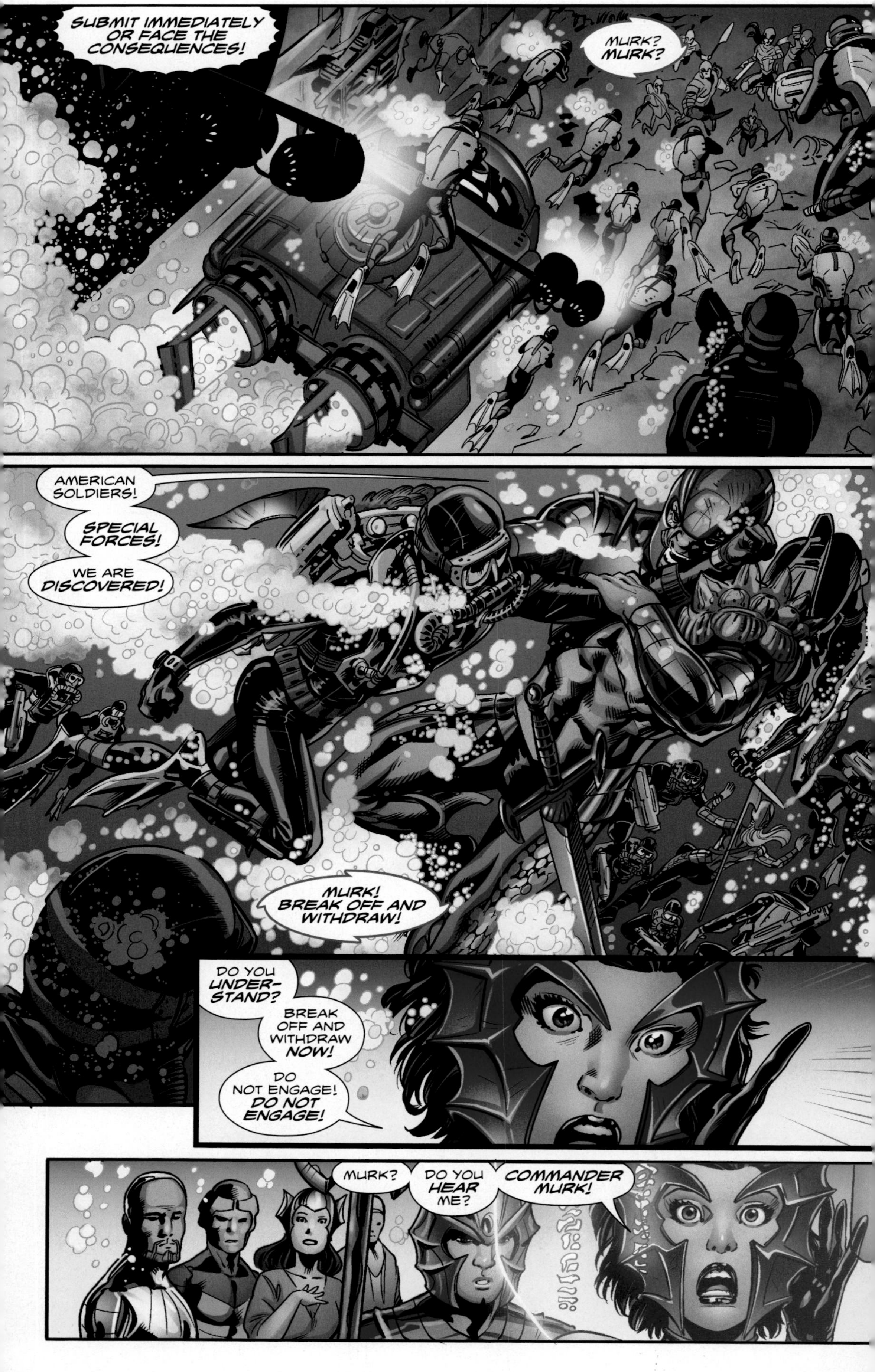
SUBMIT IMMEDIATELY OR FACE THE CONSEQUENCES!
MURK? MURK?
AMERICAN SOLDIERS!
SPECIAL FORCES!
WE ARE DISCOVERED!
MURK! BREAK OFF AND WITHDRAW!
DO YOU UNDER-STAND?
BREAK OFF AND WITHDRAW NOW!
DO NOT ENGAGE! DO NOT ENGAGE!
MURK?
DO YOU HEAR ME?
COMMANDER MURK!

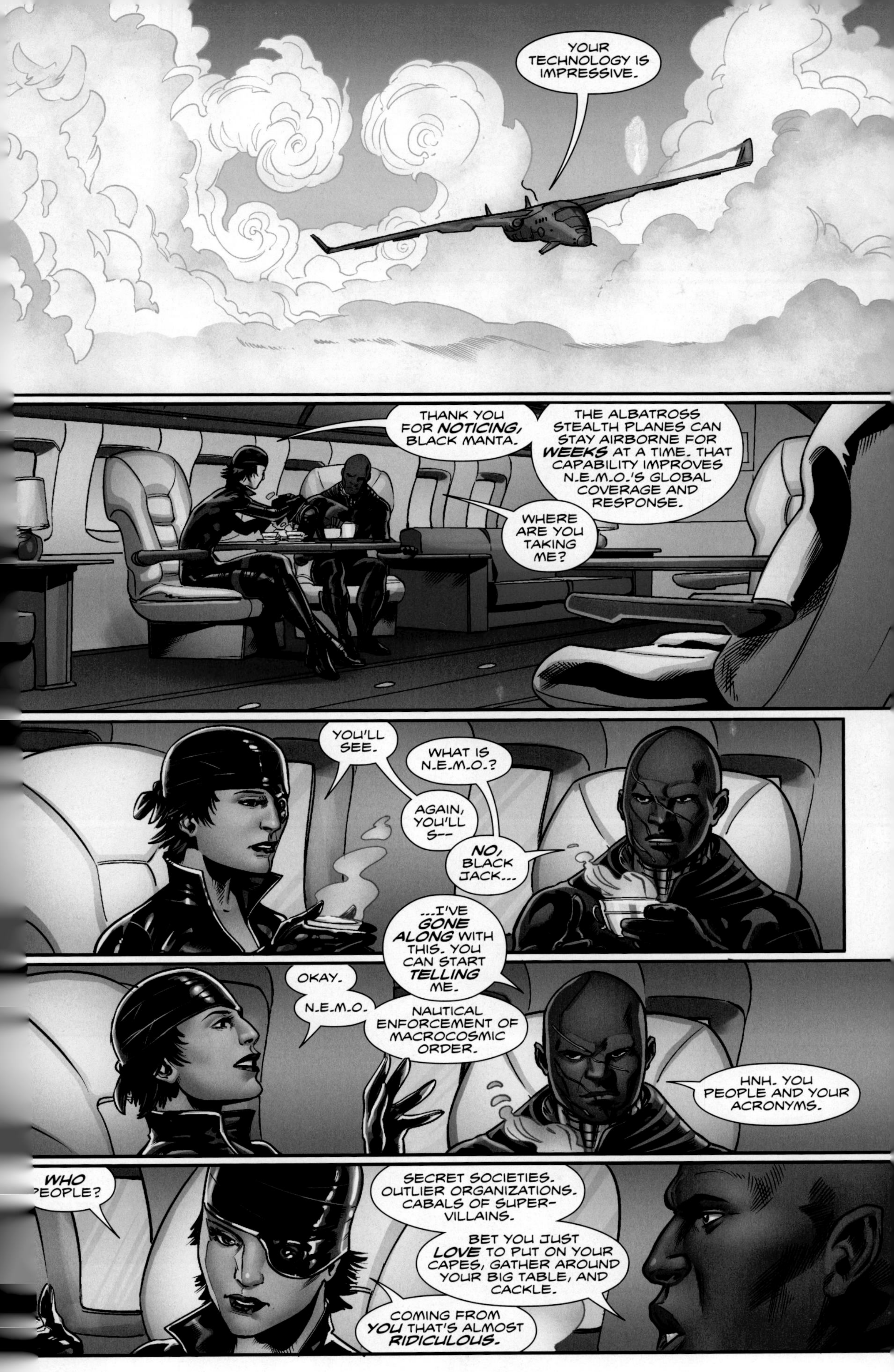
YOUR TECHNOLOGY IS IMPRESSIVE.
THANK YOU FOR NOTICING, BLACK MANTA.
THE ALBATROSS STEALTH PLANES CAN STAY AIRBORNE FOR WEEKS AT A TIME. THAT CAPABILITY IMPROVES N.E.M.O.'S GLOBAL COVERAGE AND RESPONSE.
WHERE ARE YOU TAKING ME?
YOU'LL SEE.
WHAT IS N.E.M.O.?
AGAIN, YOU'LL S--
NO, BLACK JACK...
...I'VE GONE ALONG WITH THIS. YOU CAN START TELLING ME.
OKAY.
N.E.M.O.
NAUTICAL ENFORCEMENT OF MACROCOSMIC ORDER.
HNH. YOU PEOPLE AND YOUR ACRONYMS.
WHO PEOPLE?
SECRET SOCIETIES. OUTLIER ORGANIZATIONS. CABALS OF SUPER-VILLAINS.
BET YOU JUST LOVE TO PUT ON YOUR CAPES, GATHER AROUND YOUR BIG TABLE, AND CACKLE.
COMING FROM YOU THAT'S ALMOST RIDICULOUS.

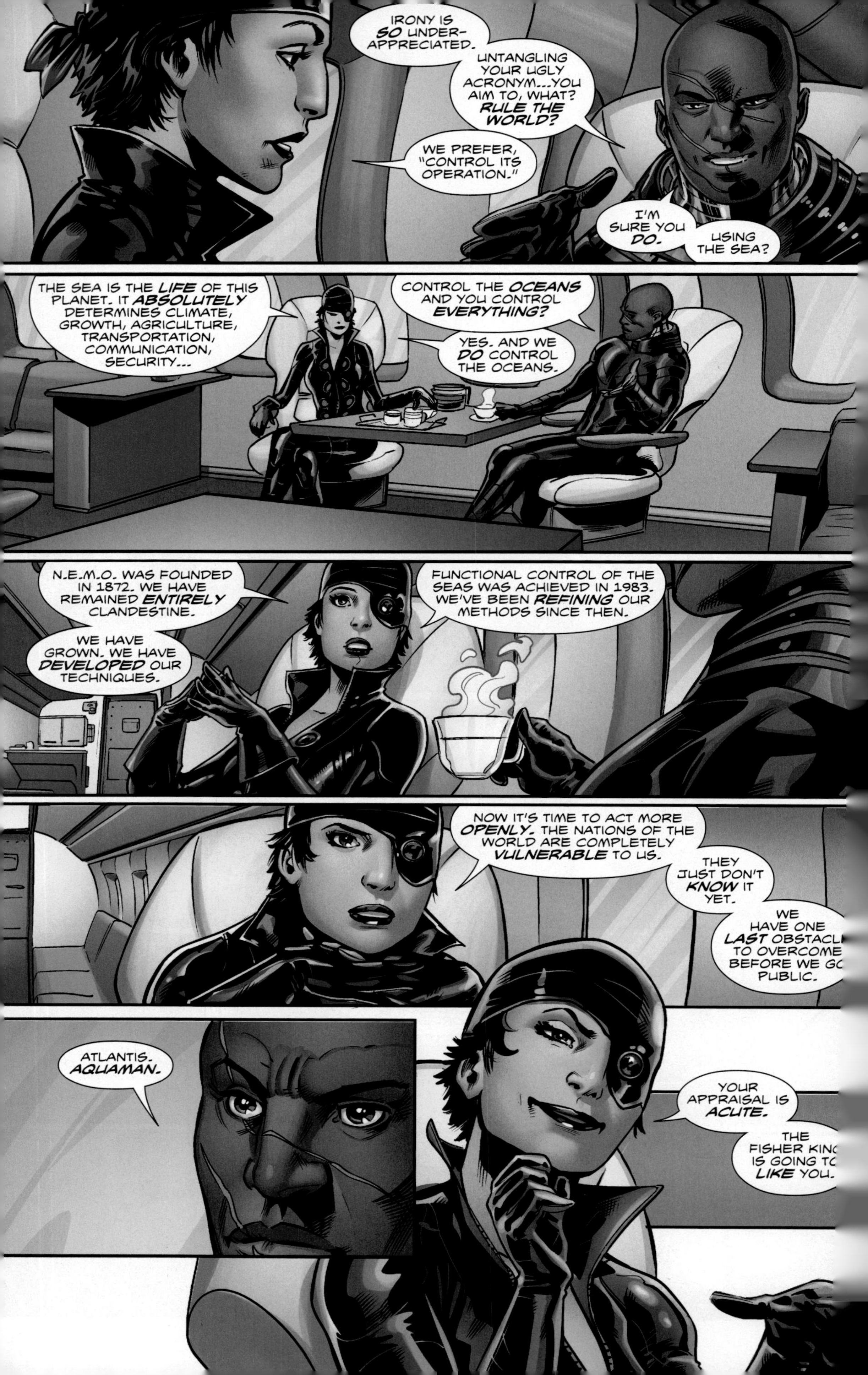
IRONY IS SO UNDER-APPRECIATED.
UNTANGLING YOUR UGLY ACRONYM...YOU AIM TO, WHAT? RULE THE WORLD?
WE PREFER, "CONTROL ITS OPERATION."
I'M SURE YOU DO.
USING THE SEA?
THE SEA IS THE LIFE OF THIS PLANET. IT ABSOLUTELY DETERMINES CLIMATE, GROWTH, AGRICULTURE, TRANSPORTATION, COMMUNICATION, SECURITY...
CONTROL THE OCEANS AND YOU CONTROL EVERYTHING?
YES. AND WE DO CONTROL THE OCEANS.
N.E.M.O. WAS FOUNDED IN 1872. WE HAVE REMAINED ENTIRELY CLANDESTINE.
WE HAVE GROWN. WE HAVE DEVELOPED OUR TECHNIQUES.
FUNCTIONAL CONTROL OF THE SEAS WAS ACHIEVED IN 1983. WE'VE BEEN REFINING OUR METHODS SINCE THEN.
NOW IT'S TIME TO ACT MORE OPENLY. THE NATIONS OF THE WORLD ARE COMPLETELY VULNERABLE TO US.
THEY JUST DON'T KNOW IT YET.
WE HAVE ONE LAST OBSTACL TO OVERCOME BEFORE WE GO PUBLIC.
ATLANTIS. AQUAMAN.
YOUR APPRAISAL IS ACUTE.
THE FISHER KING IS GOING TO LIKE YOU.

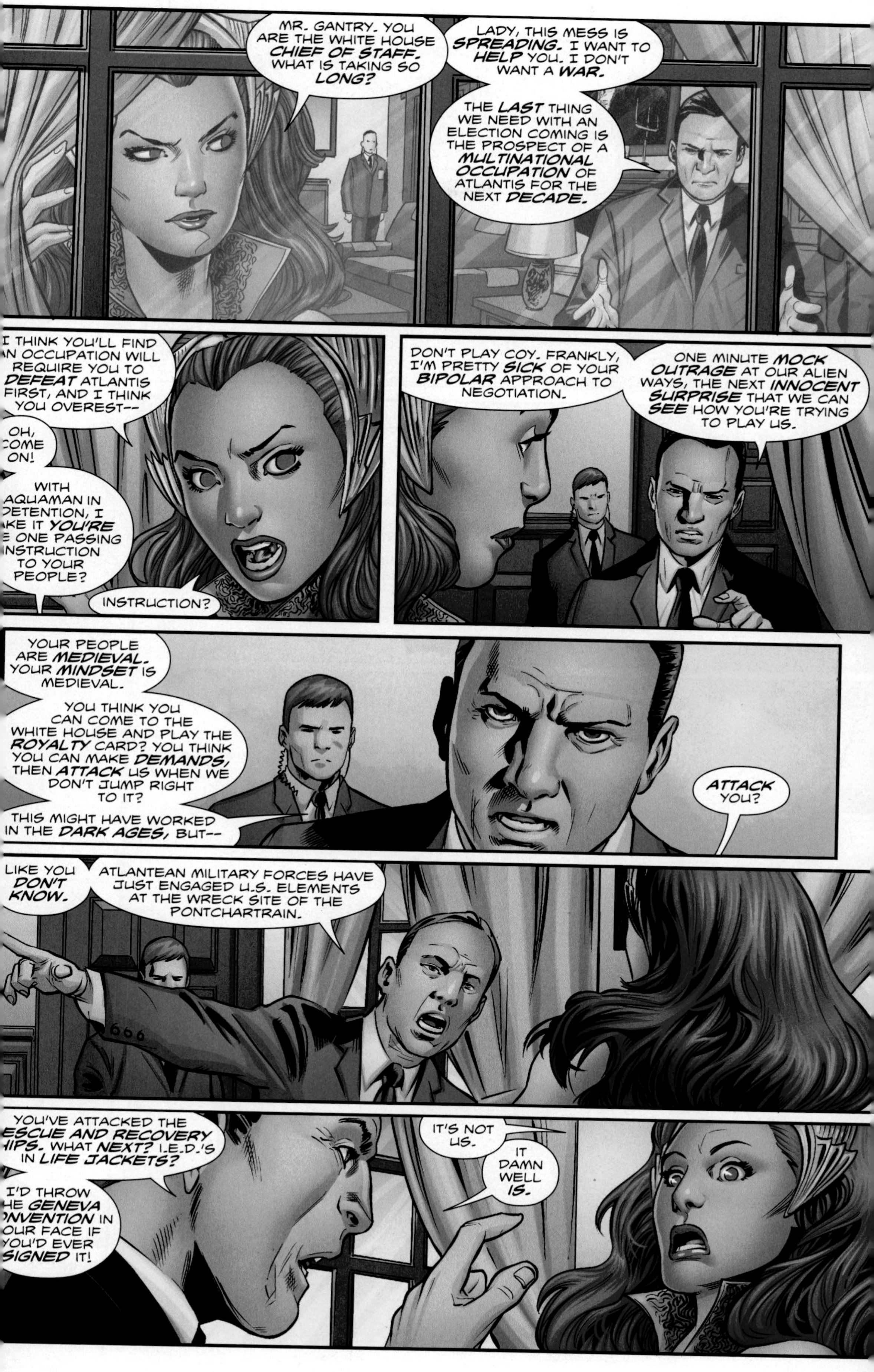

MR. GANTRY. YOU ARE THE WHITE HOUSE CHIEF OF STAFF. WHAT IS TAKING SO LONG?
LADY, THIS MESS IS SPREADING. I WANT TO HELP YOU. I DON'T WANT A WAR.
THE LAST THING WE NEED WITH AN ELECTION COMING IS THE PROSPECT OF A MULTINATIONAL OCCUPATION OF ATLANTIS FOR THE NEXT DECADE.
I THINK YOU'LL FIND N OCCUPATION WILL REQUIRE YOU TO DEFEAT ATLANTIS FIRST, AND I THINK YOU OVEREST--
OH, COME ON!
WITH AQUAMAN IN DETENTION, I AKE IT YOU'RE E ONE PASSING INSTRUCTION TO YOUR PEOPLE?
INSTRUCTION?
DON'T PLAY COY. FRANKLY, I'M PRETTY SICK OF YOUR BIPOLAR APPROACH TO NEGOTIATION.
ONE MINUTE MOCK OUTRAGE AT OUR ALIEN WAYS, THE NEXT INNOCENT SURPRISE THAT WE CAN SEE HOW YOU'RE TRYING TO PLAY US.
YOUR PEOPLE ARE MEDIEVAL. YOUR MINDSET IS MEDIEVAL.
YOU THINK YOU CAN COME TO THE WHITE HOUSE AND PLAY THE ROYALTY CARD? YOU THINK YOU CAN MAKE DEMANDS, THEN ATTACK US WHEN WE DON'T JUMP RIGHT TO IT?
THIS MIGHT HAVE WORKED IN THE DARK AGES, BUT--
ATTACK YOU?
LIKE YOU DON'T KNOW.
ATLANTEAN MILITARY FORCES HAVE JUST ENGAGED U.S. ELEMENTS AT THE WRECK SITE OF THE PONTCHARTRAIN.
YOU'VE ATTACKED THE ESCUE AND RECOVERY HIPS. WHAT NEXT? I.E.D.'S IN LIFE JACKETS?
I'D THROW HE GENEVA ONVENTION IN OUR FACE IF YOU'D EVER SIGNED IT!
IT'S NOT US.
IT DAMN WELL IS.

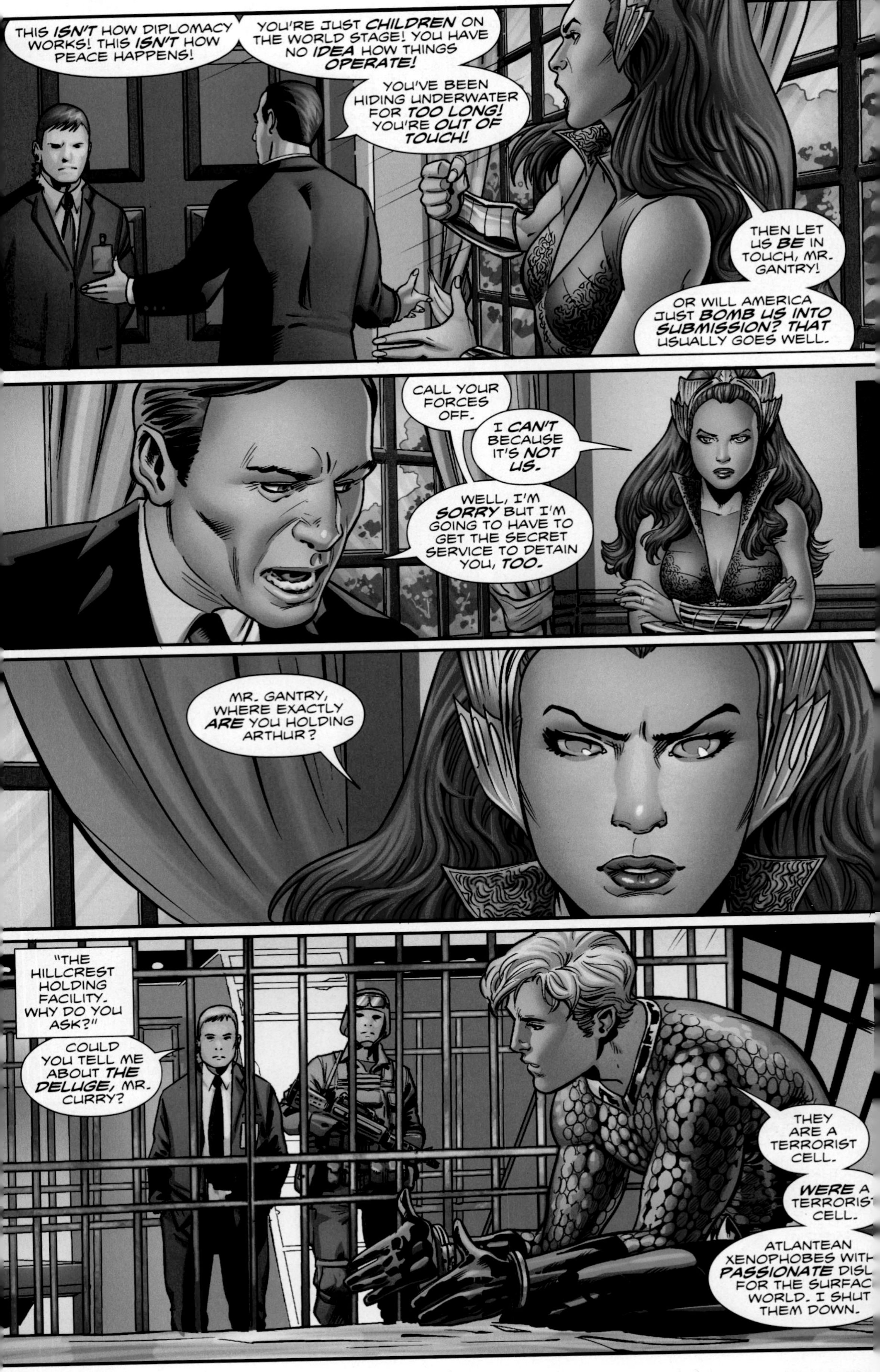
THIS ISN'T HOW DIPLOMACY WORKS! THIS ISN'T HOW PEACE HAPPENS!
YOU'RE JUST CHILDREN ON THE WORLD STAGE! YOU HAVE NO IDEA HOW THINGS OPERATE!
YOU'VE BEEN HIDING UNDERWATER FOR TOO LONG! YOU'RE OUT OF TOUCH!
THEN LET US BE IN TOUCH, MR. GANTRY!
OR WILL AMERICA JUST BOMB US INTO SUBMISSION? THAT USUALLY GOES WELL.
CALL YOUR FORCES OFF.
I CAN'T BECAUSE IT'S NOT US.
WELL, I'M SORRY BUT I'M GOING TO HAVE TO GET THE SECRET SERVICE TO DETAIN YOU, TOO.
MR. GANTRY, WHERE EXACTLY ARE YOU HOLDING ARTHUR?
"THE HILLCREST HOLDING FACILITY. WHY DO YOU ASK?"
COULD YOU TELL ME ABOUT THE DELUGE, MR. CURRY?
THEY ARE A TERRORIST CELL.
WERE A TERRORIST CELL.
ATLANTEAN XENOPHOBES WITH PASSIONATE DISL FOR THE SURFAC WORLD. I SHUT THEM DOWN.

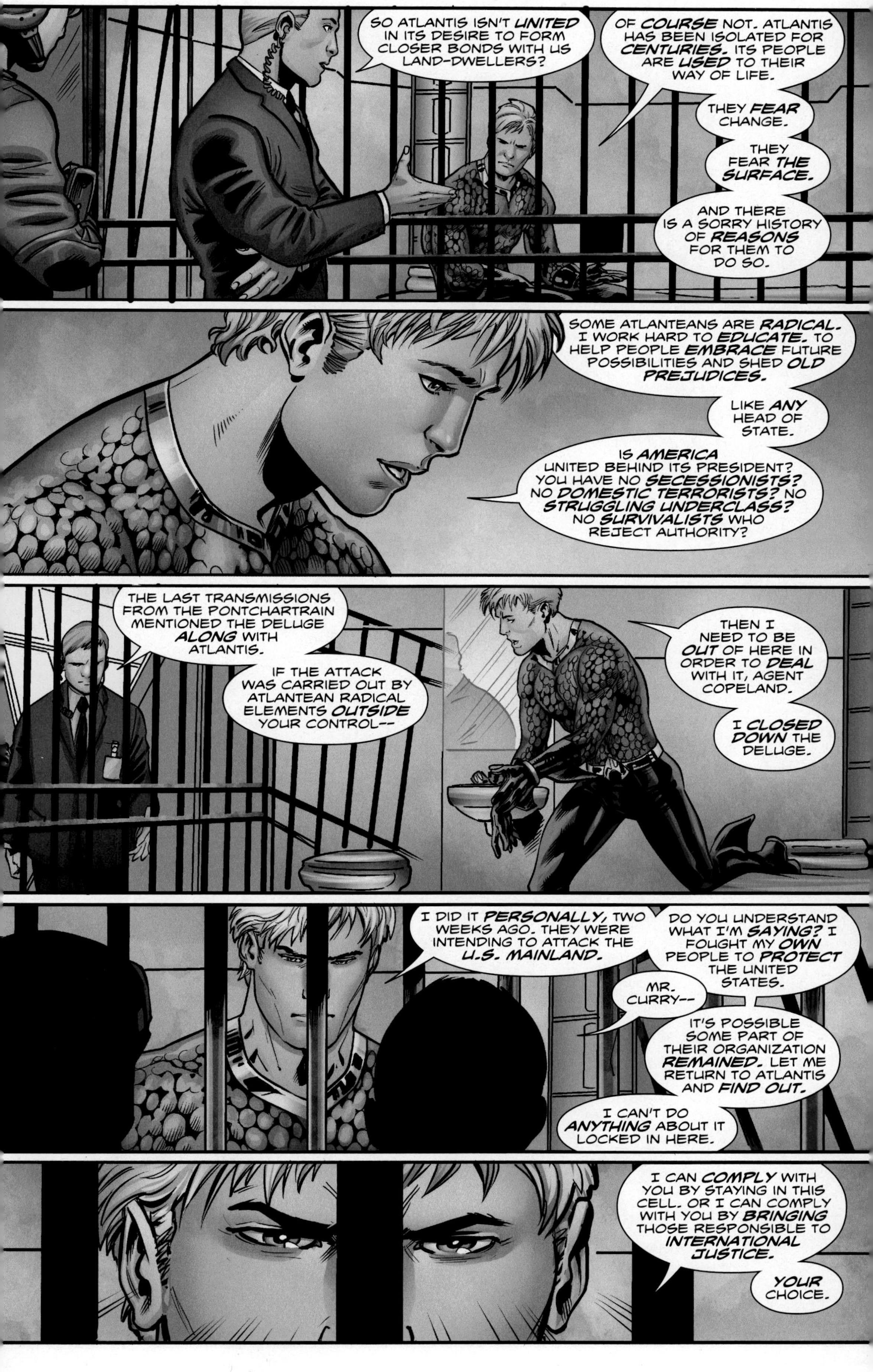
SO ATLANTIS ISN'T UNITED IN ITS DESIRE TO FORM CLOSER BONDS WITH US LAND-DWELLERS?
OF COURSE NOT. ATLANTIS HAS BEEN ISOLATED FOR CENTURIES. ITS PEOPLE ARE USED TO THEIR WAY OF LIFE.
THEY FEAR CHANGE.
THEY FEAR THE SURFACE.
AND THERE IS A SORRY HISTORY OF REASONS FOR THEM TO DO SO.
SOME ATLANTEANS ARE RADICAL. I WORK HARD TO EDUCATE. TO HELP PEOPLE EMBRACE FUTURE POSSIBILITIES AND SHED OLD PREJUDICES.
LIKE ANY HEAD OF STATE.
IS AMERICA UNITED BEHIND ITS PRESIDENT? YOU HAVE NO SECESSIONISTS? NO DOMESTIC TERRORISTS? NO STRUGGLING UNDERCLASS? NO SURVIVALISTS WHO REJECT AUTHORITY?
THE LAST TRANSMISSIONS FROM THE PONTCHARTRAIN MENTIONED THE DELUGE ALONG WITH ATLANTIS.
IF THE ATTACK WAS CARRIED OUT BY ATLANTEAN RADICAL ELEMENTS OUTSIDE YOUR CONTROL--
THEN I NEED TO BE OUT OF HERE IN ORDER TO DEAL WITH IT, AGENT COPELAND.
I CLOSED DOWN THE DELUGE.
I DID IT PERSONALLY, TWO WEEKS AGO. THEY WERE INTENDING TO ATTACK THE U.S. MAINLAND.
DO YOU UNDERSTAND WHAT I'M SAYING? I FOUGHT MY OWN PEOPLE TO PROTECT THE UNITED STATES.
MR. CURRY--
IT'S POSSIBLE SOME PART OF THEIR ORGANIZATION REMAINED. LET ME RETURN TO ATLANTIS AND FIND OUT.
I CAN'T DO ANYTHING ABOUT IT LOCKED IN HERE.
I CAN COMPLY WITH YOU BY STAYING IN THIS CELL. OR I CAN COMPLY WITH YOU BY BRINGING THOSE RESPONSIBLE TO INTERNATIONAL JUSTICE.
YOUR CHOICE.

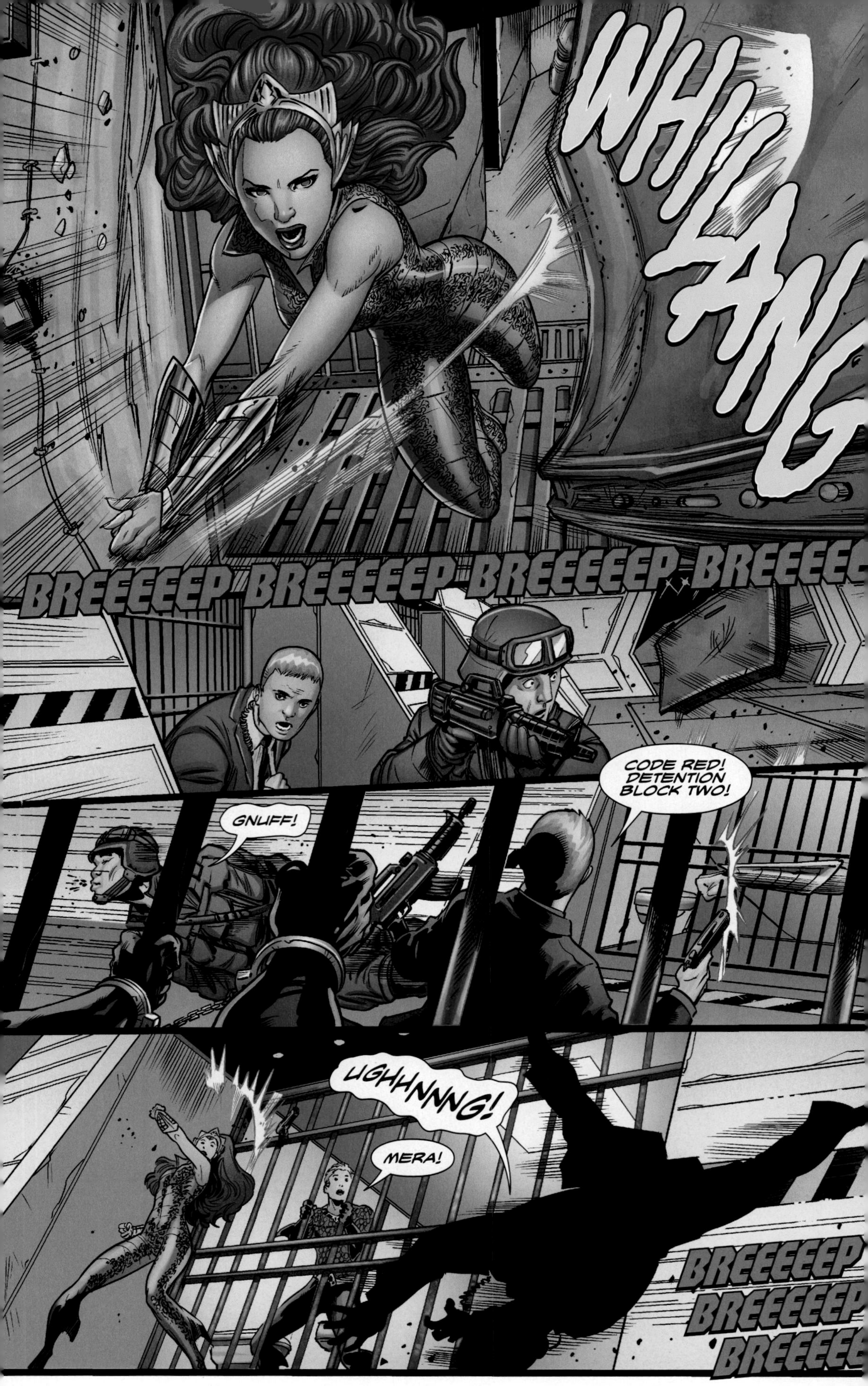
WHHLANG
BREEEEEP BREEEEEP BREEEEEP BREEEEE
CODE RED! DETENTION BLOCK TWO!
GNUFF!
UGHHNNNG!
MERA!
BREEEEEP
BREEEEEP
BREEEEE

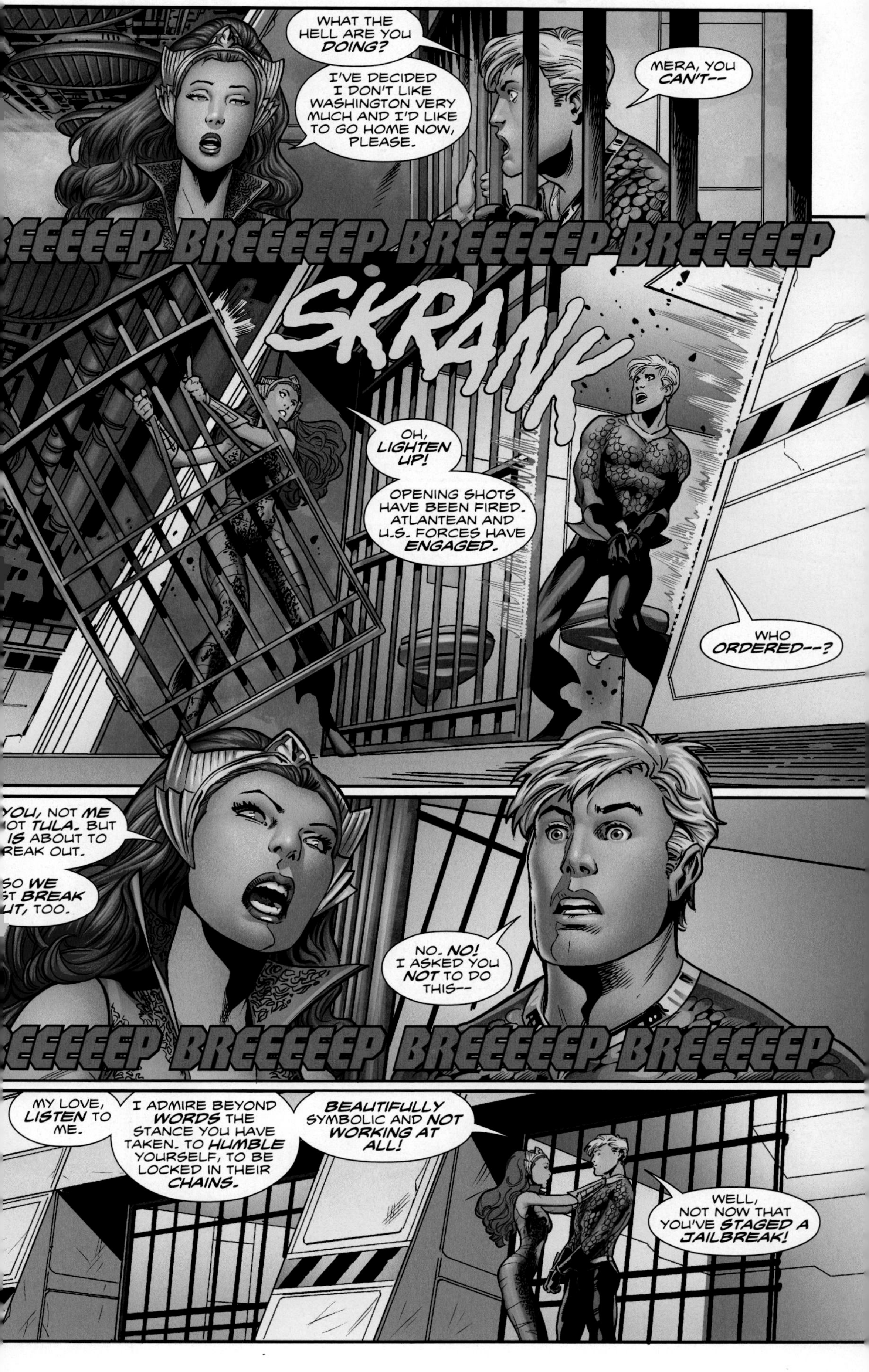
WHAT THE HELL ARE YOU DOING?
I'VE DECIDED I DON'T LIKE WASHINGTON VERY MUCH AND I'D LIKE TO GO HOME NOW, PLEASE.
MERA, YOU CAN'T--
BREEEEEP BREEEEEP BREEEEEP BREEEEEP
SKRANK
OH, LIGHTEN UP!
OPENING SHOTS HAVE BEEN FIRED. ATLANTEAN AND U.S. FORCES HAVE ENGAGED.
WHO ORDERED--?
YOU, NOT ME OT TULA. BUT IS ABOUT TO REAK OUT.
SO WE ST BREAK UT, TOO.
NO. NO! I ASKED YOU NOT TO DO THIS--
BREEEEEP BREEEEEP BREEEEEP BREEEEEP
MY LOVE, LISTEN TO ME.
I ADMIRE BEYOND WORDS THE STANCE YOU HAVE TAKEN. TO HUMBLE YOURSELF, TO BE LOCKED IN THEIR CHAINS.
BEAUTIFULLY SYMBOLIC AND NOT WORKING AT ALL!
WELL, NOT NOW THAT YOU'VE STAGED A JAILBREAK!

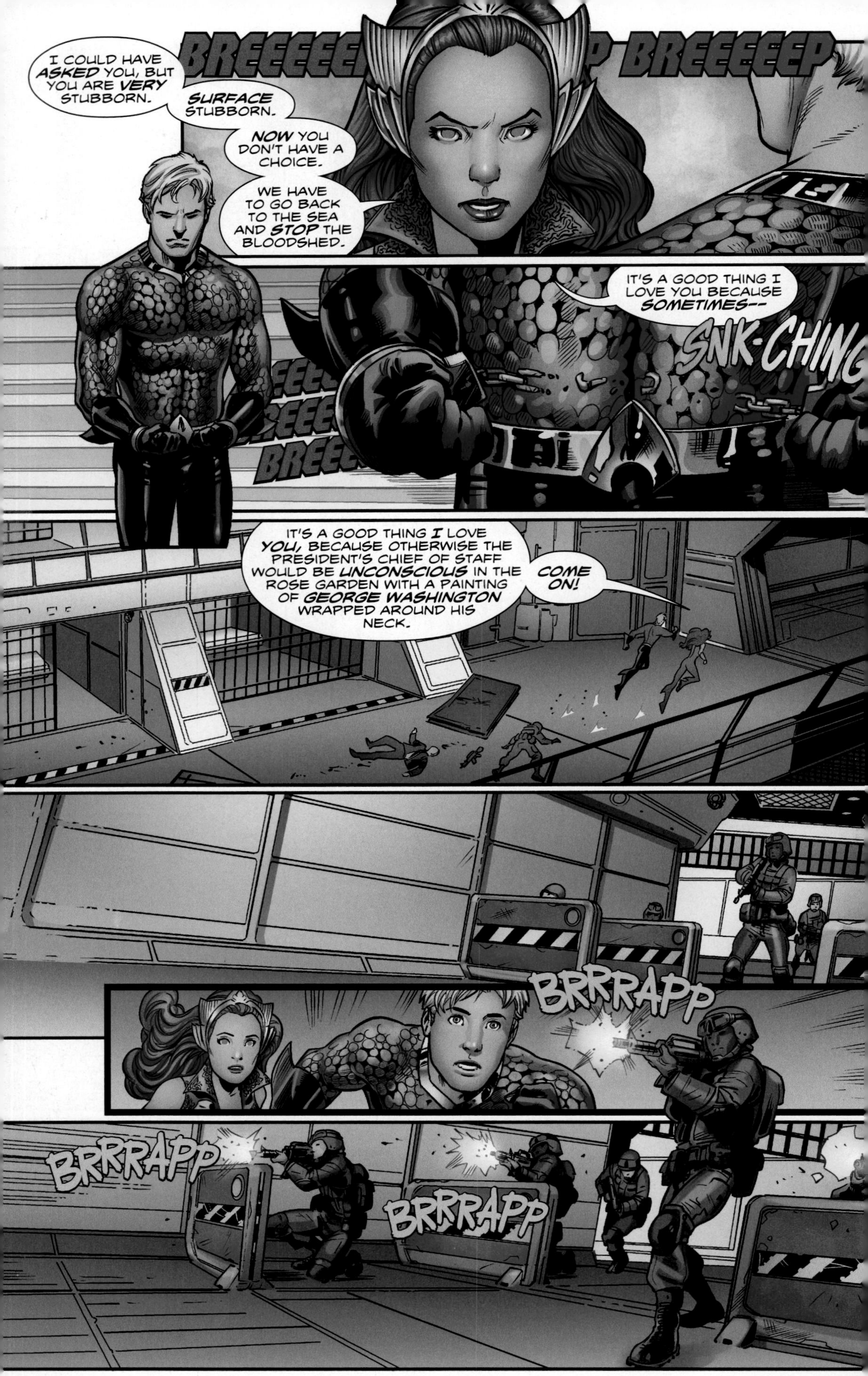
BREEEEEP BREEEEEP
I COULD HAVE ASKED YOU, BUT YOU ARE VERY STUBBORN.
SURFACE STUBBORN.
NOW YOU DON'T HAVE A CHOICE.
WE HAVE TO GO BACK TO THE SEA AND STOP THE BLOODSHED.
IT'S A GOOD THING I LOVE YOU BECAUSE SOMETIMES--
SNK-CHING
IT'S A GOOD THING I LOVE YOU, BECAUSE OTHERWISE THE PRESIDENT'S CHIEF OF STAFF WOULD BE UNCONSCIOUS IN THE ROSE GARDEN WITH A PAINTING OF GEORGE WASHINGTON WRAPPED AROUND HIS NECK.
COME ON!
BRRRAPP
BRRRAPP
BRRRAPP

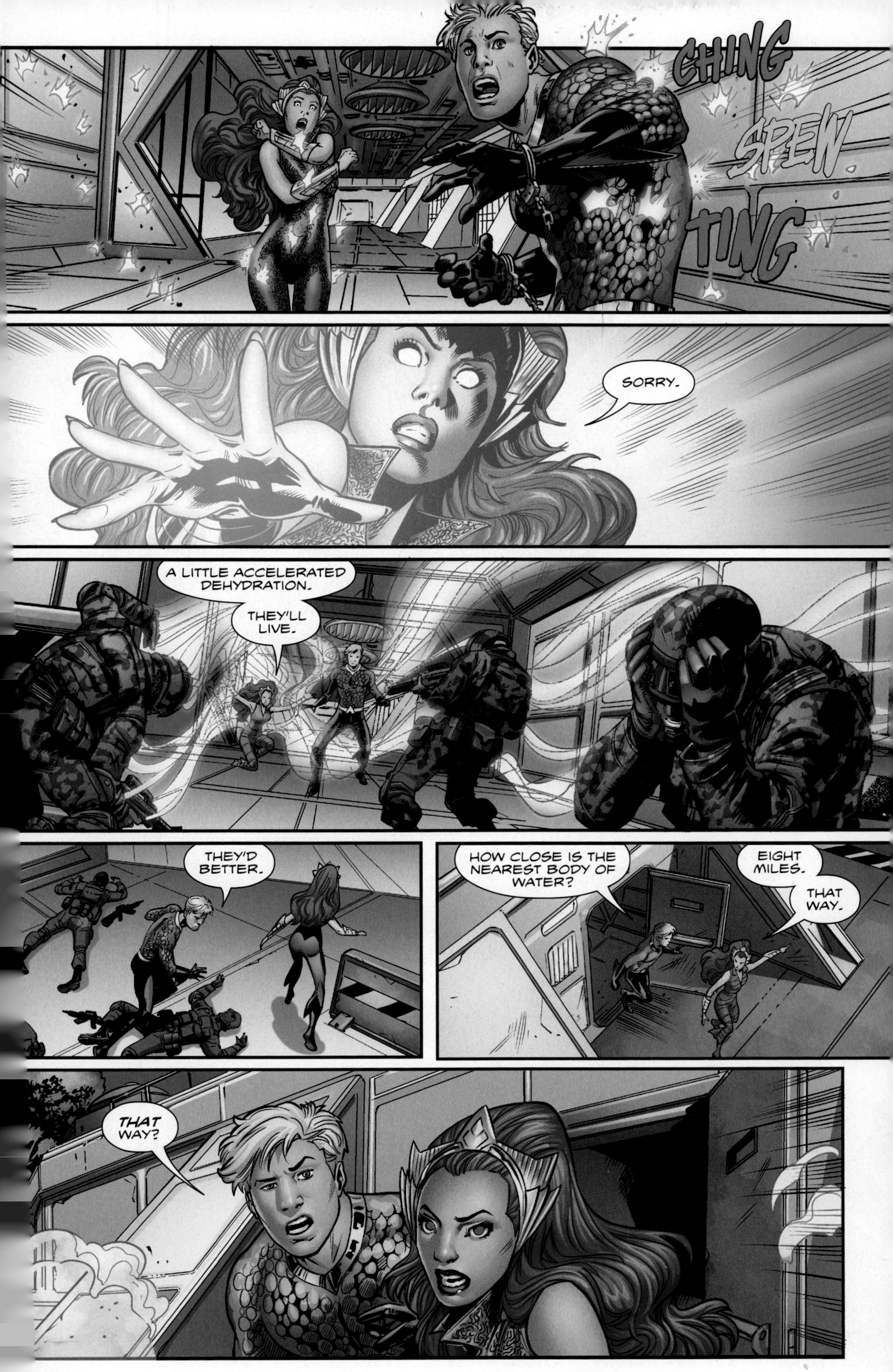
CHING
SPEW
TING
SORRY.
A LITTLE ACCELERATED DEHYDRATION.
THEY'LL LIVE.
THEY'D BETTER.
HOW CLOSE IS THE NEAREST BODY OF WATER?
EIGHT MILES.
THAT WAY.
THAT WAY?

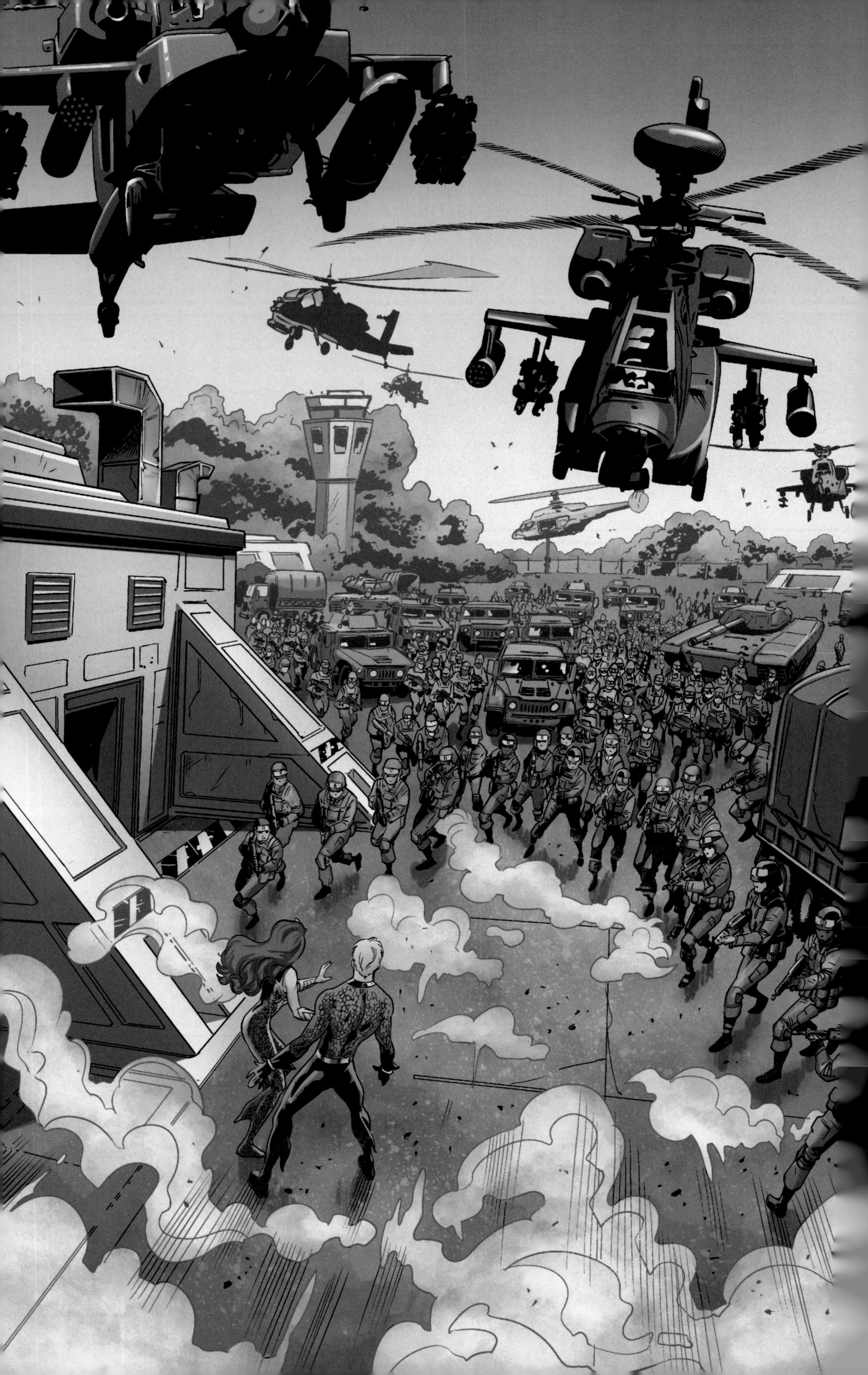

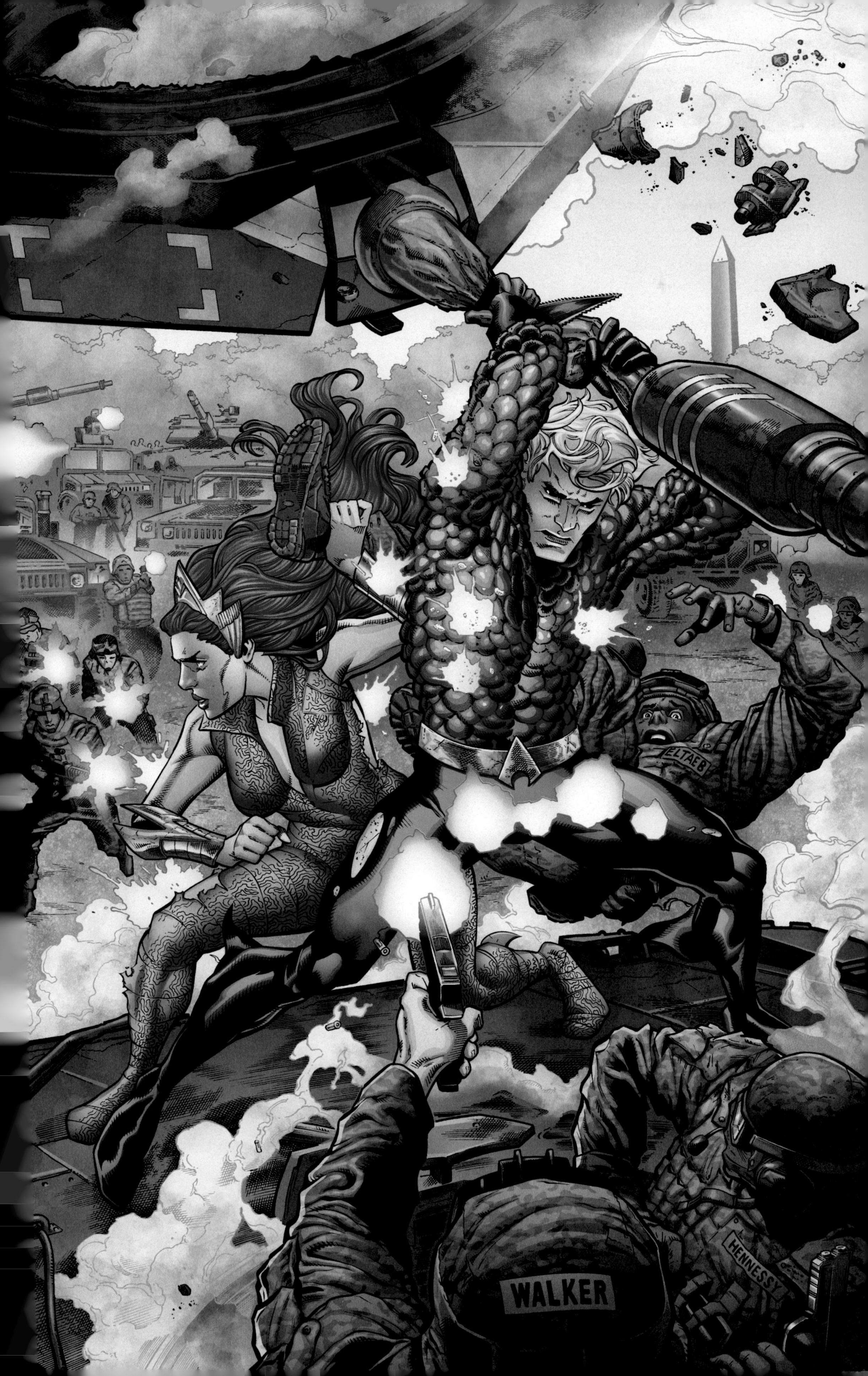
ELTAEB
HENNESSY
WALKER

PART FIVE: EXECUTIVE SANCTION

DAN ABNETT Writer * PHILIPPE BRIONES Artist * GABE ELTAEB Colorist * PAT BROSSEAU Letterer

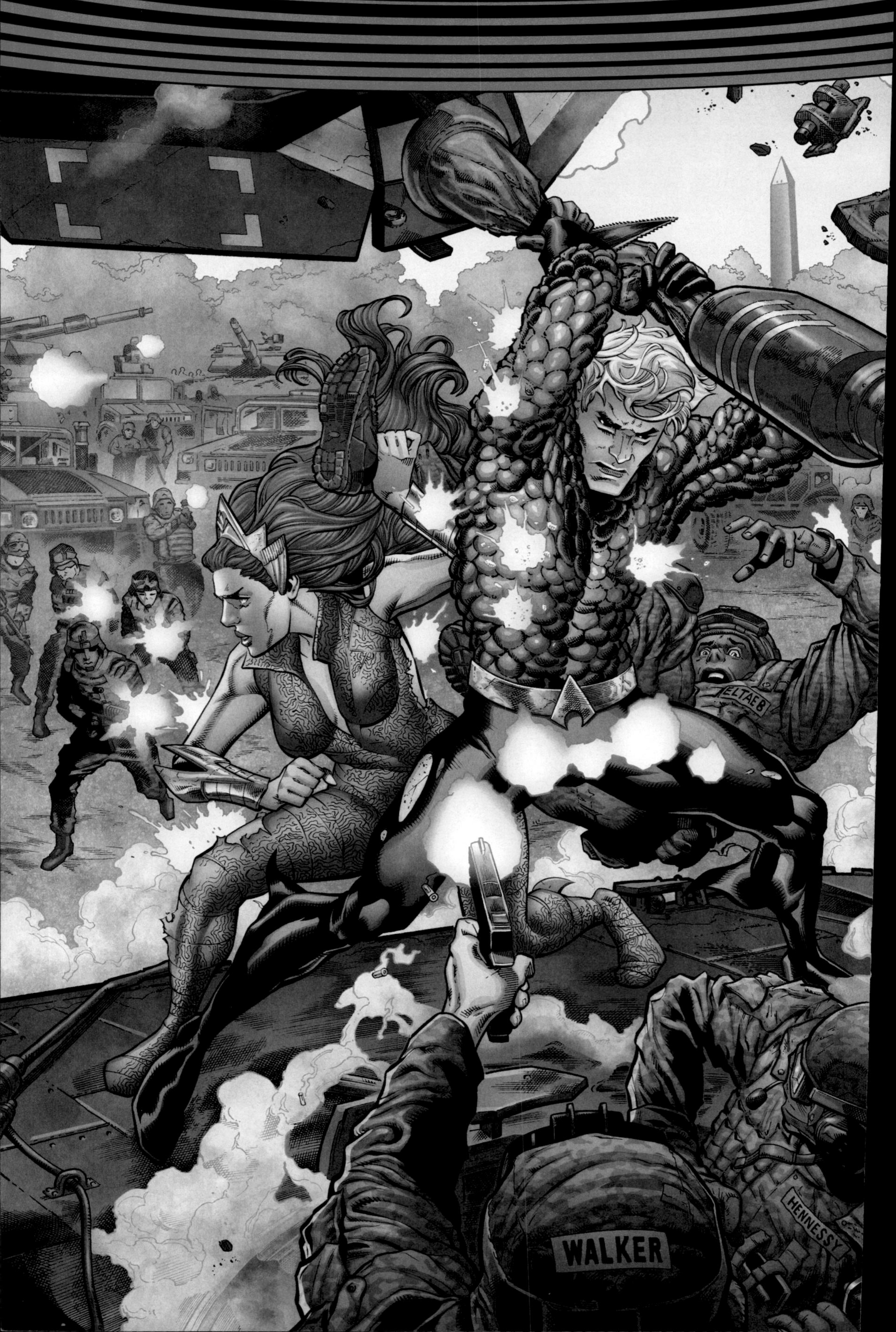

ELTAEB
HENNESSY
WALKER

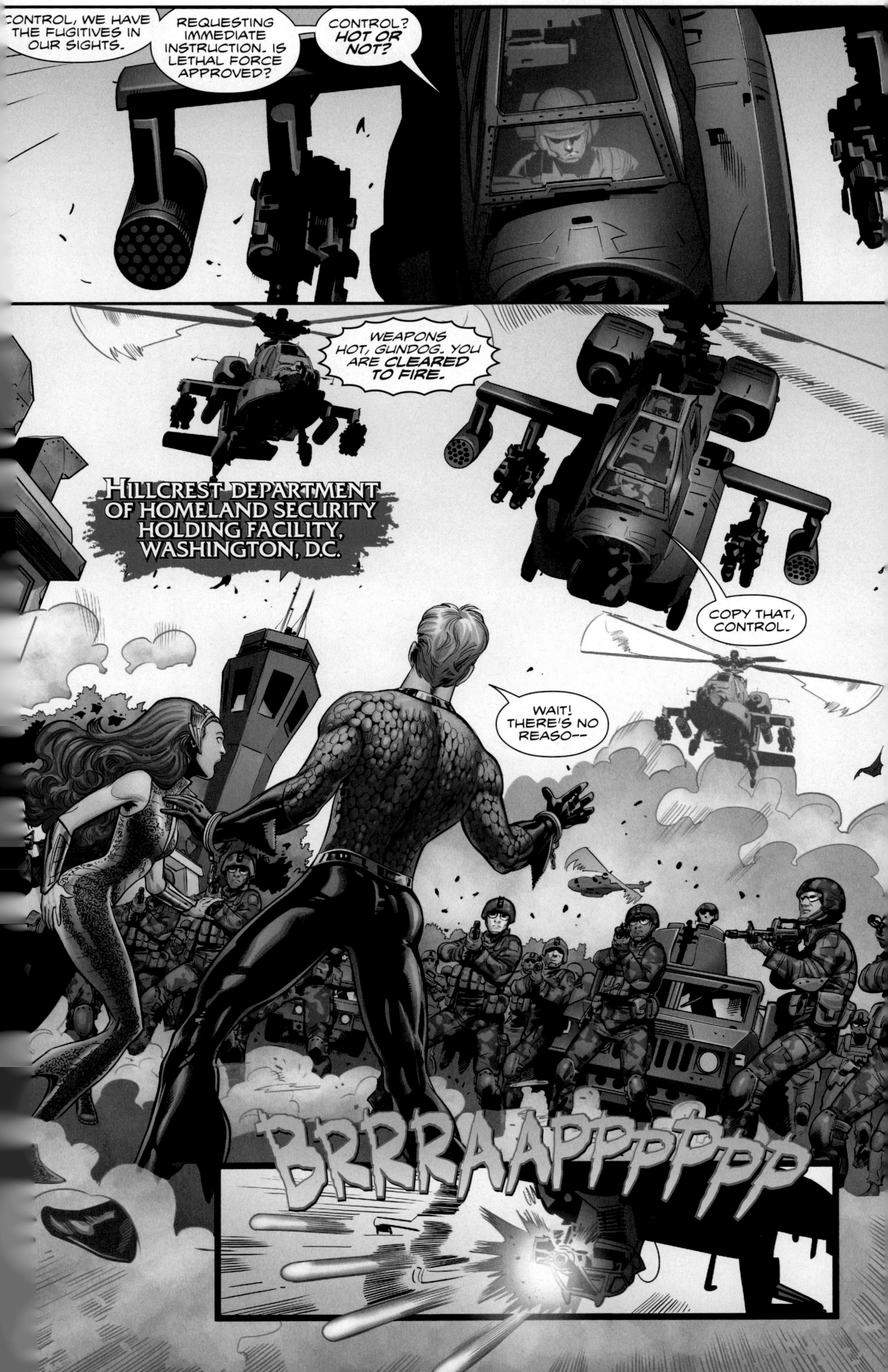

CONTROL, WE HAVE THE FUGITIVES IN OUR SIGHTS.
REQUESTING IMMEDIATE INSTRUCTION. IS LETHAL FORCE APPROVED?
CONTROL? HOT OR NOT?
WEAPONS HOT, GUNDOG. YOU ARE CLEARED TO FIRE.
HILLCREST DEPARTMENT OF HOMELAND SECURITY HOLDING FACILITY, WASHINGTON, D.C.
COPY THAT, CONTROL.
WAIT! THERE'S NO REASO--
BRRRAAPPPPPP

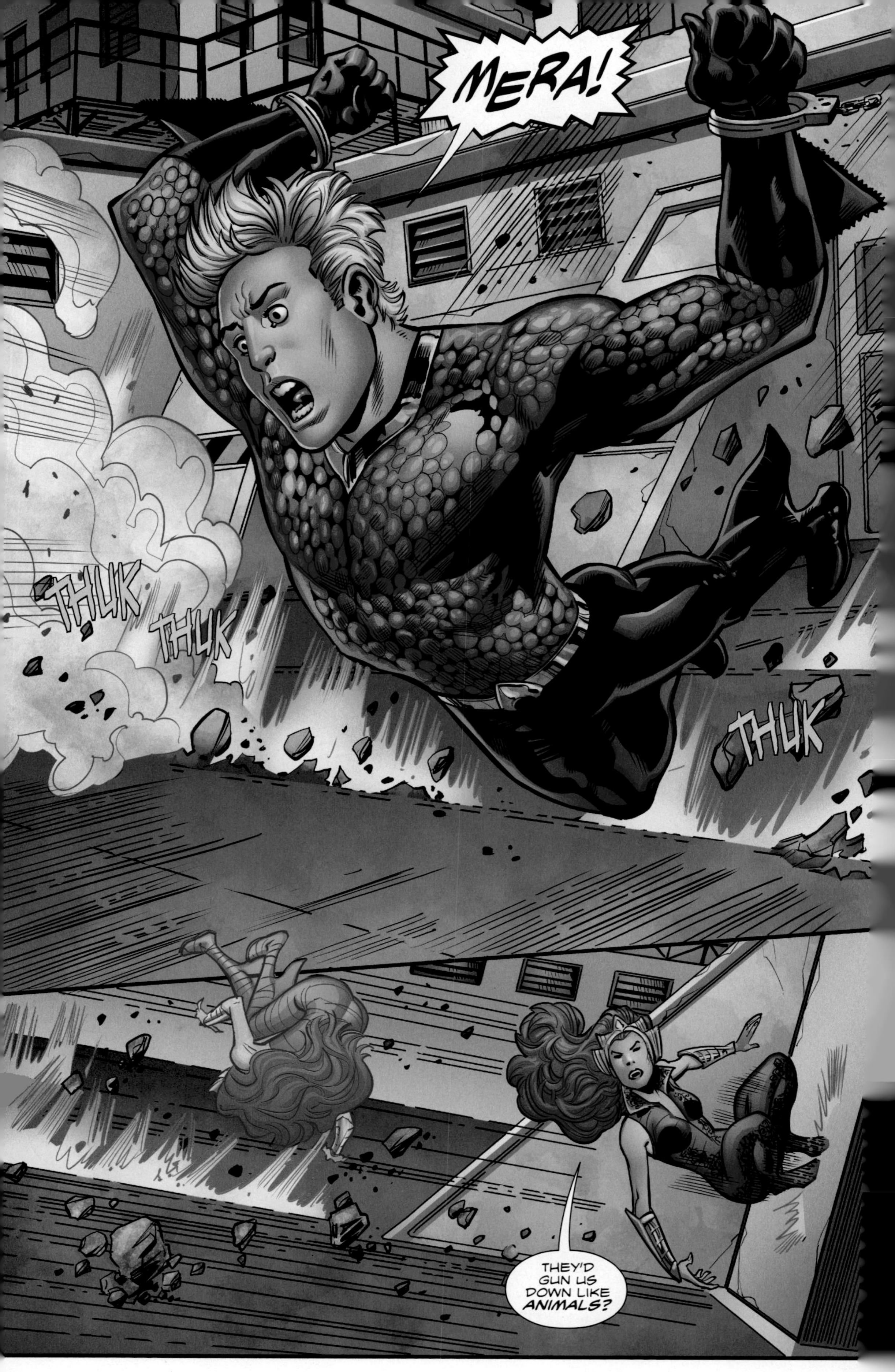
MERA!
THUK
THUK
THUK
THEY'D GUN US DOWN LIKE *ANIMALS?*

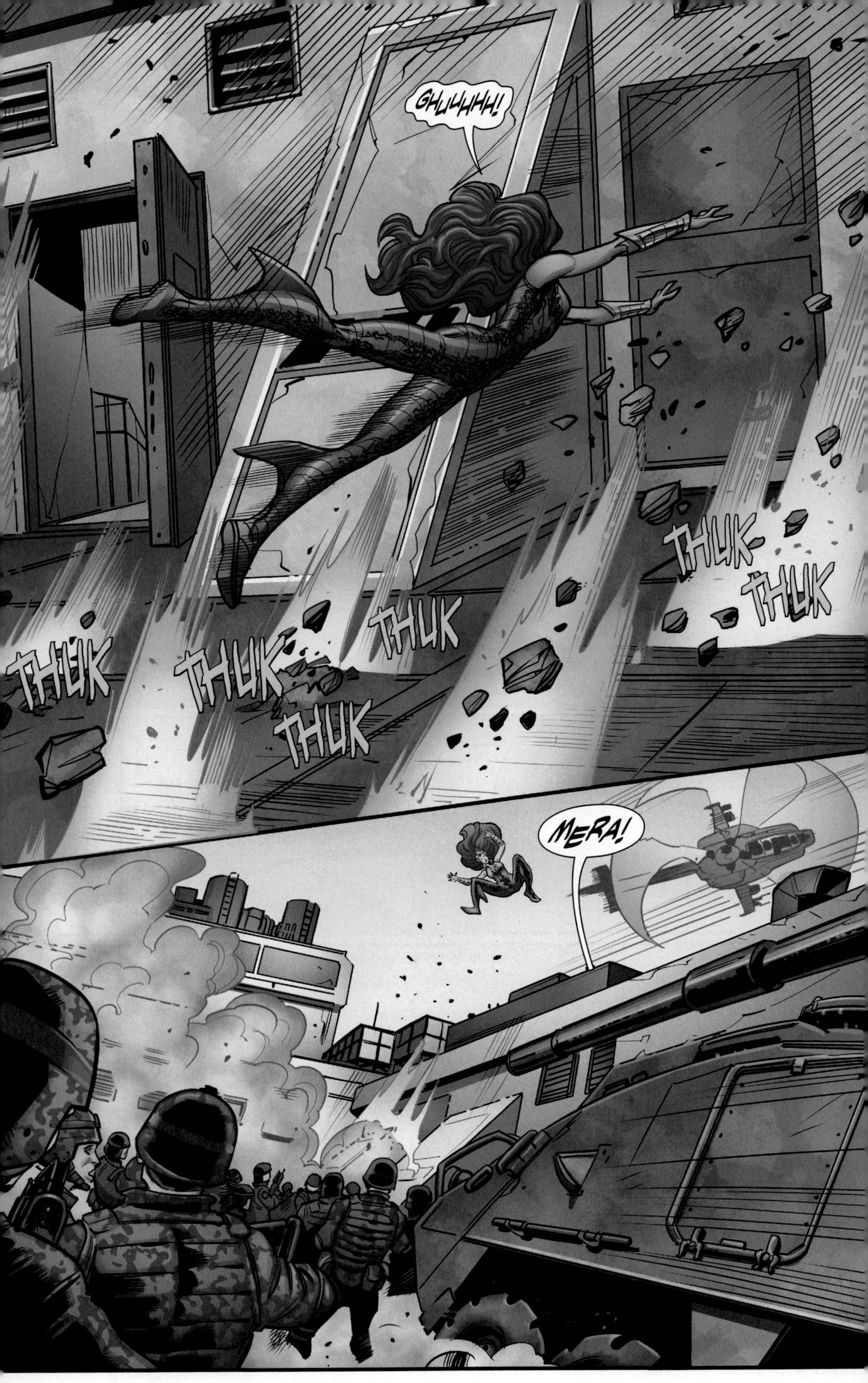
GHUUHHH!
THUK
THUK
THUK
THUK
THUK
THUK
MERA!

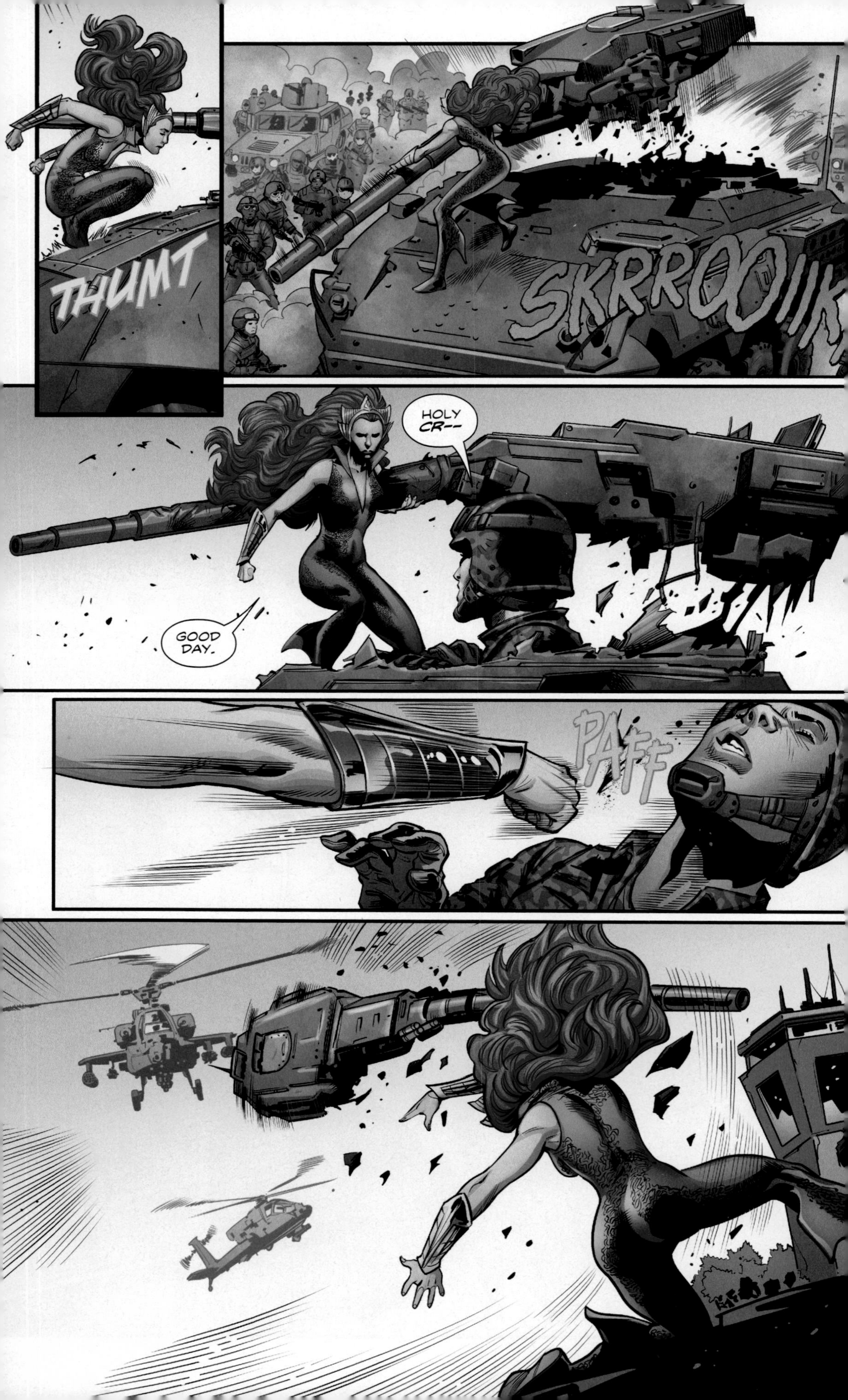
THUMT
SKRROOIK
HOLY CR--
GOOD DAY.
PAFF

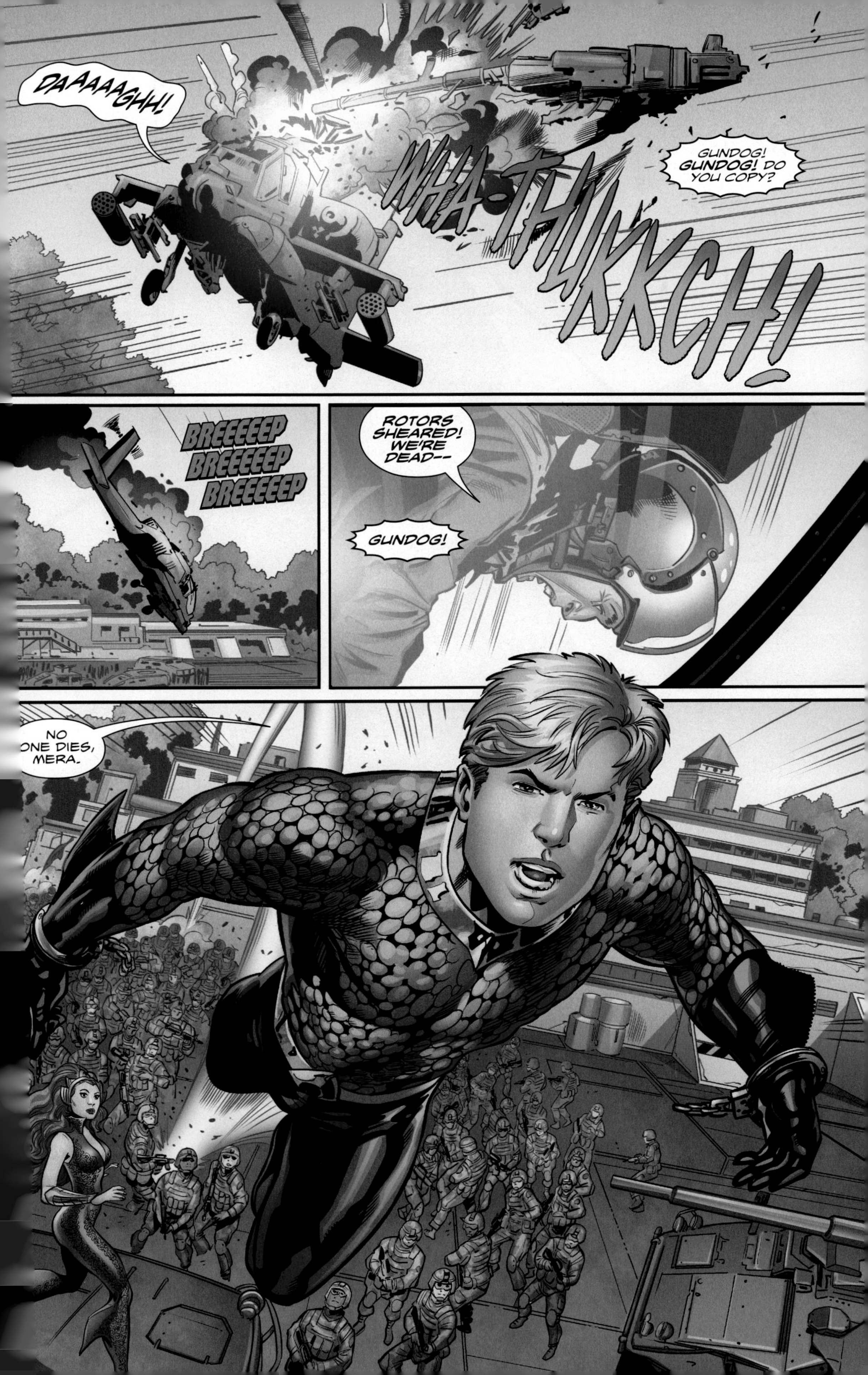
DAAAAAGHH!
WHA-THUKKCH!
GUNDOG! GUNDOG! DO YOU COPY?
BREEEEEP
BREEEEEP
BREEEEEP
ROTORS SHEARED! WE'RE DEAD--
GUNDOG!
NO ONE DIES, MERA.

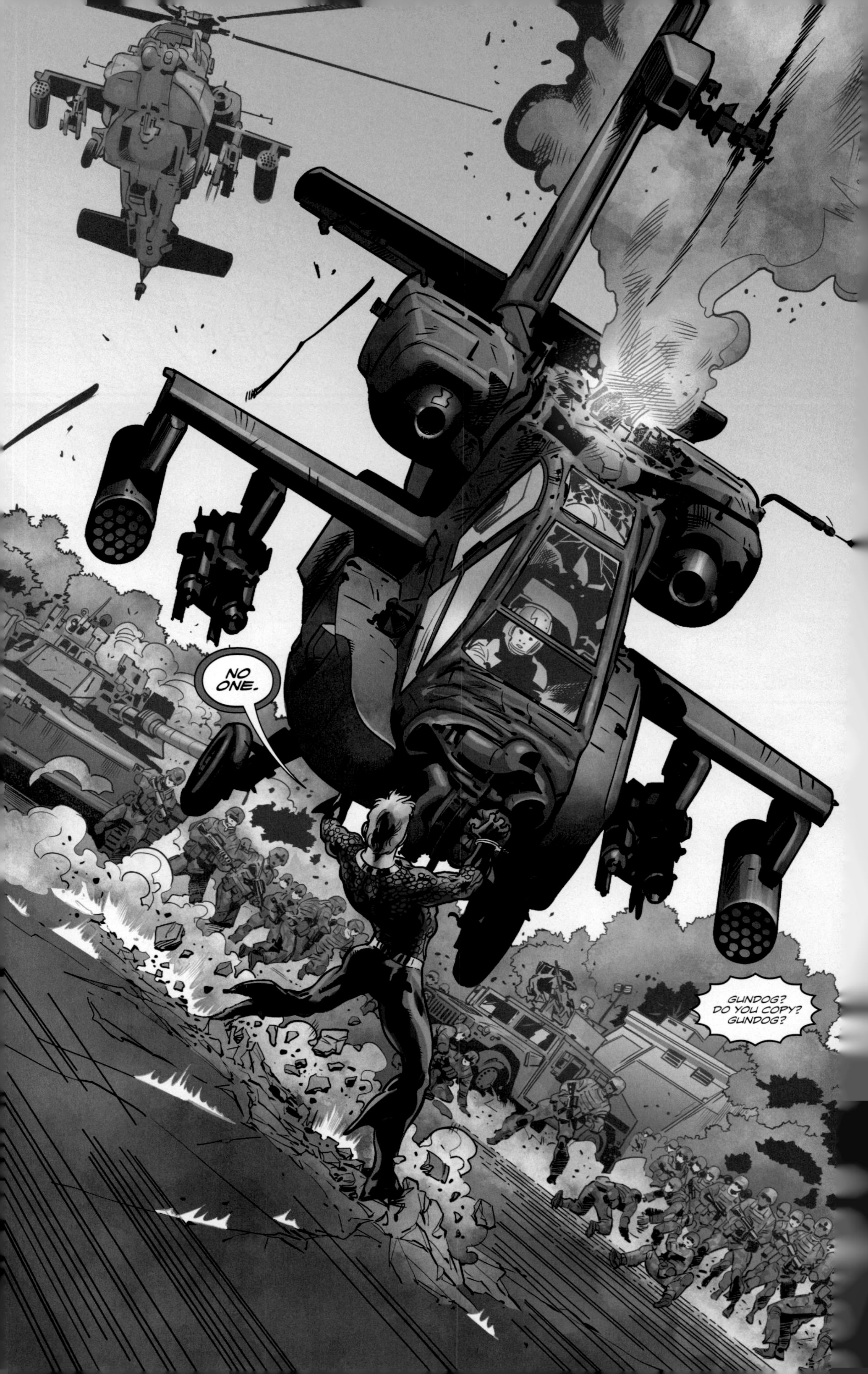
NO ONE.
GUNDOG? DO YOU COPY? GUNDOG?

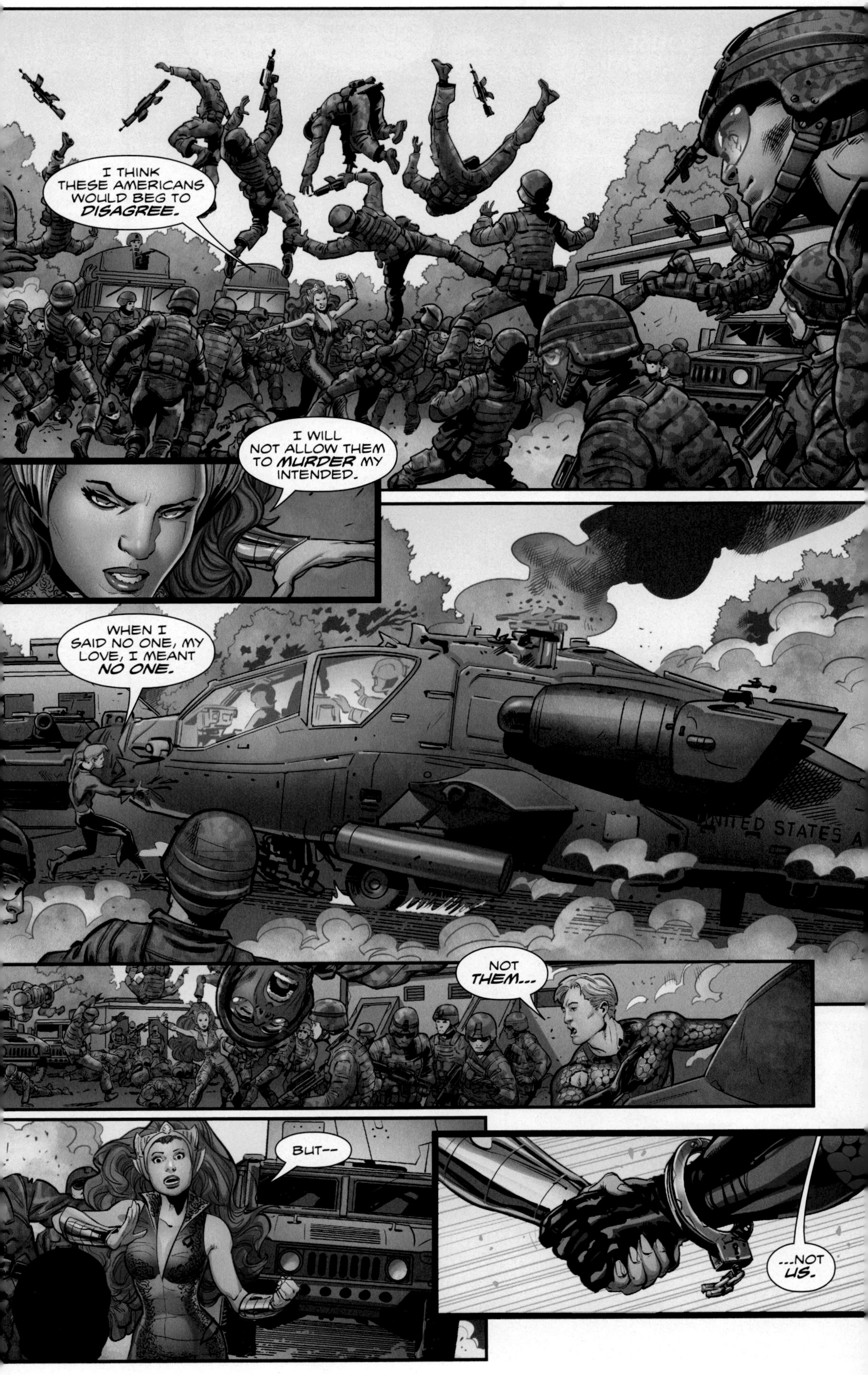
I THINK THESE AMERICANS WOULD BEG TO *DISAGREE.*
I WILL NOT ALLOW THEM TO *MURDER* MY INTENDED.
WHEN I SAID NO ONE, MY LOVE, I MEANT *NO ONE.*
UNITED STATES A
NOT *THEM...*
BUT--
...NOT *US.*

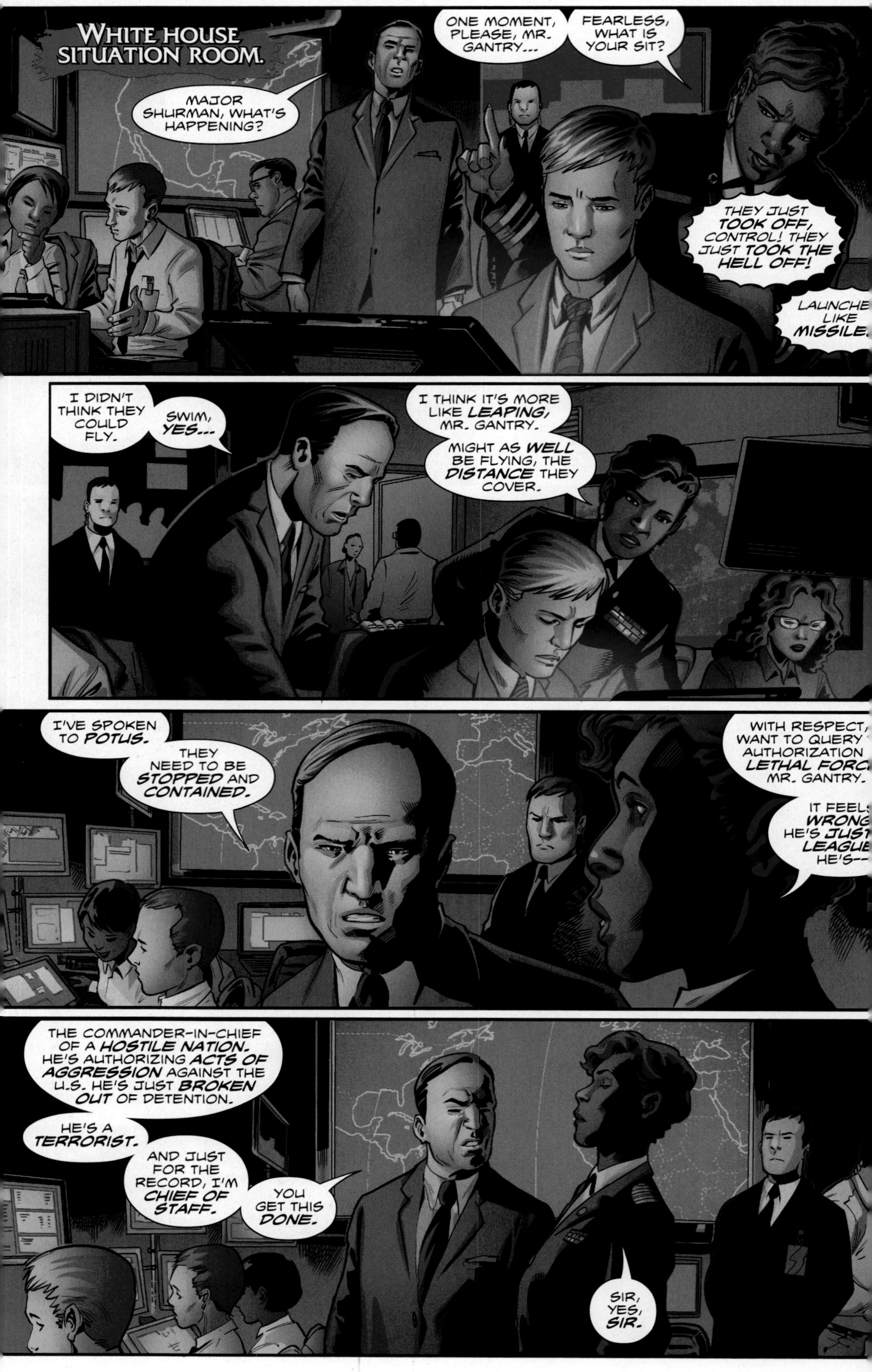
WHITE HOUSE SITUATION ROOM.
MAJOR SHURMAN, WHAT'S HAPPENING?
ONE MOMENT, PLEASE, MR. GANTRY...
FEARLESS, WHAT IS YOUR SIT?
THEY JUST TOOK OFF, CONTROL! THEY JUST TOOK THE HELL OFF!
LAUNCHE LIKE MISSILE
I DIDN'T THINK THEY COULD FLY.
SWIM, YES...
I THINK IT'S MORE LIKE LEAPING, MR. GANTRY.
MIGHT AS WELL BE FLYING, THE DISTANCE THEY COVER.
I'VE SPOKEN TO POTUS.
THEY NEED TO BE STOPPED AND CONTAINED.
WITH RESPECT, WANT TO QUERY AUTHORIZATION LETHAL FORC MR. GANTRY.
IT FEELS WRONG HE'S JUST LEAGUE HE'S--
THE COMMANDER-IN-CHIEF OF A HOSTILE NATION. HE'S AUTHORIZING ACTS OF AGGRESSION AGAINST THE U.S. HE'S JUST BROKEN OUT OF DETENTION.
HE'S A TERRORIST.
AND JUST FOR THE RECORD, I'M CHIEF OF STAFF.
YOU GET THIS DONE.
SIR, YES, SIR.

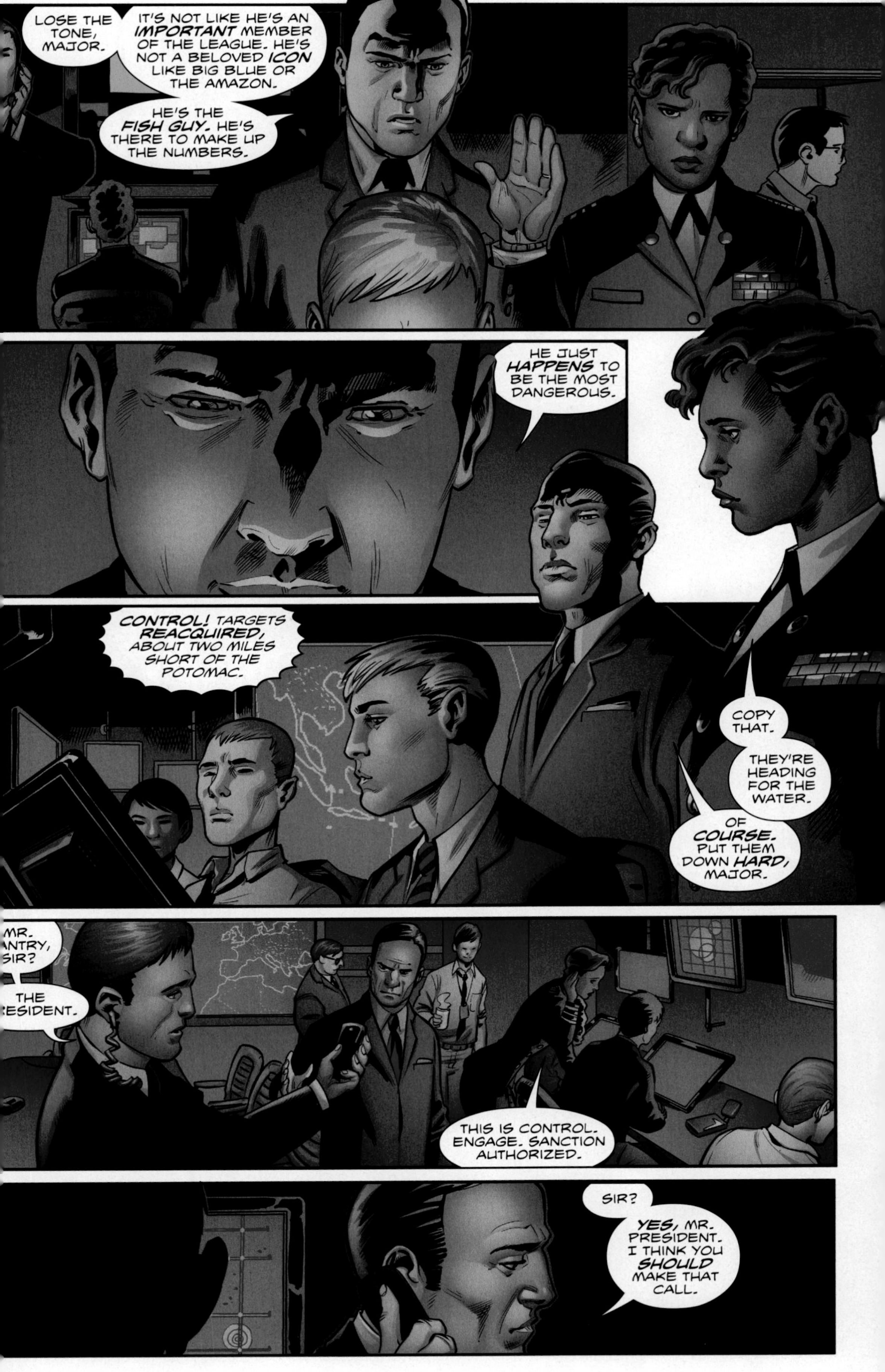
LOSE THE TONE, MAJOR.
IT'S NOT LIKE HE'S AN *IMPORTANT* MEMBER OF THE LEAGUE. HE'S NOT A BELOVED *ICON* LIKE BIG BLUE OR THE AMAZON.
HE'S THE *FISH GUY*. HE'S THERE TO MAKE UP THE NUMBERS.
HE JUST *HAPPENS* TO BE THE MOST DANGEROUS.
CONTROL! TARGETS *REACQUIRED*, ABOUT TWO MILES SHORT OF THE POTOMAC.
COPY THAT.
THEY'RE HEADING FOR THE WATER.
OF *COURSE*. PUT THEM DOWN *HARD*, MAJOR.
MR. ANTRY, SIR?
THE RESIDENT.
THIS IS CONTROL. ENGAGE. SANCTION AUTHORIZED.
SIR?
YES, MR. PRESIDENT. I THINK YOU *SHOULD* MAKE THAT CALL.

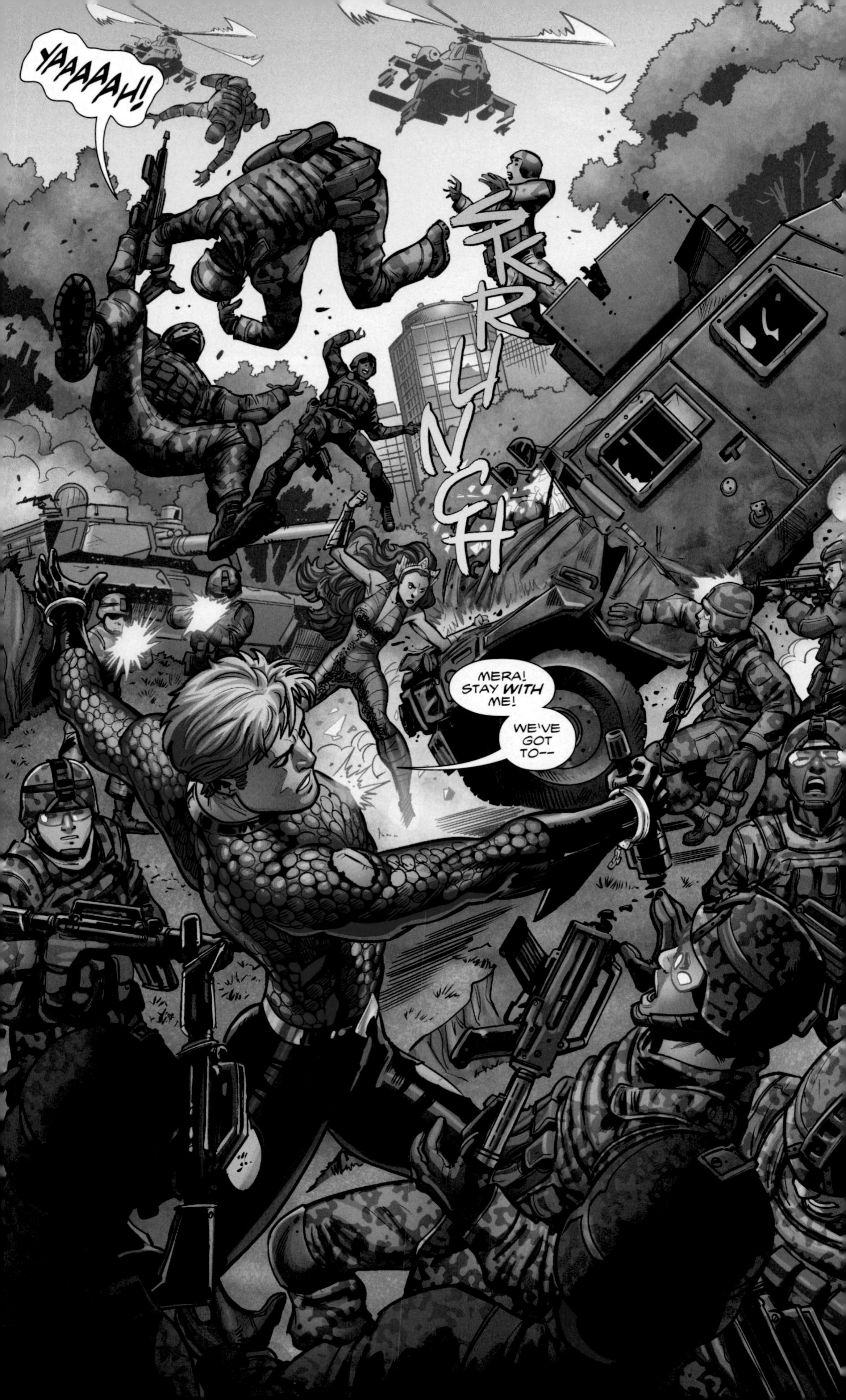
YAAAAAH!
SKRUNCH
MERA! STAY WITH ME!
WE'VE GOT TO--

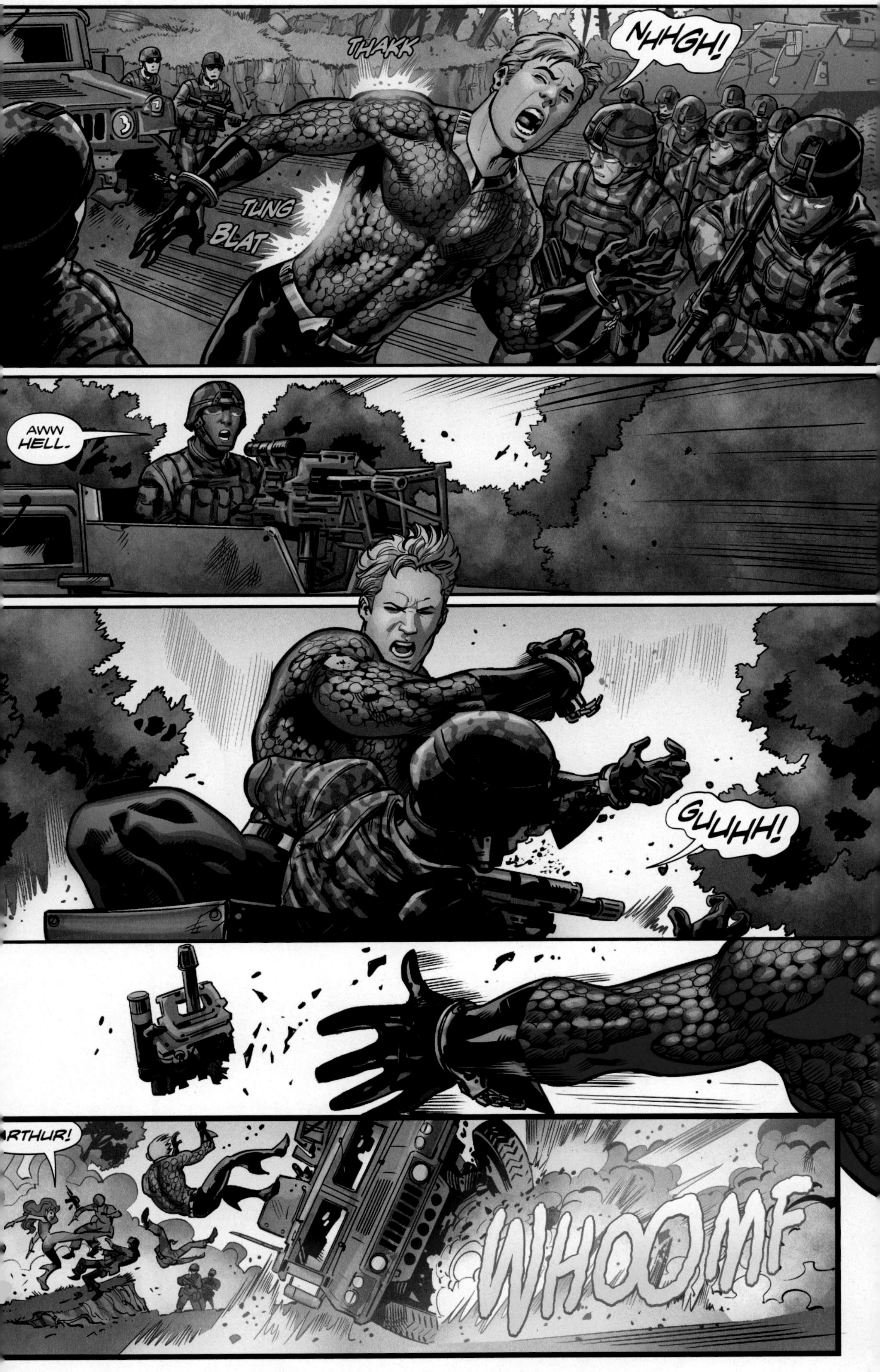
THAKK
NHHGH!
TUNG
BLAT
AWW HELL.
GUUHH!
ARTHUR!
WHOOMF

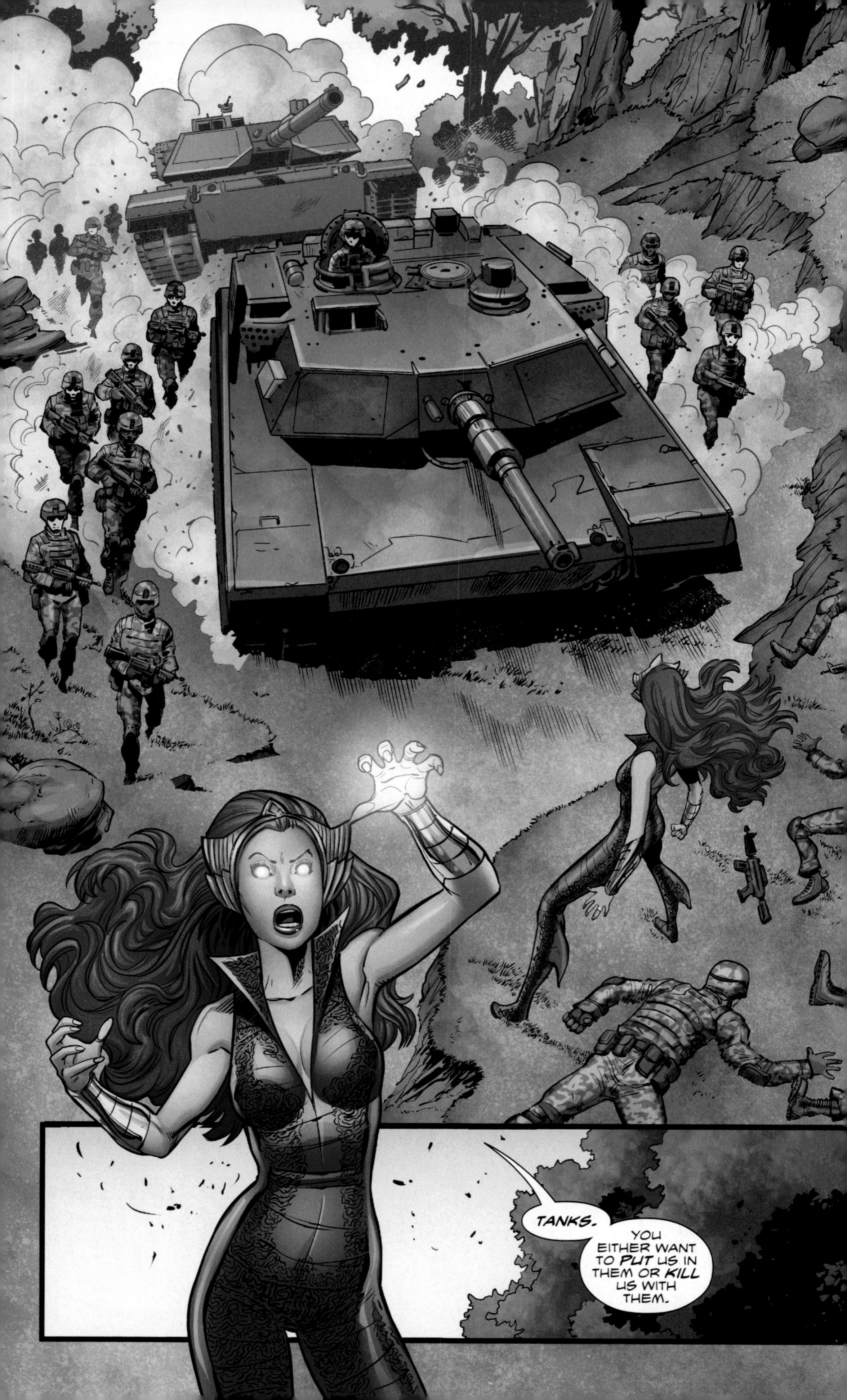
TANKS.
YOU EITHER WANT TO PUT US IN THEM OR KILL US WITH THEM.

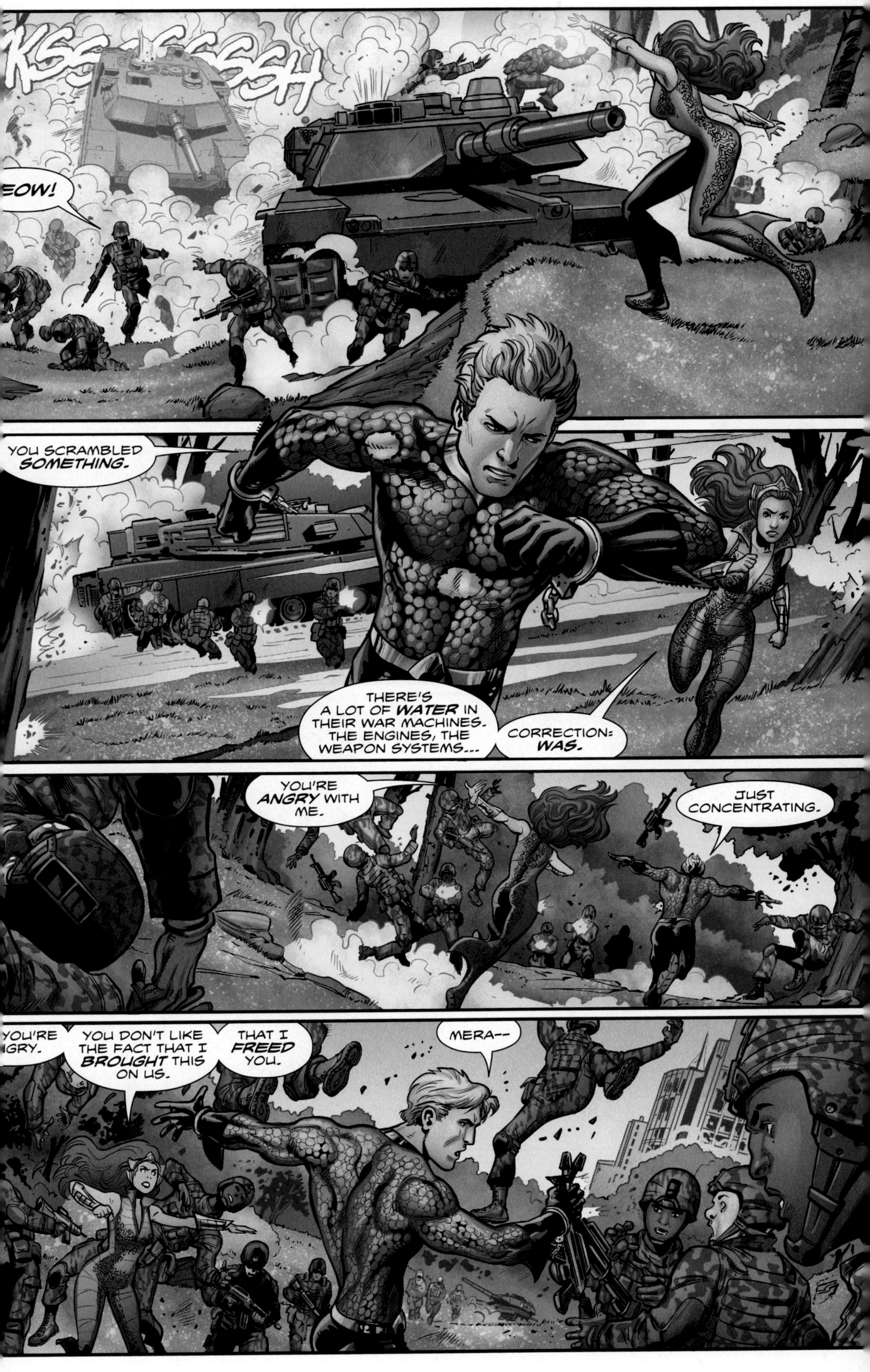
KSSSSSSSH
EOW!
YOU SCRAMBLED SOMETHING.
THERE'S A LOT OF WATER IN THEIR WAR MACHINES. THE ENGINES, THE WEAPON SYSTEMS...
CORRECTION: WAS.
YOU'RE ANGRY WITH ME.
JUST CONCENTRATING.
YOU'RE
NGRY.
YOU DON'T LIKE THE FACT THAT I BROUGHT THIS ON US.
THAT I FREED YOU.
MERA--

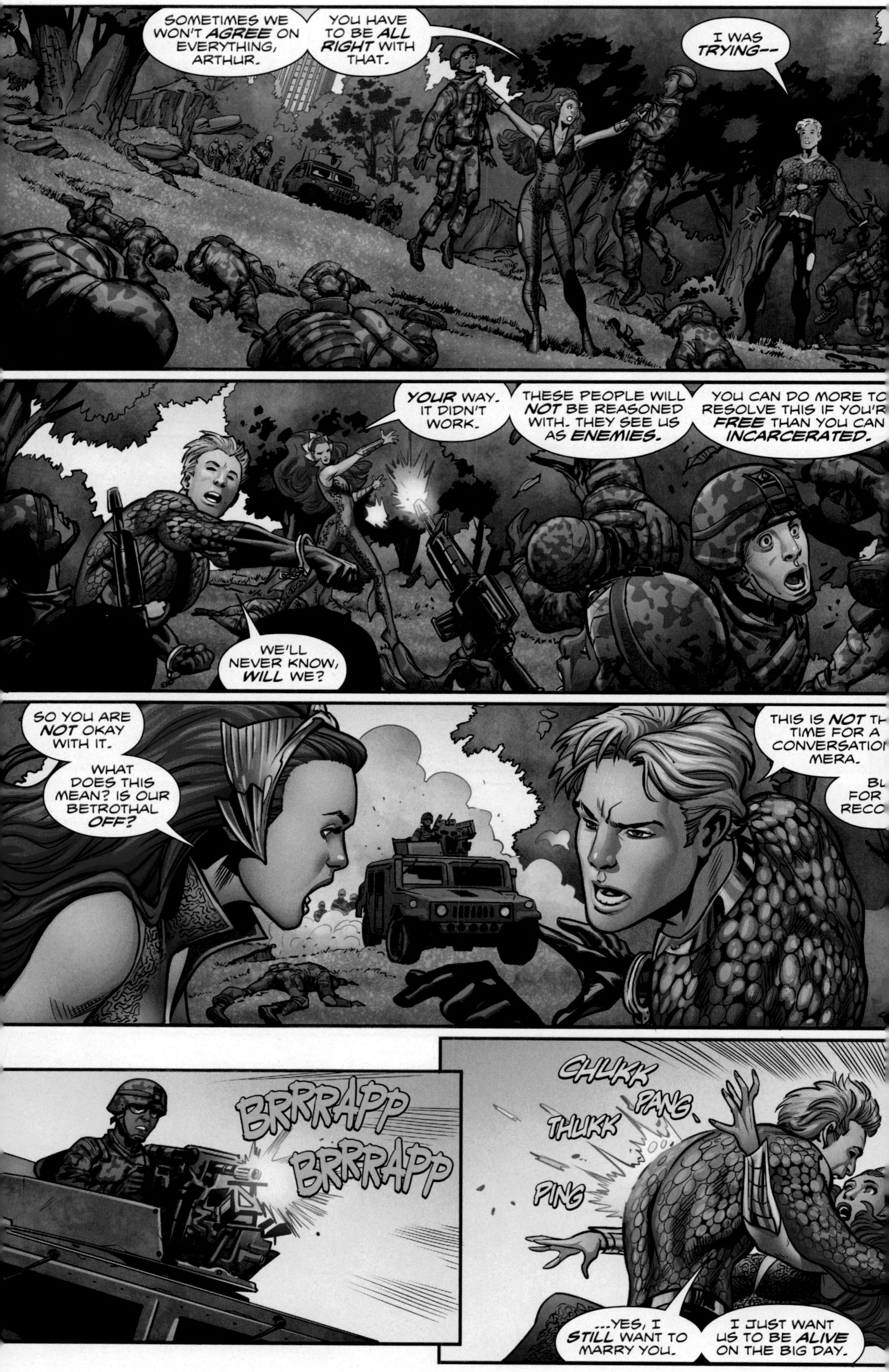
SOMETIMES WE WON'T AGREE ON EVERYTHING, ARTHUR.
YOU HAVE TO BE ALL RIGHT WITH THAT.
I WAS TRYING--
YOUR WAY. IT DIDN'T WORK.
THESE PEOPLE WILL NOT BE REASONED WITH. THEY SEE US AS ENEMIES.
YOU CAN DO MORE TO RESOLVE THIS IF YOU'R FREE THAN YOU CAN INCARCERATED.
WE'LL NEVER KNOW, WILL WE?
SO YOU ARE NOT OKAY WITH IT.
WHAT DOES THIS MEAN? IS OUR BETROTHAL OFF?
THIS IS NOT TH TIME FOR A CONVERSATION MERA.
BRRRAPP
BRRRAPP
CHUKK
PANG
THUKK
PING
...YES, I STILL WANT TO MARRY YOU.
I JUST WANT US TO BE ALIVE ON THE BIG DAY.

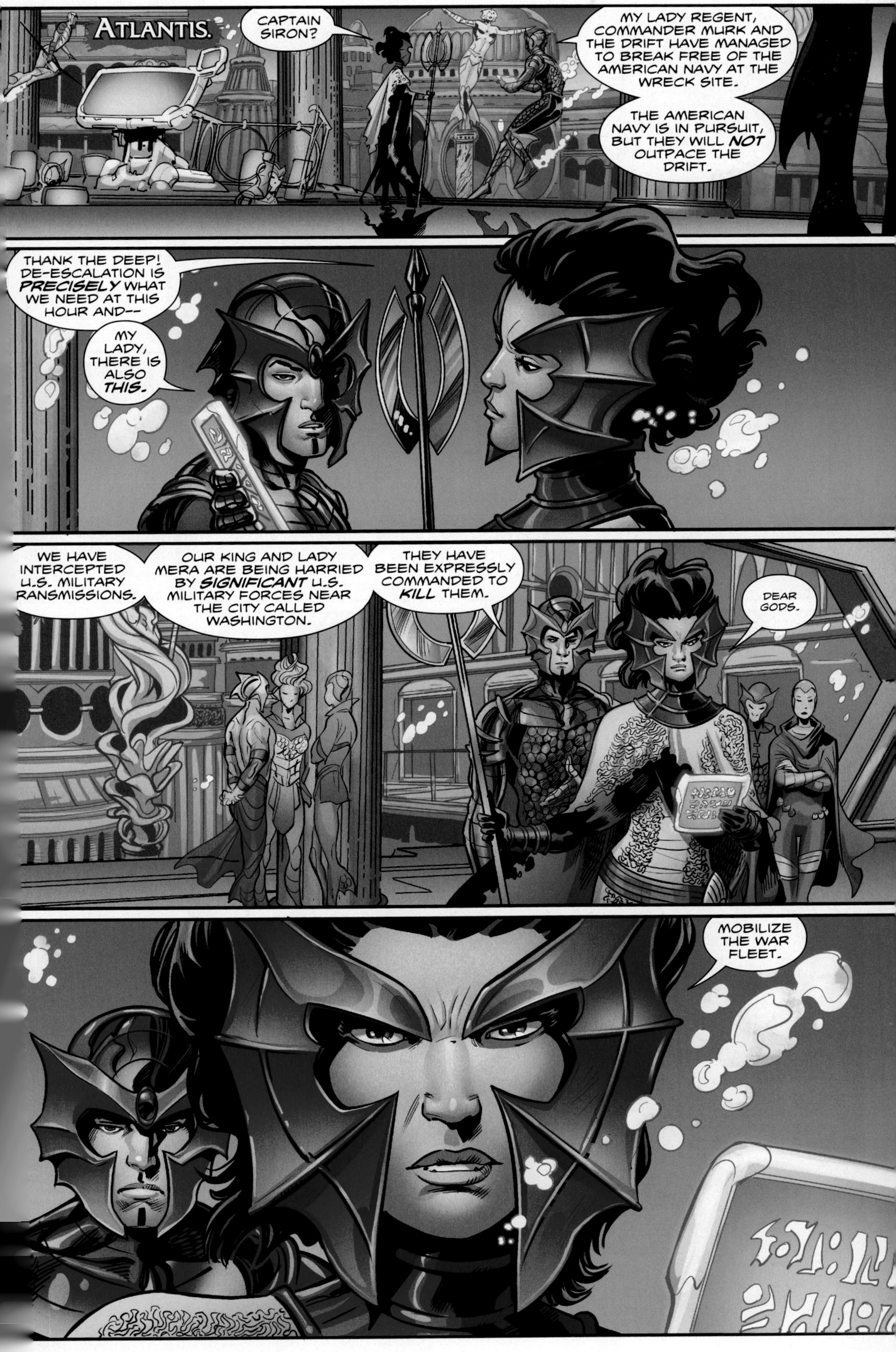
ATLANTIS.
CAPTAIN SIRON?
MY LADY REGENT, COMMANDER MURK AND THE DRIFT HAVE MANAGED TO BREAK FREE OF THE AMERICAN NAVY AT THE WRECK SITE.
THE AMERICAN NAVY IS IN PURSUIT, BUT THEY WILL NOT OUTPACE THE DRIFT.
THANK THE DEEP! DE-ESCALATION IS PRECISELY WHAT WE NEED AT THIS HOUR AND--
MY LADY, THERE IS ALSO THIS.
WE HAVE INTERCEPTED U.S. MILITARY RANSMISSIONS.
OUR KING AND LADY MERA ARE BEING HARRIED BY SIGNIFICANT U.S. MILITARY FORCES NEAR THE CITY CALLED WASHINGTON.
THEY HAVE BEEN EXPRESSLY COMMANDED TO KILL THEM.
DEAR GODS.
MOBILIZE THE WAR FLEET.

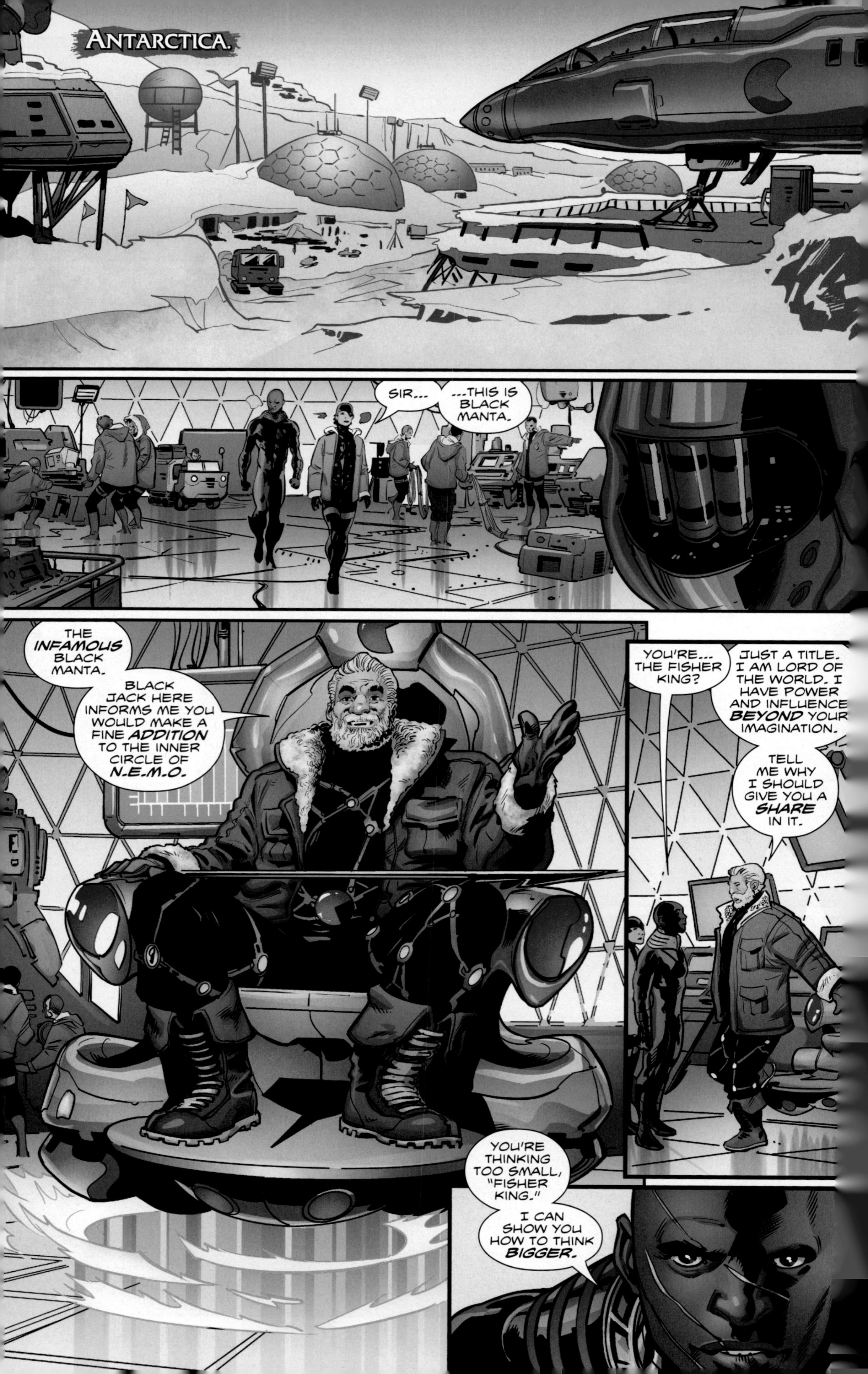

ANTARCTICA.
SIR...
...THIS IS BLACK MANTA.
THE INFAMOUS BLACK MANTA.
BLACK JACK HERE INFORMS ME YOU WOULD MAKE A FINE ADDITION TO THE INNER CIRCLE OF N.E.M.O.
YOU'RE... THE FISHER KING?
JUST A TITLE. I AM LORD OF THE WORLD. I HAVE POWER AND INFLUENCE BEYOND YOUR IMAGINATION.
TELL ME WHY I SHOULD GIVE YOU A SHARE IN IT.
YOU'RE THINKING TOO SMALL, "FISHER KING."
I CAN SHOW YOU HOW TO THINK BIGGER.

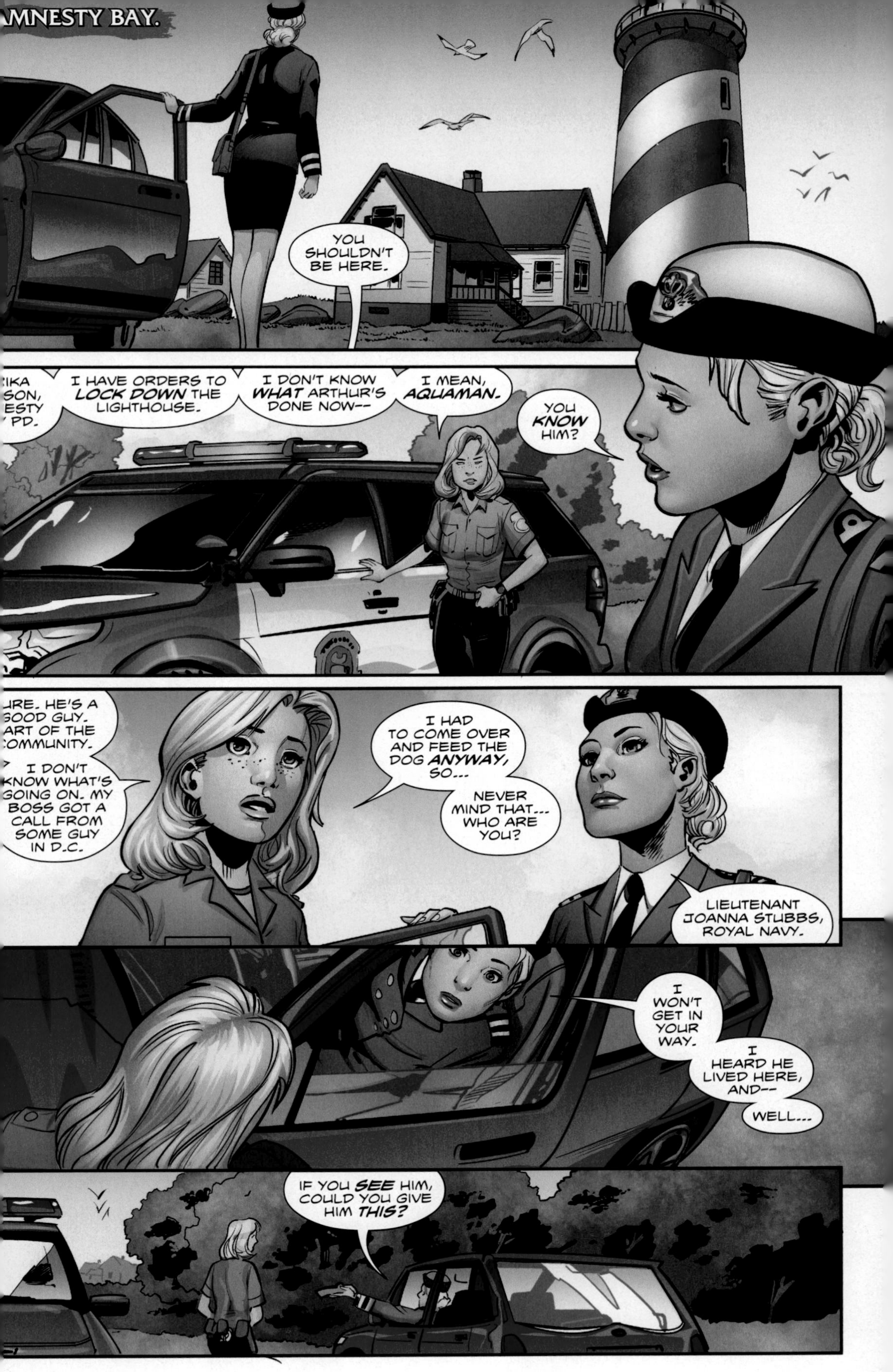
MNESTY BAY.
YOU SHOULDN'T BE HERE.
IKA SON, ESTY PD.
I HAVE ORDERS TO LOCK DOWN THE LIGHTHOUSE.
I DON'T KNOW WHAT ARTHUR'S DONE NOW--
I MEAN, AQUAMAN.
YOU KNOW HIM?
URE. HE'S A GOOD GUY. ART OF THE COMMUNITY.
I DON'T KNOW WHAT'S GOING ON. MY BOSS GOT A CALL FROM SOME GUY IN D.C.
I HAD TO COME OVER AND FEED THE DOG ANYWAY, SO...
NEVER MIND THAT... WHO ARE YOU?
LIEUTENANT JOANNA STUBBS, ROYAL NAVY.
I WON'T GET IN YOUR WAY.
I HEARD HE LIVED HERE, AND--
WELL...
IF YOU SEE HIM, COULD YOU GIVE HIM THIS?

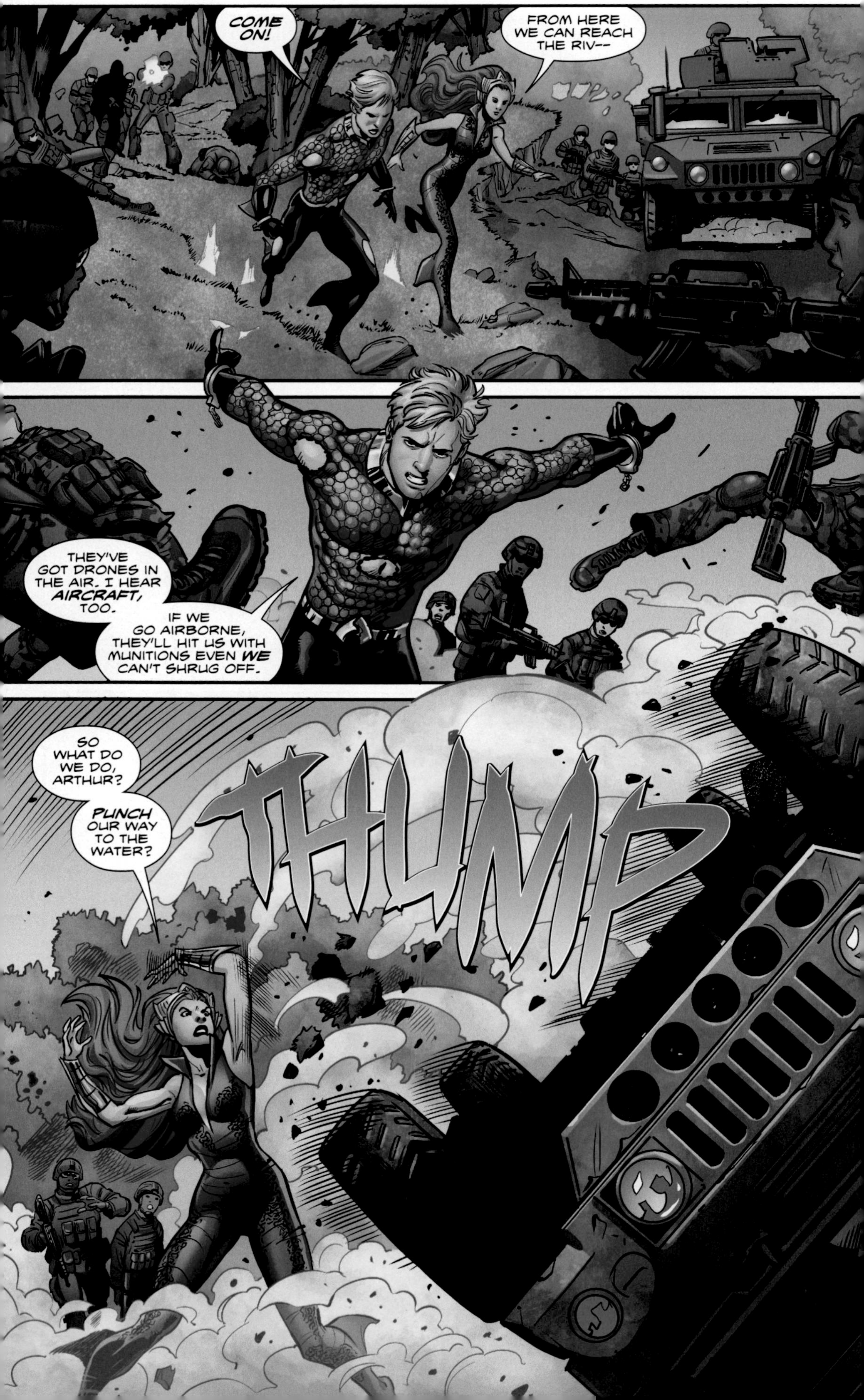
COME ON!
FROM HERE WE CAN REACH THE RIV--
THEY'VE GOT DRONES IN THE AIR. I HEAR *AIRCRAFT,* TOO.
IF WE GO AIRBORNE, THEY'LL HIT US WITH MUNITIONS EVEN *WE* CAN'T SHRUG OFF.
SO WHAT DO WE DO, ARTHUR?
PUNCH OUR WAY TO THE WATER?
THUMP

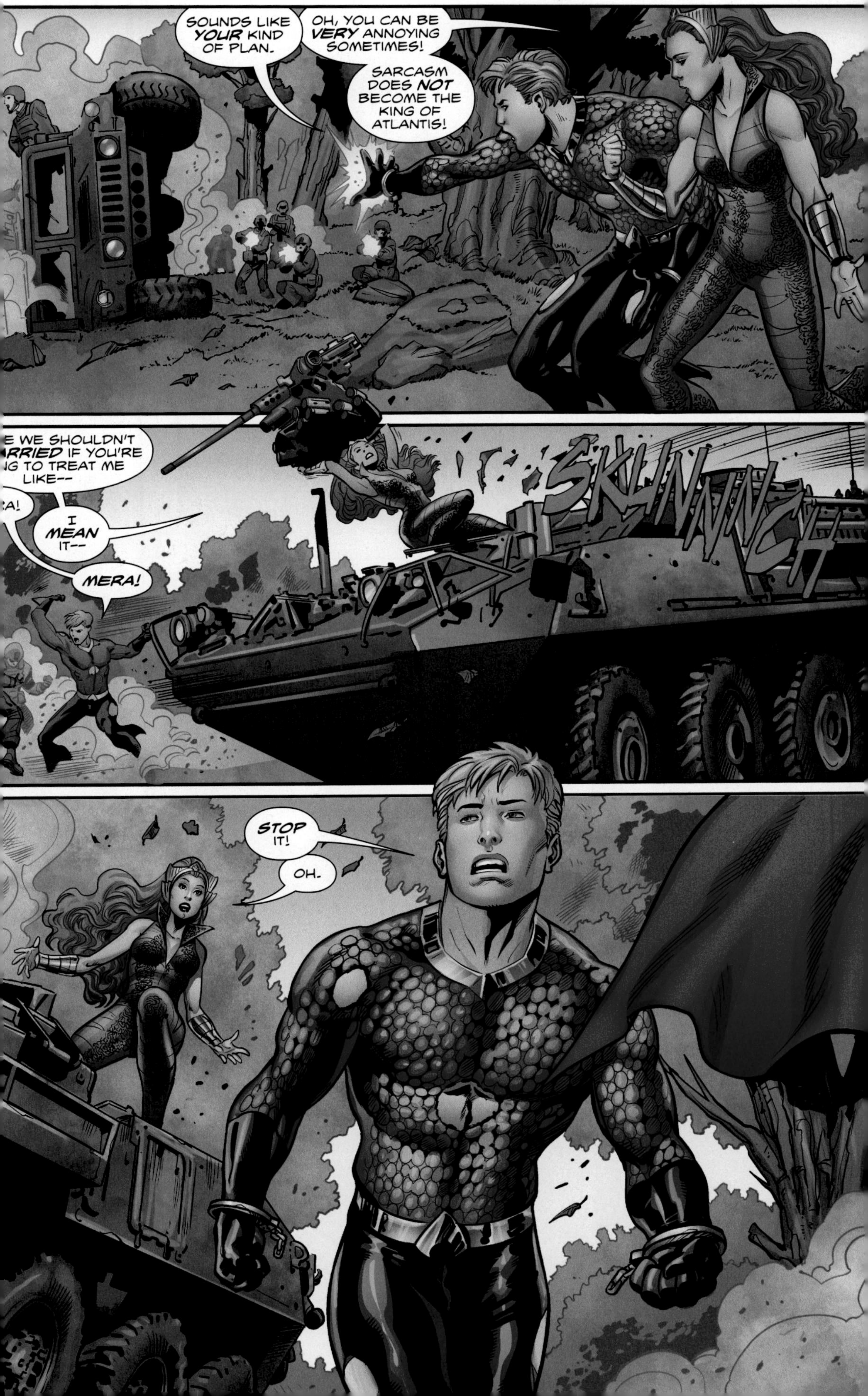
SOUNDS LIKE YOUR KIND OF PLAN.
OH, YOU CAN BE VERY ANNOYING SOMETIMES!
SARCASM DOES NOT BECOME THE KING OF ATLANTIS!
E WE SHOULDN'T ARRIED IF YOU'RE G TO TREAT ME LIKE--
I MEAN IT--
A!
MERA!
SKLUNNNCH
STOP IT!
OH.

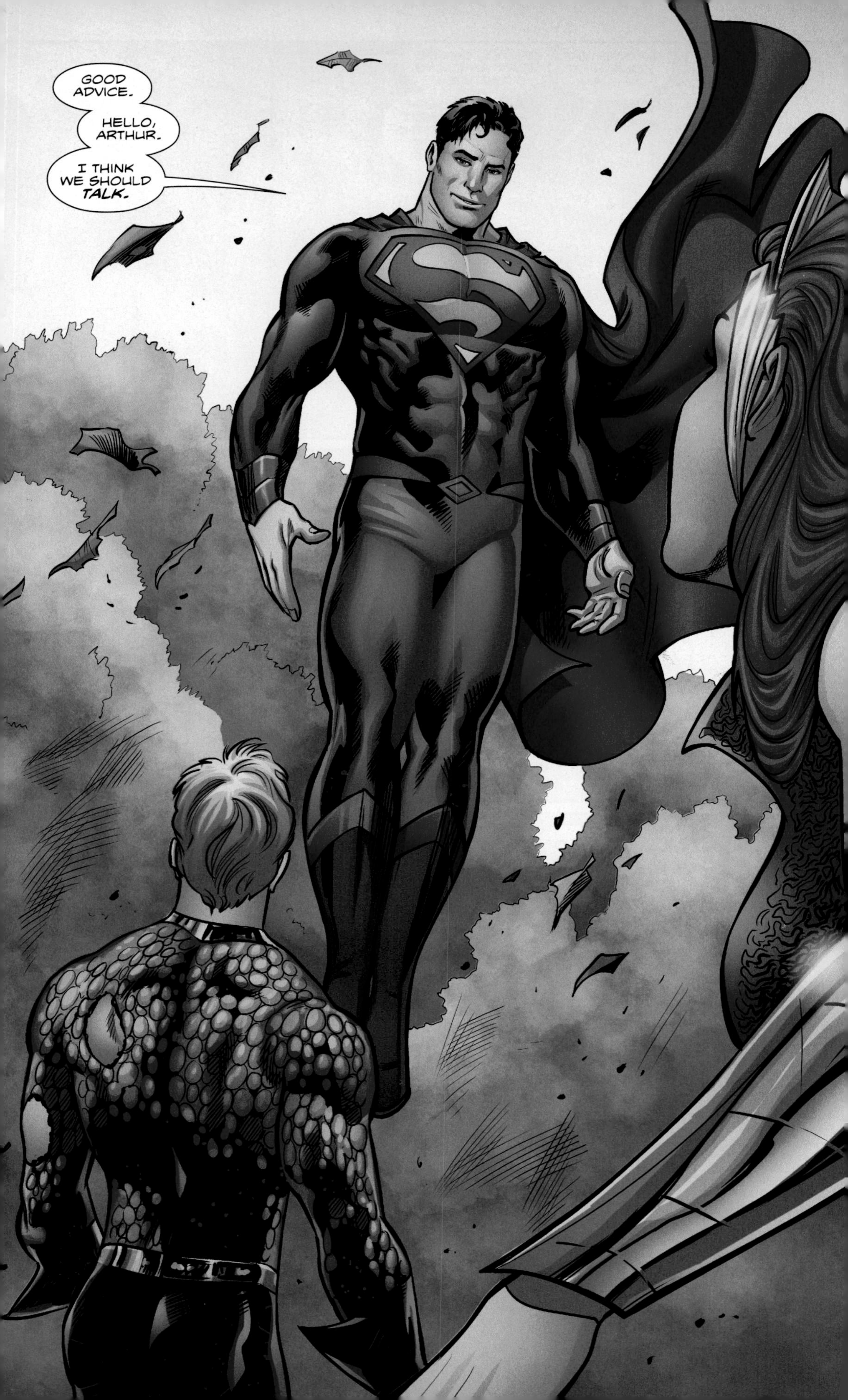
GOOD ADVICE.
HELLO, ARTHUR.
I THINK WE SHOULD TALK.

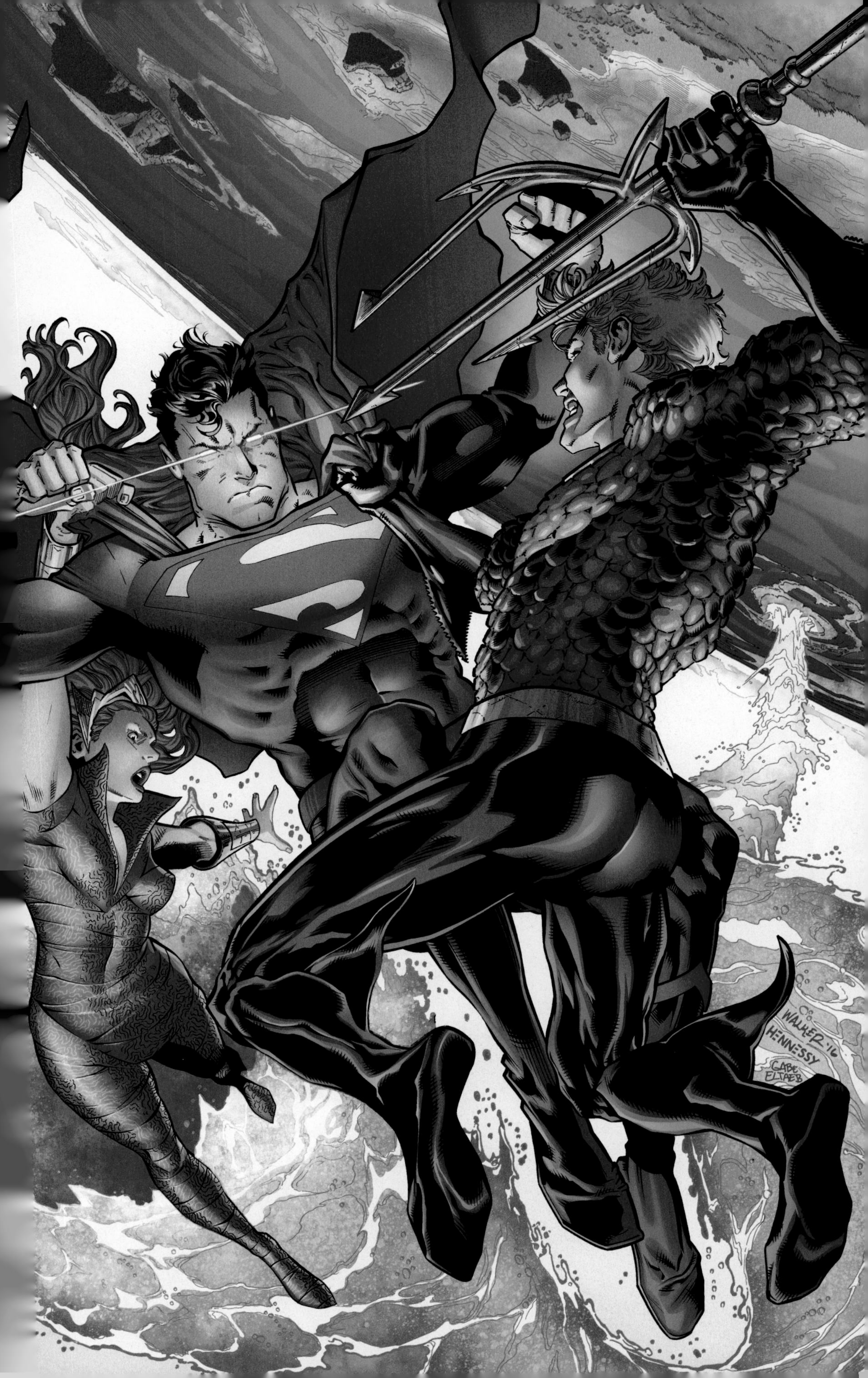
WALKER '16
HENNESSY
GABE ELTAEB

CONCLUSION: OUT OF HIS LEAGUE

DAN ABNETT Writer * BRAD WALKER Penciller * ANDREW HENNESSY Inker * GABE ELTAEB Colorist * PAT BROSSEAU Letterer

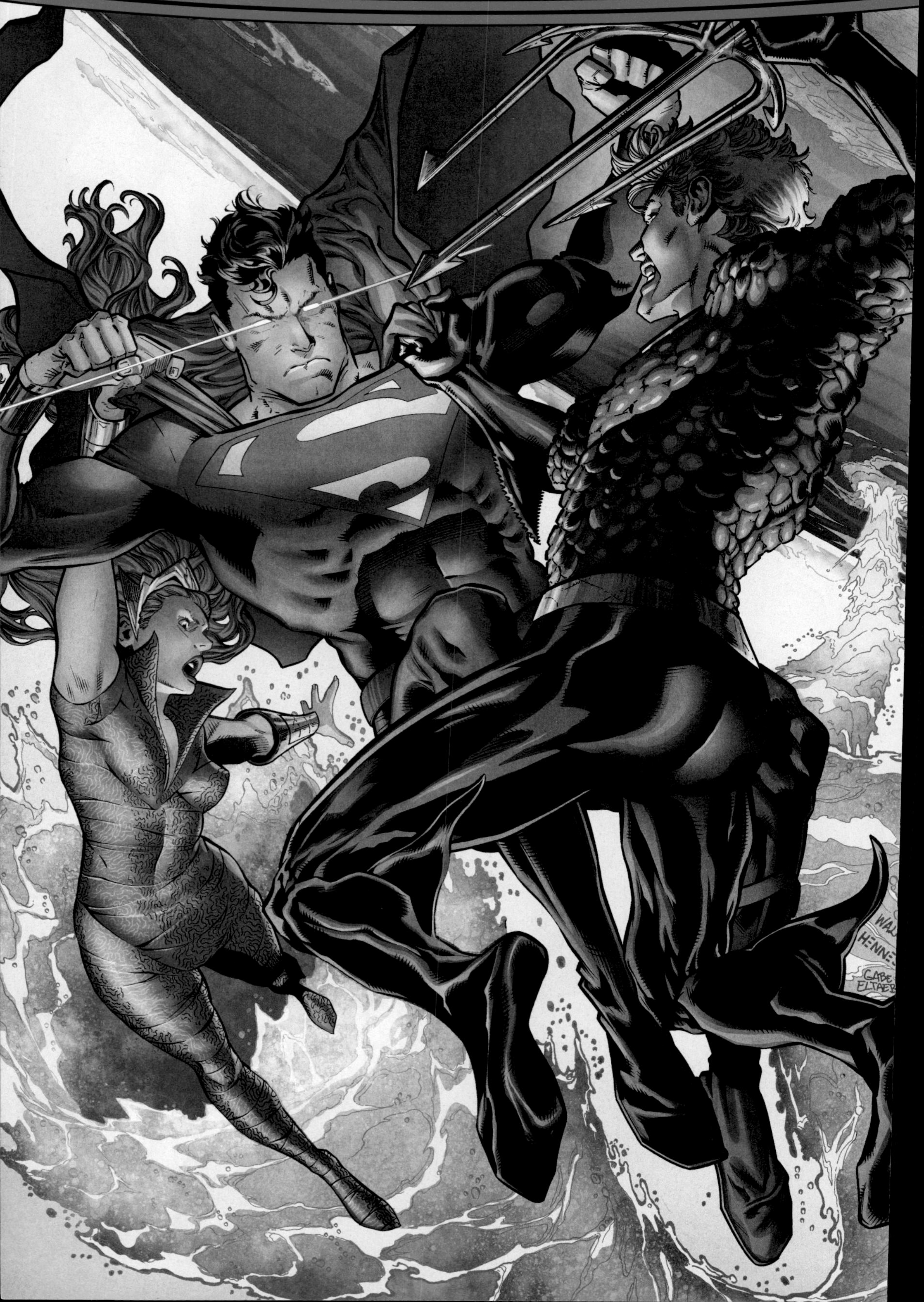

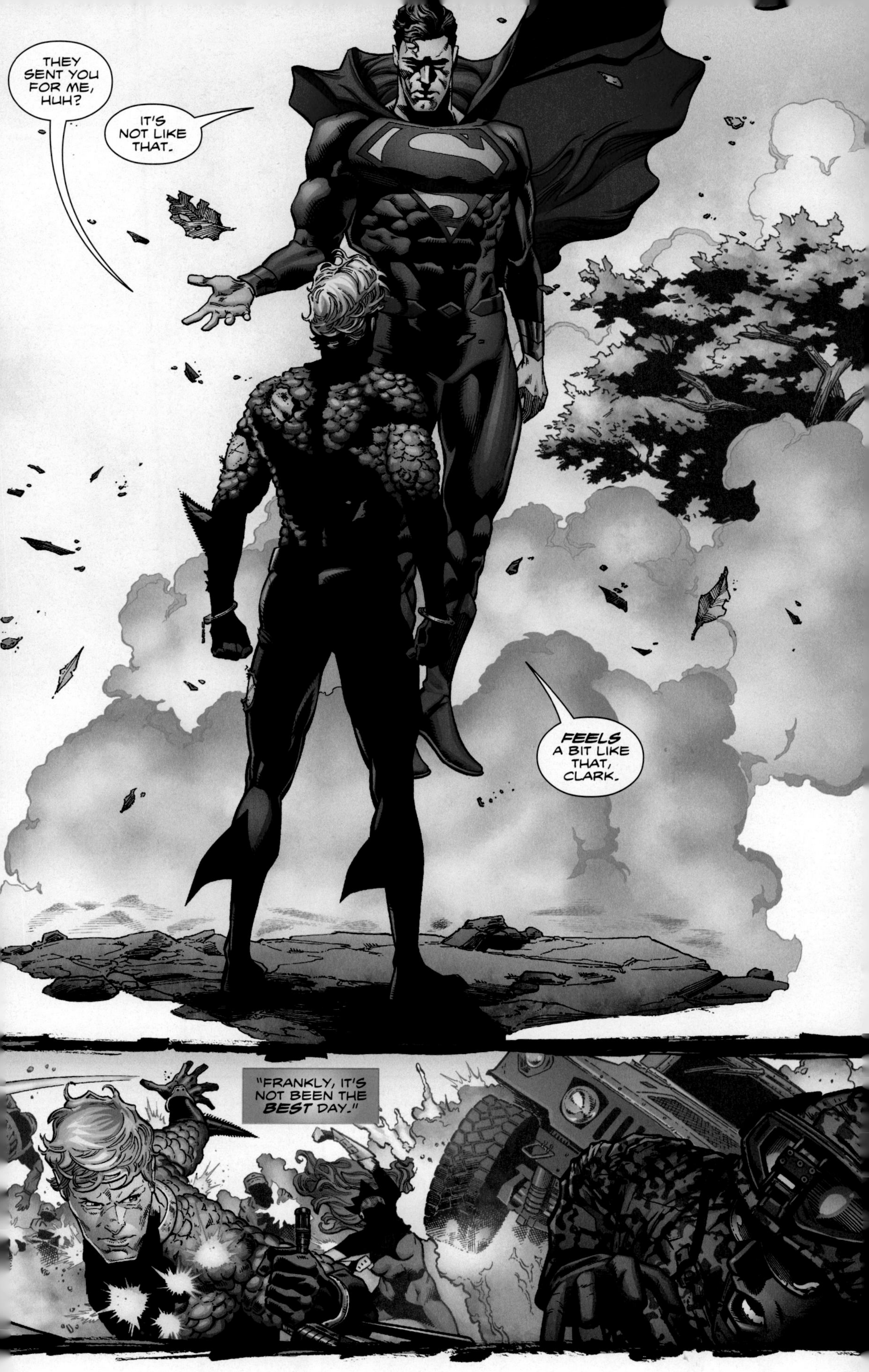
THEY SENT YOU FOR ME, HUH?
IT'S NOT LIKE THAT.
FEELS A BIT LIKE THAT, CLARK.
"FRANKLY, IT'S NOT BEEN THE BEST DAY."

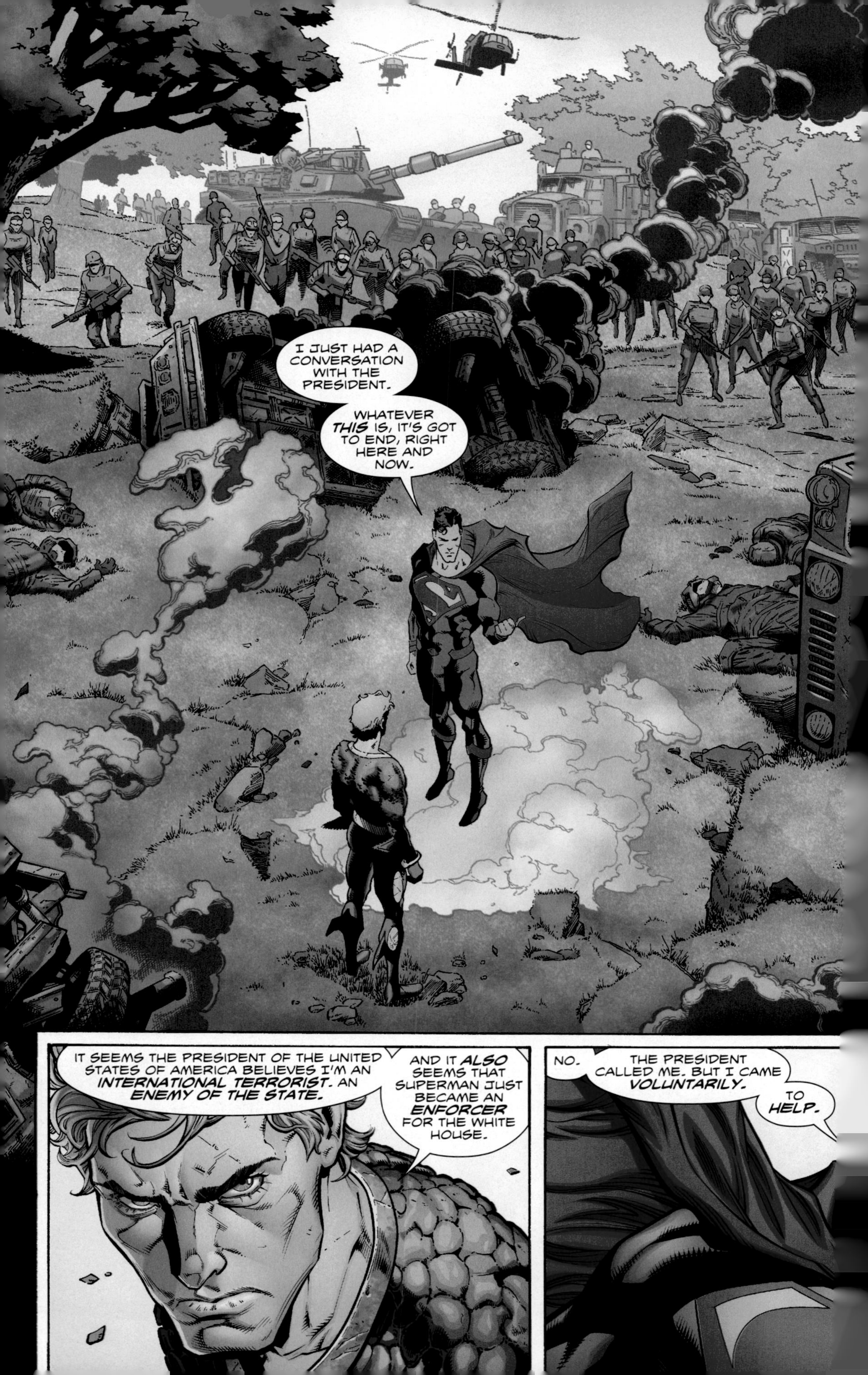

I JUST HAD A CONVERSATION WITH THE PRESIDENT.
WHATEVER *THIS* IS, IT'S GOT TO END, RIGHT HERE AND NOW.
IT SEEMS THE PRESIDENT OF THE UNITED STATES OF AMERICA BELIEVES I'M AN *INTERNATIONAL TERRORIST*. AN *ENEMY OF THE STATE.*
AND IT *ALSO* SEEMS THAT SUPERMAN JUST BECAME AN *ENFORCER* FOR THE WHITE HOUSE.
NO.
THE PRESIDENT CALLED ME. BUT I CAME *VOLUNTARILY.*
TO *HELP.*

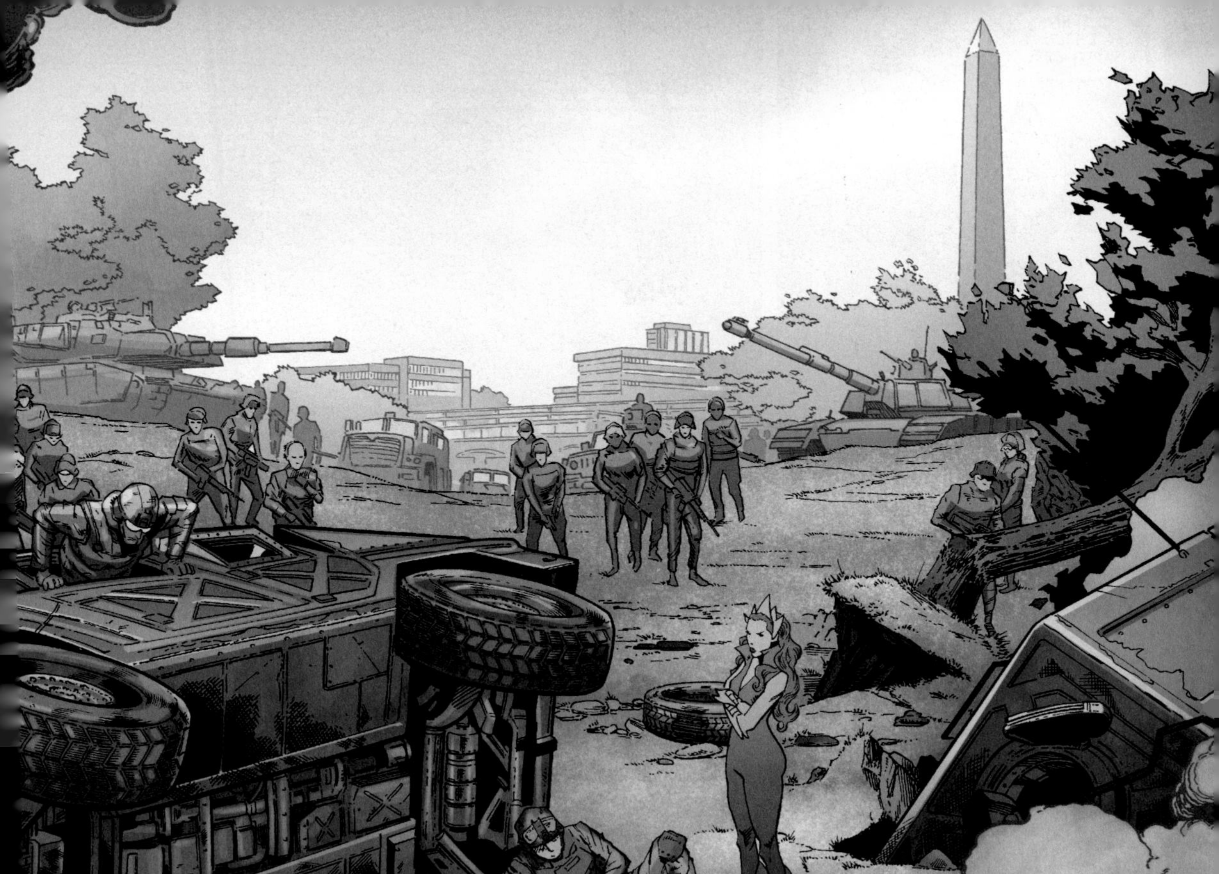

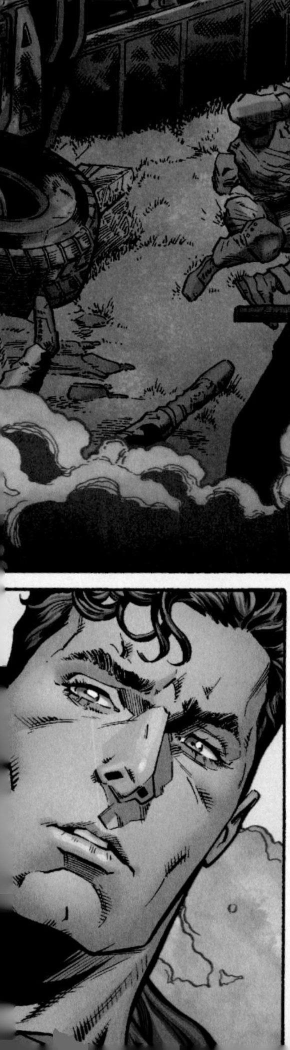

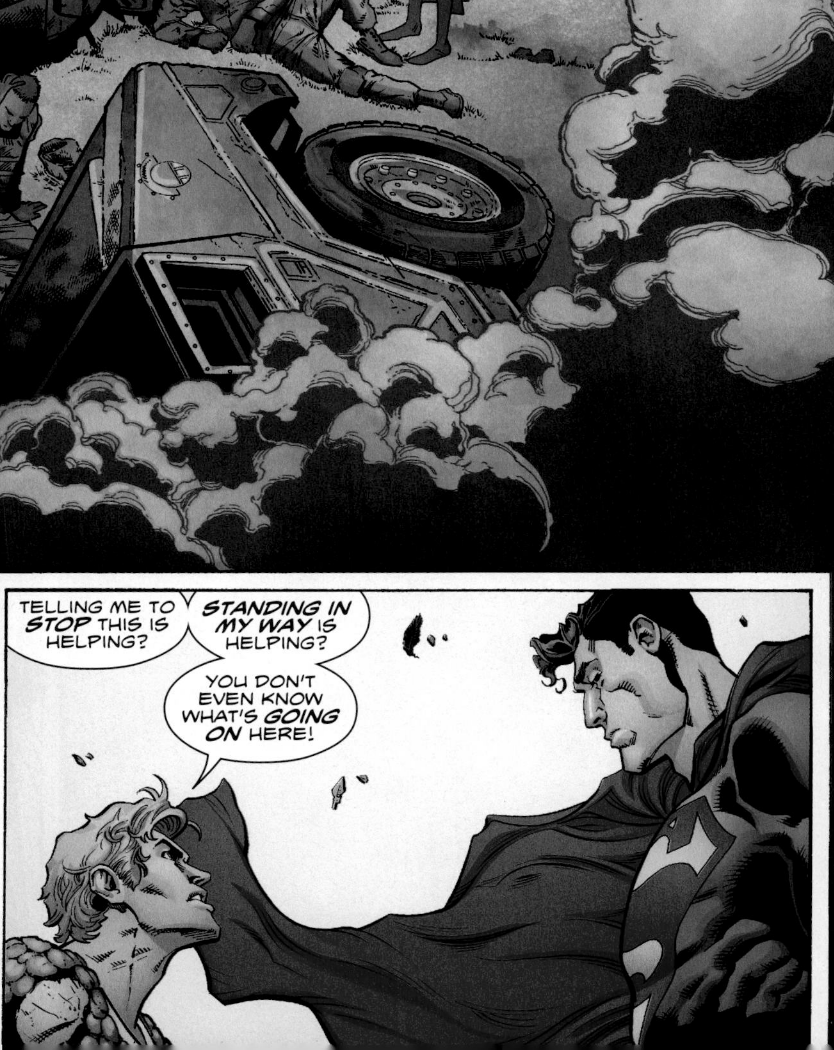
TELLING ME TO STOP THIS IS HELPING?
STANDING IN MY WAY IS HELPING?
YOU DON'T EVEN KNOW WHAT'S GOING ON HERE!

I THINK I DO, ARTHUR.

I WAS TOLD ABOUT THE USS PONTCHARTRAIN, LOST WITH *ALL HANDS* IN THE SOUTH ATLANTIC.

AND RIGHT NOW...

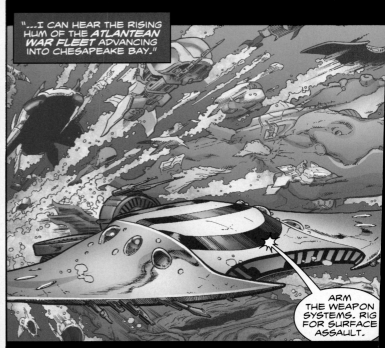

"...I CAN HEAR THE RISING HUM OF THE *ATLANTEAN WAR FLEET* ADVANCING INTO CHESAPEAKE BAY."

ARM THE WEAPON SYSTEMS. RIG FOR SURFACE ASSAULT.

THE KING WENT TO GREAT PAINS TO AVOID CONFLICT WITH THE NATIONS OF THE LAND, MY LADY REGENT.

I AM AWARE OF THAT, CAPTAIN SIRON. IN GOOD FAITH, I WILL *ALWAYS* OBEY HIS WISHES.

BUT THIS IS *BAD* FAITH. THE AMERICANS HAVE ATTACKED HIM, HOUNDED HIM, *CORNERED* HIM...

OUR KING IS *UNDER THREAT.*

ATLANTIS *CANNOT* TOLERATE THIS.

I WANT TO HELP.

THEN WH... AREN'T Y... *HELPING...*

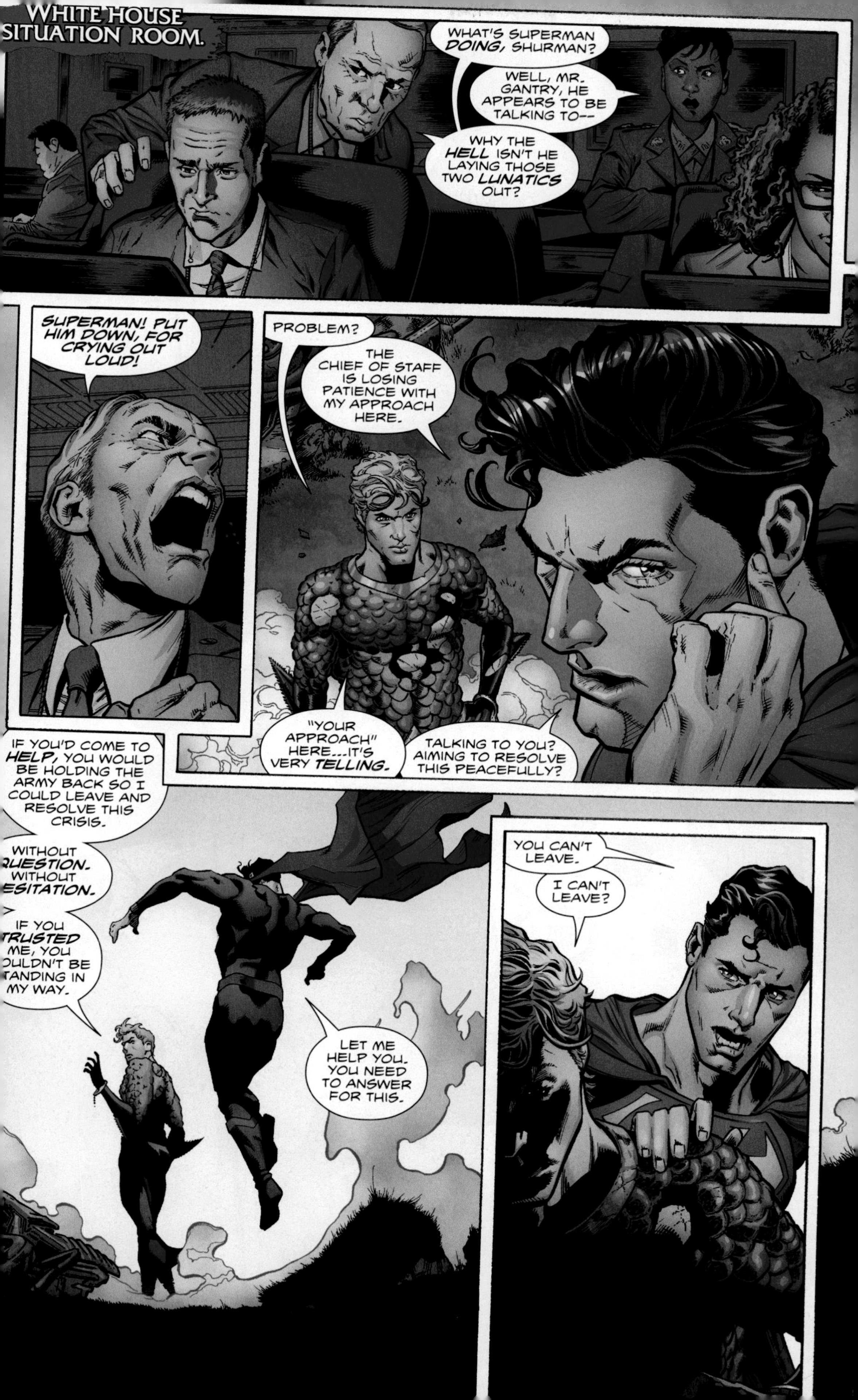
WHITE HOUSE SITUATION ROOM.
WHAT'S SUPERMAN DOING, SHURMAN?
WELL, MR. GANTRY, HE APPEARS TO BE TALKING TO--
WHY THE HELL ISN'T HE LAYING THOSE TWO LUNATICS OUT?
SUPERMAN! PUT HIM DOWN, FOR CRYING OUT LOUD!
PROBLEM?
THE CHIEF OF STAFF IS LOSING PATIENCE WITH MY APPROACH HERE.
"YOUR APPROACH" HERE...IT'S VERY TELLING.
TALKING TO YOU? AIMING TO RESOLVE THIS PEACEFULLY?
IF YOU'D COME TO HELP, YOU WOULD BE HOLDING THE ARMY BACK SO I COULD LEAVE AND RESOLVE THIS CRISIS.
WITHOUT QUESTION. WITHOUT ESITATION.
IF YOU TRUSTED ME, YOU OULDN'T BE TANDING IN MY WAY.
LET ME HELP YOU. YOU NEED TO ANSWER FOR THIS.
YOU CAN'T LEAVE.
I CAN'T LEAVE?

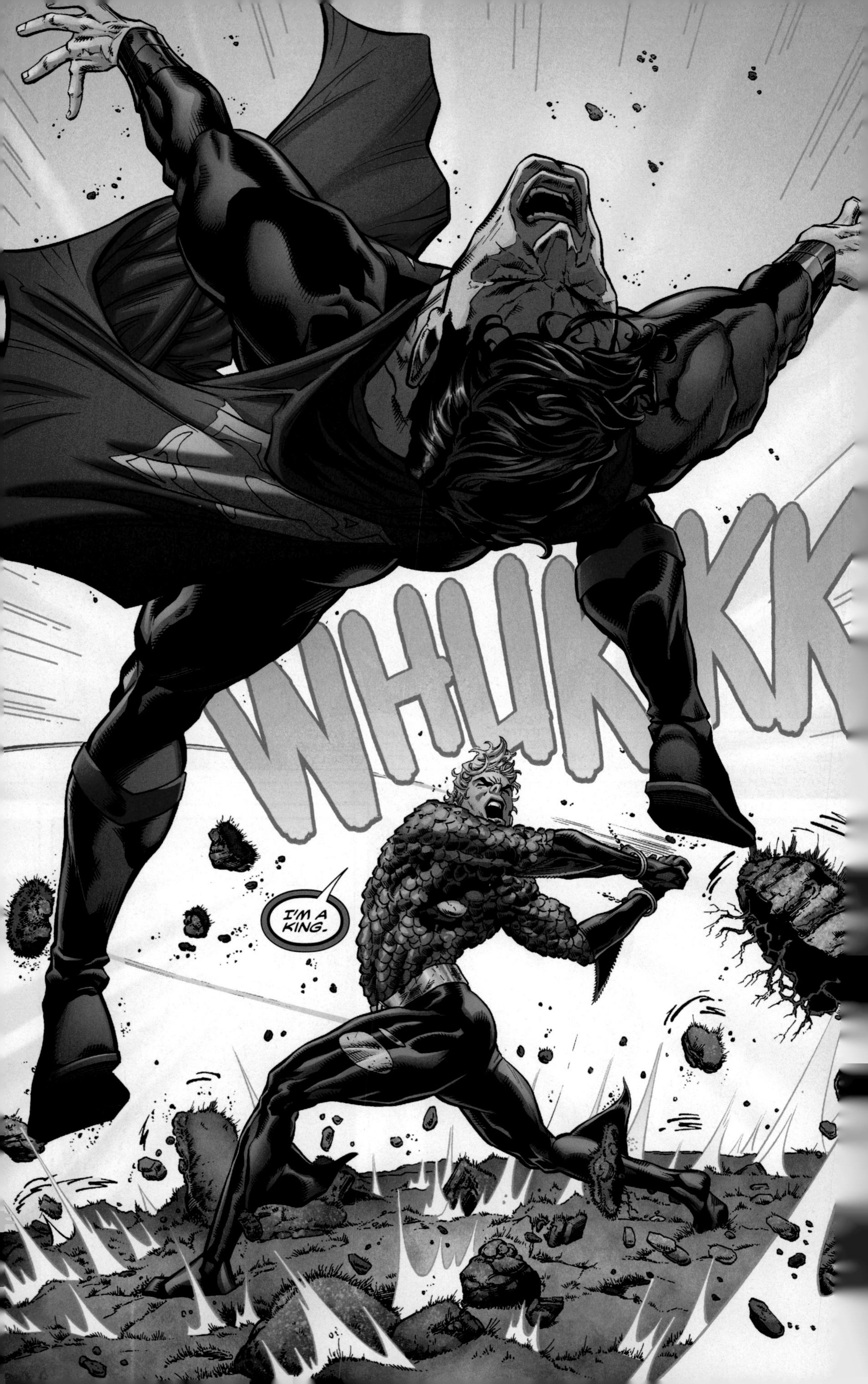
WHUKKK
I'M A KING-

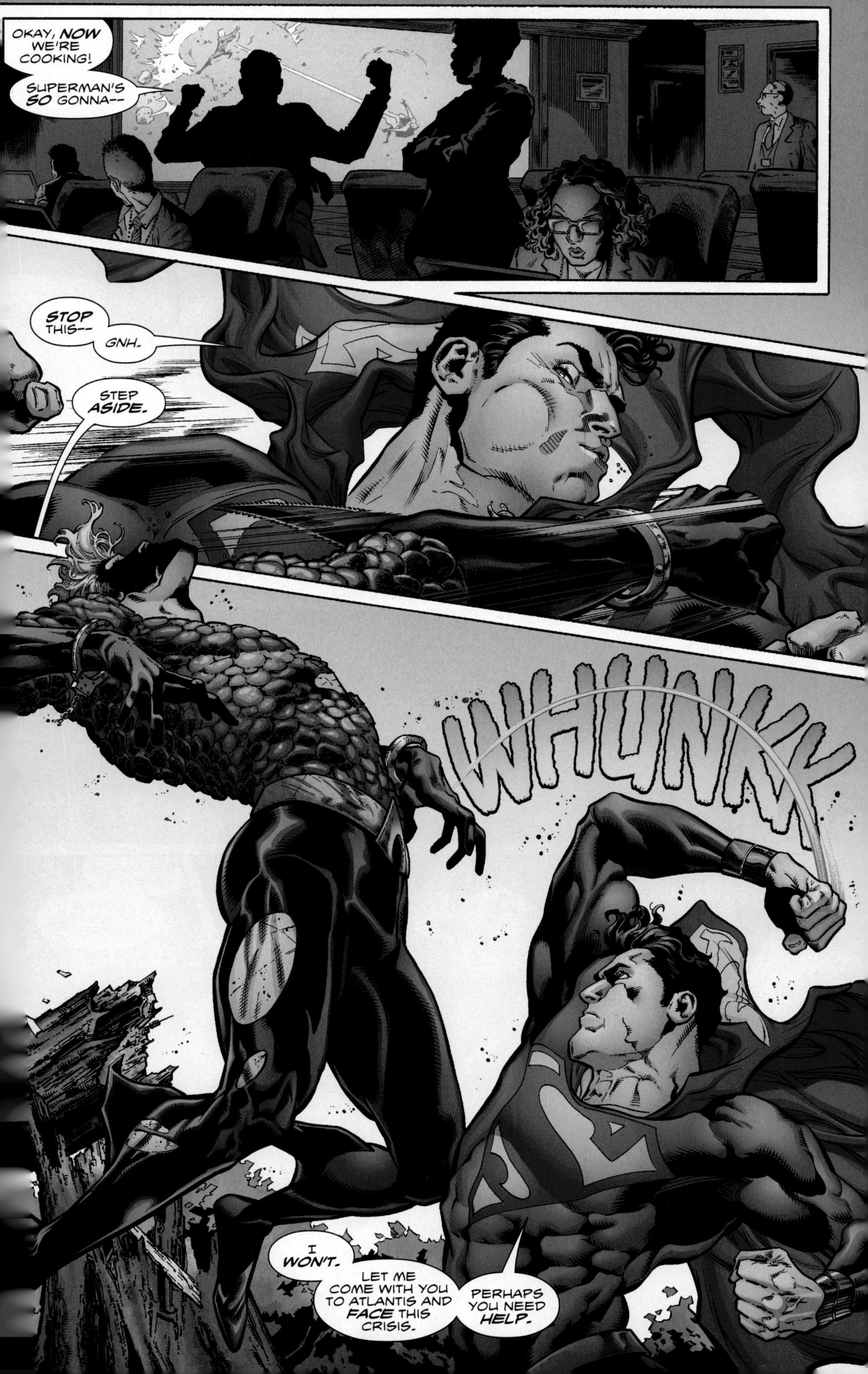
OKAY, NOW WE'RE COOKING!
SUPERMAN'S SO GONNA--
STOP THIS--
GNH.
STEP ASIDE.
WHUNKK
I WON'T.
LET ME COME WITH YOU TO ATLANTIS AND FACE THIS CRISIS.
PERHAPS YOU NEED HELP.

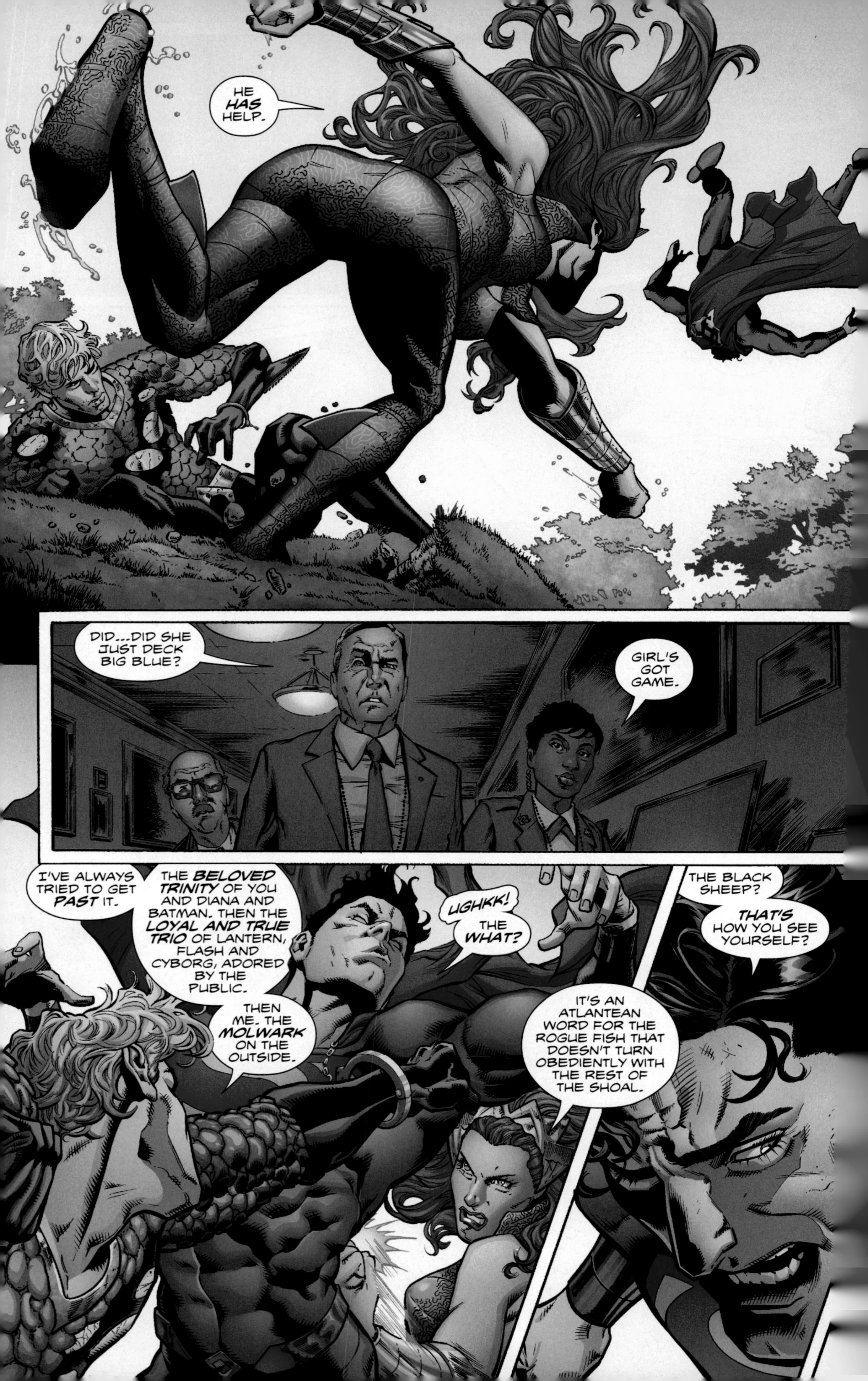
HE *HAS* HELP.
DID...DID SHE JUST DECK BIG BLUE?
GIRL'S GOT GAME.
I'VE ALWAYS TRIED TO GET *PAST* IT.
THE *BELOVED TRINITY* OF YOU AND DIANA AND BATMAN. THEN THE *LOYAL AND TRUE TRIO* OF LANTERN, FLASH AND CYBORG, ADORED BY THE PUBLIC.
THEN ME. THE *MOLWARK* ON THE OUTSIDE.
UGHKK!
THE *WHAT?*
IT'S AN ATLANTEAN WORD FOR THE ROGUE FISH THAT DOESN'T TURN OBEDIENTLY WITH THE REST OF THE SHOAL.
THE BLACK SHEEP?
THAT'S HOW YOU SEE YOURSELF?

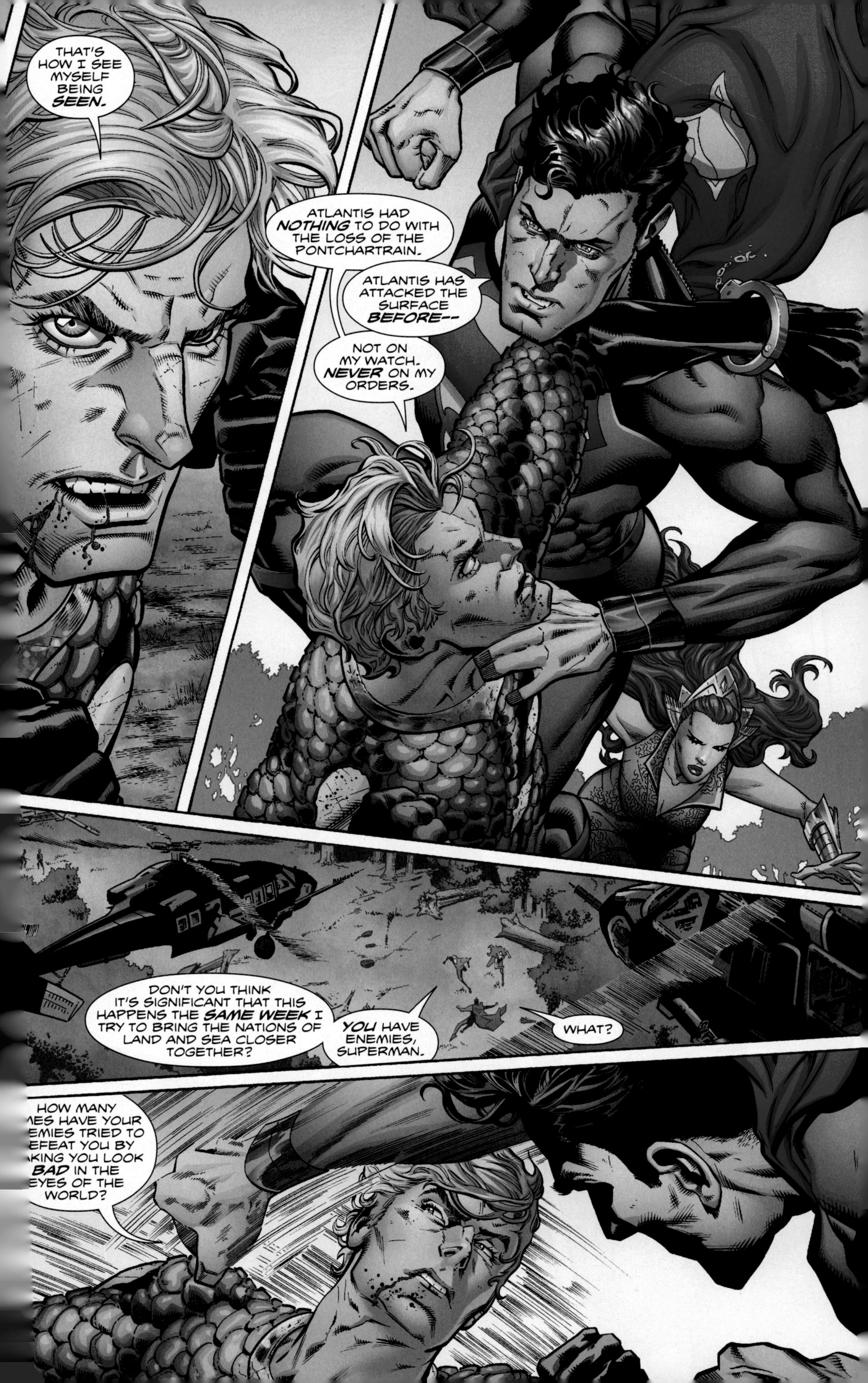
THAT'S HOW I SEE MYSELF BEING SEEN.
ATLANTIS HAD NOTHING TO DO WITH THE LOSS OF THE PONTCHARTRAIN.
ATLANTIS HAS ATTACKED THE SURFACE BEFORE--
NOT ON MY WATCH. NEVER ON MY ORDERS.
DON'T YOU THINK IT'S SIGNIFICANT THAT THIS HAPPENS THE SAME WEEK I TRY TO BRING THE NATIONS OF LAND AND SEA CLOSER TOGETHER?
WHAT?
YOU HAVE ENEMIES, SUPERMAN.
HOW MANY MES HAVE YOUR EMIES TRIED TO EFEAT YOU BY AKING YOU LOOK BAD IN THE EYES OF THE WORLD?

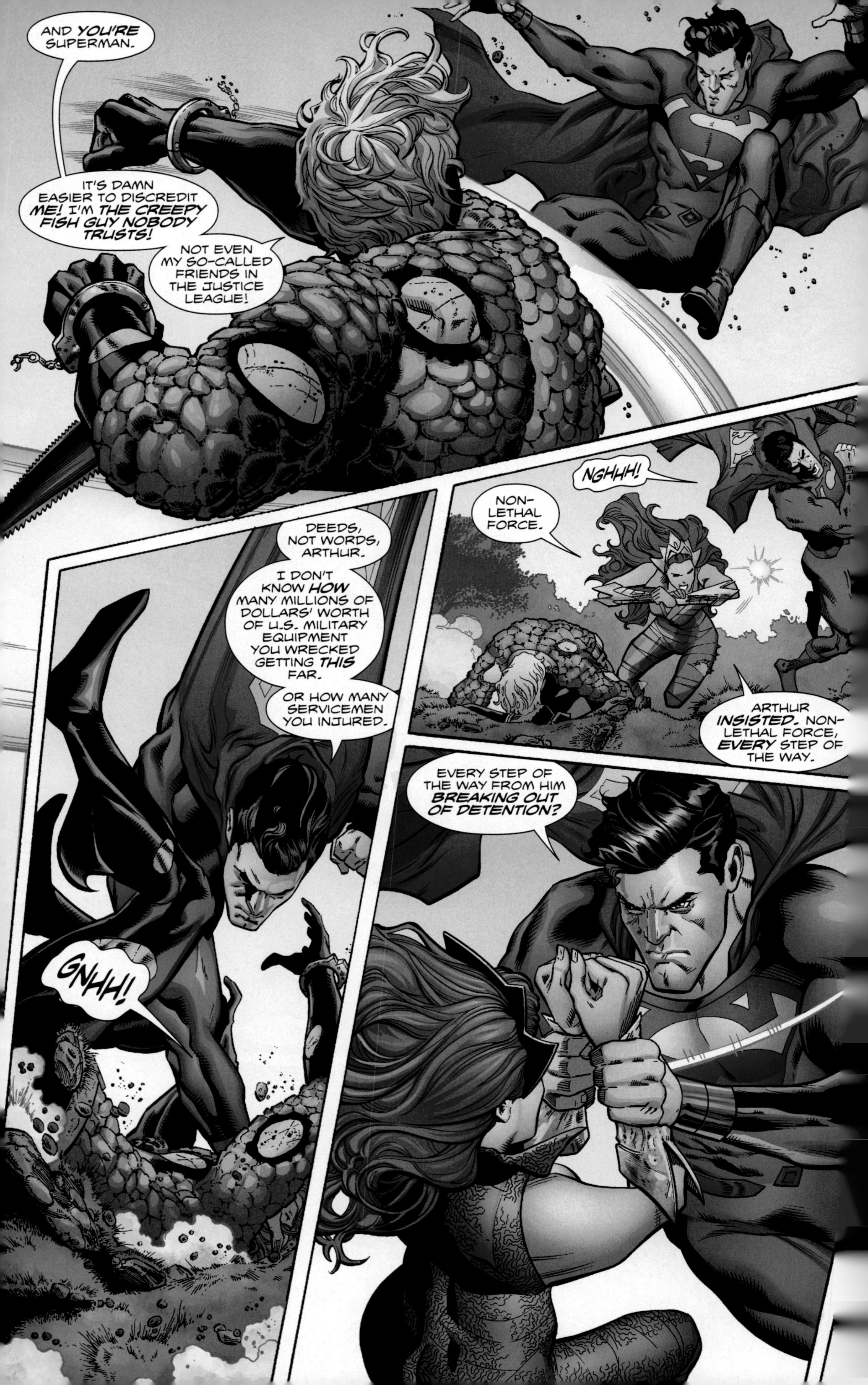
AND YOU'RE SUPERMAN.
IT'S DAMN EASIER TO DISCREDIT ME! I'M THE CREEPY FISH GUY NOBODY TRUSTS!
NOT EVEN MY SO-CALLED FRIENDS IN THE JUSTICE LEAGUE!
NGHHH!
NON-LETHAL FORCE.
ARTHUR INSISTED. NON-LETHAL FORCE, EVERY STEP OF THE WAY.
DEEDS, NOT WORDS, ARTHUR.
I DON'T KNOW HOW MANY MILLIONS OF DOLLARS' WORTH OF U.S. MILITARY EQUIPMENT YOU WRECKED GETTING THIS FAR.
OR HOW MANY SERVICEMEN YOU INJURED.
GNHH!
EVERY STEP OF THE WAY FROM HIM BREAKING OUT OF DETENTION?

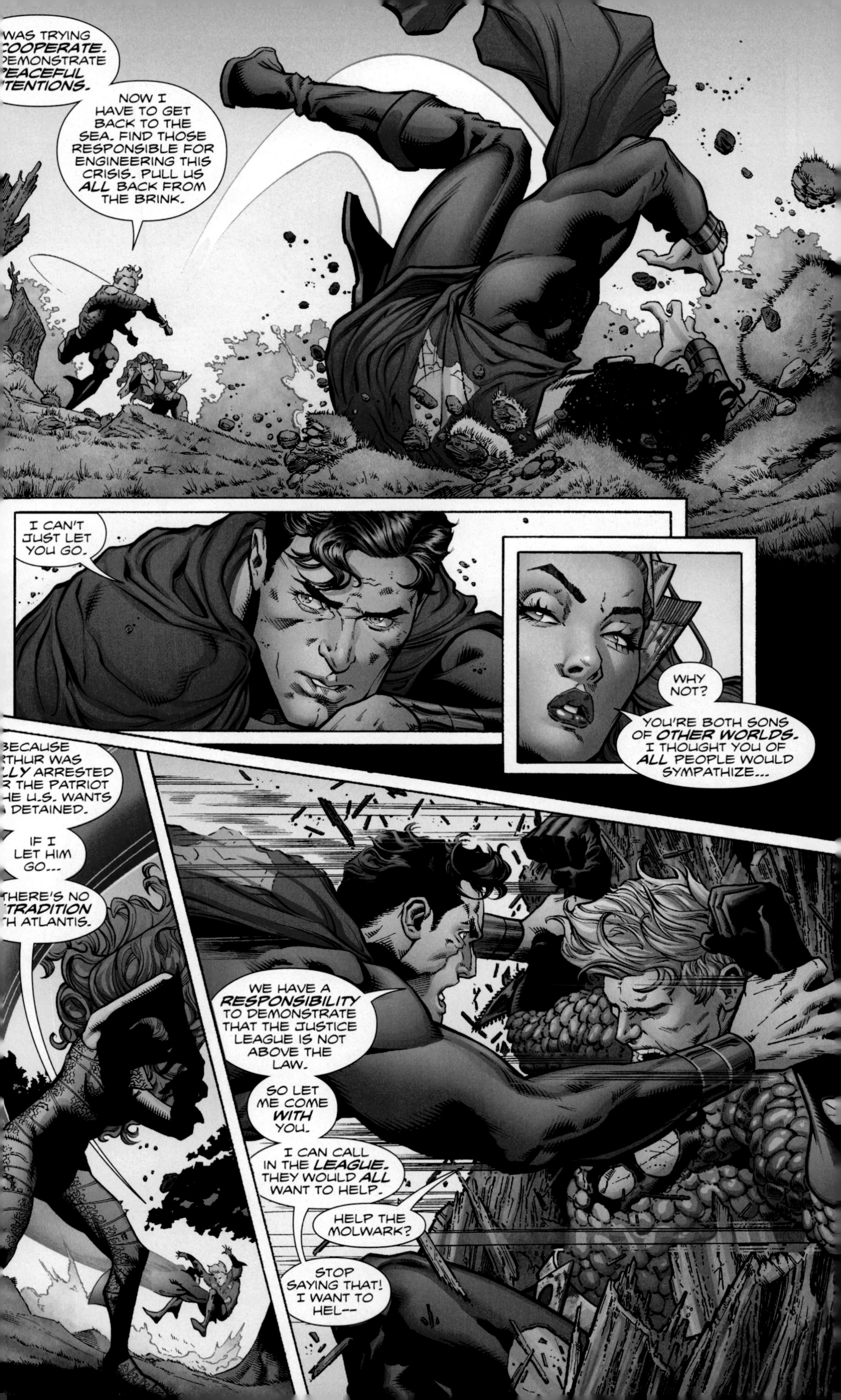

WAS TRYING COOPERATE. EMONSTRATE PEACEFUL TENTIONS.
NOW I HAVE TO GET BACK TO THE SEA. FIND THOSE RESPONSIBLE FOR ENGINEERING THIS CRISIS. PULL US ALL BACK FROM THE BRINK.
I CAN'T JUST LET YOU GO.
WHY NOT?
YOU'RE BOTH SONS OF OTHER WORLDS. I THOUGHT YOU OF ALL PEOPLE WOULD SYMPATHIZE...
BECAUSE RTHUR WAS LLY ARRESTED R THE PATRIOT HE U.S. WANTS DETAINED.
IF I LET HIM GO...
THERE'S NO TRADITION TH ATLANTIS.
WE HAVE A RESPONSIBILITY TO DEMONSTRATE THAT THE JUSTICE LEAGUE IS NOT ABOVE THE LAW.
SO LET ME COME WITH YOU.
I CAN CALL IN THE LEAGUE. THEY WOULD ALL WANT TO HELP.
HELP THE MOLWARK?
STOP SAYING THAT! I WANT TO HEL--

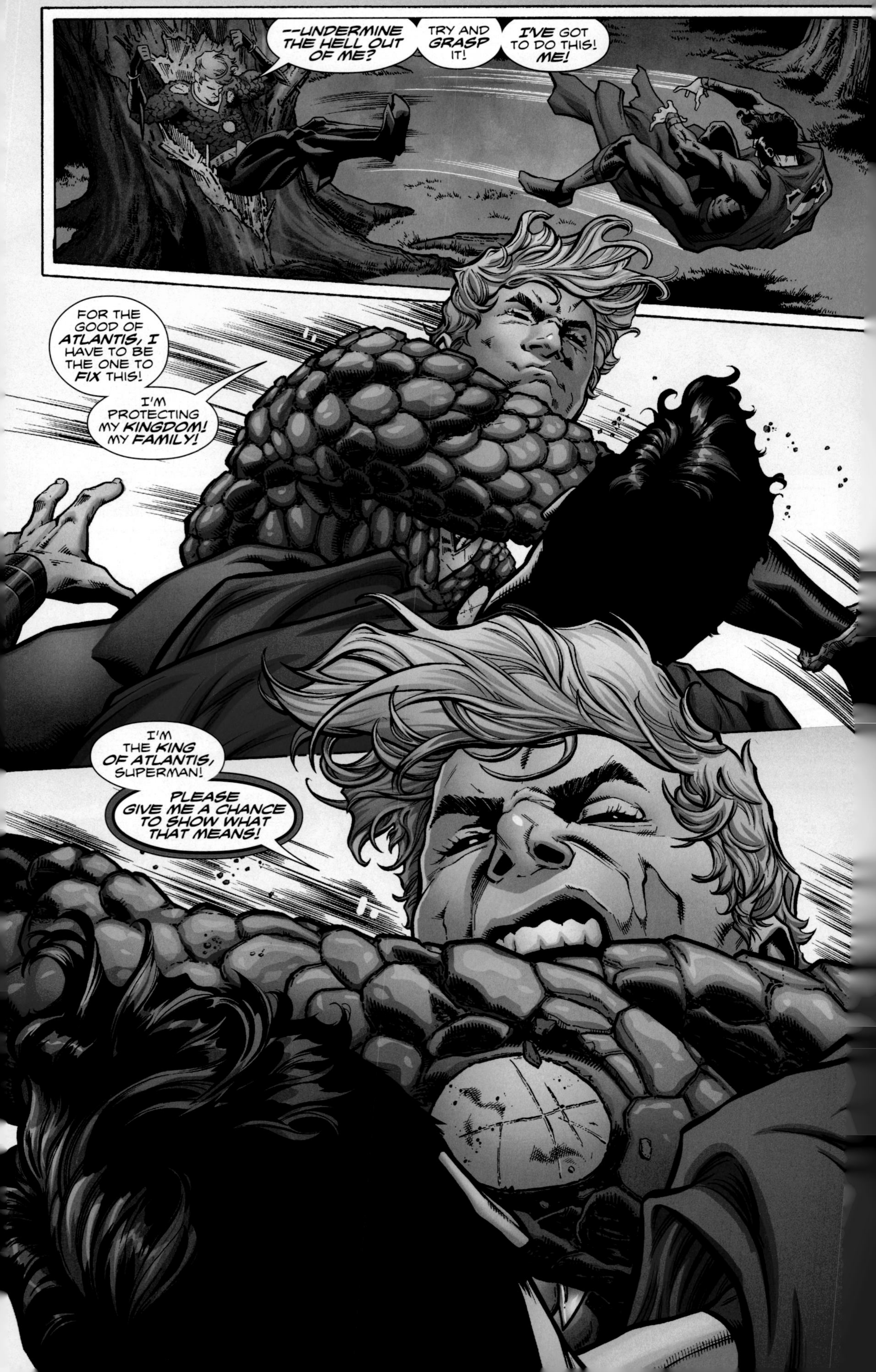
--UNDERMINE THE HELL OUT OF ME?
TRY AND GRASP IT!
I'VE GOT TO DO THIS! ME!
FOR THE GOOD OF ATLANTIS, I HAVE TO BE THE ONE TO FIX THIS!
I'M PROTECTING MY KINGDOM! MY FAMILY!
I'M THE KING OF ATLANTIS, SUPERMAN!
PLEASE GIVE ME A CHANCE TO SHOW WHAT THAT MEANS!

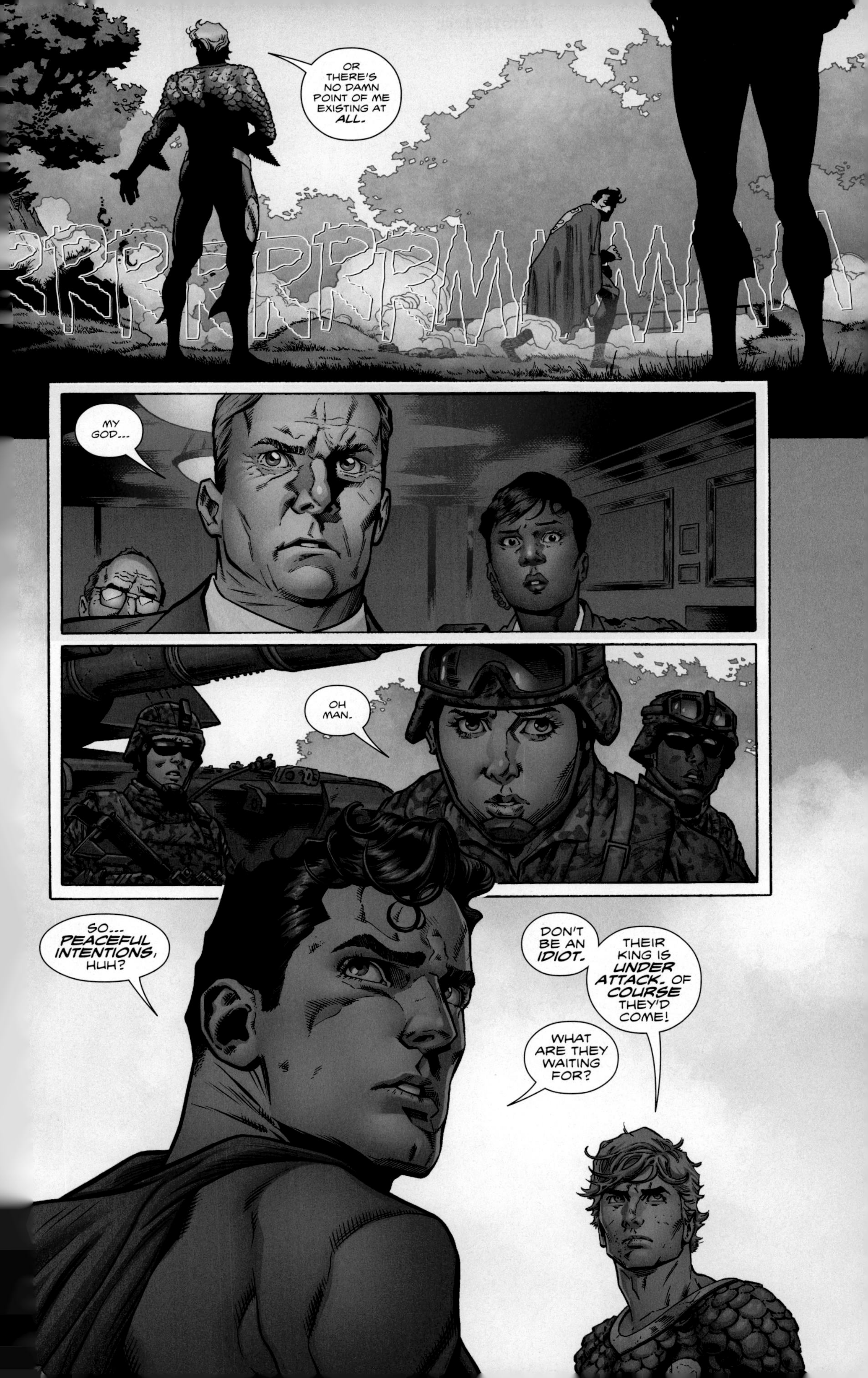
OR THERE'S NO DAMN POINT OF ME EXISTING AT ALL.
RRRRRRRMMMMM
MY GOD...
OH MAN.
SO... PEACEFUL INTENTIONS, HUH?
DON'T BE AN IDIOT.
THEIR KING IS UNDER ATTACK. OF COURSE THEY'D COME!
WHAT ARE THEY WAITING FOR?

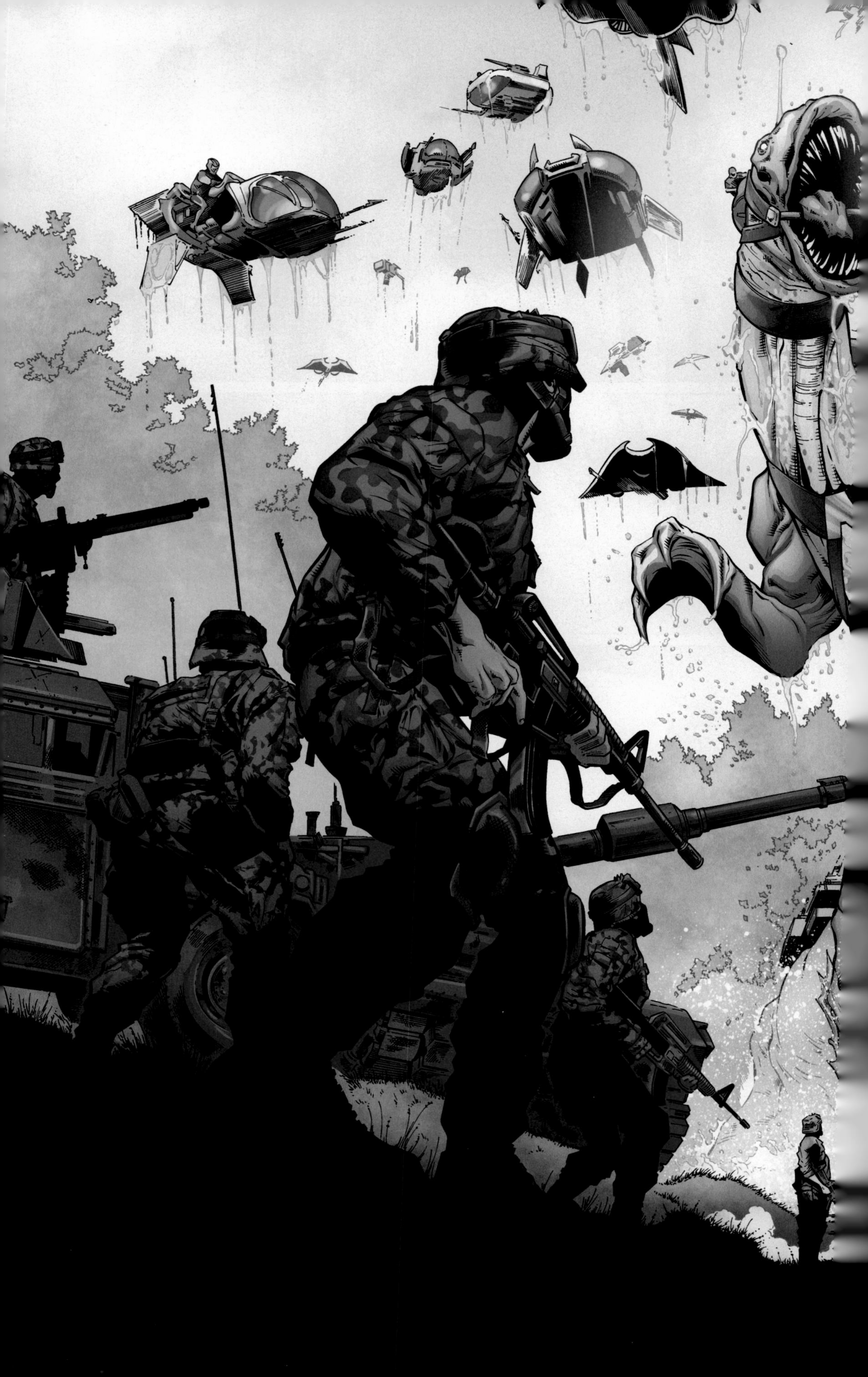

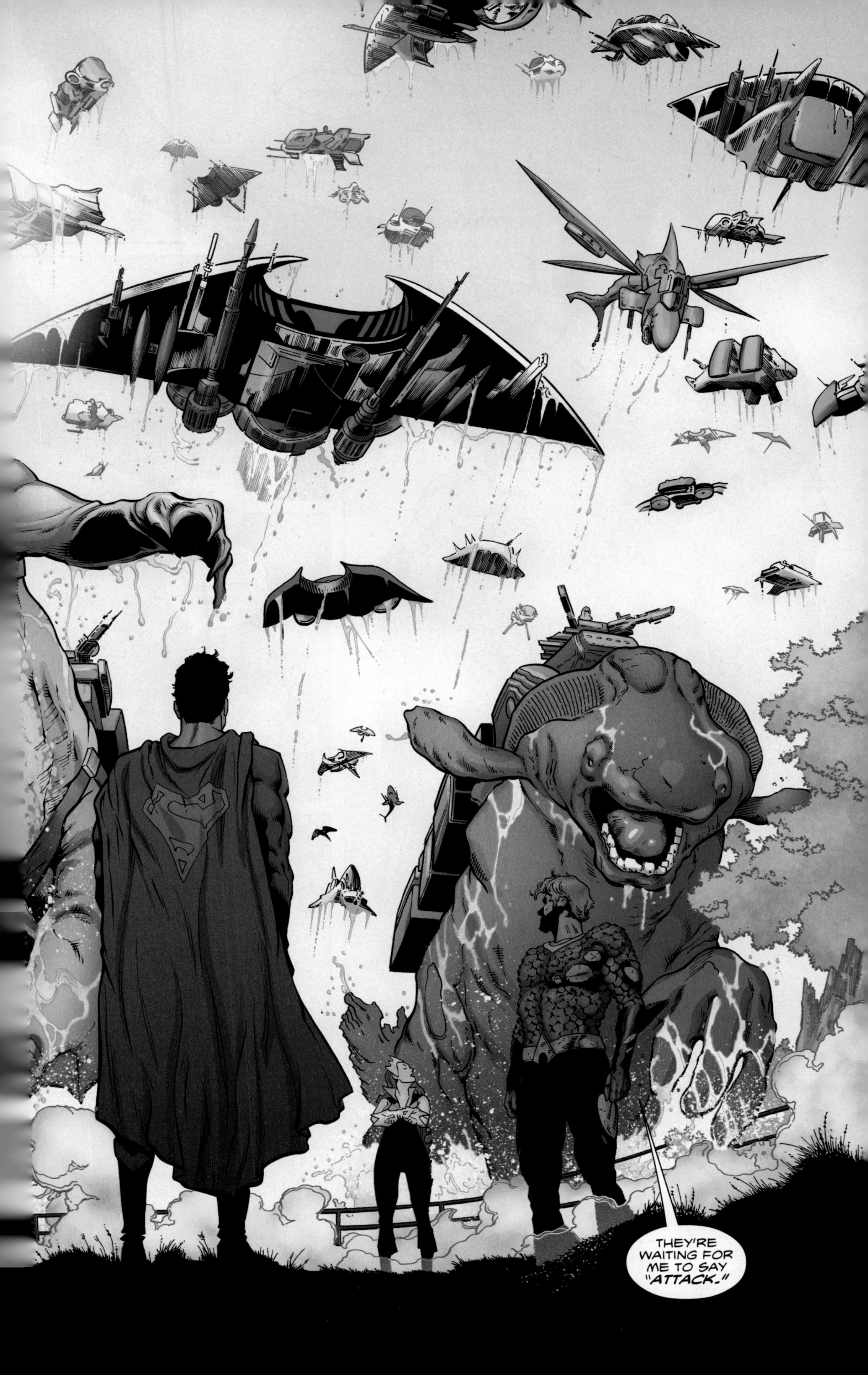
THEY'RE WAITING FOR ME TO SAY "ATTACK."

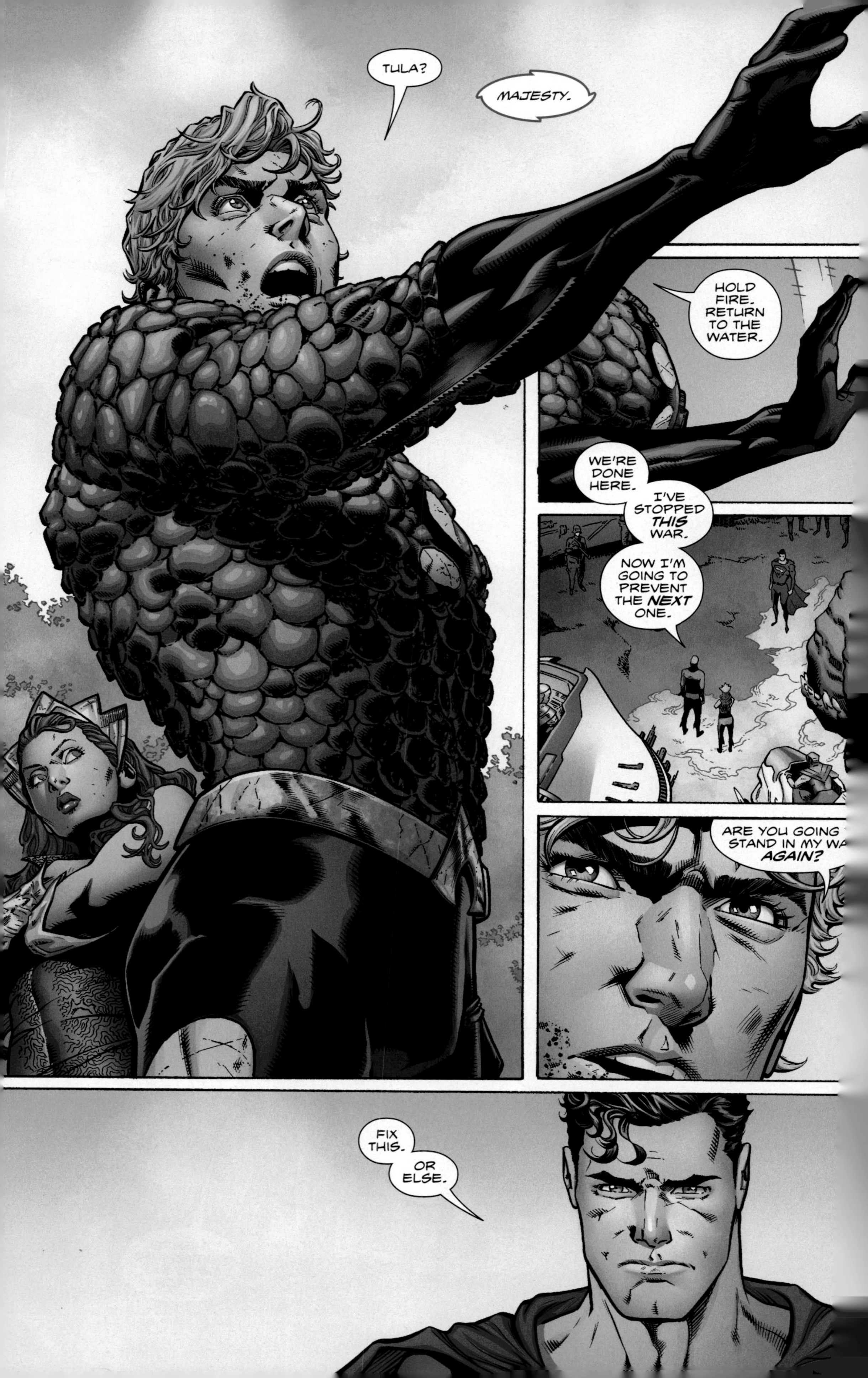
TULA?
MAJESTY.
HOLD FIRE. RETURN TO THE WATER.
WE'RE DONE HERE.
I'VE STOPPED *THIS* WAR.
NOW I'M GOING TO PREVENT THE *NEXT* ONE.
ARE YOU GOING STAND IN MY WA *AGAIN?*
FIX THIS.
OR ELSE.

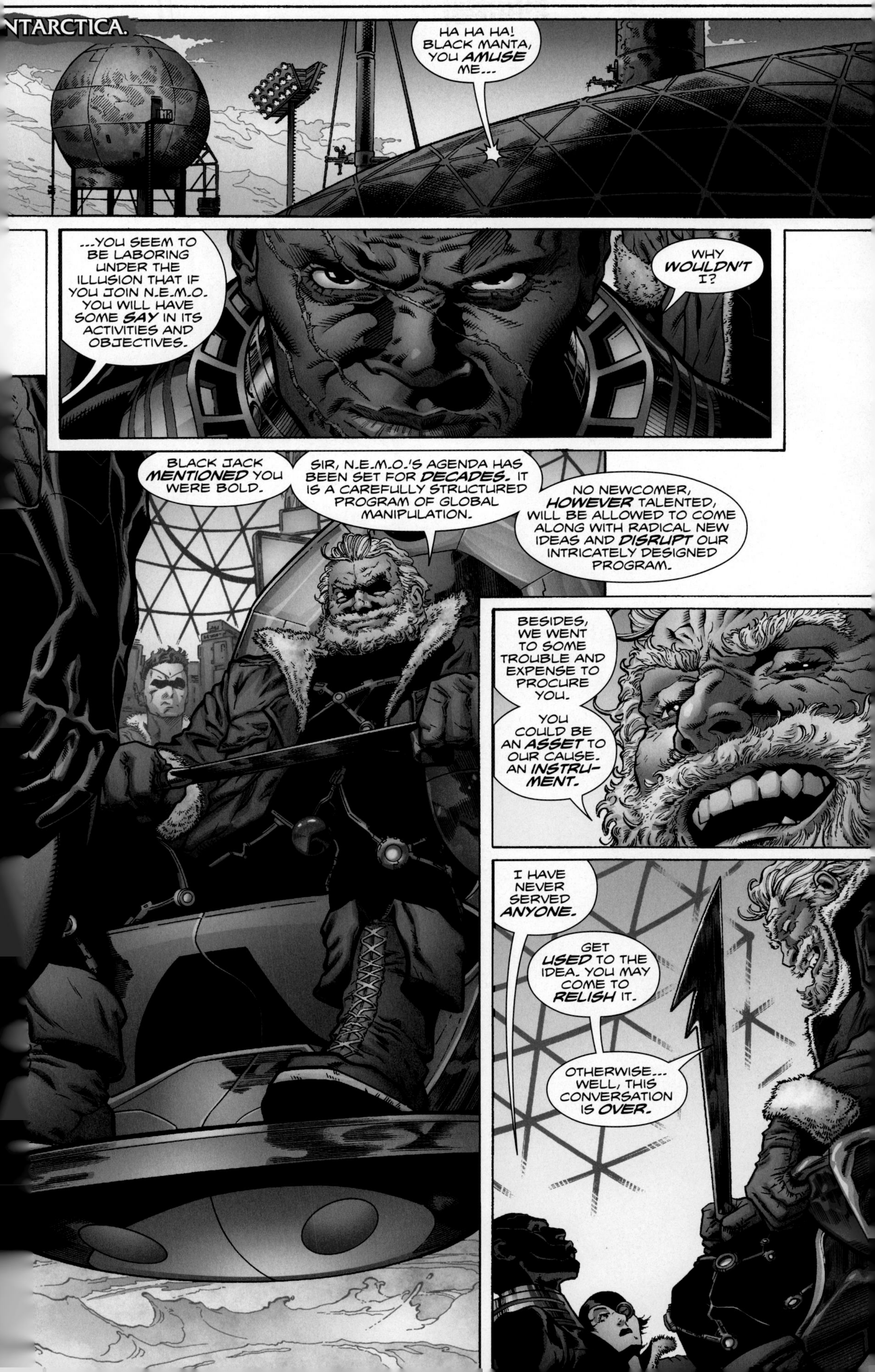
NTARCTICA.
HA HA HA! BLACK MANTA, YOU AMUSE ME...
...YOU SEEM TO BE LABORING UNDER THE ILLUSION THAT IF YOU JOIN N.E.M.O. YOU WILL HAVE SOME SAY IN ITS ACTIVITIES AND OBJECTIVES.
WHY WOULDN'T I?
BLACK JACK MENTIONED YOU WERE BOLD.
SIR, N.E.M.O.'S AGENDA HAS BEEN SET FOR DECADES. IT IS A CAREFULLY STRUCTURED PROGRAM OF GLOBAL MANIPULATION.
NO NEWCOMER, HOWEVER TALENTED, WILL BE ALLOWED TO COME ALONG WITH RADICAL NEW IDEAS AND DISRUPT OUR INTRICATELY DESIGNED PROGRAM.
BESIDES, WE WENT TO SOME TROUBLE AND EXPENSE TO PROCURE YOU.
YOU COULD BE AN ASSET TO OUR CAUSE. AN INSTRU-MENT.
I HAVE NEVER SERVED ANYONE.
GET USED TO THE IDEA. YOU MAY COME TO RELISH IT.
OTHERWISE... WELL, THIS CONVERSATION IS OVER.

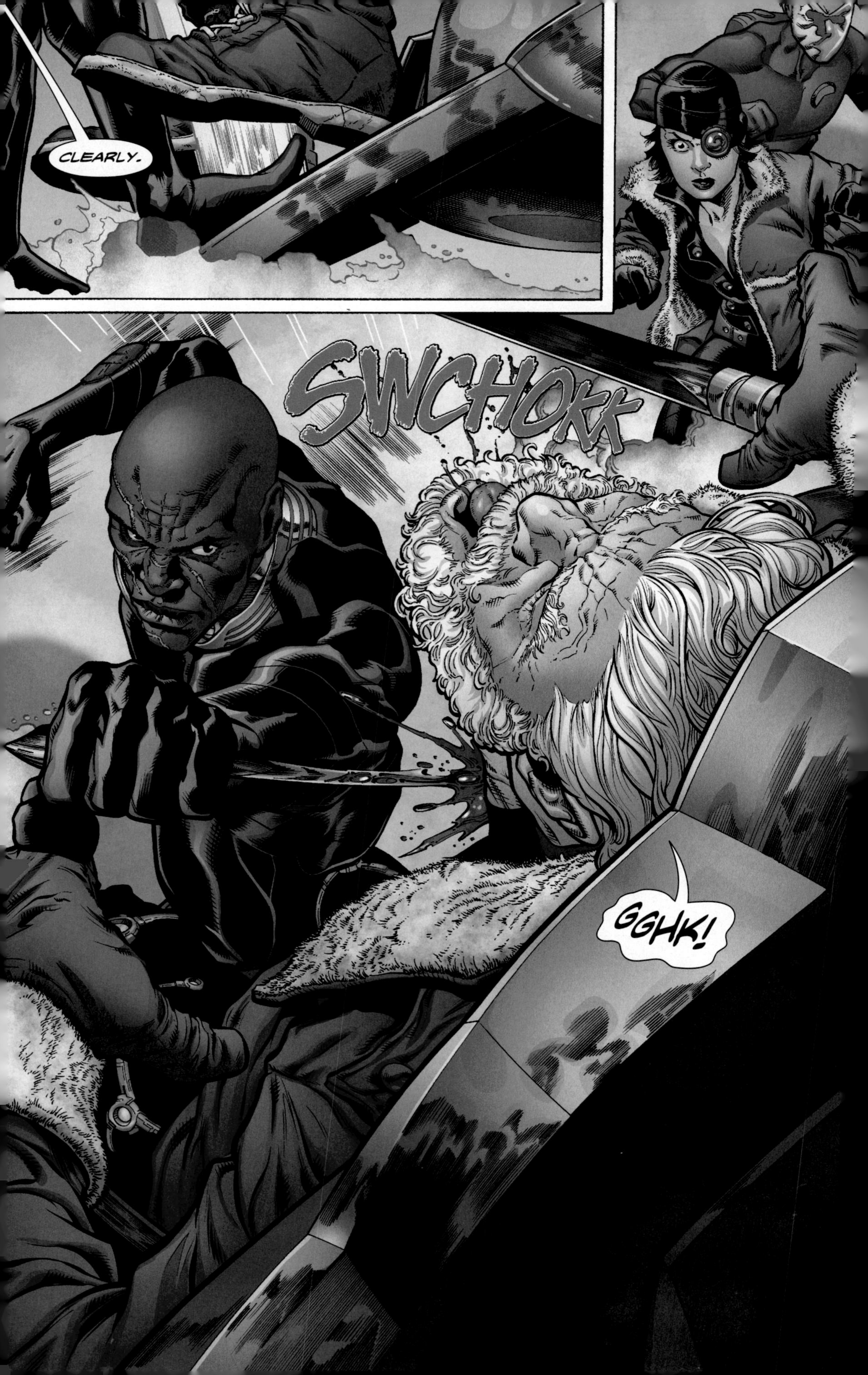
CLEARLY.
SWCHOKK
GGHK!

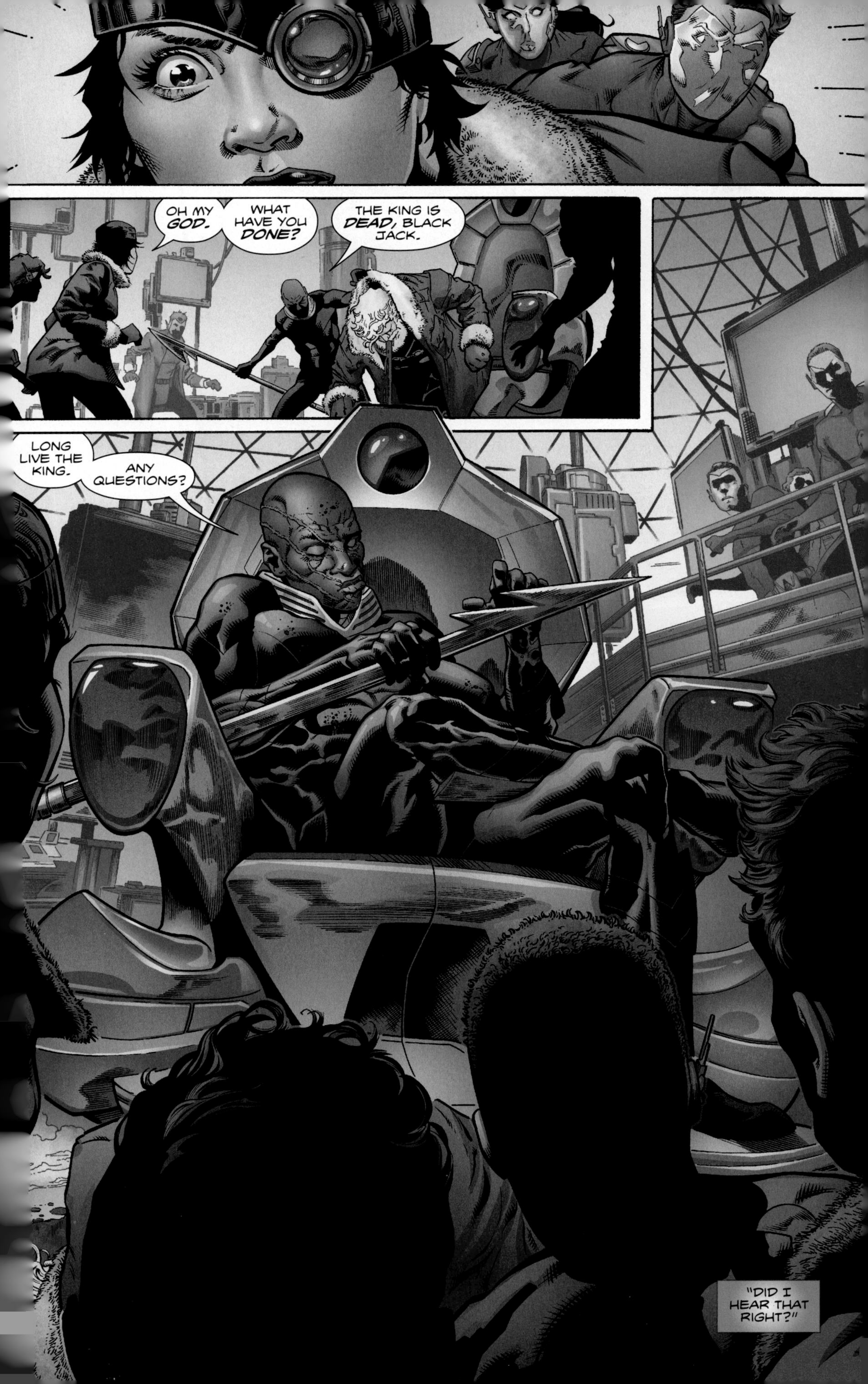
OH MY GOD.
WHAT HAVE YOU DONE?
THE KING IS DEAD, BLACK JACK.
LONG LIVE THE KING.
ANY QUESTIONS?
"DID I HEAR THAT RIGHT?"

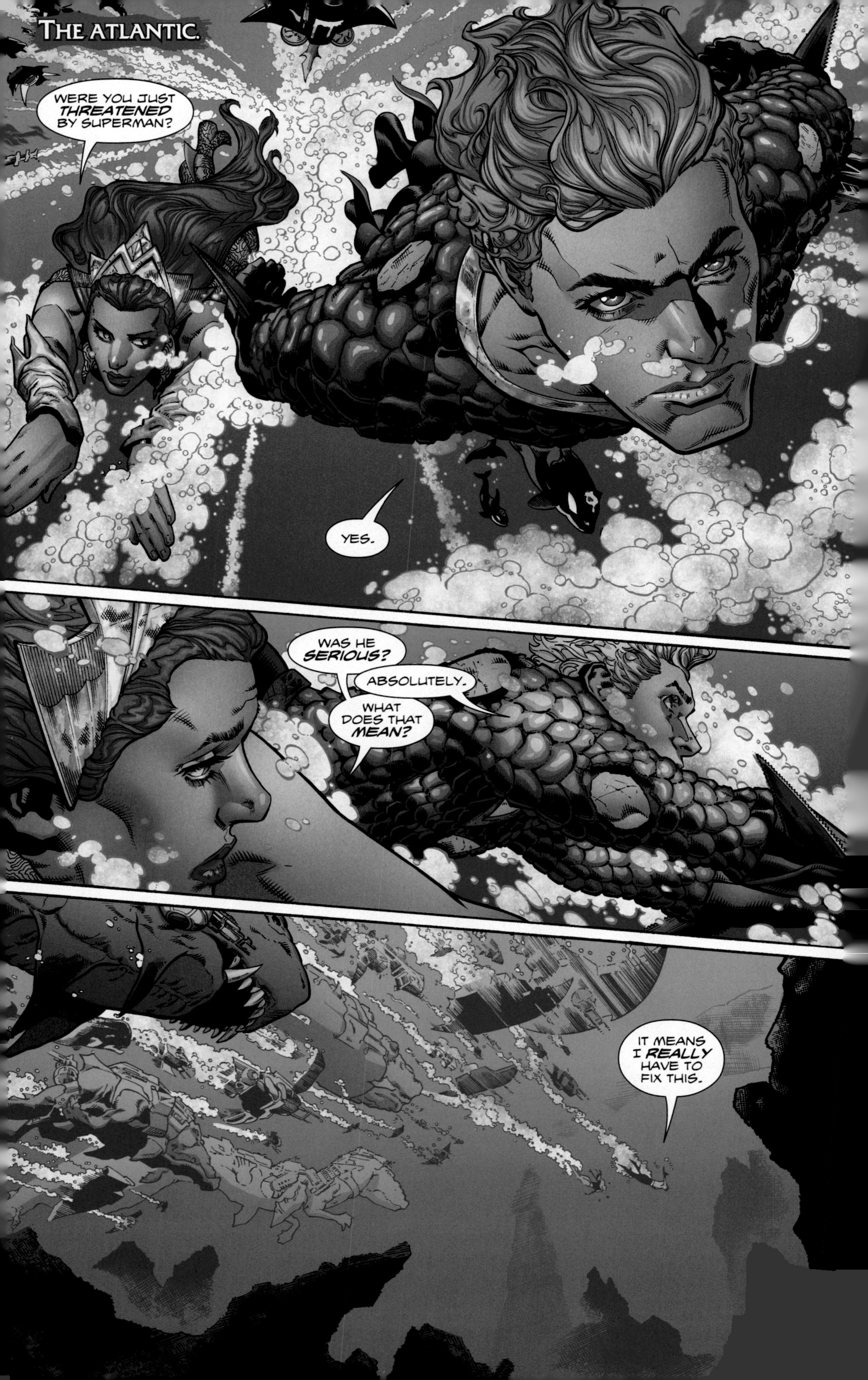
THE ATLANTIC.
WERE YOU JUST THREATENED BY SUPERMAN?
YES.
WAS HE SERIOUS?
ABSOLUTELY.
WHAT DOES THAT MEAN?
IT MEANS I REALLY HAVE TO FIX THIS.

AQUAMAN: REBIRTH #1 variant cover by Ryan Benjamin

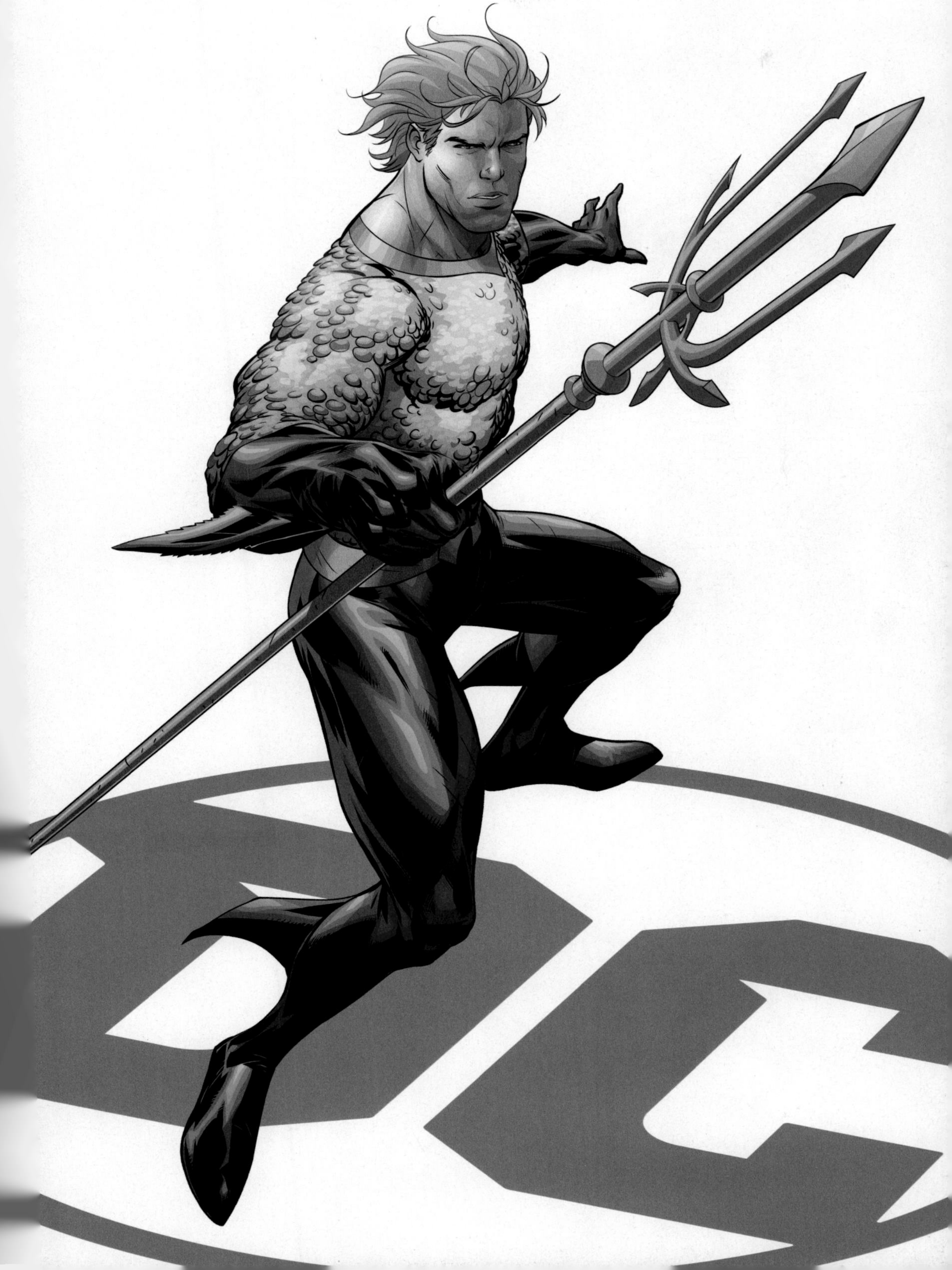

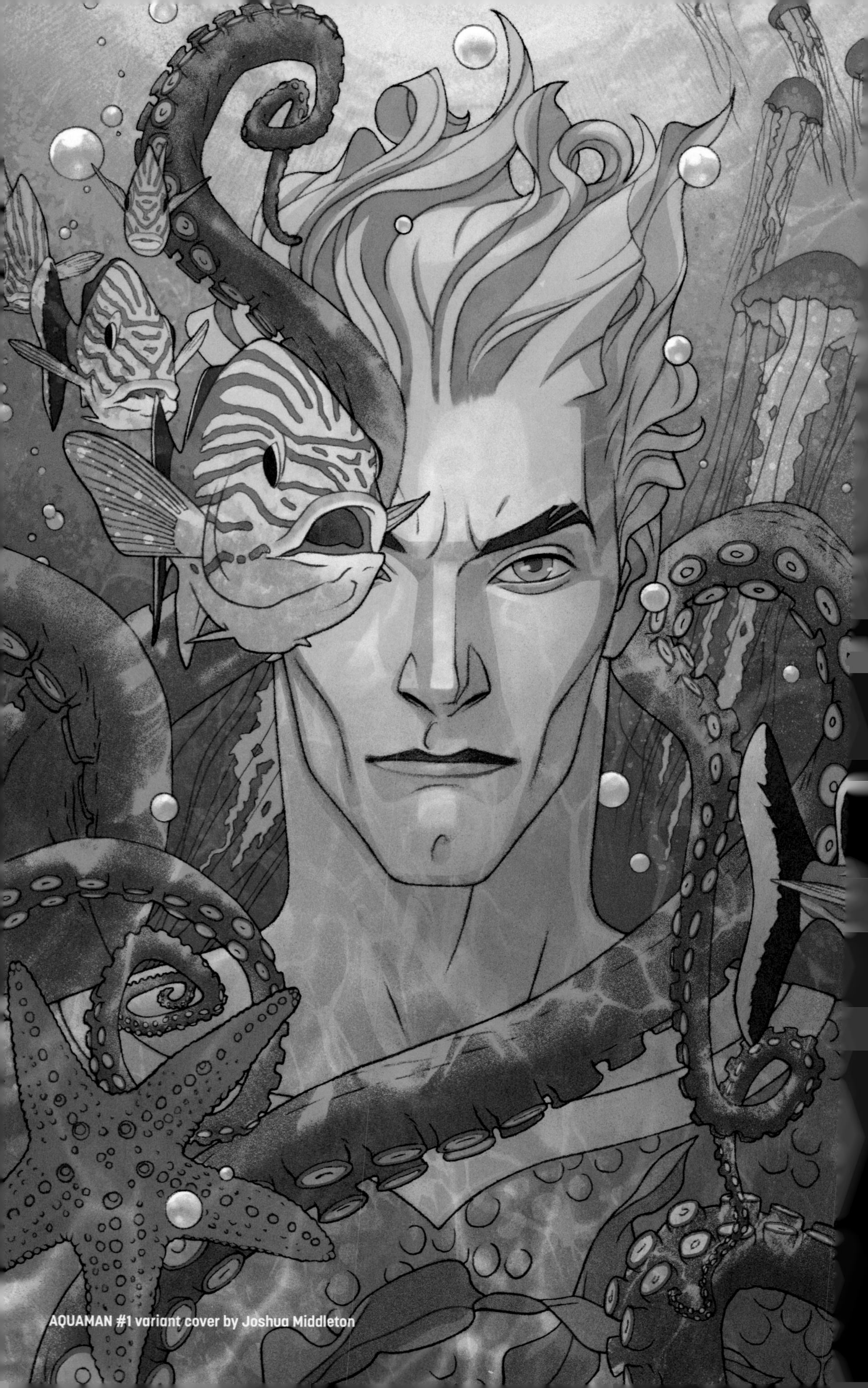

AQUAMAN #1 variant cover by Joshua Middleton

AQUAMAN #2 variant cover by Joshua Middleton

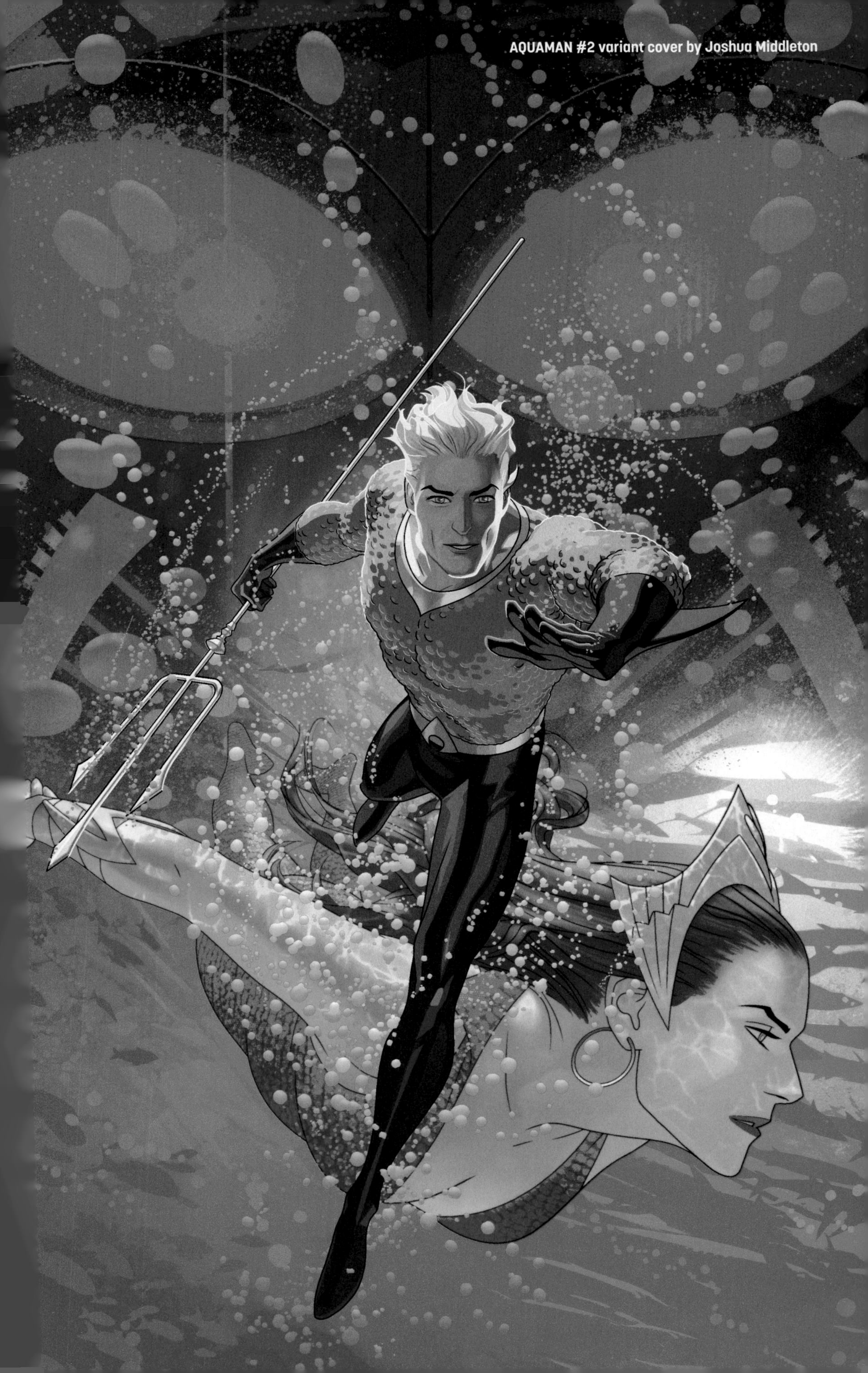

AQUAMAN #3 variant cover by Joshua Middleton

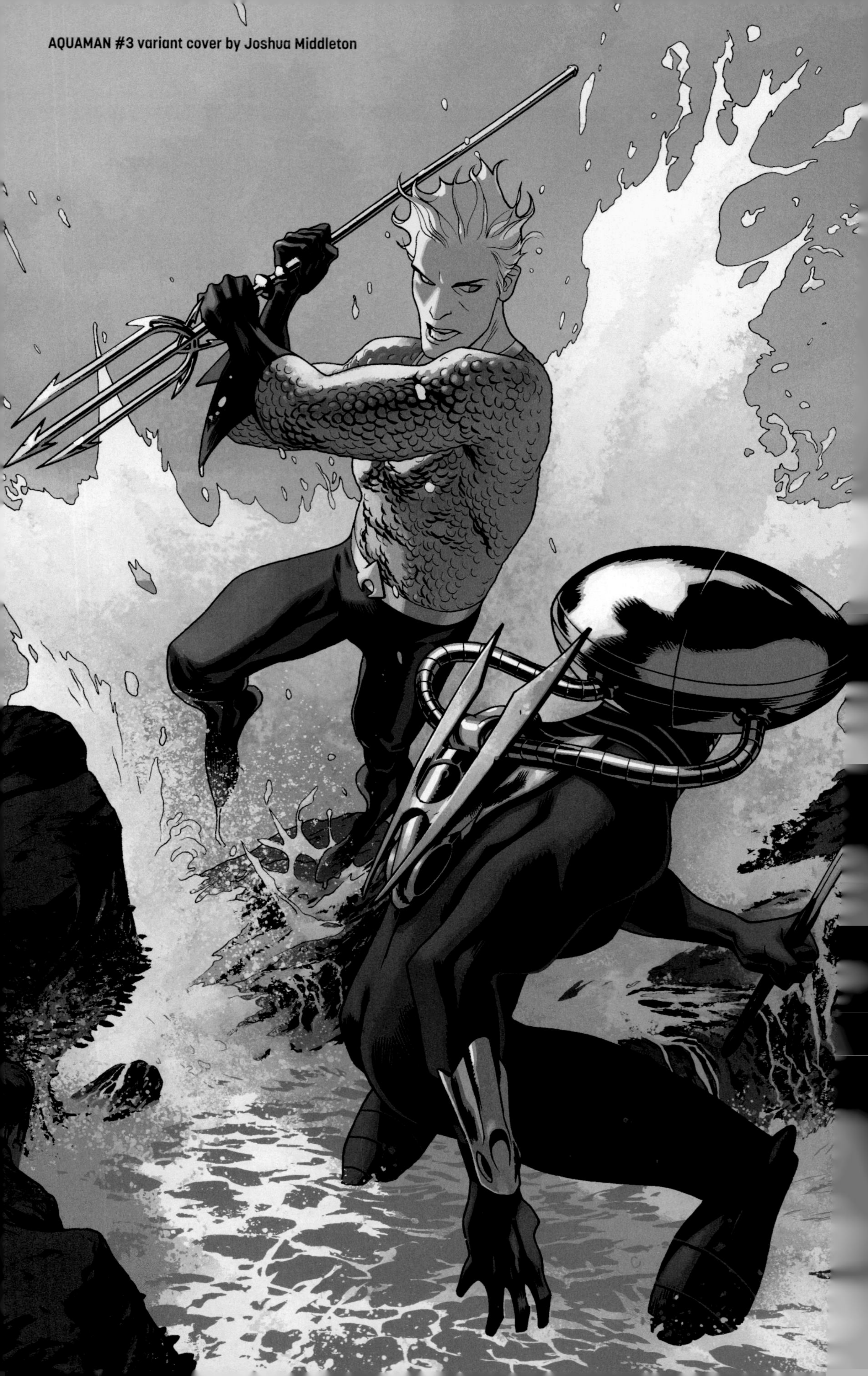

AQUAMAN #4 variant cover by Joshua Middleton

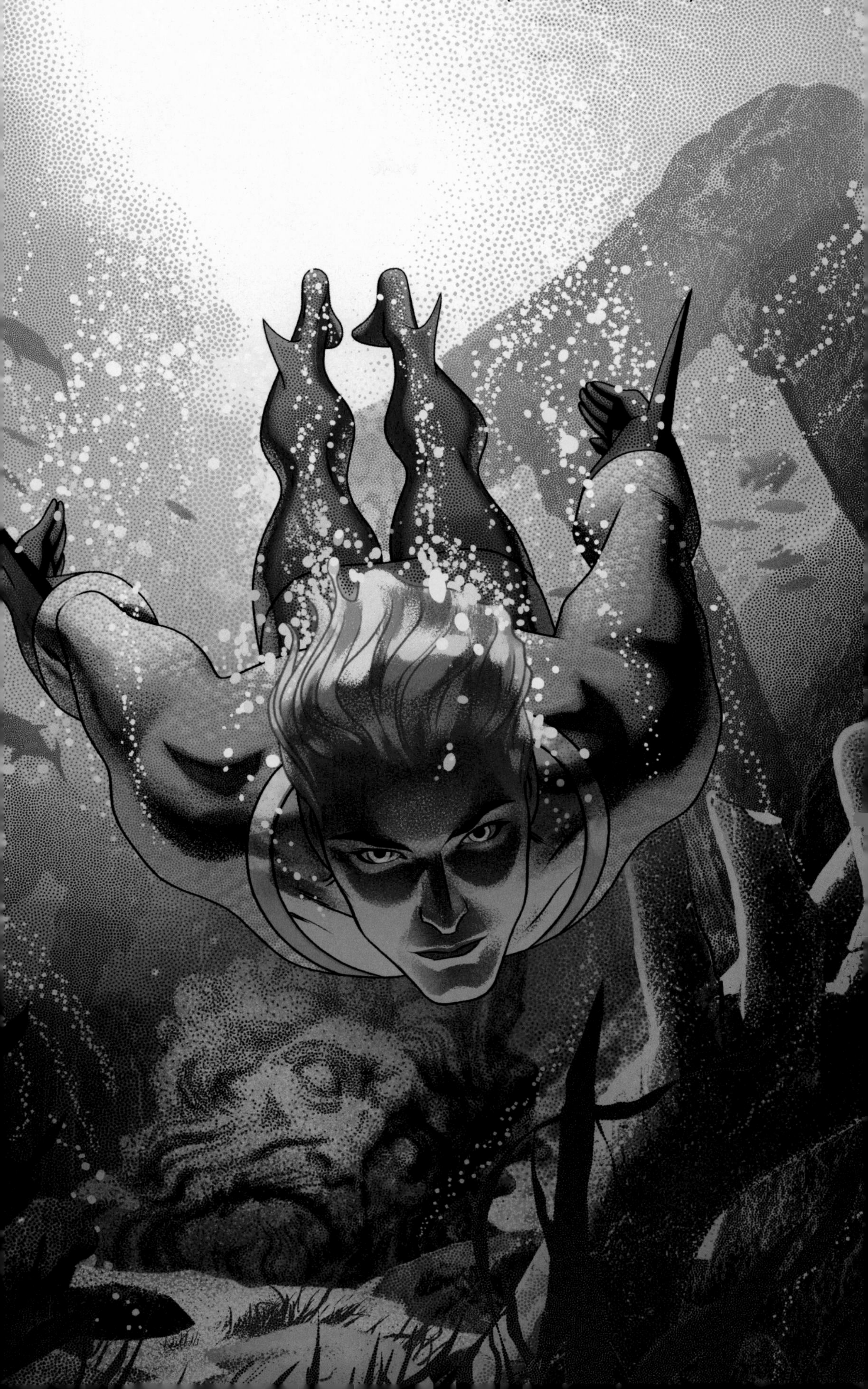

AQUAMAN #5 variant cover by Joshua Middleton

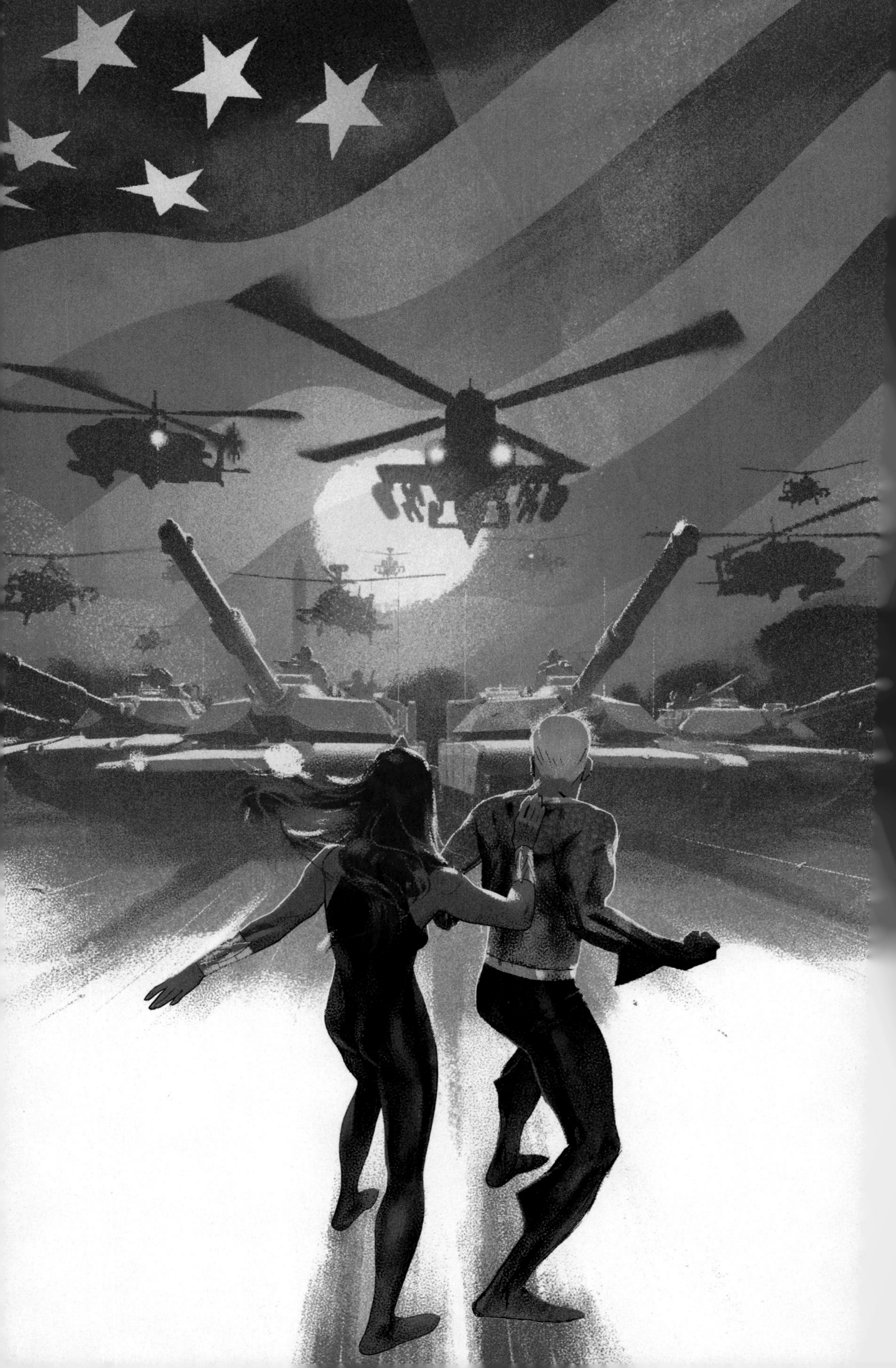

AQUAMAN #6 variant cover by Joshua Middleton

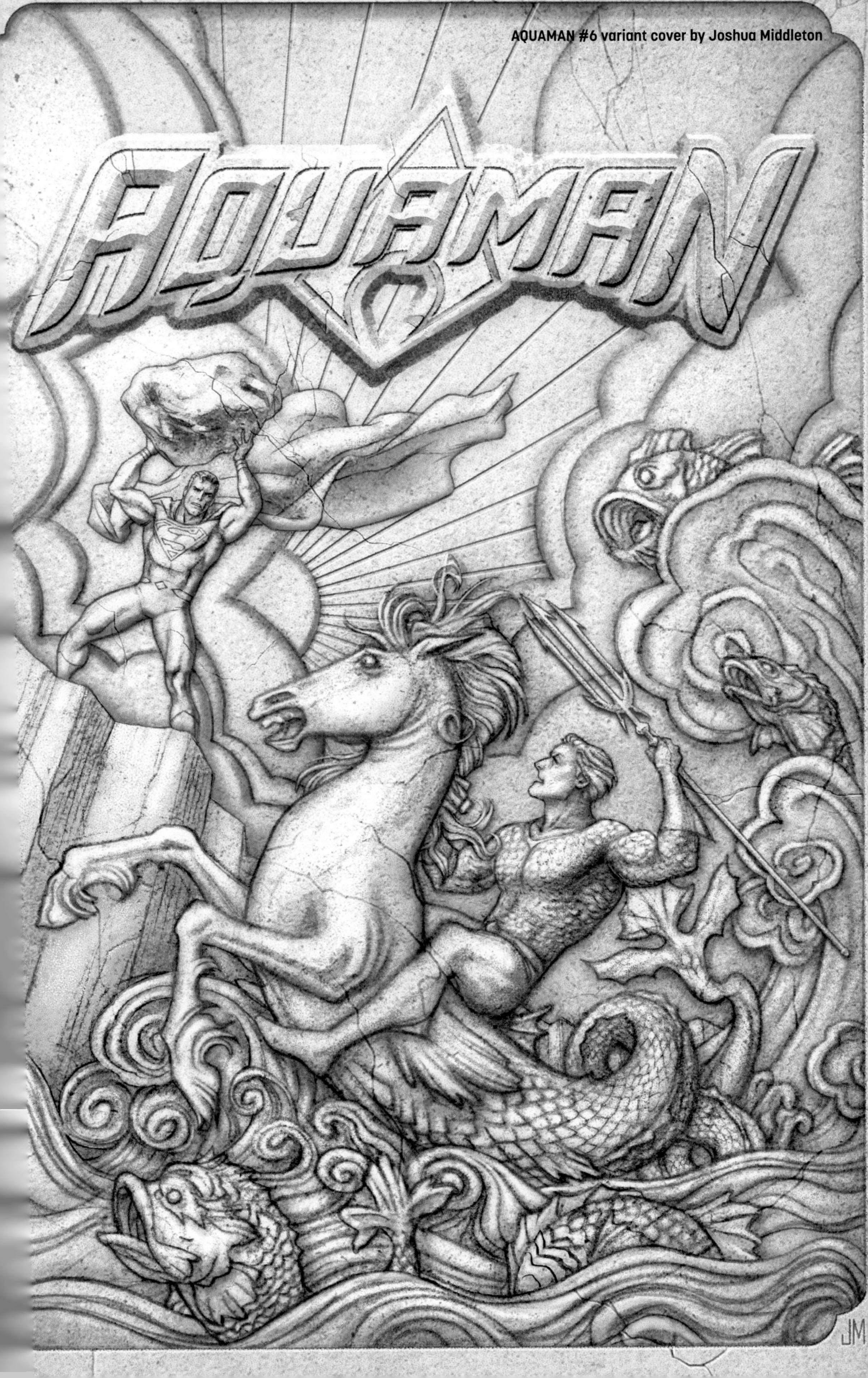
AQUAMAN
JM

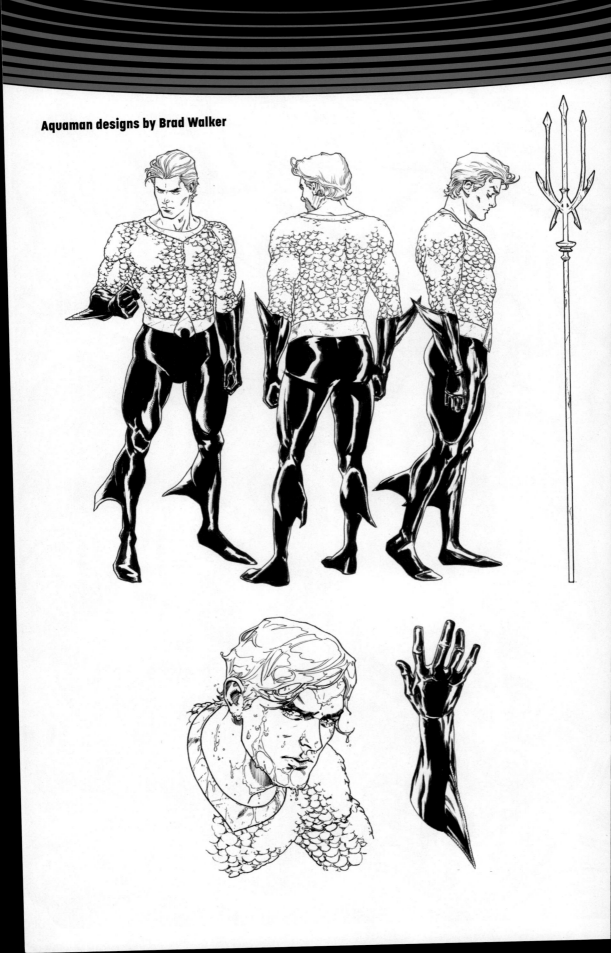

Aquaman designs by Brad Walker

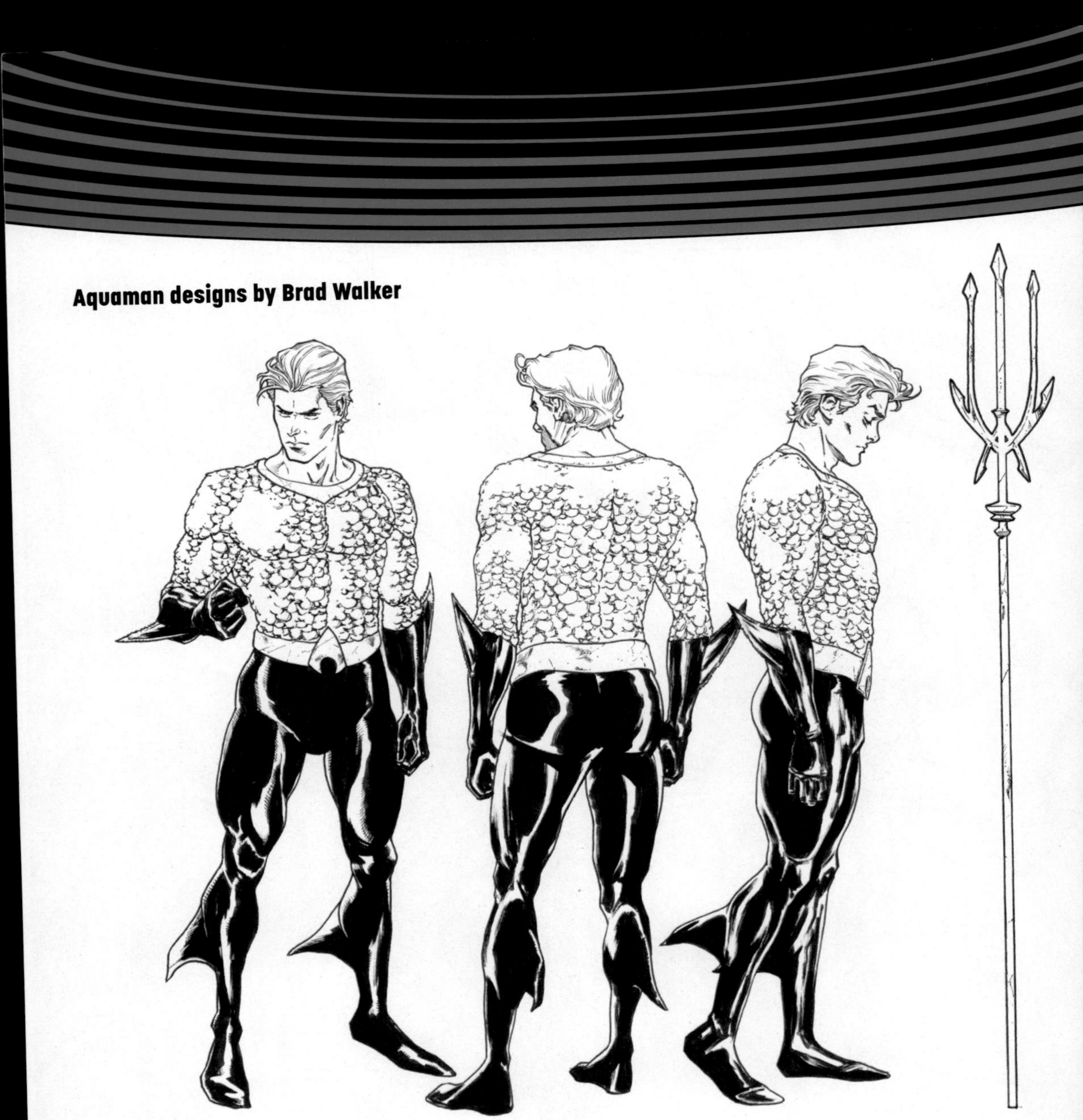

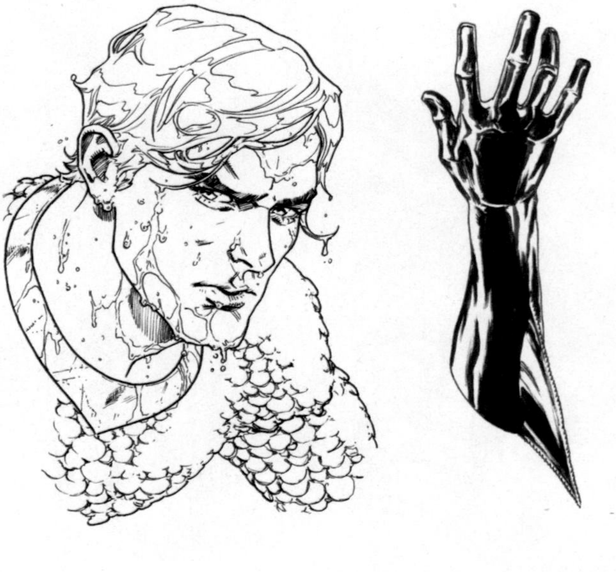

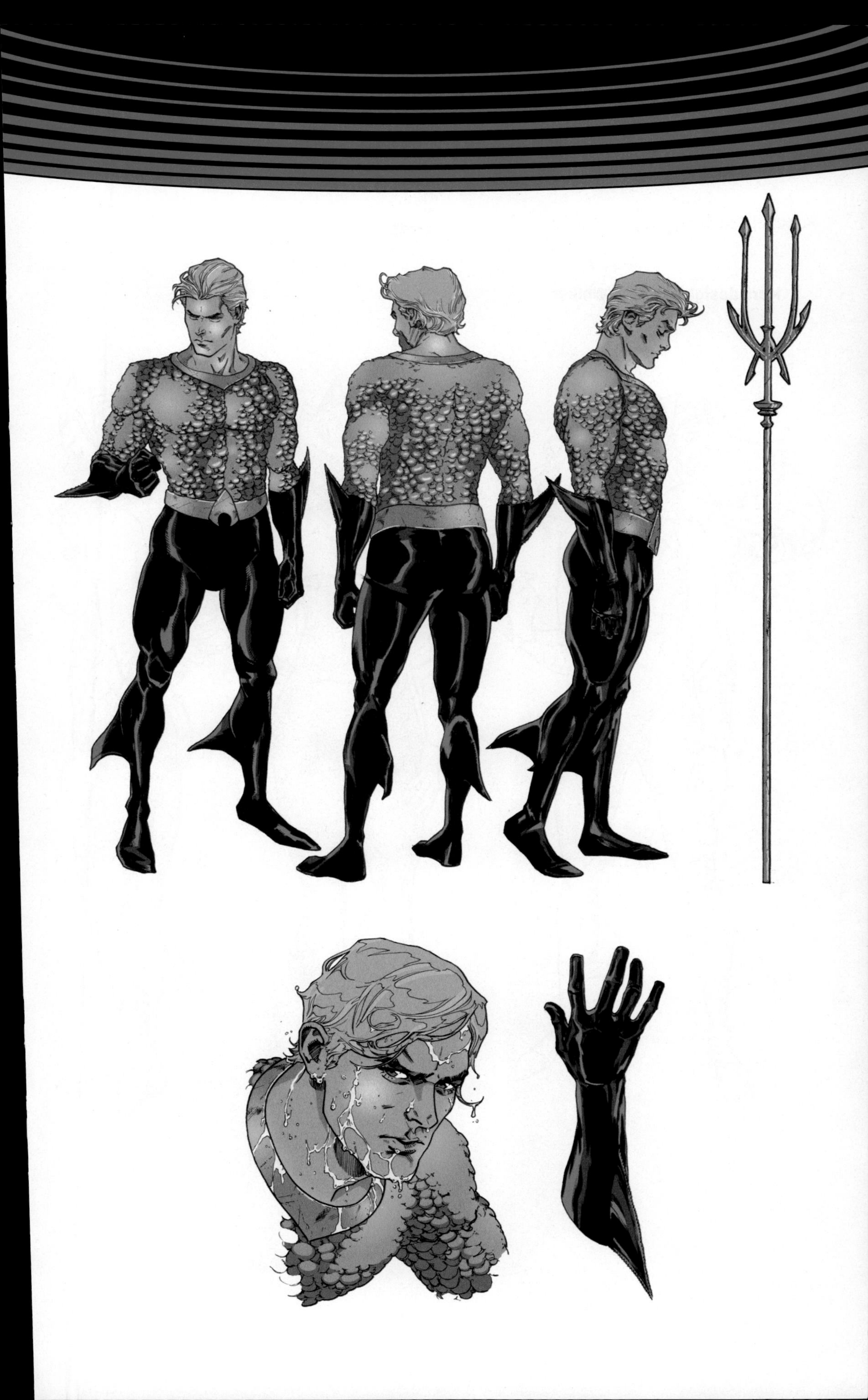

Mera designs by Brad Walker

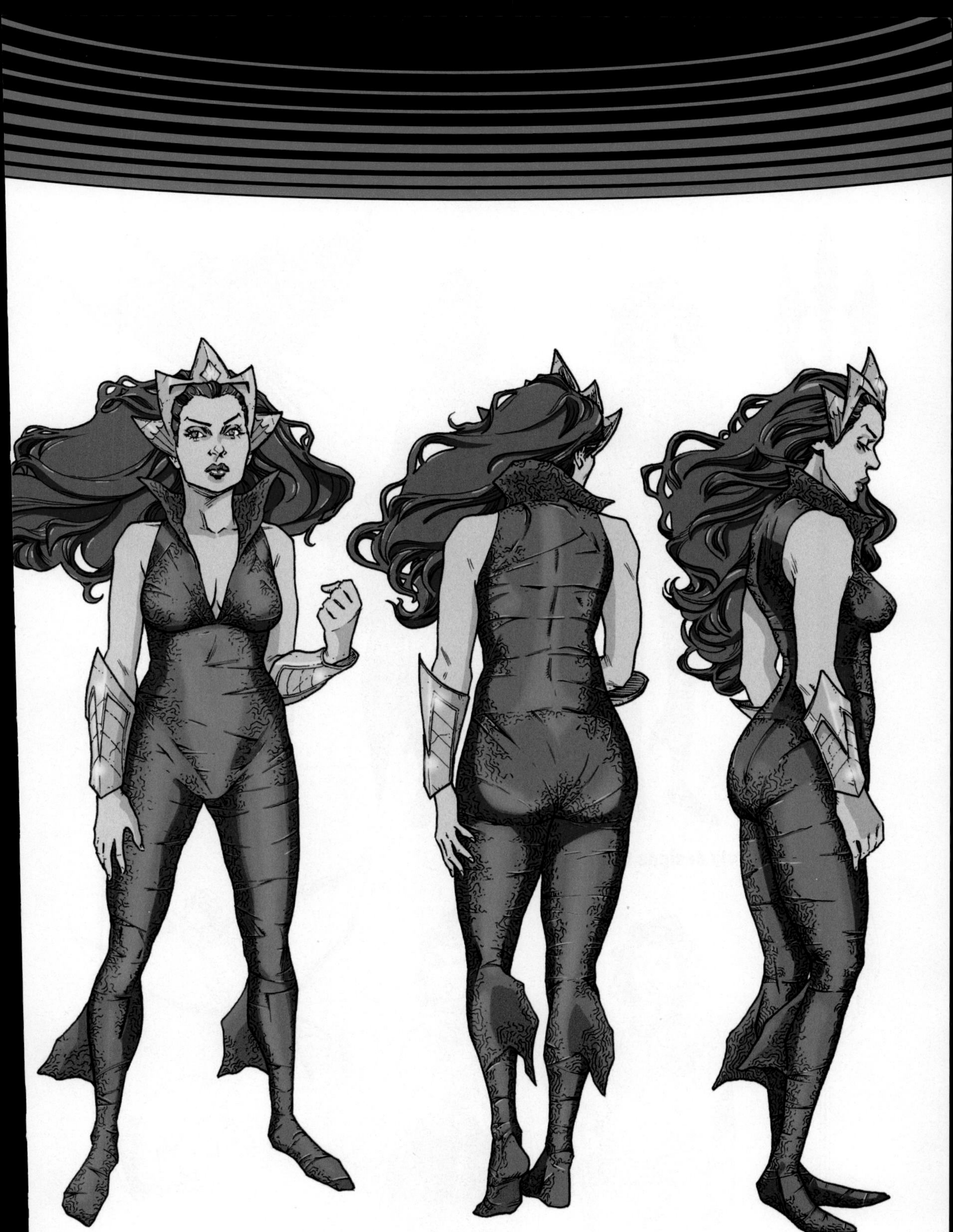

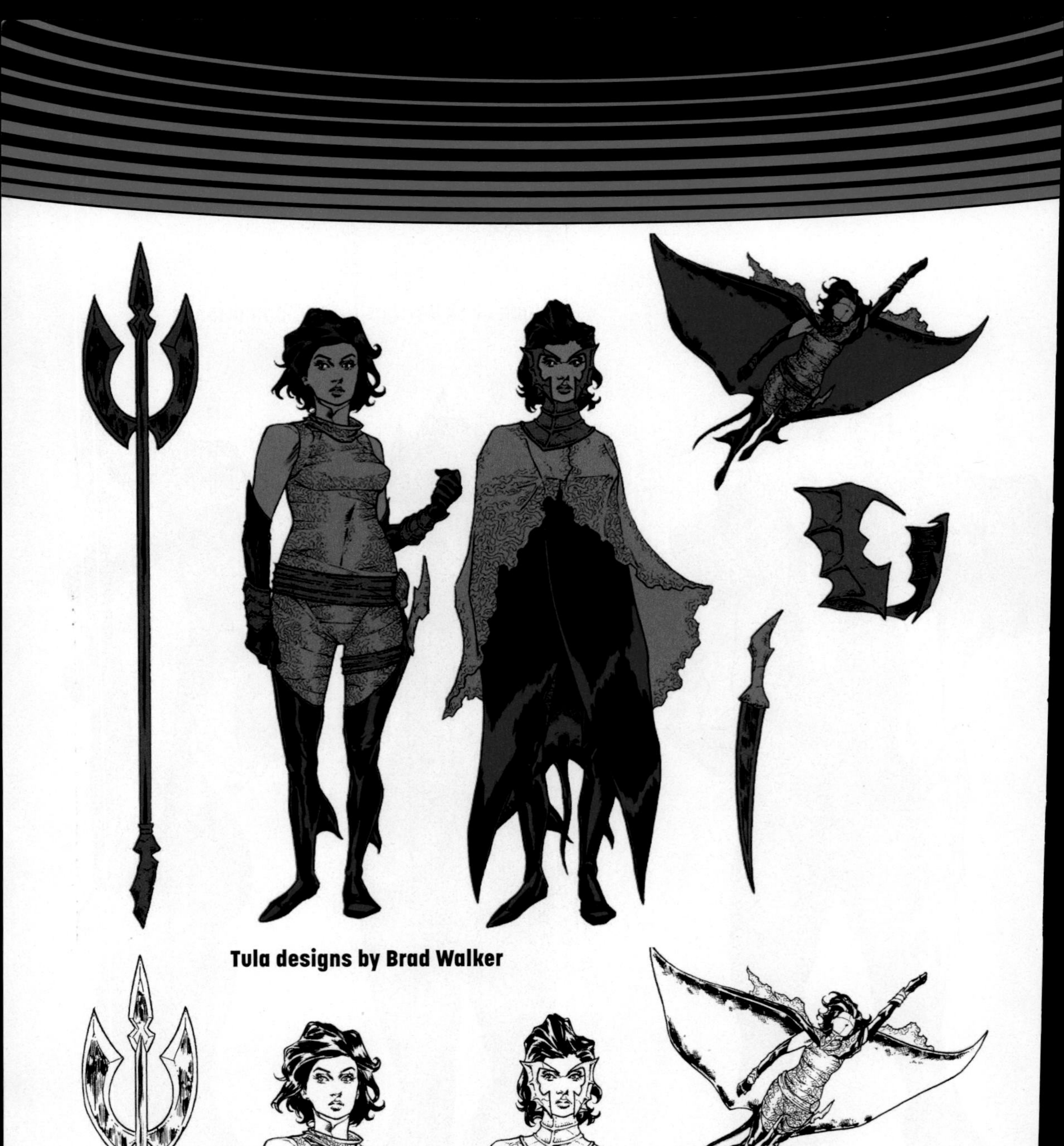

Tula designs by Brad Walker

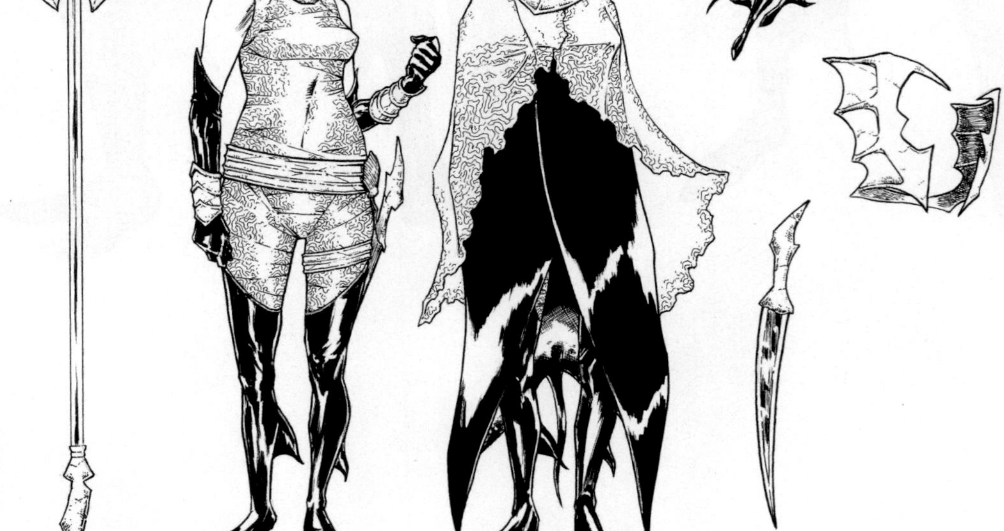

Black Jack designs by Philippe Briones

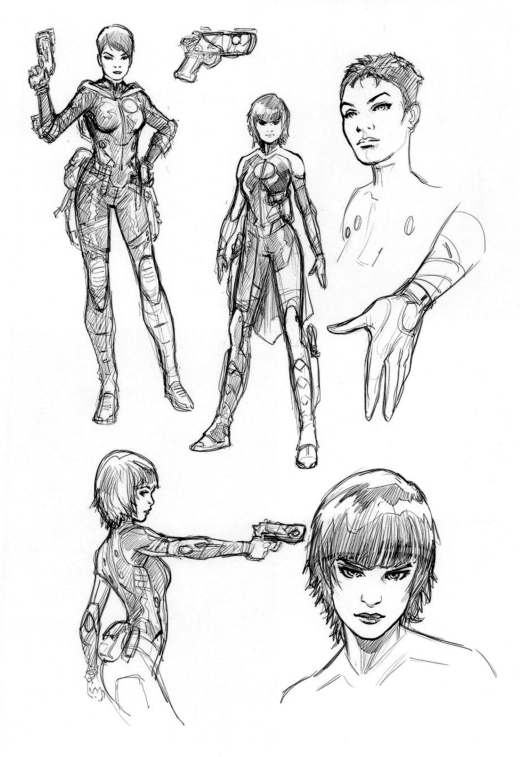

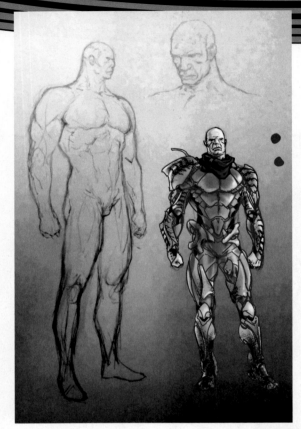

Rath designs by Oscar Jiménez

Fisher King designs by Brad Walker

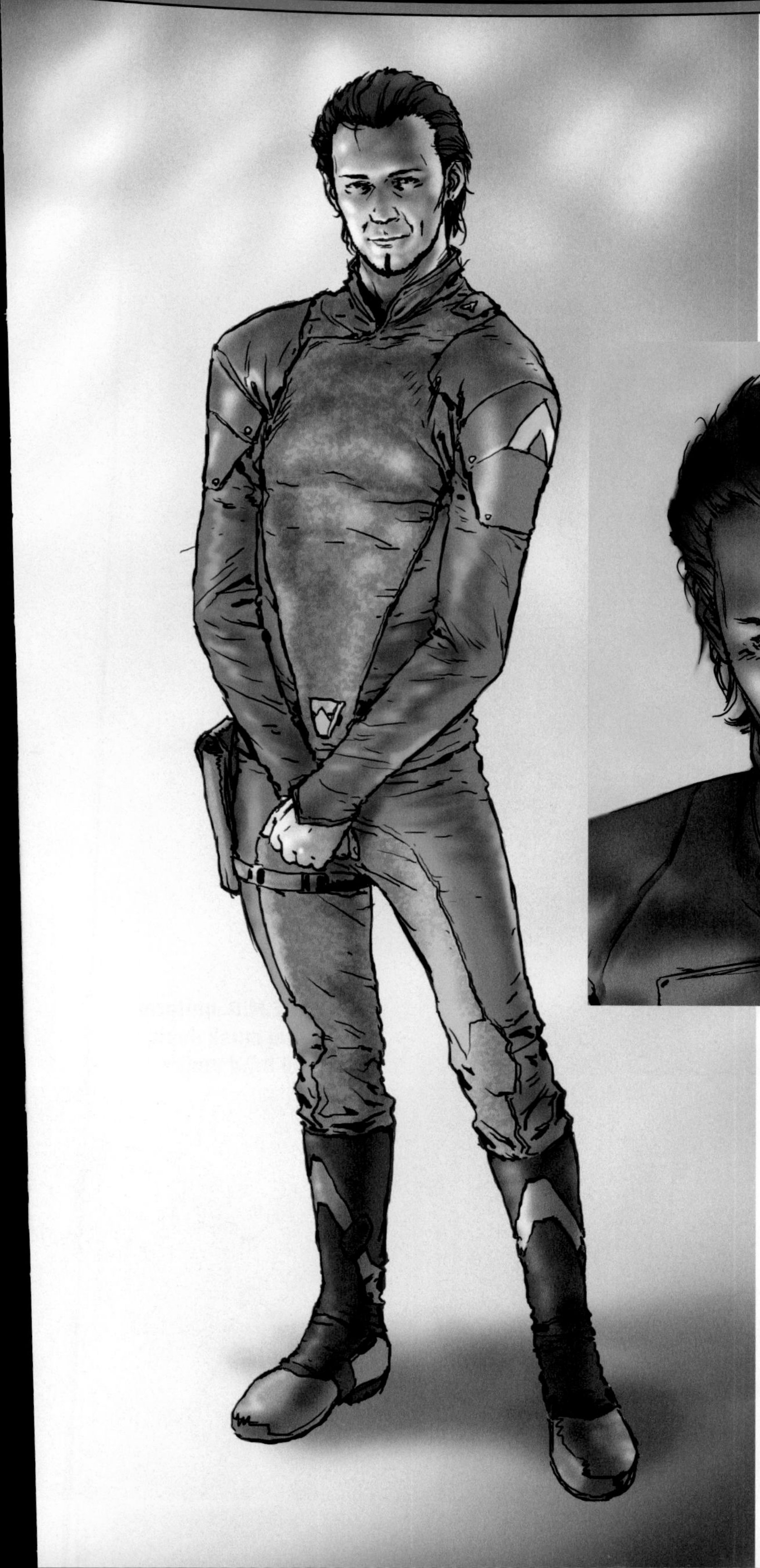

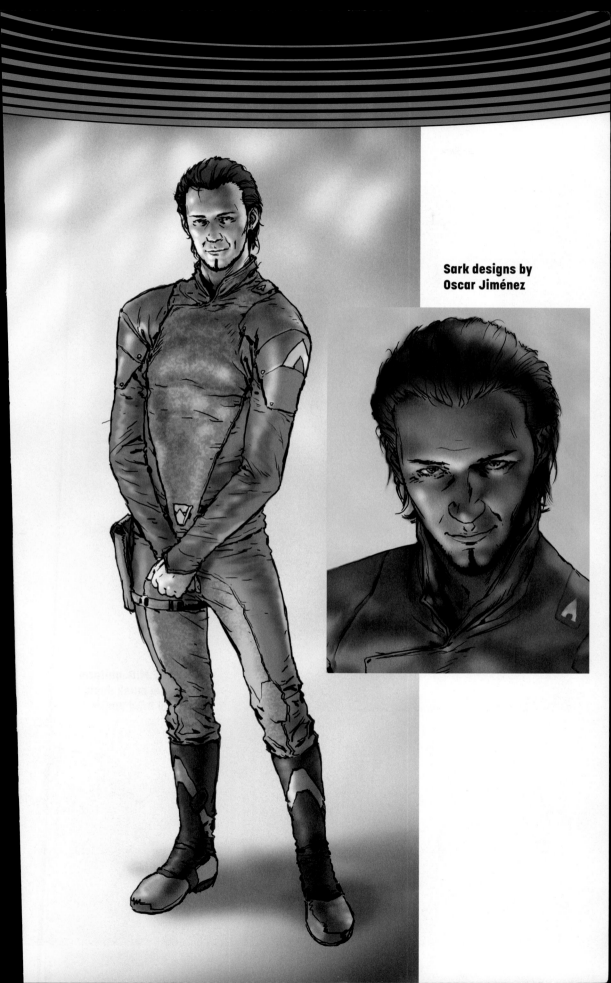

Sark designs by
Oscar Jiménez

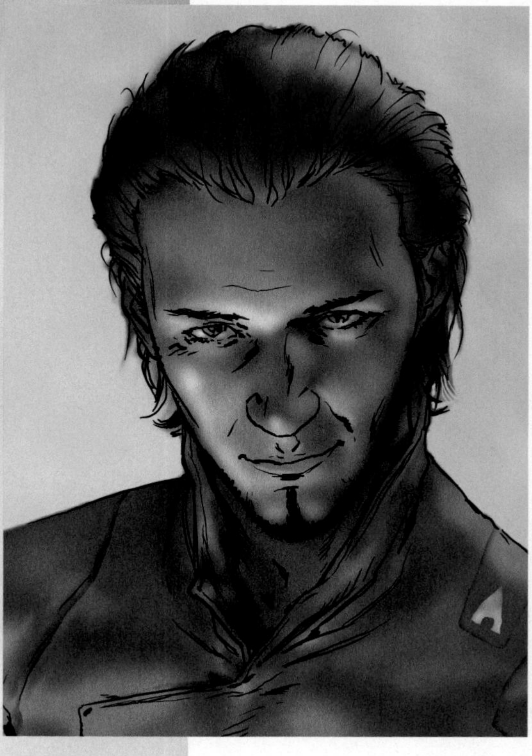

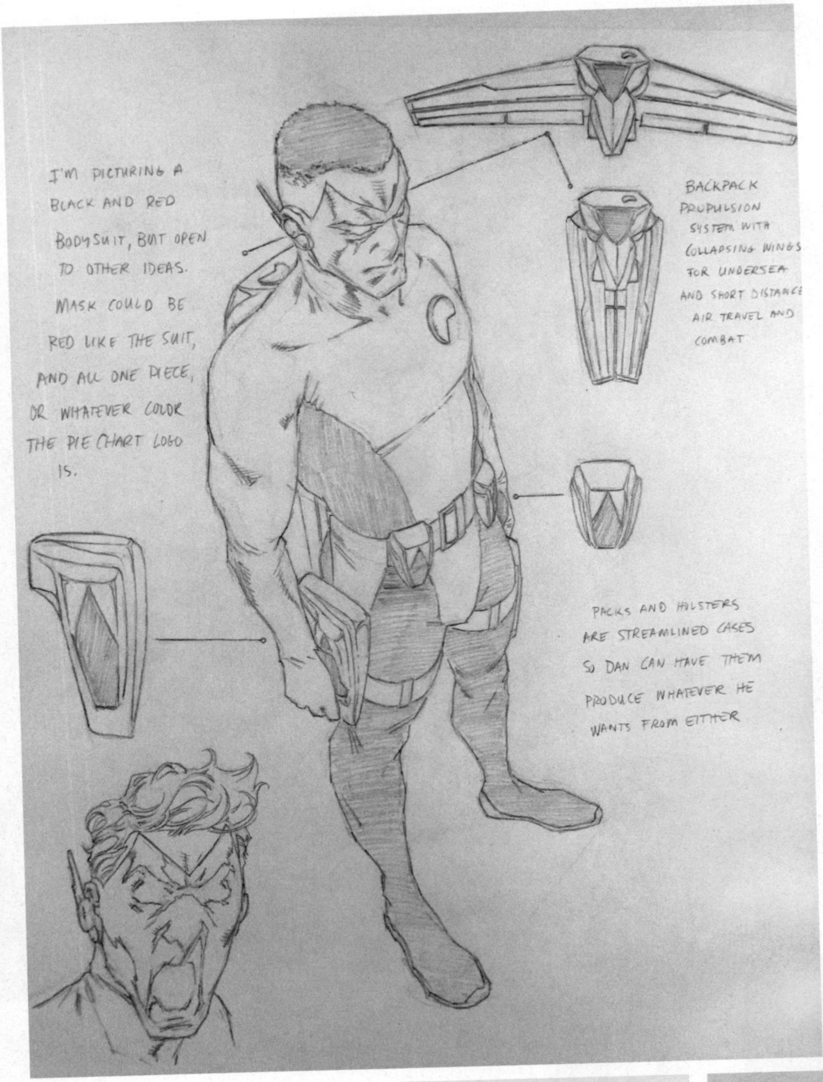
I'M PICTURING A BLACK AND RED BODYSUIT, BUT OPEN TO OTHER IDEAS.
MASK COULD BE RED LIKE THE SUIT, AND ALL ONE PIECE, OR WHATEVER COLOR THE PIE CHART LOGO IS.
BACKPACK PROPULSION SYSTEM WITH COLLAPSING WINGS FOR UNDERSEA AND SHORT DISTANCE AIR TRAVEL AND COMBAT
PACKS AND HOLSTERS ARE STREAMLINED CASES SO DAN CAN HAVE THEM PRODUCE WHATEVER HE WANTS FROM EITHER

N.E.M.O. uniform and mask designs by Brad Walker

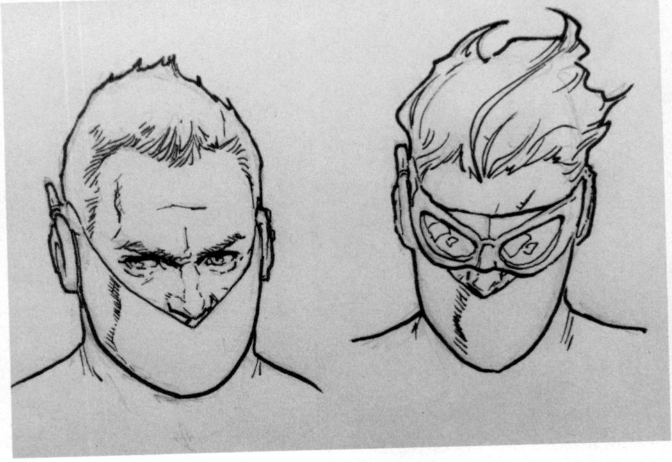

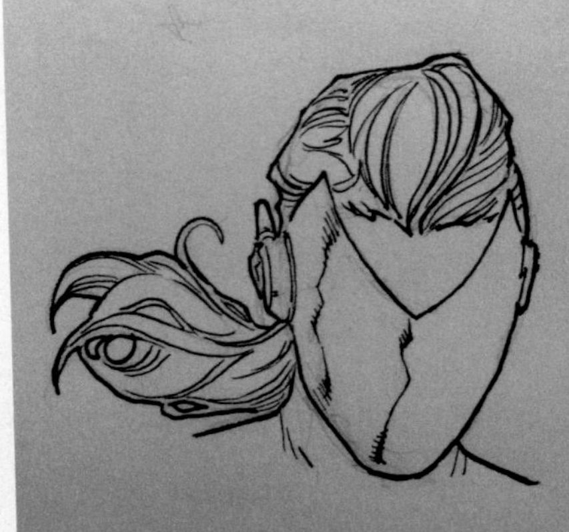

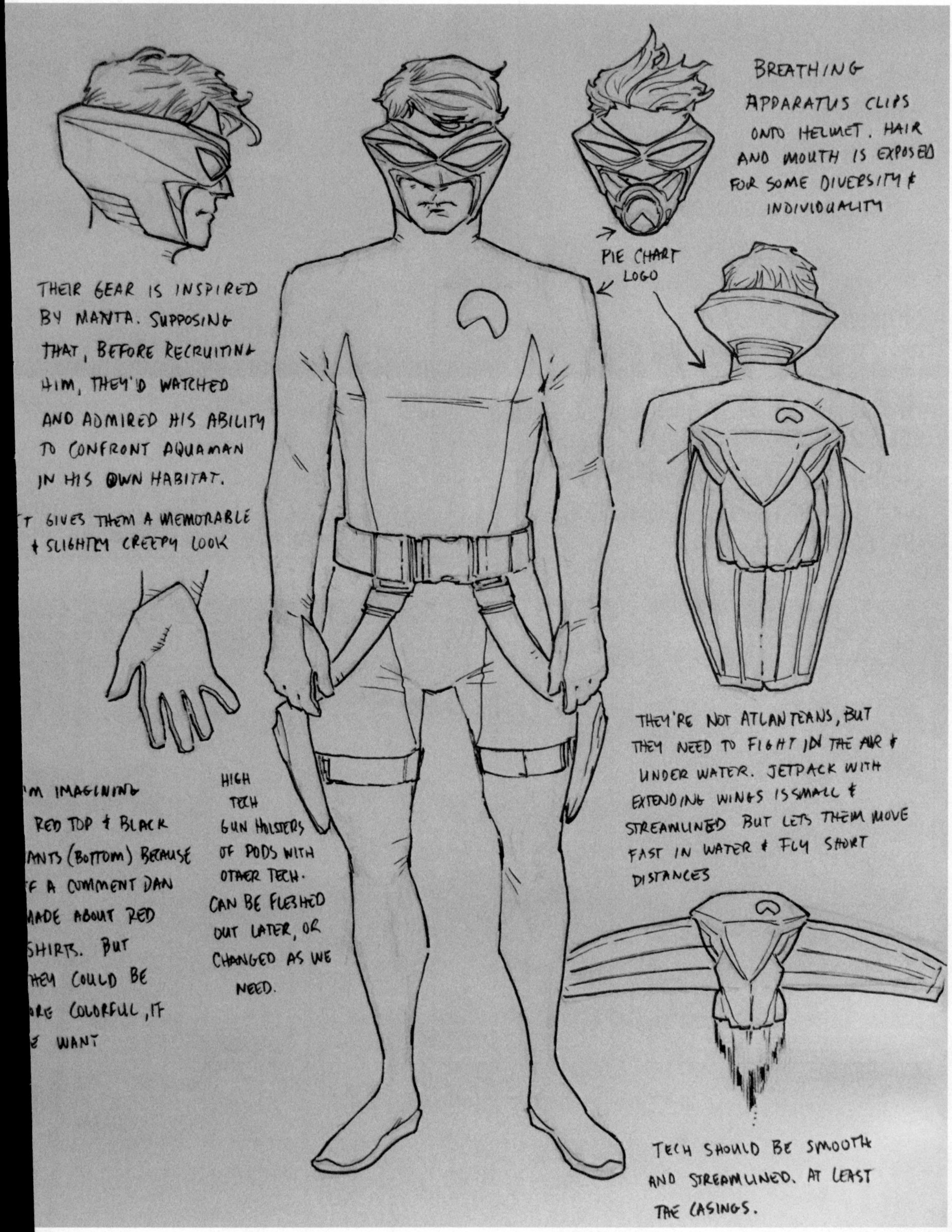

BREATHING APPARATUS CLIPS ONTO HELMET. HAIR AND MOUTH IS EXPOSED FOR SOME DIVERSITY & INDIVIDUALITY
PIE CHART LOGO
THEIR GEAR IS INSPIRED BY MANTA. SUPPOSING THAT, BEFORE RECRUITING HIM, THEY'D WATCHED AND ADMIRED HIS ABILITY TO CONFRONT AQUAMAN IN HIS OWN HABITAT.
T GIVES THEM A MEMORABLE & SLIGHTLY CREEPY LOOK
M IMAGINING RED TOP & BLACK ANTS (BOTTOM) BECAUSE F A COMMENT DAN MADE ABOUT RED SHIRTS. BUT HEY COULD BE ORE COLORFUL, IF E WANT
HIGH TECH GUN HOLSTERS OF PODS WITH OTHER TECH. CAN BE FLESHED OUT LATER, OR CHANGED AS WE NEED.
THEY'RE NOT ATLANTEANS, BUT THEY NEED TO FIGHT IN THE AIR & UNDER WATER. JETPACK WITH EXTENDING WINGS IS SMALL & STREAMLINED BUT LETS THEM MOVE FAST IN WATER & FLY SHORT DISTANCES
TECH SHOULD BE SMOOTH AND STREAMLINED. AT LEAST THE CASINGS.

DC UNIVERSE: REBIRTH

THE FLASH

VOL 1: LIGHTNING STRIKES TWICE

JOSHUA WILLIAMSON

with CARMINE DI GIANDOMENICO
and IVAN PLASCENCIA

VOL. 1 LIGHTNING STRIKES TWICE

JOSHUA WILLIAMSON • CARMINE DI GIANDOMENICO • IVAN PLASCENCIA

**JUSTICE LEAGUE VOL 1:
THE EXTINCTION MACHINES**

**TITANS VOL 1:
THE RETURN OF WALLY WEST**

**HAL JORDAN AND
THE GREEN LANTERN CORPS V
SINESTRO'S LAW**